Problems in Marketing

Second Edition

Applying Key Concepts and Techniques

Luiz Moutinho & Charles Chien

SAGE Publications
Los Angeles ▪ London ▪ New Delhi ▪ Singapore

First published 2008

SAGE Publications Ltd
1 Oliver's Yard
55 City Road
London EC1Y ISP

SAGE Publications Inc.
2455 Teller Road
Thousand Oaks, California 91320

SAGE Publications India Pvt Ltd
B 1/I 1 Mohan Cooperative Industrial Area
Mathura Road
New Delhi 110 044

SAGE Publications Asia-Pacific Pte Ltd
33 Pekin Street #02-01
Far East Square
Singapore 048763

Library of Congress Control Number: 2006940458

British Library Cataloguing in Publication data

A catalogue record for this book is available from the British Library

ISBN 978–0–7619–7178–8
ISBN 978–0–7619–7179–5 (pbk)

Typeset by Newgen Imaging Systems (P) Ltd., Chennai, India
Printed and bound in India by Replika Press Pvt. Ltd.
Printed on paper from sustainable resources

To my true friends
Luiz Moutinho

To Sharly, Edward and Andrew
Charles Chien

Contents

Contents

List of Figures

List of Tables

Preface and Acknowledgements

Welcome to the second edition of *Problems in Marketing: Applying Key Concepts and Techniques*. I am very pleased that I had the good sense of inviting my good friend Dr Charles S. Chien, from Feng China University in Taiwan, to co-author this new edition. Apart from being an accomplished researcher and solid academic, his impact to this new edition was invaluable, incisive and of extreme importance. I am therefore very grateful to him. Although there is a time lag since the first edition of this book appeared on the academic market 12 years ago, my special attachment for this book and its innovative features have always remained high and it is one of my favourite textbooks.

The ethos of the book has remained the same – it should be used primarily as a supplementary teaching and learning tool for any major marketing textbook. It can also be used for specialised electives at postgraduate levels and final-year undergraduates. The content of the book is still designed to provide many examples of marketing management practice, with each analytical problem concentrating on particular concepts or techniques.

I would like to thank all those adopters of the book who, at the time of its launch, were brave enough to be challenged with the degree of innovative traits provided in the text – its very nature in terms of analytical reasoning, its mostly quantitative content, as well as the computer-aided problems. Furthermore, I would like to thank all those adopters, reviewers and academic peers who have provided me with feedback over several years, as well as my many MBA students who were exposed to the book. I have taken into account all their suggestions, comments and criticisms. Moreover, I have used their valuable input to redesign this new edition of *Problems in Marketing: Applying Key Concepts and Techniques*.

What are then the new features of this edition? First, there are 72 analytical problems in total, covering 11 key areas of marketing management. This number represents a 20 per cent increase in the total number of analytical problems available to marketing lecturers. Three brand new sections have been added, reflecting the contemporary importance of these topics: Environmental Scanning; Internet Marketing; and Issues and Trends Shaping the Future. Also, one of the previous sections has been repositioned as 'Integrated Marketing Communication' and two of the previous sections have been combined into a new one – 'Marketing Research and Market Forecasting'. 'Consumer Behaviour' has become a stand-alone section and, finally, 'Positioning' has been combined with 'Product Policy Branding and New Product Development'.

As a response to a direct request from previous adopters, 60 per cent of all analytical problems included in the book are of a qualitative nature, with the remaining 40 per cent being clearly quantitative.

The make-up of the book with regard to the level of difficulty associated with the solving of the problems is pretty much halved. We now have 30 introductory problems,

24 problems of a medium level of complexity and 18 analytical problems that are applied at a more advanced level. As in the case of the first edition, we have developed ten of the quantitative problems so that they can be used and designed as computer-aided problems, meaning that they can be solved through the use of the software package which accompanies this text. Overall, this new edition represents almost a new book, since over 70 per cent of the analytical problems included are brand new!

The most important purposes behind this book are still valid – to help bring the subject of marketing management to life and to provide students with a new range of challenging situations and examples that will help them 'digest' hybrid marketing concepts, techniques and methodologies. This has been achieved by coming 'mind-stretching', robust, up-to-date and 'thought-provoking problems' which reflect 'managerial reality'.

This book only became a manageable project with the outstanding cooperation, help and support of Claire Leitch, who did a superb job in typing the manuscript. I would also like to thank my SAGE editors – Rosemary Nixon, Kiren Showman and Delia Martinez Alfonso – for all the encouragement, patience and support provided during the preparation of this text. To all of you who gave us motivation and assistance, please accept our gratitude.

We hope that you will continue to find *Problems in Marketing* a useful learning/ teaching resource. Many improvements can still be made, so we are counting on you to provide us with the necessary feedback, advice and positive criticism so that, jointly we can increase once again the book's substantiality and usefulness. Thanks once again!

Enjoy!

Luiz Moutinho and Charles S. Chien
Glasgow, Scotland
January 2007

1

Environmental Scanning

A marketing-oriented firm looks outwards to the environment in which it operates, adapting to take advantage of emerging opportunities and to minimise potential threats. In this section we shall examine the marketing environment, and how to monitor it. In particular, we shall look at some of the major forces acting on companies, such as the economic, social, legal, physical and technological issues which affect corporate activities.

The *marketing environment* consists of the actors and forces that affect a company's capability to operate effectively in providing products and services to its customers. It is useful to classify these forces into the micro-environment and the macro-environment. The *micro-environment* consists of the actors in the firm's immediate environment that affect its capabilities to operate effectively in its chosen markets. The key actors are suppliers, distributors, customers and competitors.

The *macro-environment* consists of a number of broader forces that affect not only the company but also the other actors in the micro-environment. These can be grouped under economic, social, legal, physical and technological forces. These shape the character of the opportunities and threats facing a company, and yet are largely uncontrollable.

The process of monitoring and analysing the marketing environment of a company is called environmental scanning. Two key decisions that management need to make are what to scan and how to organise the activity. Clearly, in theory every event in the word has the potential to affect a company's operations but to establish a scanning system which covers every conceivable force would be unmanageable. The first task, then, is to define a feasible range of forces that require monitoring. These are the *potentially relevant environmental forces* that have the most likelihood of affecting future business prospects. The second prerequisite for an effective scanning system is to design a system which provides a fast response to events that are only partially predictable and emerge as surprises and grow very rapidly. This is essential because of the increasing turbulence of the marketing environment. Ansoff proposes that environmental scanning monitors the company's environment for signals of the development of *strategic issues* which can have an influence on company performance.

1   *Line management* functional managers (e.g. sales, marketing, purchasing) can be required to conduct environmental scanning in addition to their existing duties. This approach can falter because of line management resistance to the imposition of additional duties, and the lack of specialist research and analytical skills required of scanners.

2   *Strategic planner* environment scanning is made part of the strategic planner's job. The drawback of this approach is that a head-office planner may not have the depth of understanding of a business unit's operations to be able to do the job effectively.

3   *Separate organisational unit* regular and ad hoc scanning is conducted by a separate organisational unit and is responsible for disseminating relevant information to managers. General Electrics use such a system with the unit's operations funded by the information recipients. The advantage is that there is a dedicated team concentrating their efforts on this important task. The disadvantage is that it is very costly and unlikely to be feasible except for large, profitable companies.

4   *Joint line/general management teams* a temporary planning team consisting of line and general (corporate) management may be set up to identify trends and issues that may have an impact on the business. Alternatively, an environment tread or issue may have emerged which requires closer scrutiny. A joint team may be set up to study its implications.

The most appropriate organisational arrangement for scanning will depend on the unique circumstances facing a firm. A judgement needs to be made regarding the costs and benefits of each alternative. The size and profitability of the company and the perceived degree of environment turbulence will be factors which impinge on this decision:

Brownlie (1987) suggests that a complete environment scanning system would perform the following:

1   Monitor trends, issues and events and study their implications.
2   Develop forecasts, scenarios and issues analysis as input to strategic decision-making.
3   Provide a focal point for the interpretation and analysis of environmental information identified by other people in the company.
4   Establish a library or database for environmental information.
5   Provide a group of internal experts on environmental affairs.
6   Disseminate information on the business environment through newsletters, reports and lectures.
7   Evaluate and revise the scanning system itself by applying new tools and procedures.

The benefits of formal environmental scanning were researched by Diffenbach (1983), who found that practitioners believed that it provided the following:

1   Better general awareness of and responsiveness to environment changes.
2   Better strategic planning and decision-making.
3   Greater effectiveness in dealing with government.
4   Improved industry and market analysis.
5   Better foreign investment and international marketing.
6   Improved resource allocation and diversification decisions.
7   Superior energy planning.

Environmental scanning provides the essential informational input to strategic fit between strategy, organisation and the environment. Marketing strategy should reflect the environment even if it means a fundamental organisation of operations.

(I) *Problem 1.1* Environmental scanning procedure

Introductory comments

Like any other new programme, the scanning activity in a corporation evolves over time. There is no way to introduce a foolproof system from the beginning. If conditions are favourable, that is if there is an established system of strategic planning in place and the CEO is interested in a structured effort at scanning, the evolutionary period shortens, of course, but the state of the art may not permit the introduction of a fully developed system at the outset. Besides, behavioural and organisational constraints require that things be done over a period of time.

The level and type of scanning activity that a corporation undertakes should be custom designed, and a customised system takes time to emerge into a viable system.

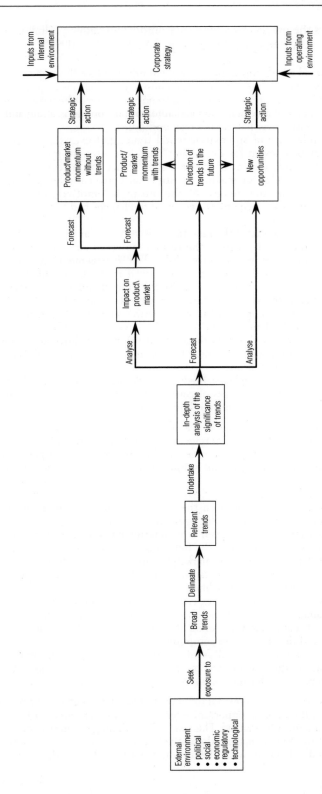

Figure 1.1 Linking environmental scanning to corporate strategy.

Figure 1.1 shows the process by which environmental scanning is linked to marketing strategy. Listed below are the procedural steps which explain this relationship.

1   Keep a tab on broad trends appearing in the environment. Once the scope of environmental scanning is determined, broad trends in the chosen areas may be reviewed from time to time. For example, in the area of technology, trends in mastery of energy, material science, transportation capability, mechanisation and automation, communications and information processing, and control over natural life may be studied.

2   Determine the relevance of an environmental trend. Not everything happening in the environment may be relevant for a company. Therefore attempts must be made to select those trends in the environment which have significance for the company. There cannot be any hard-and-fast rules for making a distinction between 'relevant' and 'irrelevant'. Consider, for example, the demise of the steam locomotive industry. Perhaps its constituencies would have been more receptive to changes had these come from within the industry itself.

I would hypothesise that if the new threat is very similar to a firm's traditional way of meeting consumer needs, such as the turbine-powered automobile being similar to the internal combustion-powered automobile, then management often would perceive the new development as threatening. However, if it meets consumer needs in very different ways, it is less likely to be recognised at an early point. For instance, I suspect that one of the major threats to the future growth of commercial airlines is originating not with transportation companies, but rather with communication firms. I am thinking in particular of the US Telephone and Telegraph's development of the 'television phone'. As that product is perfected and as the costs of using it are lowered, it may eliminate completely the need for many business flights, and consequently substantially impact upon the future growth of airlines.

Management's creativity and farsightedness would play an important role in a company's ability to pinpoint the relevant areas of concern. Described below is one way (for a large corporation) of identifying relevant trends in the environment:

*   Place a senior person in charge of scanning.
*   Identify a core list of about 100 relevant publications worldwide.
*   Assign these publications to volunteers within the company, one per person. Selected publications considered extremely important should be scanned by the scanning manager.
*   Each scanner reviews stories/articles/news items in the assigned publication that meet predetermined criteria, based on the company's aims. Scanners might also review books, conference proceedings, lectures and presentations.
*   The scanned information is given a predetermined code. For example, a worldwide consumer goods company used the following codes: subject (e.g. politics); geography (e.g. Middle East); function (e.g. marketing); application (e.g. promotion, distribution); and 'uniterm' or keyword for organising the information. An abstract is prepared on the story, and so forth, in a few lines.
*   The abstract, along with the codes, is submitted to a scanning committee consisting of several managers, to determine the relevance in terms of effect on corporate/ SBU/product market strategy. An additional relevance code is added at this time.
*   The codes and the abstract are computerised.
*   A newsletter is prepared to disseminate the information company-wide. Managers whose areas are directly affected by the information are encouraged to contact the scanning department for further analysis.

3   Study the impact of an environmental trend on a product/market. An environmental trend can pose either a threat or an opportunity for a company's product/market; which one it will turn out to be must be studied. The task of determining the impact of a change is the responsibility of the SBU manager. Alternatively, it may by assigned to another executive who is supposedly familiar with the product/market. If the whole subject appears

controversial, it may be safer to have an ad hoc committee look into it, or even consultants, either internal or external, may be approached. There is a good chance that a manager who has been involved with a product or service for a good many years would look at any change as a threat. He or she may therefore avoid the issue by declaring the impact to be irrelevant at the outset. If such sabotage is feared, perhaps it would be better to rely on the committee or a consultant.

4   Forecast the direction of an environmental trend into the future. If an environmental trend does appear to have significance for a product/market, it is desirable to determine the course that the trend is likely to adopt in the future. In other words, attempts must be made at environmental forecasting.

5   Analyse the momentum of the product/market business with the environmental trend. Assuming the company takes no action, what will be the shape of the product/market performance in the midst of the environmental trend and its direction into the future? The impact of an environmental trend is usually gradual. While it is helpful to be 'first' to recognise freedom of action, a serious effort would have to be undertaken to 'open up' line managers to new ideas and to encourage innovation in their plans.

CONDUCTING ENVIRONMENTAL SCANNING

Following the steps in Table 1.1 an attempt is made here to illustrate how specific trends in the environment may be systematically scanned.

A *literature search* in the area of politics shows the following laws:

1   Eliminating inside directors.
2   Requiring companies to meet the cost of 'unfriendly' proxy contests.
3   Barring nominee ownership of stock.
4   Reducing a company's right to fire workers at will.
5   Guarding worker privacy.
6   Mandating due-process procedures for grievances.
7   Disclosing lobbying efforts in detail.
8   Requiring that all ad claims be substantiated.
9   Publishing corporate actions that endanger workers or the environment.

Table 1.1 Systematic approach to environmental scanning

1   Pick up events in different environments (via literature search)
2   Delineate events of interest to the SBU in one or more of the following areas: production, labour, markets (household, business, government, foreign), finance, R&D. This could be achieved via trend-impact analysis of the events
3   Undertake cross-impact analysis of the events of interest
4   Relate the trends of the noted events to current SBU strategies in different areas
5   Select the trends which appear either to provide new opportunities or to pose threats
6   Undertake trends' forecasts
   Wild card prediction
   Most probable occurrence
   Conservative estimate
7   Develop three scenarios for each trend based on three types of forecast
8   Pass on the information to strategists
9   Strategists may repeat steps 4–7 and develop more specific scenarios vis-à-vis different products/markets. These scenarios will then be incorporated in SBU strategy

SCANNING TECHNIQUES

Environmental scanning has been implemented mainly with the use of conventional methodologies such as marketing research, economic indicators, demand forecasting and industry studies. But the use of such conventional techniques for environmental scanning has not been without pitfalls, for two major reasons. One, these techniques have failed to provide reliable insights into the future. As Ewing has said, 'the most careful and sophisticated forecasts of market demand have gone awry, and there is no technical improvement in sight that promises to change matters'. Two, these techniques, in any event, provide a narrow view of the environment:

Direct competition...is only one of the basic dimensions of the company's total strategic environment. The competitive audit must be augmented by assessment of the broader governmental, social, economic, ideological and other forces which all influence the company's character, purpose and strategies over the longer term. (J. Thomas Cannon (1972), Auditing the competition environment, in John W. Bonge and Bruce P. Coleman (eds), Concepts of Corporate Strategy, New York: Macmillan Co., pp. 263–4.)

Discussed below are a variety of techniques which have been adapted for use in environmental scanning.

Extrapolation procedures. These procedures require the use of information from the past to explore the future. Obviously their use assumes that the future is some function of the past. There are a variety of extrapolation procedures which range from a simple estimate of the future (based on past information) to regression analysis.

Historical analogy. Where past data cannot be used to scan an environmental phenomenon, the phenomenon may be studied by establishing historical parallels with other phenomena. Assumed here is the availability of sufficient information on the other phenomena. The turning points in the progression of these phenomena become the guideposts for predicting the behaviour of the phenomenon under study.

Missing-link approach. The missing-link approach combines morphological analysis and the network method. Many developments and innovations that appear promising and marketable may be held back because something is missing. Under such circumstances this technique may be used to scan new trends to see if they provide answers to the missing links.

Model building. This technique emphasises construction of models following deductive or inductive procedures. Two types of models may be constructed: phenomenological models and analytic models. Phenomenological models identify trends as a basis for prediction but make no attempt to explain the underlying causes. Analytic models seek to identify the underlying causes of change so that future developments may be forecast on the basis of a knowledge of their causes.

Delphi technique. The Delphi technique is the systematic solicitation of expert opinion. Based on reiteration and feedback, this technique gathers opinions of a panel of experts on happenings in the environment.

Intuitive reasoning. This technique bases the future on the 'rational feel' of the scanner. Intuitive reasoning requires free thinking unconstrained by past experience and personal biases. This technique, therefore, may provide better results when used by freelance think tanks than when used by managers on the job.

Scenario building. This technique calls for developing a time-ordered sequence of events bearing a logical cause–effect relationship to one another. The ultimate forecast is based on multiple contingencies, each with its respective probability of occurrence.

Cross-impact matrices. When two different trends in the environment point towards conflicting futures, this technique may be used to study these trends simultaneously for their effect. As the name implies, this technique uses a two-dimensional matrix, arraying one trend along the rows and the other along the columns. Some of the features of cross-impact analyses that make them attractive for strategic planning are that (1) they can accommodate all types of eventuality (social or technological, quantitative or qualitative, and binary events or continuous functions); (2) they rapidly discriminate important from unimportant sequences of developments; and (3) the underlying rationale is fully retraceable from the analysis.

Morphological analysis. This technique requires identification of all possible ways to achieve an objective. For example, the technique can be employed to anticipate innovations and to develop the optimum configurations for a particular mission or task.

Network methods. There are two types of network method: contingency trees and relevance trees. A contingency tree is simply a graphical display of logical relationships among environmental trends that focuses on branch-points where several alternative outcomes are possible. A relevance tree is a logical network similar to a contingency tree, but drawn in a way that assigns degrees of importance to various environmental trends with reference to an outcome.

Problem – example

The marketing strategist of a consumer goods company may want to determine if these trends have any relevance for the company. To do so the marketing strategist will undertake *trend-impact analysis.* This will require the formation of a Delphi panel to determine the desirability (0–1) technical feasibility (0–1), probability of occurrence (0–1) and probable time of occurrence of each event listed above. The panel may also be asked to suggest the area(s) which may be affected by each event that is production, labour, markets (household, business, government, foreign), finance, or R&D.

The above information about an event may be studied by managers in areas which, according to the Delphi panel, are likely to be affected by the event. If their consensus is that the event is indeed important, the scanning may continue (see Table 1.2).

Next, *cross-impact analysis* may be undertaken. This type of analysis is planned to study the impact of an event on other events. Where events are mutually exclusive, such analysis may not be necessary. But where an event seems to reinforce or inhibit other events, the cross-impact analysis is highly desirable for uncovering the true strength of an event.

The cross-impact analysis amounts to studying the impact of an event (given its probability of occurrence) upon other events. The impact may be delineated either in qualitative terms (such as critical, major, significant, slight or none) or in quantitative terms in the form of probabilities.

Table 1.3 shows how cross-impact analysis may be undertaken. The cross-impact ratings or probabilities can best be determined with the help of another Delphi panel. To sharpen the analysis further, it may also be determined whether the impact of an event on other events will be felt immediately or after a certain number of years.

Table 1.2 Trend-impact analysis: an example

Event	Requiring that all ad claims be substantiated	Reducing a company's right to fire workers at will
Desirability	.8	.5
Feasibility	.6	.3
Probability of occurrence	.5	.1
Probable time of occurrence	2003	2010
Area(s) impacted	Household markets Business markets Government markets Finance R&D Production	Labour Finance
Decision	Carry on scanning	Drop from further consideration

Note: Two to three rounds of Delphi would be needed to arrive at the above probabilities.

Table 1.3 Cross-impact analysis: an example

Event	Probability of occurrence	Impact								
		a	b	c	d	e	f	g	h	i
(a) Eliminating inside directors	.6									
(b) Requiring companies to meet the cost of 'unfriendly' proxy contests	.3		.3*							
(c) Barring nominee ownership of stock	.5									
(d) Reducing a company's right to fire workers at will	.1									
(e) Guarding worker privacy	.4									
(f) Mandating due-process procedures for grievances	.3									
(g) Disclosing lobbying efforts in detail	.4									
(h) Requiring that all ad claims be substantiated	.5									
(i) Publishing corporate actions that endanger workers or the environment	.4								.7**	

Notes
* This means that elimination of inside directors has no effect on the probability of event (b).
** This means that if publishing corporate actions that endanger workers or the environment occurs (probability .4), the probability of requiring that all ad claims be substantiated increases from .5 to .7.

The cross-impact analysis provides the 'time' probability of occurrence of an event and indicates other key events which may be monitored to keep track of the first event. Cross-impact analysis is more useful for project-level scanning than for general scanning.

To relate the environmental trends to strategy, consider the following assumed environmental trends and strategies of a cigarette manufacturer.

Trends

T_1 Requiring that all ad claims be substantiated
T_2 Publishing corporate actions that endanger workers or the environment
T_3 Disclosing lobbying efforts in detail
T_4 Reducing a company's right to fire workers at will
T_5 Eliminating inside directors

Strategies

S_1 Heavy emphasis on advertising, using emotional appeals
S_2 Seasonal adjustments in labour force for agricultural operations of the company
S_3 Regular lobbying effort against further legislation imposing restrictions on the cigarette industry
S_4 Minimum number of outside directors on the board

The analysis in Table 1.4 shows that strategy S_1, heavy emphasis on advertising, is most susceptible and requires immediate management action. Among the trends, trend T_5, eliminating inside directors, will have the most positive overall impact. Trends T_1 and T_2, requiring that all ad claims be substantiated and publishing corporate actions that endanger workers or the environment, will have a devastating impact. This type of analysis indicates where management concern and action should be directed.

Table 1.4 Use of matrix to determine the impact of selected trends on different corporate strategies

Trends	Strategies				Impact (I_1)	
	S1	S2	S3	S4	+	−
T_1	−8	0	+2	−2		8
T_2	−4	−2	−6	0		12
T_3	0	+4	−4	+2	2	
T_4	0	−4	0	+6	2	
T_5	−2	+6	+4	+2	10	
Impact(I_2) +	−	4	−	8		
−	14	−	4	−		

(*Table 1.4 continued*)

Table 1.4 Continued

Scale

Scale		
+8	Enhance the implementation of strategy	Critical
+6		Major
+4		Significant
+2		Slight
0		
−2	Inhibit the implementation of strategy	Slight
−4		Significant
−6		Major
−8		Critical

Thus, it will be desirable to undertake forecasts of trends T_1 and T_2. The forecasts may predict when the legislation will be passed, what the major provisions of the legislation will be, and so forth. Three different forecasts may be obtained:

1 Extremely unfavourable legislation.
2 Most probable legislation.
3 Most favourable legislation.

Three different scenarios (using three types of forecast) may be developed, indicating the impact of each trend. This information may then be passed on to product/market managers for action. Product/market managers may repeat steps 4–7 (see Table 1.1) to study the selected trend(s) in depth.

Questions

1 Define both areas and discuss the link between the concepts of environmental scanning and strategic planning.
2 Give and explain some examples of classic market opportunity analyses which have recognised key environmental trends.
3 What are the organisational behaviour implications of environmental scanning, especially when dealing with (1) responsibility; (2) key tasks to be implemented; and (3) staff training and motivation?
4 Describe and comment on the trend impact analysis approach as well as on the Delphi technique.

(I) *Problem 1.2* Assessing the social environment

Introductory comments

The ultimate test of a business is its social relevance. This is particularly true in a society where survival needs are already met. It therefore behoves the strategic planner to be familiar with emerging social trends and concerns. The relevance of the social environment to a particular business will of course vary depending on the nature of the business. For a technologically oriented business, the scanning of the social environment will be limited to aspects of pollution control and environmental safety. For a consumer products company, however, the impact of the social environment will go much further.

An important aspect of the business environment is the values people hold. In recent years changes in these values have stimulated massive regulations, deep criticisms, new demands and challenges of the very foundation on which business rests. For example, a substantial percentage of people in the USA are less and less willing to accept the impartial operation of the market mechanism as the best way to allocate resources. They expect government to intervene on their behalf. Another interesting value shift is what Daniel Bell calls the Revolution of Rising Entitlements, challenging the traditional concept of egalitarianism. Equality had meant that conditions should permit individuals, whatever, their origins, to make a life on the basis of ability and character. It was believed that everyone should have an equal place at 'the starting line'. More recently the emphasis has shifted to the finish line, a guarantee of an equal outcome for all. A central tenet of the new egalitarianism argues that because people are born with different natural abilities and are raised under different circumstances, not everyone approaches the starting line equally. In this light, it is argued, fairness and justice necessitate equalisation of results.

Observers have noted many other value shifts that directly or indirectly influence business. For example, people today seek self-gratification now rather than later. They want the good things of life immediately. They want to lead lives that are continuously improving in quality. There is a growing attitude of cynicism towards authority. There seems to be an erosion of that part of the Protestant ethic that motivates people to high standards of work performance. People seem to want a more comfortable and less risky life. People are no longer willing to accept traditional rights of property ownership but want to influence how property is used. Profit is no longer universally accepted as the end purpose of business. Society is coming more and more to expect that societal interests be considered, as well as business self-interest, in pursuing profit objectives. Some observers see in such trends a serious erosion of the fundamental institutional values of the classical free enterprise system.

Information on social trends may be derived from published sources. The impact of social trends on a particular business can be studied in-house or with the help of outside consultants. A number of consulting firms specialise in making this kind of study. Table 1.5 shows 31 social trends which, according to the firm of Yankelovich, Skelley and White, Inc., will have a tremendous effect on business in the coming years. One of these, female careerism (trend 30 in Table 1.5), is of particular interest to the retail industry. This structural social change leads retailers to ask such questions as: Where does the working wife like to do most of her shopping? What type of store does she prefer? How fashion-conscious is she? What sources of information does she use before she makes a purchase? What kinds of service does she expect retailers to provide?

A proprietary study on the subject (conducted for a major department store) with which the author was associated brought out interesting findings. It was found that in general, working wives are better educated, are more experienced metropolitans and have more sophisticated tastes than wives who do not work outside the home. Their shopping behaviour is considerably different from that of the traditional woman shopper.

Table 1.5 Social trends having marketing significance

Psychology of affluence trends, reflecting the increasing assumption that the essentials of economic survival are assured, leading to a focus on having more or doing more to improve the quality of living.

Trends
1   Personalisation
2   Physical self-enhancement
3   Physical fitness and well-being
4   Social/cultural self-expression
5   Personal creativity
6   Anti-materialism
7   Meaningful work

Anti-functionalism trends, reflecting reaction to the emphasis on the functional and 'scientific', seen as leading to drabness and boredom in everyday life.

Trends
8   Mysticism
9   Sensuousness
10   New romanticism
11   Introspection
12   Novelty and change
13   Beauty in the home

Reaction against complexity trends, reflecting the belief that life has become excessively complicated, that the individual has lost control of his/her destiny, and that there is much to be gained by returning to a more natural and more simple style of life.

Trends
14   Return to nature
15   Simplification
16   Anti-bigness
17   Scientism and technology
18   Ethnic orientation
19   Local community involvement

Trends related to the weakening of the 'Protestant ethic', reflecting a questioning of a value system, termed the 'Protestant ethic' by sociologists, which, put very simply, is based on the belief that ambition, striving, hard work, self-sufficiency, self-denial and other familiar virtues will lead to a successful life.

Trends
20   Living for today
21   Hedonism
22   Away from self-improvement
23   Non-institutional religion
24   Liberal sex attitudes
25   Blurring of the sexes
26   Acceptance of drugs

Trends reflecting permissiveness in child rearing, deriving from the psychological guidelines which have been widely used in the upbringing of our current youth population. These guidelines were based largely on concern about the negative after-effects of a rigid, demanding, punishment-oriented childhood.

Trends
27   Anti-hypocrisy
28   Rejection of authority
29   Tolerance for chaos and disorder
30   Female careerism
31   Familism

The working-wife market cannot be served by a store that is 'all things to all customers'. It is predicted that a new kind of store is on the horizon which may emerge either within a department store or as a separate institution to cater for this market. The working wife was found to prefer suburban stores to downtown stores even though she may be working downtown. She is likely to be interested in the latest fashions and looks for clothing that is stylish but practical on the job. The above findings bear heavily on retailers' strategies in such areas as merchandising, the role of the suburban store, store positioning, fashion orientation, promotion and store services.

Let us take two additional trends – physical fitness and well-being (trend 3 in Table 1.5) and meaningful work (trend 7) – and examine their impact on marketing strategy.

Physical fitness and well-being

Salads and fish are replacing the traditional American dinner of meat and potatoes. Increasing varieties of decaffeinated coffee and tea and substitutes for sugar and salt are crowding supermarket shelves. Shoppers are reading the small print to check for artificial ingredients in foods and beverages they once bought without a thought. Smoking is finally declining. Manufacturers and retailers of natural foods are building a healthy 'health industry' in the midst of a slow economy.

The dramatic new awareness of health is prompting these changes. The desire to feel better, look younger and live longer exerts a powerful influence on what people put into their bodies, and this strong force is now moving against a well-entrenched habit that affects millions and dates back to biblical times – the consumption of too much alcohol.

Health substitutes for alcoholic beverages, labelled 'dealcoholised', are now being offered to US consumers. For some time, gourmet food shops have stocked champagne-like bottles of carbonated grape juice and cans containing a not-fully brewed mixture of water, malt, corn, yeast and hops. Except for the packaging, these alcohol-free imitations failed to resemble wine and beer, especially in the crucial area of taste. The new dealcoholised beverages, however, are fully fermented or brewed before their alcohol is separated out – either by pressure or heat – to below an unnoticeable 0.5 per cent, which is the federal maximum before classifying a drink as alcoholic. The taste and body of the beverages match that of their former alcoholised selves.

This 0.5 per cent level is so low that a drinker would need to consume 24 glasses of dealcoholised wine or eight cans of dealcoholised beer to obtain the same amount of alcohol as in one 4-ounce glass of regular wine or one 12-ounce can of regular beer. Thus the drinker avoids not only intoxication but also worthless calories, as a regular glass of wine or beer has about 150 calories, while their dealcoholised copies contain about 40–60 calories respectively. And their prices are the same.

Introduced in Europe around 2001, dealcoholised wines are just now entering the USA.

Meaningful work

The following changes are producing a new challenge at work. First, people want good jobs, not make-work. Second, workers want their individual rights to be respected. Third, the concept of the professional appears to be under siege. It is increasingly difficult for professionals to maintain their special status in a society that is becoming more knowledge-oriented, more bureaucratic and more participatory. The growth of the two-income family is also blurring status distinctions, as it has brought a new degree of affluence to the so-called working class. For example, a secretary and her labourer husband can have a family income of £30,000 a year, while a family headed by a sole-earner college professor or attorney can have an income well under that. Fourth, the oncoming generation has doubts about the ideals of efficiency. They are unwilling to pay the crushing price of loss of pride, mind-killing monotony, dehumanisation and stress diseases in return for the highest wages in history. Fifth, today a woman's place can be wherever she wants it to be, and so a greater number of women are expected to find their place in the labour market.

Problem

LIFESPAN is a new company in the insurance market in Scotland. The company is a niche player pursuing specific types of segment (i.e. work-related insurance services) as well as developing a range of new financial services products, such as the 'housewife insurance plan' which takes into account the new life demands (e.g. dual-income families, the difficulties associated with the fulfilment of housework chores and duties, etc.) and work/social pressures which affect many layers of the population. Mike O'Leary, the marketing manager of the company, is considering the implementation of a marketing scanning study to take into account social trends which will impact directly on his strategic marketing plans.

Questions

1   What are the strategic implications derived from the main source trends which will impact on LIFESPAN with regard to the job market and working patterns?
2   What is your assessment of the future developments linked with the women's job market, their employment situation as well as their specific needs for life insurance?
3   What lessons can LIFESPAN learn from the environmental scanning exercise with regard to equal employment opportunities and group coverage?

(M) Problem 1.3 Scanning and forecasting methods

Introductory comments

Market measurement is an activity of critical importance for a wide range of decisions. Market-potential estimates and industry and company sales forecasts are essential for the development of corporate marketing strategies and produce objectives. Middle-management decisions regarding the size and allocation of marketing expenditures depend heavily on sales forecasts and on the relationship between forecasts and measures of profitability and productivity. By understanding the purpose and assumptions behind a given market measurement, a manager will find it easier to specify the kind of information needed in a given situation and to understand the degree of reliability that should be placed on a given market-measurement estimate.

Additionally, managers should be aware of the available data sources that can be used to develop market-measurement estimates. When environmental changes can be expected to create a shift in the historical pattern of sales, then time-series models are likely to prove unsatisfactory. In such situations, managers are more likely to use forecasting techniques that link sales to one or more factors thought to cause or influence sales. Descriptive models such as multiple-regression models are used when a number of factors have an impact on sales. Multiple-regression forecasts allow managers to incorporate the expected effects of any controllable marketing variables likely to be significant when one is forecasting company sales. The goal is to assess the relationship between these controllable variables and sales. Can the variation in sales for different time periods be explained by levels of price, promotion, distribution and so on, in those time periods? A multiple-regression model, with sales as the dependent variable and the controllable factors as predictor or independent variables, will address this question.

JUDGEMENTAL APPROACHES

Frequently, it is not possible to rely on statistical approaches to forecasting. Time-series methods may be inappropriate because of wide fluctuations in sales or because of anticipated changes in trends. Regression methods may not be feasible because of a lack of historical data or because of management's inability to determine (or even identify) causal factors. The judgemental approach may be management's only possible avenue for forecasting in these situations.

Even when statistical estimates are available, managers may want to use judgement to supplement these approaches because even the most sophisticated statistical models cannot anticipate all the potential external factors that can influence sales (such as strikes at customers' facilities or major competitive innovations). Two prevalent judgemental techniques are jury of executive opinion and Delphi techniques. The jury of executives opinion invites the input from senior-level executives. In some cases the executives are asked to give an optimistic, pessimistic and most probable level of sales for some future period. The forecasting managers first determine a forecast for each executive and then combine the levels of all the executives. The Delphi technique asks members of a team to submit their forecasts and the assumptions behind the forecasts. These are then reviewed by a team leader and given back to the participants, with a summary of the first round, for a second round of forecasts. When an acceptable consensus is reached the process stops.

INTERPRETING THE FORECAST

In evaluating the managerial implications of a sales forecast, managers should be fully aware of both the sensitivity of forecast results to slight changes in forecast assumptions or techniques and the costs of forecasting errors.

SENSITIVITY ANALYSIS

If several techniques give essentially the same results, the reliability of a forecast should be greater. Accordingly, some firms develop parallel forecasts based on alternative techniques. Knowing how different techniques or assumptions lead to alternative estimates enables a manager to determine how sensitive the forecast is to a change in these factors. When forecasts are highly sensitive, managers should expect greater imprecision and should closely monitor the environment to find out which model and which assumptions most closely approximate reality.

THE COSTS OF FORECAST ERRORS

Companies that make or sell products with long lifetimes and steady sales are less concerned with the costs of forecast errors because the forecasts in these cases are likely to be close to actual sales. However, when the sales forecast given to management has a large standard error, managers need to consider the costs of overestimating and underestimating sales.

As Table 1.6 indicates, different kinds of consequence are associated with overestimating and underestimating company sales. For some firms, the cost of holding excess inventory may be extremely high (perhaps because the product is perishable), whereas the amount of sales lost because of delayed shipments is very low (perhaps because the company has loyal customers). Accordingly, if a firm is in that situation, management will be more willing to risk underestimation than overestimation. This willingness to risk underestimation occurs because the cost of excess inventory resulting from excess production will outweigh the lost revenue from an inadequate level of production. Because the costs of overestimation are greater for that firm, managers will probably want to base decisions on a forecast that is more conservative than the sales forecast.

Problems

Consider Table 1.6(a), which presents data on market shares for a leading brand of biscuits. Notice that market share varies from a low of 46.61 per cent in period 14 to a high of 61.08 per cent in period 21. The factors used to explain the variation in sales are relative levels of price, distribution and advertising. The relative levels are the ratio

---

Table 1.6 Possible results of company sales forecast errors

Results of overestimation
Excess capacity leading to layoffs, loss of skilled labour
Price cuts or additional marketing expenses to move product
Distributor ill-will because of excess distributor inventories
Inventory costs
Cash flow problems and cost of capital tied up in finished goods, components, raw materials
Technical obsolescence or damage
Storage or warehousing costs

Results of underestimation
Lost sales or customer goodwill
Overtime costs
Costs of expediting shipments
Reduced quality control because of reduced maintenance of machinery at full production capacity
Production of bottlenecks because of lack of material and parts

---

Table 1.6(a) Leading brand of biscuits

Period	Market share	Relative price	Relative distribution	Relative advertising
1	0.518667	0.99596	1.05763	0.83048
2	0.558001	0.99112	1.03970	0.42723
3	0.545538	0.98112	1.04589	0.24783
4	0.493883	1.00633	1.03959	0.55797
5	0.502510	0.98687	1.03284	1.00000
6	0.553169	0.97524	1.04448	1.00000
7	0.561195	0.97223	1.04752	0.97441
8	0.535317	0.99437	1.05605	0.51284
9	0.540326	0.99321	1.05296	0.51284
10	0.522628	0.98322	1.03618	0.56120
11	0.536117	1.00383	1.04714	0.80892
12	1.558861	0.99705	1.04960	1.00000
13	0.524293	1.00225	1.04838	0.22737
14	0.466122	1.00172	1.04868	0.32652
15	0.471938	1.00017	1.02406	0.32546
16	0.497760	0.98295	1.03772	0.80955
17	0.511327	0.97971	1.06260	0.87337
18	0.554894	0.98837	1.09686	0.73084
19	0.590279	0.99098	1.10962	0.95759
20	0.572970	0.98397	1.06835	1.00000
21	0.610783	0.97863	1.11071	0.46047

of the company's level to the industry average. The multiple-regression model based on the data in Table 1.6(a) is

Market share = .61 − 1.11 (relative price) + .97 (relative distribution)
$\qquad$ + .01 (relative advertising)

Although many other factors could explain why market share varies from one period to another, the model explains greater than 60 per cent of the variation in market share, based solely on relative levels of price, distribution and advertising.

Additionally, as in any statistical forecast, the company was able to determine the standard error of the forecast – in this case .025; that is, there is always some imprecision in terms of past sales and past forecasts. Two-thirds of the time the forecast estimate of sales will be within one standard error (in this case .025) of actual market share; 95 per cent of the time, forecasted share will be within two standard errors (in this case .05) of the actual market share.

Multiple-regression models allow managers to predict values of the dependent variable (e.g. market share) for different levels of the predictor variables (e.g. price, distribution and advertising). If we set the relative price at .95, relative distribution at 1.06, and relative advertising at 1.0, the estimated level of market share, based on the multiple-regression model described above, is:

Market share = .61 − 1.11 (.95) + .97 (1.06) + .01 (1.0)
$\qquad$ = .5937

When constructing and interpreting multiple-regression models, managers need to address a number of important questions in order to assess the reliability of the regression forecasts. Two of the more important questions regarding multiple-regression models are:

- Have any important factors been left out of the model?
- Are the independent or predictor variables correlated among themselves?

The first question deals with the specification of the model. If any factors that have a significant impact on sales have been left out of the model, the impact will not be included in the forecast and, therefore, the forecast can be seriously biased.

The second question deals with the manager's ability to isolate the effects of predictor variables on the dependent variable. Consider the multiple-regression model for estimating the market shares for the biscuit manufacturer. The coefficients for price, distribution and advertising are 1.11, .97 and .01 respectively. There is a temptation to conclude that distribution is highly related to changes in market share and advertising is not. However, if the two variables, distribution and advertising, are themselves highly correlated, one cannot make this conclusion.

Assume that a manager has been given a company sales forecast of 200,000 units with a standard error of 10,000 units. Statistical theory tells us that there is a 95 per cent chance that the actual level sales will be within two standard errors. Thus, there is a 95 per cent chance that sales will be within the range of 180,000–220,000 units. If the manager sets production at the lower end – 180,000 units – and demand is higher, the underestimation will lead to stockouts or shortages of the product. If the manager sets production at the high end – 220,000 units – and demand is less, the overestimation will lead to excess inventory. Either of these consequences adds to the cost of the products. In some industries characterised by highly volatile demand, like the fashion industry, the costs of stockouts for underestimation and markdowns for overestimation can actually exceed the original cost of manufacturing.

Questions

1   What are some of the key issues that you need to address in order to evaluate the reliability of regression forecasts?
2   Comment of the methodology behind these two judgemental forecasting methods: jury of executive opinion and Delphi technique.
3   Discuss the different kinds of consequences associated with overestimating and under-estimating company sales.

(M) *Problem 1.4* Data mining

Introductory comments

Analysing large databases has become known as *data mining*, and businesses hope it will allow them to boost sales and profits by better understanding their customers. The analysis of databases is not new – what is new and challenging is the extraordinary size of these databases.

The availability of huge databases began with scanner purchase data. Estimates suggest that marketing managers in packaged goods companies are inundated with 100 to 1,000 times more bits of data than even a few years ago because of the adoption of scanner technology in their channels of distribution. Some data mining techniques also arose in response to 'database marketing' or 'direct marketing' (e.g. by catalogue vendors or coupon distribution providers) in which a company is trying to form relationships with its individual customers, as marketing attempts to proceed from 'mass' (one media message for all potential buyers) to 'segments' (some targeting and positioning differences) to 'one-to-one' marketing. In order to achieve such tailored market offerings, a company has to know a lot about its customers, hence the data contain many pieces of information on each of the company's many customers.

Traditionally, a company's database would have contained only current business information, but many now contain historical information as well. These 'data warehouses' literally dwarf those available even a few years ago. For example, Wal-Mart has contracted with NCR Corporation to build a data warehouse with 24 terabytes (1 terabyte = 1,000 gigabytes) of data storage, which will make it the world's largest data warehouse. The system will provide information about each of Wal-Mart's 3,000 plus stores in multiple countries. Wal-Mart plans to use the information to select products that need replenishment, analyse seasonal buying patterns, examine customer buying trends, select markdowns, and react to merchandise volume and movement.

In response to the increasingly massive data sets, firms have been working to create increasingly sophisticated data mining technologies (hardware and software) to analyse the data. Data mining uses *massively parallel processing* (MPP) and *symmetric multi-processing* (SMP) supercomputer technologies (during which multiple data points and sub-routines may be processing simultaneously, compared with old-fashioned 'serial' processing, in which one datum is processed after another). These huge machines support 'relational' database programs that can slice massive amounts of data into dozens of smaller, more manageable pools of information.

Sometimes these intensive approaches are applied to databases that are being analysed with fairly traditional statistical techniques. For example, regression is still a premier analytical tool, because many predictors can be used to capture complex consumer decision-making and market behaviour – forecasting sales as a function of season, price, promotions, sales force, competitor factors and delivery delays. Other popular techniques of data mining include cluster analysis for segmentation and neural networks. Businesses regularly use data mining analytical tools to mathematically model customers who respond to their promotional campaigns versus those who do not. The effects of direct mailing efforts, for example, are easily measured and compared as a function of customer information (demographics such as age, household size, income) and purchase behaviour (past buying history, cross-sales). Data mining can also be used to measure incremental business (additional traffic, sales, profits) that may be directly attributed to a recent promotion by deliberately withholding the promotional mailing from a 'control' group 'experimental' techniques.

In addition to standard techniques being applied to these huge data sets, marketing research methodologists are creating techniques and software especially for data mining analyses of large data sets. Sales of such customer management software are currently growing at five times the rate of the overall software market, as managers struggle to track every encounter with each customer, to facilitate call-centre interactions between customers and customer service representatives, and to manage internal customers, for example, one's sales force. Some of these relational database systems include NCR's Teradata system or Unix or Windows NT machines, IBM's Intelligent

Miner and SAS's Enterprise Miner. Other software companies offer 'content aggregator' services that synthesise multiple databases – company financial information, histories, executive profiles and the like.

As an illustration of a data mining exercise, Farmers Insurance used IBM's DecisionEdge software to look at the 200 pieces of information the company maintained on its database of 10 million automobile insurance policy owners. Think of a sports car owner and 'you probably imagine a twenty-something single guy flaming down the highway in his hot rod'. This profile fit many of its customers, but the data mining exercise identified another segment of sports car owner – married baby boomers with kids and more than one car. These customers produced fewer claims, yet had been paying the same sports-car surcharge. With this information in hand, Farmers could charge them less, providing greater value and customer satisfaction.

There is no question that the explosion in databases, computer hardware and software for accessing those databases, and the World Wide Web are all changing the way marketing intelligence is obtained. Not only are more companies building DSSs, but those that have them are becoming more sophisticated in using them for general business and competitive intelligence. This, in turn, has produced some changes in the organisation of the marketing intelligence function. One change has been the emergence of the position of chief information officer, or CIO.

The CIO's major role is to run the company's information and computer systems like a business. The CIO serves as the liaison between the firm's top management and its information systems department. He or she has the responsibility for planning, coordinating and controlling the use of the firm's information resources, and is much more concerned with the firm's outlook than with the daily activities of the department. CIOs typically know more about the business in general than do the managers of the information systems department, who are often more technically knowledgeable. In many cases, the managers of the information systems department will report directly to the CIO. Information systems are not intended to be simply data warehouses – the management of information is ideally designed as an electronic library that allows all employees access to the 'firm's collective wisdom'.

FROM ACCOUNTS TO CUSTOMERS

The data extracted from the customer information system had one row per account. This reflects the usual *product-centric* organisation of a bank where managers are responsible for the profitability of particular products rather than the profitability of customers or households. The best next offer project required pivoting the data to build *customer-centric* models.

To be useful for cross-selling, the 1.2 million account-level records extracted from the customer information system had to be transformed into around a quarter of a million household-level records. This was accomplished using SAS to group all the accounts for a given tax identification number and then transpose them into a single customer record with a set of columns for each account type. In cases where the bank was aware that multiple members of a household had accounts, one of them was chosen as the primary ID (identifiers) for the household and used to identify all house-hold members. This allowed each newly created customer record to represent all accounts belonging to an entire household. The new customer record contains a count for each product, indicating how many accounts of that type the household has (zero in most cases) along with the associated balances. The resulting table had many more fields than the original extract of account data. The abbreviated Table 1.7 gives a feel for the kinds of variables that were available as inputs to the model.

Table 1.7 Illustrative sample of variables used as input to models

Household-level field descriptions
Account county
Address state
Age of latest asset management product
Age of latest business brokerage product
Age of latest business credit card
Age of latest business time deposit
Age of latest business interest checking
Age of latest business instalment direct loan
Age of latest business loan
Age of latest business credit line

The variables whose names start with age say how many months the customer has had an account of this type. This information is derived from the account open date.
America Online user flag
Acquired from
Time with bank
Credit card declined flag
Express check card #1 flag
Express check card #2 flag
Bank territory
Bank county
Months since express check card was used
Bank employee household

Household-level field descriptions
Number of people in household
Microvision household description code
Premier (high value) household
Time between becoming bank customer and going online (months)
True if delay greater than 30 days
Number of credits
Number of debits
Months online
Number of products held
Pseudo tax ID (real tax IDs not used to protect customer privacy)
Count of asset management products
Count of business brokerage products
Count of business credit cards
Count of business time deposit accounts
Count of business interest checking accounts

Banking products fall into families such as 'credit cards' or 'demand deposit accounts'. The variables starting with the word 'counts' are derived variables that say how many the customer has in each account family.
Uses Quicken
Number of balance inquiries last 60 days – card one

(*Table 1.7 continued*)

Table 1.7 Continued

Number of ATM payments last 60 days – card one
Number of POS uses last 60 days – card one
Number of balance inquiries last 60 days – card one
Network ATM use last 60 days – card one
Bank ATM use last 60 days – card one
True if customer has any business product
True if customer uses Quicken bill paying feature
True if customer uses MS Money
True if customer uses Quicken

Many of the fields are flags that are true if the customer uses a particular service or has exhibited a certain behaviour.
True if customer has at least one student loan
True if customer has at least one time deposit
True if customer has at least one unsecured line of credit

Household-level field descriptions
True if customer has at least one wholesale DDA product
True if customer has private banking services
Balance for asset management products
Balance for business brokerage products
Balance for business credit cards
Balance for business time deposit accounts
Balance for business interest checking

Clearly, account balances can be very predictive.
Total balance over all customer's accounts
True if customer has total balance over $50,000
County of residence or 'other'
Customer tenure bin
Telephone area code or 'other'
Household standard metropolitan statistical area or 'other'
First three digits of postal zip code or 'other'

Note that many of the variables used as inputs to the model-building process are derived variables that were not part of the original extract. Some values, such as length of tenure, have been binned into ranges. Others, such as total balance, are values calculated from the original fields. A few are flags added to reflect groups of people that the bank considered interesting, such as people who tried online banking within 30 days of becoming a bank customer and people whose total deposits with the bank were over $50,000.

DEFINING THE PRODUCTS TO BE OFFERED

The customer information system recognised several hundred different products, many of which are simply small variations on a theme. This level of product differentiation is too detailed for the kind of marketing campaign we were supporting. For example, the bank might make someone an offer of a savings account without trying to determine which of several variants would be most likely to appeal. These variants offer different interest rates based on total balances at the bank, other types of account, and so on. In fact, there are business rules for determining which savings account is most appropriate for a given customer – data mining can figure out that a savings account is appropriate and then business rules take over to determine which one in particular.

Often the number of product codes is often dauntingly large. And, when there are too many codes (more than a few dozen) it is difficult to develop good cross-sell models – there are simply too few instances for each one. Often, many of the codes refer to the same type of thing, such as a current account or a home mortgage, with just minor (from the point of view of marketing) differences between them. Look for a hierarchy that describes the products at the right level.

There is a budgeting application that rolls up account types into a hierarchy of product category, account type and subtype. The four major categories are deposit account, loan, service and investment. The marketing people decided that, with a few modifications, the account-type level of this pre-existing hierarchy would serve well. From a marketing perspective, some of the account types are essentially the same, such as certificates of deposit (CDs) and time deposits (TDs). These account types were combined into a single category.

The product categories were used as the target variables for modelling. That is, a model predicted who would have CD/TD, or home mortgages, or whatever. The individual product types were retained as input variables. Table 1.8 shows the 45 product types used for the best next offer model. Of these, 25 products are ones that may be offered to a customer as part of this campaign. Information on the remaining (business-oriented) account types are used only as input variables when building the models.

Problem – example

Pillsbury's internal network allows its employees in over 70 countries access to data of several kinds, including consumer feedback that has been logged into a massive database (based on 3,500 calls a day to the 800 number printed on every Pillsbury product), manufacturing (testing equipment at new plants, statistics on production quality and packaging) and so on. Any employee, at a plant or at a sales call pitching new products to a grocer, can access the company's data.

Hallmarks Cards assists its 15,000 store managers in 'stock-keeping unit (SKU) optimisation', the allocation of store square footage to its 40,000 products. It can determine which cards and gifts are selling on any given day at any given retail outlet.

CONSUMER INSIGHTS GAINED FROM DATA MINING

Loyalty cards, such as those offered at supermarket retailers, offer consumers discounted prices and coupon incentives. In the past ten years, more than 100 million loyalty cards and key tags have been issued: 30 per cent of supermarket customers have them and, of those, 70 per cent use them. Companies know that all customers are not equal, and loyalty cards enable one-to-one marketing, customising the shopping

Table 1.8 Product types used in the best next offer model

Product code	Product description	To be modelled	Account holders	Combine with
ASM	Asset management	No		
BBK	Business brokerage	No		
BCC	Business credit card	No		
BCD	Business certificate of deposit	No		
BIC	Business interest bearing checking			
BIL	Bill pay	Yes	106,949	
BLD	Business loan division	No		
BLN	Business line of credit	No		
BMM	Business money market	No		
BMR	Business market rate	No		
BMS	Business money market savings	No		
BNC	Business non-interest checking	No		
BSV	Business savings	No		
CC	Credit card	Yes	154,738	
CD	Certificate of deposit	Yes	10,646	
CUS	Custody	No		
DLR	Instalment dealer loans	Yes	2,693	
ELC	Equity line of credit	Yes	10,952	
EXL	Express lease	Yes	2,792	
GRP	Group retirement programmes	No		
GUR	Wholesale loan guarantors	No		
IBC	Interest bearing checking	Yes	40,233	
IL	Instalment direct loans	Yes	12,545	
IRA	Individual retirement account	Yes	13,074	
IRB	Individual retirement account brokerage	Yes	2,045	
IRF	Individual retirement account mutual funds	Yes	5,339	
LOC	Line of credit	Yes	53	
ML2	Second mortgage	Yes	519	
MMA	Money market access	Yes	1,823	
MMS	Money market savings	Yes	35,841	
MRA	Market rate account	Yes	19,467	
MTG	Mortgage	Yes	2,444	
NIC	Non-interest bearing checking	Yes	370,420	
PAN	Platform annuities	No		
PMR	Premier	No		
RBR	Retail brokerage	Yes	5,297	
RP	Retirement programmes	No		
RPS	Retirement programmes securities	No		

experience for households with different purchasing profiles (e.g. sensitivities to price, value, brand and quality). Loyalty cards and grocery purchases have yielded consumer insights and marketing actions such as these:

1   Of Diet Coke drinkers, 13 per cent consume 83 per cent of its volume. Taster's Choice is even more extreme – it generates 73 per cent of its sales from only 4 per cent of its customers.
2   Gillette used a direct marketing mailing campaign to send its razors and coupons to men and women who purchased competitors' razors.
3   Coca-Cola strengthened its relationship and power with retailers when it demonstrated that customers who purchased Coke as one of the items in their shopping trolleys were more profitable to the retailer (for the entire basket of purchases) than consumers who did not purchase Coke.

Federal Express data mines to obtain customer segments to pinpoint their desires for greater profitability. Customer service representatives are empowered to go to different lengths to satisfy customers who have been segmented as more and less profitable. This customer relationship management effectively creates a profit-and-loss statement per customer and customer segment.

Rubbermaid data mines its warehouse to determine promotional effectiveness. It can model the likely sales resulting from a 25 per cent reduction on prices with two-page ads compared with 40 per cent price cuts with smaller ads. They also use their data for merchandise optimisation and claim that this careful category management also enhances their relationships with their retailers, such as Wal-Mart, Pamida and Ames.

Hotels regularly collect a great deal of information on their guests. They supplement guest history data with guest preferences, and can thereby provide better quality and customised service. Implementers of such data systems find greater customer satisfaction and loyalty, and increased revenue per customer.

Questions

1   Explain some of the reasons behind the advent and availability of large databases to help companies/organisations increase their marketing effectiveness.
2   Discuss the role and managerial implications of some of the key data mining technologies.
3   Comment on the emergence of the position of a chief information officer (CIO) and its appearance on an organisational chart and its main functions.

(I) *Problem 1.5* Elements of a global information system

Introductory comments

Information, or useful data, is the raw material of executive action. The global marketer is faced with a dual problem in acquiring the information needed for decision making. In advanced countries the amount of information available far exceeds the absorptive capacity of an individual or an organisation. The problem is super-abundance, not scarcity. While advanced countries all over the world are enduring an information explosion, there is relatively little information available on the marketing characteristics of less developed countries. Thus the global marketer is faced with the problem of information abundance and information scarcity. The global marketer must know where to go to obtain information, the subject areas that should be covered, and the different ways that information can be acquired. The process of information acquisition is known as *scanning*. The section that follows presents a scanning model for multinational marketing. The chapter continues with an outline of how to conduct global marketing research.

ELEMENTS OF A GLOBAL INFORMATION SYSTEM

Information subject agenda

A subject agenda, or list of subjects for which information is desired, is a basic element of a global marketing information system. Because each company's subject agenda should be developed and tailored to the specific needs and objectives of the company, it is not possible to suggest an ideal or standard agenda. Therefore any framework, such as that proposed in Table 1.9, consists of six broad information areas with 31 information

Table 1.9 Categories for a global business intelligence system

Category	Coverage
I Market information	
1 Market potential	Information indicating potential demand for products, including the status and prospects of existing company products in existing markets
2 Consumer/customer attitudes and behaviour	Information and attitudes, behaviour, and needs of consumers and customers of existing and potential company products. Also included in this category are attitudes of investors towards a company's investment, merit
3 Channels of distribution	Availability, effectiveness, attitudes and preferences of channel agents
4 Communications media	Media availability, effectiveness and cost
5 Market sources	Availability, quality and cost
6 New products	Non-technical information concerning new products for a company (this includes products that are already marketed by other companies)
II Competitive information	
7 Competitive business strategy and plans	Goals, objectives. Definition of business; the 'design' and rationale of the company
8 Competitive functional strategies, plans and programmes	Marketing: target markets, product, price, place, promotion. Strategy and plan, finance, manufacturing, R&D and human resource strategy, plans, and programmes
9 Competitive operations	Detailed intelligence on competitor operations. Production, shipments, employee transfers, morale, etc.
III Foreign exchange	
10 Balance of payments	Government reports
11 Nominal and real interest rates	Expert estimation
12 Inflation rate compared with weighted trading partner average	Secondary information report
13 Estimate of international competitiveness	Expert judgement

(*Table 1.9 continued*)

Table 1.9 Continued

Category	Coverage
14 Attractiveness of country currency and assets to global investors	Currency demand
15 Government policy regards: country competitiveness	Expert assessment
16 Country monetary and fiscal policy	Expert assessment
17 Spot and forward market activity	Market reports
18 Expectations and opinions of analysts, traders, bankers, economists, business people.	General assessment
IV Prescriptive information	
19 Foreign taxes	Information concerning decisions, intentions and attitudes of foreign authorities regarding taxes upon earnings, dividends and interest
20 Other foreign prescriptions and laws	All information concerning local, regional or international authority guidelines, rulings, laws, decrees other than foreign exchange and tax matters affecting the operations, assets or investments of a company
21 Home country prescriptions	Home country incentives, controls, regulations, restraints, etc., affecting a company
V Resource information	
22 Human resources	Availability of individuals and groups, employment candidates, sources, strikes, etc.
23 Money	Availability and cost of money for company uses
24 Raw material	Availability and cost
25 Acquisitions and mergers	Leads or other information concerning potential acquisitions, mergers or joint ventures
VI General conditions	
26 Economic factors	Macro-economic information dealing with broad factors, such as capital movements, rates of growth, economic structure, and economic geography
27 Social factors	Social structure of society, customs, attitudes, and preferences
28 Political factors	'Investment climate', meaning of elections, political change
29 Scientific technological factors	Major developments and trends
30 Management and administrative practices	Management and administrative practices and procedures concerning such matters as employees compensation, report procedure
31 Other information	Information not assignable to another category

categories. The framework satisfies two essential criteria. First, it is exhaustive: it accepts all the subject areas of information encountered by a company with global operations. Second, the categories in the framework are mutually exclusive: any kind of information encompassed by the framework can be correctly placed in one and only one category.

Prescriptive information covers the rules for action in the foreign market. This category incorporates information from guidelines to regulations, rulings and laws by public and private groups and authorities.

Scanning modes: surveillance and search

Once the subject agenda has been determined, the next step in formulating a systematic information-gathering system in the organisation is the actual collection of information. There are two important modes or orientations in information collection or scanning: surveillance and search.

In *surveillance* the scanner is oriented towards acquiring relevant information that is contained in messages that cross his or her scanning attention field. In *search* the scanner is deliberately seeking information, either informally or by means of an organised research project. The two orientations and their components are briefly described in Table 1.10.

The significance of determining scanning mode is the measure it offers (1) of the extent that a scanner actively seeks out information, as contrasted to the more passive acquisition of information and (2) of the scanner's attention state at the time of acquiring information.

Table 1.11 shows that the bulk of information acquired by headquarters' executives of major US multinational firms is gained through surveillance as opposed to search (73 per cent versus 27 per cent). However, viewing (general exposure), the least oriented of the surveillance modes, generates only 13 per cent of important external information acquired, where monitoring generates 60 per cent.

Table 1.10 Scanning modes

Modes	Coverage
Surveillance orientation	
Viewing	General exposure to external information where the viewer has no specific purpose in mind other than exploration
Monitoring	Focused attention, not involving active search, to a clearly defined area or type of external information
Search orientation	
Investigation	A relatively limited and informal seeking of specific information
Research	A formally organised effort to acquire specific information usually for a specific purpose

Table 1.11 Relative importance of scanning modes in acquiring global information

	Percentage of information acquired	
Surveillance		73
Viewing	13	
Monitoring	60	
Search		27
Investigation	23	
Research	4	
Total	100	100

This paucity of information generated by viewing is the result of two factors. One is the extent to which executives are exposed to information that is not included in a clearly defined subject agenda. The other is their receptiveness to information outside this agenda. Both factors operate to limit the relative importance of viewing as a scanning mode. Every executive limits his or her exposure to information that will not have a high probability of being relevant to the job or company. This is a rational and necessary response to the basic human mental limitations. A person can handle only a minute fraction of the data available to him or her. Because exposure absorbs limited mental resources, exposure must be selective.

Nevertheless, receptiveness by the organisation as a whole to information not explicitly recognised as important is vital. The effective scanning system must ensure that the organisation is viewing areas where developments that could be important to the company might occur. This may require the creation of a full-time scanning unit that would have explicit responsibility for acquiring and disseminating information on subjects of importance to the organisation.

SOURCES OF INFORMATION

Human sources

As can be seen in Table 1.12, people are the most important source of information for headquarters executives of global companies. The most important human source of external information is company subsidiaries, affiliates and branches. The importance of executives abroad as a source of information about the world environment is one of the most striking features of the modern global corporation. The general view of headquarters executives is that company executives overseas are the people who know best what is going on in their areas. Typical comments of headquarters executives are:

Our principal sources are internal. We have a very well informed and able overseas establishment. The local people have a double advantage. They know the local scene and they know our business. Therefore, they are an excellent source. They know what we are interested in learning, and because of their local knowledge they are able to effectively cover available information from all sources.

The presence of an information network abroad in the form of company people is a major strength of the global company. It may also be a weakness in the scanning posture of a company that has only partially extended the limits of its geographical operations because inside sources abroad tend to scan only information about their own countries or region. Although there may be more attractive opportunities outside existing areas of operation, the chances of their being noticed by inside sources in a domestic company are very low because the horizons of domestic executives tend to end at national borders.

Table 1.12 Sources of information (percentage)

Location of sources		Types of source	
Inside organisation	34	People	67
Outside organisation	66	Documentary	27
		Physical phenomena	6

A man may be perfectly rational, but only within a limited horizon. As a consumer, he will normally restrict his expenditures to those goods offered to him through customary channels. As a producer, he will sell his goods typically in a given ambit. Over his horizon there may be brilliant opportunities to improve his welfare as a consumer or his income as a producer, but unless he is made aware of them, they will avail him nothing.

Distributors, consumers, customers, suppliers and government officials are also important information sources. Information from these sources is largely obtained by country-operating personnel as opposed to headquarters' staff. Other sources are friends, acquaintances, professional colleagues, 'freelance' university consultants, and candidates for employment, particularly if they have worked for competitors. As shown in Table 1.13, personal sources of information far exceed impersonal sources in importance. Eighty-six per cent of the human sources utilised by respondents are personal. Interestingly, when human sources inside and outside the company are compared, 97 per cent of sources inside the company are personal. The comparison suggests that lack of acquaintanceship is a barrier to the flow of information in an organisation, thus underlining the importance of travel and contact.

Significantly, three-quarters of the information acquired from human sources is gained in face-to-face conversation. Why is face-to-face communication so important? There are many factors involved. Some information is too sensitive to transmit in any other way. Political information from government sources, for example, could be damaging to the source if it were known that the source was transmitting certain information. In such cases, word of mouth is the most secure way of transmitting information. Information that includes estimates of future developments or even appraisals of the significance of current happenings is often considered too uncertain to commit to writing. One executive in commenting upon this point said:

People are reluctant to commit themselves in writing to highly 'iffy' things. They are not cowards or overly cautious; they simply know that you are bound to be wrong in trying to predict the future, and they prefer to not have their names associated with documents that will someday look foolish.

Other information does not have to be passed on immediately to be of value. For example, a division president said:

Information of relevance to my job [strategic planning] is not the kind of information which must be received immediately. Timeliness is not essential; what is more important is that I eventually get the information.

Table 1.13 Comparison of personal and impersonal human sources (percentage)

Source relationship	Inside sources	Outside sources	All human sources
Personal sources	97	80	86
Impersonal sources	3	20	14
Total	100	100	100
Number of instances	$N = 33$	$N = 60$	$N = 93$

The great importance of face-to-face communication lies in the dynamics of personal interaction. Personal contact provides an occasion for executives to get together for a long enough time to permit communication in some depth. Face-to-face discussion also exposes highly significant forms of communication, such as the tone of voice, the expression of a person's eyes, movements, and many other forms of communication that cannot be expressed in writing.

Documentary sources

Of all the changes in recent years affecting the availability of information, perhaps none is more apparent than the outpouring of documentary information. This outpouring has created a major problem, the so-called 'information explosion'. The problem is particularly acute for international marketers who must be informed about numerous national markets.

Although executives are overwhelmed with documentary information, only a handful of companies employ a formal system for monitoring documentary information. The absence of formal monitoring systems has resulted in a considerable amount of duplication. A typical form of duplication is the common practice of an entire management group reading one publication covering a particular subject area when several excellent publications covering the same area are available.

The best way to identify unnecessary duplication is to carry out an audit of reading activity by asking each person involved to list the publications he or she reads regularly. A consolidation of the lists will reveal the reading attention of the group. In a surprisingly large number of instances, the reading attention of the group will be limited to a handful of publications to the exclusion of other publications of considerable merit. An elaboration of this procedure could involve consultation with experts outside the company regarding the availability and quality of publications in relevant fields.

External documentary sources are a valuable source of information for part of every company's international information requirement, and they are also a particularly valuable source of information for the student who typically does not have the human and written sources that are available to a long-time professional working in the field.

Perception sources

Direct perception is the source of a very limited proportion of the information acquired by executives, as measured by message volume. However, it provides a vital background for the information that comes from human and documentary sources. There are three types of direct perception. One type is information easily available from other sources, but it requires sensory perception of the actual phenomena to register the information in the respondent's mind.

Another type of direct perception is information not readily available from alternative sources. An example is the information that a company is erecting a plant in a country capable of producing a competitive product. Local executives in the country drive by the new plant every day on their way to their offices but are unaware of the product X potential of the plant under construction. The company erecting the plant had announced that it was for product Y, and local executives have accepted this announcement. The headquarters executive realises immediately that it is potentially capable of producing product X. He possesses technical knowledge that enables him to perceive information in a physical object (the plant) that his local executives are unable to perceive.

The third type of direct perception is perhaps the most important. This is the background information that one gets from observing a situation. Of course, in multinational marketing, direct perception requires travel. Thus the independent variable in the use of this source is travel. Travel should be seen not only as a tool for management control of existing operations, but also as a vital and indispensable tool in information scanning.

Information perception and media

The medium is the channel through which information is transmitted. Any marketing information system is based on three basic media: the human voice for transmitting words and numbers; printed words and numbers; and direct perception through the senses of sight, hearing, smell, taste and touch. Each of these basic information system media has been extended in recent years by important innovations in electronic and travel technologies. Of particular importance to the marketing information system have been the impressive developments in the Internet, e-mail, satellite communication networks for voice and data, and transportation via jet aircraft.

Comparability of international data

International statistics are subject to more than the usual number of caveats and qualifications concerning comparability. An absence of standard data-gathering techniques is the basis for some of the lack of comparability in international statistics. In Germany, for example, consumer expenditures are estimated largely on the basis of turnover tax receipts, whereas in the UK consumer expenditures are estimated on the basis of data supplied not only by tax receipts but also from household surveys and production sources.

Even with standard data-gathering techniques, definitional differences would still remain internationally. In some cases, these differences are minor; in others, they are quite significant. Germany, for example, classifies the purchase of a television set as an expenditure for 'recreation and entertainment', whereas the same expenditure falls into the 'furniture, furnishings and household equipment' classification in the USA.

Problem – example

Survey data are subject to perhaps even more comparability problems. When Pepsico International, a typical user of international research, reviewed its data, it found a considerable lack of comparability in a number of major areas. Table 1.14 shows how age categories were developed in seven countries surveyed by Pepsico.

While flexibility may have the advantage of providing groupings for local analysis that are more pertinent (e.g. 14–19 might be a more pertinent 'youth' classification in one country, whereas 14–24 might be a more useful definition of the same segment in another country), the marketing research group at Pepsico's headquarters pointed out that if data were reported to the company's headquarters in standard five-year

Table 1.14 Age classifications from consumer surveys, major markets

South Korea	Brazil	Chile	Slovenia	Portugal	Ireland	Taiwan
14–18	10–14	14–18	14–19	15–24	13–20	14–18
19–25	15–24	19–24	20–29	25–34	21–25	19–25
26–35	25–34	25–34	30–39	35–44	26–35	26–35
36–45	35–44	35–44	40–49	45–54	36–45	36–50
46+	45+	45–65	50+	55–64	46–60	
				65+		

Table 1.15 Definition of consumption used by Pepsico market researcher

Mexico	Count of number of occasions product was consumed on day prior to interview
Venezuela	Count of number of occasions product was consumed on day prior to interview
Argentina	Count of number of drinks consumed on day prior to interview
Germany	Count of number of respondents consuming 'daily or almost daily'
Spain	Count of number of drinks consumed 'at least once a week'
Italy	Count of number of respondents consuming product on day prior to interview
Philippines	Count of number of glasses of product consumed on day prior to interview

intervals, it would be possible to compare findings in one country with those in another. Without this standardisation, such comparability was not possible. The company's headquarters marketing research group recommended, therefore, that standard five-year intervals be required in all reporting to headquarters, but that any other intervals that were deemed useful for local purposes were perfectly allowable. Pepsico also found that local market definitions of consumption differed so greatly that it was unable to make inter-market comparisons of brand share figures. Representative definitions of consumption are shown in Table 1.15.

One important qualification about comparability in multi-country survey work is that comparability does not necessarily result from sameness of method. A survey asking the same question and using the same methods will not necessarily yield results that are comparable from country to country. For example, if the data were recorded by household, the definition of *household* in each of these countries could vary. The point is that comparability of results has to be established directly; it does not simply follow from the sameness of method. Establishing that results will be comparable depends upon either knowing that methods will produce identical measurements or knowing how to correct any biases that may exist.

Questions

1 Define the scanning modes of surveillance and search.
2 Comment on the role of documentary sources.
3 Analyse the relevant issues that can be raised when a marketing manager is addressing the subject of comparability of international data.

Reference and further readings

Berry, M. and Linoff, G.S. (2000) *Mastering Data Mining*, New York: John Wiley & Sons.

Bishop, W.S., Graham, J.L. and Jones, M.H. (1984) Volatility of derived demand in industrial markets and its management implications, *Journal of Marketing*, Fall: 95–103.

Brownlie, D. (1987) Environmental analysis, in Baker, M.J. (ed.) *The Marketing Book*, Oxford: Butterworth-Heinemann.

Churchill, G. and Iacobucci, D. (2002) *Marketing Research: Methodological Foundations*, Mason, OH: South-Western.

Dalrymple, D., Strahle, W. and Bock, D. (1989) How many observations should be used in trend regression in forecasts? *Journal of Business Forecasting*, Spring: 7–10.

Daniel Bell (1975) The revolution of rising entitlements, *Fortune*, April: 98–185.

Dickinson, C. and Tabernilla, M. (1999) A new customer relationship management approach, *Lodging Hospitality*, 15 May: R11–12.

Diffenbach, J. (1983) Corporate environmental analysis in large US corporations, *Long Range Planning*, 16(3): 107–16.

Frisbie, G. and Mabert, V.A. (1981) Crystal ball vs. system: the forecasting dilemma, *Business Horizons*, September–October: 72–6.

Georgoff, D.M. and Murdick, R.G. (1986) Manager's guide to forecasting, *Harvard Business Review*, January–February: 110–19.

Guiltinan, J.P., Paul, G. and Madden, T. (1997) *Marketing Management: Strategies and Programs*, New York: McGraw-Hill.

Hagdorn-van der Meijden, Jo, van Nunen, A.E.e. and Ramondt, A. (1994) Forecasting – bridging the gap between sales and manufacturing, *International Journal of Production Economics*, 101–14.

Jobber, D. (1988) *Principles and Practice of Marketing* (second edition), London: McGraw-Hill.

Judge, P.C. (1998) What've you done for us lately? *Business Week*, 14 September: 140–6.

Keegan, W.C. (1989) *Global Marketing Management*, Englewood Cliffs, NJ: Prentice-Hall.

Mahajan, V., Muller, E. and Bass, F. (1990) New product diffusion models in marketing: a review and directions for research, *Journal of Marketing*, January: 1–26.

Mentzer, J.T. and Gomes, R. (1994) Further extensions of adaptive extended exponential smoothing and comparison with the M-comparison, *Journal of the Academy of Marketing Science*, 22 (4): 372–82.

Norton, P. (1994) Welcome to the fast lane, *Sales and Marketing Management*, August: 65–6.

Proctor, R.A. (1989) A different approach to sales forecasting: using a spreadsheet, *European Management Journal*, Fall: 358–65.

Raider, A.M. (1999) Programs make results out of research, *Marketing News*, 33 (21 June): 14.

Schnaars, S.P. (1984) Situational factors affecting forecast accuracy, *Journal of Marketing Research*, August: 290–7.

Sobek, R. (1973) A manager's primer on forecasting, *Harvard Business Review*, May–June: 6–15.

Thomas Cannon, J. (1972) Auditing the competition environment, in John W. Bonge and Bruce P. Coleman (eds) *Concepts of Corporate Strategy*, New York: Macmillan Co. pp. 263–4.

Wang, G.C.S. (1993–94) What you should know about regression-based forecasting, *The Journal of Business Forecasting*, Winter: 15–21.

2

Consumer Behaviour

Consumer behaviour is important from a number of different points of view. From the perspective of marketing, the study of consumer behaviour is important as it helps forecast and understand consumer demand for products as well as brand preferences. From the perspective of consumer policy, it is important to inform consumers about the alternatives open to them and to avoid being deceived. Consumers also need to gain insight into their own behaviour if they are to spend their income optimally. From the perspective of science, the study of consumer behaviour is a rich domain to test economic, cognitive, economic-psychological and social-psychological theories.

The concept of a 'consumer' is only a century old. In an economy of scarcity, the challenge is to 'survive' and to fulfil basic needs. Only if households earn more income than is necessary for their basic needs, do they become free to make choices about how they spend and save. In such cases, we speak of 'discretionary income'. Originally, discretionary income only applied to the higher classes of nobility, the clergy and other wealthy citizens. It was only after the Second World War that most people acquired discretionary income. Consumers held more power because they were able to make choices about their purchases. This increasing freedom of choice makes it important to gain insight into consumer behaviour to help explain preferences for products and brands.

With the development of new interactive media, consumers have acquired even more power. By using the Internet and intelligent search agents, consumers can obtain considerable information on the various prices and qualities of products. Markets become more transparent to them. With new interactive media, consumers can take the initiative to communicate, retrieve any information they need anytime and any where, and then, if they choose to, order various products and services.

The study of consumer behaviour may be approached from a number of different perspectives. Marketing, market research, consumer advice and consumer policy have all been mentioned. But it is also important to distinguish the objectives of consumer behaviour studies. Is the aim to describe and explain consumer behaviour as accurately as possible? Is there an attempt to predict consumer behaviour? Is the purpose to help consumers to make good decisions and to maximise their utility? In these respects, normative, prescriptive, predictive and descriptive approaches to consumer research can be distinguished.

In the normative approach to consumer behaviour, it is assumed that structuring the choice problem and the available information will help consumers to take optimal decisions. So, the most important aim is to improve the process of decision-making and to prevent consumers from neglecting important information. If consumers are assisted in this way, they learn how to decide best and not necessarily what to decide.

In economics, normative rules are used to explain consumer behaviour, assuming rationality in decision-making. This assumes that people maximise utility or optimise decision-making. Obviously, consumers frequently try to behave reasonably and rationally. However, in practice, it appears that consumers do not always behave according to normative rules.

The normative approach is also emphasised in consumer education. Here, consumers are taught how to make the best decisions. Impulsiveness is discouraged in favour of comparing and evaluating alternatives. In consumer advice, too, normative elements appear. The aim of consumer advice is for consumers to spend their budgets 'as effectively as possible'. Marketing also includes normative elements. Sometimes, in advertising, choice rules are suggested to be 'the best' for consumers.

The prescriptive approach goes one step further. Here, it is prescribed what consumers should decide, given their budget and their objectives. Budgeting advice frequently makes prescriptive recommendations regarding spending and saving to encourage consumers to make best use of their resources. Consumer advice almost always includes prescriptive elements.

The predictive approach mainly deals with predictions of consumer behaviour. For example, how will consumers react to an advertising campaign? Or, what will the market share of a new product be? Economists strongly emphasise prediction, sometimes at the expense of descriptive or explanatory power. Marketing managers, too, are chiefly interested in the prediction of behaviour rather than the underlying model of consumer behaviour, although an effective underlying model clearly makes it possible to make predictions in new situations.

(I) *Problem 2.1* Emotions and consumer behaviour

Introductory comments

The last two decades have witnessed a growing interest in models of consumer behaviour that emphasise situational influences, such as emotions and feelings, in order to understand economic behaviours. These behaviours are often difficult, if not impossible, to explain with the neoclassical economic approach, which suggests that people are 'reasonable' and try to maximise some utility function. This approach could also be observed in psychology, where the so-called 'cognitive turn' dominated for several decades, using an analogy of the individual as an information-processing mechanism. Emotions, feelings and affect were then regarded as being irrational, even dysfunctional. It became, however, more and more obvious that many consumer behaviours cannot be sufficiently explained within the information-processing paradigm: gambling for high stakes, watching fear-arousing movies, collecting teddy bears, engaging in risky sports such as skydiving, buying from impulse, or browsing leisurely through shopping malls. As Scitovsky (1986) has pointed out, when applying optimal arousal theory in an economic context, the tremendous increase in security and safety as a result of social, economic and technological progress seems to have triggered the need for finding sources of excitement in consumption-related areas.

Consumer behaviour research outside economics departments has reflected psychology's so-called 'rediscovery of affect' and increasingly acknowledged the influence of emotional states in evaluating such situations as service encounters, responding to point-of-purchase stimuli, high versus low involvement in products, attitudes towards advertising, extent of perceived risk, or processing of marketing communications. On the other hand, it is also recognised that any encounter with the world of goods can trigger various emotions during the consumption experience, either actively sought out by the consumer or involuntarily evoked by dis/satisfaction with products and services.

The term 'emotion' will be used here as an umbrella term for feelings, moods and affect-based personality characteristics. Feelings are high in intensity, mainly of short duration and highly specific, while moods are less intense, last longer and are of intermediate specificity. Affective personality characteristics refer to the pleasure, arousal, dominance (PAD) paradigm by differences in preferred pleasure, arousal and dominance levels. They are low in intensity, long in duration, and low in specificity.

FUNCTIONS OF EMOTIONS

Emotions serve at least four functions in human behaviour. These functions are important for the understanding of the role of emotions as antecedents, correlates and consequences of consumer actions (compare Pieters and van Raaij, 1988).

1   Interpretation and organisation of information and knowledge about one's own somatic and psychic functioning as well as about one's physical and social environment.
2   Mobilisation and allocation of resources. Emotions change people's states of readiness for action through arousal or performance enhancement (e.g. fear or anger), motivation (e.g. pleasure), or interrupting an ongoing task.
3   Sensation-seeking and avoidance in order to pursue an optimum level of arousal between the extremes of boredom and stress, reflected in a need for stimulation.
4   Interpersonal communication via facial expressions and body language, revealing to and sharing one's feelings and preferences with others.

EMPIRICAL EVIDENCE

Multiple studies have investigated the interaction of emotions with concepts such as impulse buying, self-gifts, gift-exchange processes, recreational shopping, self-regulatory (eating) behaviour, need for stimulation, perceived risk and satisfaction.

Using the PAD paradigm, Rook and Gardner (1993) found that impulsive buying is most likely in the case of low arousal mood states such as boredom, low pleasure/high arousal mood states such as anxiety, and low to mid-range dominance mood states such as frustration. This indicates that impulsive shoppers are prone to act impulsively under many different circumstances or that they may have developed behavioural heuristics for coping with their moods that non-impulsive shoppers have not. Here, the above-mentioned functions (1) and (3) of emotions seem to apply.

Somewhat related to impulse buying is the notion of self-gift behaviours. Mick and DeMoss (1990) suggest that self-gifts are a complex class of personal acquisition that are premeditated and context bound. They are a form of personally symbolic self-communication, and for women they are precipitated by personal situations such as significant life transitions, work situations and disrupted interpersonal relations (Mick et al., 1992). The factors in the retail setting that affect self-gift giving include novelty of the brand, price and the salesperson's empathy for the buyer's personal situation. Functions (2) and (3) of emotions are here the most prominent.

Not only self-gifts but also gift-exchange processes involve emotions: the types of event and situation that lead to the expression of certain emotion through gift-giving on the one hand, and the types of emotions that are experienced by givers and recipients under various conditions of gift exchange. It was found in various studies that both givers and recipients are quite specific about the types of emotion (to be) expressed at various gift-giving occasions (Ruth, 1996). For instance, joy was associated with birthdays and weddings, pride with graduation and awards, hope with house-warming and retirement, gratitude with hostess/host gifts, and affection with anniversary, courtship and funerals. These examples illustrate functions (1) and (4) of emotions.

Recreational shopping, that is, browsing in shopping malls or department stores as a leisure activity, is another area of consumer behaviour in which emotions play an important role to ensure an enjoyable use of time in a sensually stimulating environment. Within a Finnish setting and based on the PAD paradigm, it was found that the recreational shopping tendency is a manifestation of a more general exploratory tendency and that it is dependent on an individual's preferred emotional state, particularly on the preferred arousal level (Boedeker, 1997). In other words, recreational shopping is a consumer activity aimed at satisfying a need for stimulation, thus being a case in point for function (3) of emotions.

There have been a number of studies dealing with the emotional content of advertising, based on the assumption that in a world where material needs are satisfied, the need for informational content becomes less important. But there seem to be individual differences in preferred levels of stimulation. In an exploratory study using a series of fear-appeal advertisements, it was shown that 'need for stimulation' (NST) is a key moderating variable between the arousal potential of a stimulus and the evaluation of that stimulus. Further, the effect of arousal potential on arousal was stronger for individuals with higher NSTs, and the level of arousal at which stimulus evaluation reaches a maximum is higher for individuals with higher NSTs (Steenkamp et al., 1996). This result is an example of function (3).

It has been suggested that emotions in the consumption experience are linked to perceived risk, with negative emotions being positively related and positive emotions being negatively related (Chaudhuri, 1997). Studies with both products and services as units of observation revealed that emotional dimensions such as joy, affection, sadness, anger and anxiety, in conjunction with product involvement and perceived differences between alternatives, account for a substantial amount of perceived risk. Perceived risk was also shown to mediate the effect of negative emotion and perceived differences on brand loyalty and information search while positive emotions were not related to any of these variables. Function (2) seems to be represented in these findings.

Another way of looking at perceived risk is to assess product satisfaction in the post-consumption experience. A study in which respondents evaluated both high- and low-involvement products in current use reported affective responses. Their assessment of their levels of satisfaction did reveal that two primary dimensions of product evaluation, namely utilitarian and hedonic judgement, are causal antecedents to the affect dimensions of pleasantness and arousal and to product satisfaction (Mano and Oliver, 1993). This covers especially function (1).

Problem – example

JCB approached The Licensing Company (TLC) with a brief to extend its appeal beyond its industrial heritage to fashion-conscious young people, children and the DIY hobbyist – effectively to develop a brand lifestyle relevant to an individual from childhood to adulthood. The first task was to look at its existing appeal, and how to market to different audiences.

BRAND ASSESSMENT

An early step was to assess the values the brand epitomised to the different age groups. 'Yellow', 'diggers' and 'durable' were three themes common to all audiences, and whereas adults saw the brand as a British one of quality and functionality, children saw it as big, muddy and thus 'fun'. The three areas of business TLC and JCB decided to target with sub-brands were fashion, toys and hardware.

Competition in the marketplace was already strong, and TLC were careful to differentiate themselves from the positioning of existing, potentially competitive brand extensions by names such as Jeep, Land Rover and Cat. 'We recognised from the start that there was a finite number of quality licensees for each range who would be suitable for partnerships with the JCB brand', says Farrugia, managing director of TLC. 'It took careful managing of the brand aspirations and close ongoing partnerships with the respective licensees on where the products are going.'

'We are always weighing up where the PR and ads are going – in the case of JCB, the weight of this activity is concentrated at the adult level, which retains the value for adults and increases its value for the kids', says Farrugia. 'The pull-through then comes from aiming the proposition at adults, and attracting the kids through the aspirational virtue of being part of a grown-up brand.'

The positive consumer reaction has led to roll-out into Europe and the launch of more products in each range. A sign of things to come, then, as other brands go for a cradle-to-grave approach?

'I would advise caution to any brand considering something so ambitious', says Farrugia. 'Very few brands can cope with the demographic range required to maintain appeal from childhood to adulthood. It is TLC's ability to recognise values such as these which sets it apart as a licensing agency.'

THE THREE JCB BRAND RANGES

Fashion: JCB works

Epitome of urban credibility. Designed to reflect JCB brand qualities of strength, integrity, and functionality. Outdoor and 'rugged' clothing items such as combat trousers, fleeces and funnel-neck jumpers, footwear and sports equipment. *Partners*: Secured Debenhams as exclusive partner in the fashion range. Other partners are Indigo Shoes Ltd and Quaser Sports.

Toys: JCB junior

'Big things for little people.' Reliable and built-to-last toys which represent a return to traditional values. Children can now dress up in construction worker overalls and a hard hat, play next to their father with their own workbench, drive their own digger, steer infra-red diggers up the rugged mud and rock challenge. Toys incorporate the spirit of learning, play and fun. The theme for the junior range is 'dads and lads'; unpatronising, and not detracting from the adult level. *Partners*: David Halsall International Ltd, Joal, Rolly Toys, Smoby UK Ltd, the ERTL Company, Best Lock Group.

DIY: JCB Sitemaster

The name of an actual JCB digger, the Sitemaster range comprises quality power tools, outdoor power products and hand tools. *Partners*: Alba, Pacific Brands.

Questions

1   Describe and provide your own examples of the functions of emotions.
2   Explain the antecedents and consequences of impulse buying, self-gift behaviours and recreational shopping.
3   How do you assess the effectiveness of JCB's brand strategy in terms of emotions and consumer behaviour?

(I) *Problem 2.2* Consideration sets

Introductory comments

Not only must consumers decide on the criteria to use in pre-purchase alternative evaluation, they must also determine the alternatives for the choice that is made. These alternatives define what is known as the consideration set (also known as the evoked set). As suggested by the information presented in Table 2.1, the consideration set will typically contain only a subset of the total number of alternatives available to the consumer. These results represent the average size of the consideration set. Thus, some consumers will have even larger consideration sets, whereas the consideration sets for other consumers will be smaller. Some consumers, such as those extremely loyal to a particular brand, will have only one brand in their consideration set.

Table 2.1 Average size of consumers, consideration sets by product category

Average consideration set size	Up to 3	3 to 5	Above 5
Product category	• Air freshener • Chili • Insecticides • Laxative • Razors	• Analgesic • Antacid • Bar soap • Bleach • Coffee • Cookies • Deodorant • Frozen dinners • Laundry detergent • Peanut butter • Sinus medicine • Soap • Yoghurt	• Bathroom cleaner • Beer • Shampoo • Shortening • Soda

Gaining entry into the consideration set is a top priority. Failure to do so means that a competitor's offering will be purchased. Marketers must therefore take steps to see that their products gain consideration during decision-making. Notice how it plays on consumers' fears about making a mistake during decision-making as a means of gaining consideration. Another tactic used by companies to gain consideration is to offer incentives. Automobile manufacturers sometimes offer consumers gifts or money to simply test drive their cars. Coupons can play essentially the same role. A decision to eat out in a restaurant might involve an external search, such as scanning the restaurants listed in the Yellow Pages, mentally noting those worth further consideration. A more likely scenario, however, would involve an internal search through memory, which is likely to yield several possibilities. In the latter situation, the consideration set would depend on the recall of alternatives from memory (i.e. the retrieval set).

Obviously, consumers cannot construct a consideration set based on an internal search of memory without prior knowledge of at least some alternatives. Yet, in the case of first-time buyers for some product categories, consumers may lack knowledge about what alternatives are available to choose from. When this occurs, the consideration set may be developed in any one of several ways. The consumer might talk to others, search through the Yellow Pages, consider all brands available at the store, and so on. Thus, external factors such as the retail environment have a greater opportunity to affect the consideration set of less knowledgeable consumers.

The manner in which the consideration set is constructed can shape marketing strategy. Consider those situations in which consumers construct a consideration set based on an internal memory search. When this occurs, the odds of a given offering being chosen are dependent on its being recalled from memory. Accordingly, when consideration sets are based on internal search, it is very important that consumers are able to *recall* the company's offering.

At other times, *recognition* rather than recall becomes more important in determining the consideration set. Take the consumer who quickly scans the shelf at a grocery store to determine what is available and makes a choice among those brands that are recognised (i.e. look familiar) by the consumer. Recognition of alternatives available at the point of purchase would therefore determine the consideration set. Beyond making sure its offering is available at the store, a company would also want to teach consumers about what its product packaging looks like so that it can be easily recognised.

Is the evaluation and choice of a given alternative affected by what other alternatives are included in the consideration set? Several studies have reported an attraction effect, in which a given alternative's attractiveness is enhanced when an inferior alternative is added to the set of choice alternatives. Although the robustness of this effect is not well understood, it does suggest the possibility that a product might benefit from encouraging consumers to consider weaker offerings.

Problem

COCOBIZ is a new brand name for an instant coffee manufactured by a Brazilian company called Cafeeirado NATAL. It will soon be launched in Europe and Wilson Sequeira, the marketing manager responsible for COCOBIZ, is well aware that his first line of thinking should be associated with consumer behaviour analysis. How do consumers in Britain (since this will be the first market targeted for the introduction of the product) perceive the attributes of instant coffee? What are their coffee consumption habits? What are the main competitive brands in the market? How are these competitive brands featured in the consideration sets of consumers? How easy is it for a newcomer like COCOBIZ to have a presence in the average consumer's consideration set as a precursor to the evaluation of alternatives leading to choice and product purchase? How easy is it to gain the collaboration and cooperation of retailers to reach the necessary level of consumer awareness needed to have COCOBIZ included in consumers' consideration sets?

Questions

1   Define what is meant by a consumer's internal search and explain its importance and role when dealing with 'consideration sets'?
2   Analyse the difference between the concepts of 'recognition' and 'recall' when related to consideration sets.
3   How can COCOBIZ use an effective programme of sales promotion and packaging as a key inducer to gain prominence of the brand in consumers' 'consideration sets'?

(M) *Problem 2.3* Attitudes and behaviour

Introductory comments

Under certain conditions the behaviour of consumers can be predicted from their attitudes towards products, services and brands. There are many ideas about the relationship between attitude and behaviour. The interaction is also related to the way in which attitude is measured, and to factors other than the attitude which are linked to behaviour.

MEASUREMENT OF ATTITUDE

Ajzen and Fishbein give some conditions for the measurement of attitude to optimally predict behaviour. These conditions apply to the action (behaviour), the subject of the action, the situation, and the time of the action. By 'action' we usually mean purchasing behaviour. The subject of the action is the product or service being purchased. If one tries to predict the purchase of a single good or service, the measurement of attitude needs to agree with the behaviour on at least the first two points. The measurement then needs to deal with the *purchase* (act) of the *product* or *brand* in question (the subject of the act). An example is the measurement of an evaluative component: 'How important is the lifetime of a colour television set for you when you buy one?' The prediction can be improved by including a reference to the situation and the time of the act. An example of this is the measurement of the belief component: 'If I buy a Philips colour television set next week, I expect it to have a lifetime of at least ten years.'

In the prediction of complex behaviour, such as environmentally friendly car driving, a reference to the subject of the behaviour is, in principle, enough to predict the behaviour. The environmentally friendly use of cars consists of a complex group of acts, such as the purchase of a car with a catalyser, economic fuel consumption, using unleaded petrol, not driving at high speed, and accelerating slowly. Such behaviour can be predicted by an attitude measurement with a reference to the subject. For example: 'How important is environmentally friendly car use for you?' If needed, other questions may be asked about the different elements of environmental car use.

OTHER FACTORS IN THE EXPLANATION OF BEHAVIOUR

Behavioural intention is a mediating variable in the explanation of behaviour. This implies that the intention to purchase directly predicts the behaviour, and that the intention is explained by the attitude. The attitude alone has less predictive value than the behavioural intention.

In the extended model by Fishbein and Ajzen (see Figure 2.1), the influence of the social norm is included along with attitude. The social norm indicates to what extent the social environment agrees with the behaviour of the individual. The social norm is a system of weighted opinions of different groups in the social environment, such as the normative beliefs of family members, weighted according to the extent to which one complies with these normative beliefs (motivation to comply). Compliance with the normative beliefs of others is a form of conformism. Besides family members, normative beliefs of other reference people, such as friends, acquaintances and colleagues, can also play a role. In fact, it is not so much the *actual* normative beliefs of reference people but the normative beliefs which are *attributed to them*. The social norm is the weighted sum of the normative beliefs and motivation to comply with these norms.

As mentioned earlier, one's own attitude (A) consists of beliefs and the evaluations of these beliefs. In a similar manner, the social norm consists of normative beliefs (NB) and the extent to which one complies with the normative beliefs (motivation to comply, MC). A weighted combination of attitude and social norms gives the behavioural intention (BI). A woman might have a positive attitude towards the use of contraceptives, but knows that the social norm of her reference group is negative. The relative weight of her own attitude (w_1) and of the social norm (w_2) then determines whether she will use contraceptives. Note that $i = 1, \ldots, N$ for N beliefs and $j = 1, \ldots, M$ for M reference persons. This can be shown as follows:

$$B \approx BI = w_1 \times A + w_2 \times SN = w_1(\Sigma_i B_i \times E_i) + w_2(\Sigma_j NB_j \times MC_j) + w_3 \times PBC$$

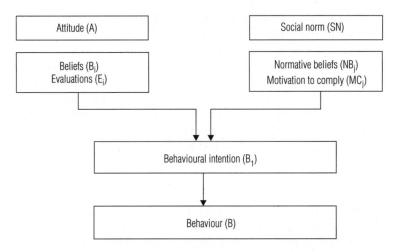

Figure 2.1 Extended attitude model for the prediction of behaviour (based on Ajzen and Fishbein).

In the extended attitude model of Figure 2.1 it is assumed that subjects have some degree of freedom and control of their behaviour. They can choose between a number of alternatives and weigh these alternatives against each other. This is called the perceived behavioural control. Perceived behavioural control (PBC) may be regarded as a third component.

The social norm can be seen as a factor in the purchase of a product. Consumers take it into account to a certain extent. Other factors are behavioural limitations such as the financial situation of the consumer and the available time. Self-applied norms and values are largely represented in personal attitudes. Purely on the basis of these restrictions, consumer behaviour can be reasonably well predicted. Within these limitations, the extended model by Fishbein and Ajzen can improve predictions.

Habits may have their own influence on purchasing behaviour besides that of attitude and social norms. In this way the purchase of tomato ketchup could be led by the brand one always buys (habit), the attitude regarding a certain brand (brand loyalty; the weighted judgements pertaining to the taste, price, thickness and other characteristics) and the social norm (the opinion of others about the purchase of the brand of ketchup by the consumer in question).

In the model by Triandis, behaviour is explained by the behavioural intention and habits multiplied by certain facilitating factors. The behavioural intention is explained, just as in the model by Fishbein and Ajzen, by the attitude and the social norm. In the example above, the purchase of tomato ketchup is explained by the buying intention and the brand one has always bought (e.g. Heinz), while the strength of these factors is influenced by facilitating factors, such as the frequency of purchase. With a high purchase frequency the habit will have more influence.

Besides intention and habit, situational factors may also have an effect on purchasing behaviour. If Heinz ketchup is coincidentally sold out, or another brand is being discounted, the purchase of Heinz will be less probable. Apart from this, emotions can also be seen as situational determinants of behaviour. Many emotions and moods are unpredictable. They are strongly dependent on the situation, place, time and preceding experiences of the individual.

Personality factors may contribute to purchasing behaviour. The need for cognition (NfC) is a personality trait which contributes to a more differentiated attitude and to a strong influence of the attitude on behaviour. Self-monitoring is a property which contributes to social norms strongly influencing behaviour. People with a high level of self-monitoring are more sensitive to the social consequences of their behaviour. People with low self-monitoring are more likely to behave how they feel. Furthermore, the action orientation of the individual influences how far attitudes and social norms can predict behaviour. For people who are strongly inclined to convert preferences into action, attitude has a relatively strong influence on purchasing behaviour. People less inclined to take action are more influenced by the social norms.

LOV

Table 2.2 compares the values of Rokeach (1973) and listing of value (LOV) is an alternative to the Rokeach values. It seems that LOV values are easier to apply for market segmentation purposes than Rokeach values. LOV values are closer to the reality of everyday life of consumers and products.

Table 2.2 Seven domains of Rokeach and LOV values

Domain	Rokeach values	LOV values
Pleasure	Pleasure A comfortable life Happiness Cheerfulness	Pleasure An exciting life
Security	Family security National security A world at peace Freedom	Security
Achievement	A sense of accomplishment Social recognition Ambition Capability Courageousness	Accomplishment Being respected
Independence	Imagination Independence Being intellectual Being logical	Self-esteem Self-realisation
Maturity	Wisdom Mature love True friendship A world of beauty Inner human balance	Belonging Good relationships with others
Conformism	Obedience Politeness Cleanliness Self-control	
Social	Equality Helpfulness Forgiving others Being loving to others Taking responsibility	

On the basis of the Rokeach values and a number of other values from the literature, an attempt has been made to organise values into two-dimensional space. One dimension should capture whether the values serve individual or collective interests – individual autonomy (self-directedness) versus status quo. This also implies that values serving the same interest are more closely correlated than those serving different interests. The second dimension distinguishes power distance and achievement values from equity resolution and human balance with nature. The two dimensions also imply that some values conflict with each other. Seven value domains have been distinguished empirically in 86 samples of teachers from 38 nations. Teachers were selected because they are considered to be important agents in transmitting cultural values to new generations. They were asked to rate the importance of 56 values using a scale of 7 (of supreme importance) to 0 (not important) and -1 (opposed to my values). It appeared that 45 values had equivalent meanings across the samples, which were selected to form the final domains. They are derived from biologically based needs, social interaction requirements for interpersonal cooperation and social institution demands for group welfare and survival.

The seven value domains are:

- *Status quo domain* This domain includes values associated with maintaining the conservatism and common interests of individuals and society (i.e. social order, honouring elders, preserving public image, politeness, reciprocation of favours, self-discipline, devotion and respect for tradition). This domain also includes the Rokeach values of family security, national security, obedience, wisdom, cleanliness and being forgiving.
- *Affective autonomy domain* This domain is associated with the emotionally self-directed individual who values an enjoyable, varied life and pleasure. Rokeach's value of an exciting life is also included.
- *Thinking freedom domain* This domain captures the intellectually self-directed individual who values curiosity and creativity. The Rokeach value of broadmindedness is also included.
- *Power distance domain* This domain includes values of social power, authority, wealth, influence and humility. No Rokeach value corresponds with this domain.
- *Achievement domain* This domain includes the values of successfulness, daring, capability and choosing one's own goals. Rokeach's values of independence and ambition are also included.
- *Equity resolution domain* This domain captures social justice, loyalty and accepting one's lot. The Rokeach values of equality, responsibility, freedom, honesty, helpfulness and world peace are also included.
- *Human balance domain* This domain includes protecting the environment and unity with nature. The Rokeach value world of beauty is also included.

A sketch of the seven domains in two-dimensional space is shown in Figure 2.2. The sketch shows adjacent domains (e.g. equity resolution and human balance) and opposite domains (e.g. thinking freedom and status quo). Tables 2.3 and 2.4 show the average scores of different samples from Europe, the USA, Japan and Australia. It appears that Eastern European countries find conservative values more important than Western European countries. As autonomy values contrast with status quo, so these values of autonomy are more important in Western than in Eastern Europe. The other parts of the world score in between. With respect to the power distance and masterly values and the equity resolution and human balance values no clear pattern emerges. Turkey scores the highest and Italy the lowest with respect to power distance values. The USA, Japan, Portugal and Greece score the highest on achievement values whereas Estonia and Finland score the lowest. The USA scores relatively low on human balance values.

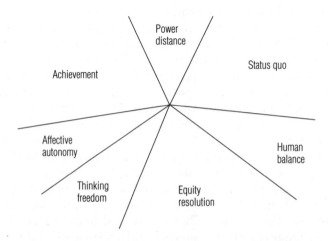

Figure 2.2 Value domains in two-dimensional space adapted from Schwartz (1994).

Table 2.3 The average importance of status quo and autonomy values in various countries

	Status quo	Affective autonomy	Thinking freedom
Bulgaria (Turks)	4.43	3.13	3.78
Estonia (rural)	4.37	3.03	3.69
Poland	4.31	3.13	4.09
Slovakia	4.28	2.76	4.03
Slovenia	4.27	3.76	5.03
Turkey	4.27	3.25	4.12
Estonia (urban)	4.26	3.08	3.93
Hungary	3.97	3.34	4.44
Finland	3.84	3.51	4.62
Italy	3.82	2.95	4.60
Portugal	3.76	3.54	4.12
Greece	3.68	3.96	4.09
The Netherlands	3.68	3.51	4.44
Denmark	3.64	4.01	4.58
East Germany	3.50	4.16	4.47
West Germany	3.42	4.03	4.75
Spain	3.42	3.97	4.90
France	3.35	4.41	5.15
Switzerland (Fr)	3.25	4.24	5.33
USA	3.90	3.65	4.20
Japan	3.87	3.54	4.68
Australia	4.06	3.50	4.12

Table 2.4 The average importance of power distance, achievement, equity resolution and human balance values in various countries

	Power distance	Achievement	Equity resolution	Human balance
Turkey	3.30	3.90	5.12	4.26
Bulgaria (Turks)	3.07	4.04	4.83	4.32
East Germany	2.69	4.16	5.29	4.08
Poland	2.53	4.00	4.82	4.10
Hungary	2.42	3.96	4.87	4.51
West Germany	2.27	4.07	5.37	4.42
The Netherlands	2.26	3.98	5.39	3.98
Switzerland	2.20	4.18	5.19	4.50
Estonia (rural)	2.18	3.64	5.02	4.53
France	2.16	3.89	5.45	4.31
Slovakia	2.11	4.09	4.98	4.40
Portugal	2.08	4.25	5.62	4.29
Spain	2.03	4.11	5.55	4.53
Finland	2.03	3.63	5.26	4.54
Greece	2.01	4.53	5.35	4.39
Estonia (urban)	2.00	3.73	4.96	4.65
Denmark	1.86	3.97	5.52	4.16
Slovenia	1.76	3.76	4.36	4.72
Italy	1.69	4.08	5.57	4.80
USA	2.39	4.34	5.03	3.70
Japan	2.86	4.27	4.69	4.07
Australia	2.36	4.09	4.98	4.05

Using an earlier vision of the value system, a Danish study has found positive correlations between human balance, equity resolution and thinking freedom values and favourable attitudes towards the environment, and negative correlations between conservative and power distance values and favourable attitudes towards the environment and no relationship with achievement and affective autonomy values. This result indicates that general values have implications for specific attitudes.

Questions

1   In what ways would the measurement of attitude be able to optimally predict behaviour?
2   How would you explain your buying behaviour on a particular purchasing experience by an extended attitude model?
3   Name and critically assess the seven value domains associated with the list of values (LOV) framework.

(A) *Problem 2.4* Brand loyalty

Introductory comments

Brand loyalty is a topical subject. We discuss briefly: (1) how far there is such a thing; (2) what form it takes; (3) how it can be predicted; and (4) some practical applications. Four questions for the reader to answer are:

	Tick one box per row		
	Yes	No	Don't Know
1 Is there such a thing as 'loyalty'?	( )	( )	( )
2 Is loyalty the same for different brands?	( )	( )	( )
3 Are loyalty levels predictable?	( )	( )	( )
4 Are 100 per cent loyal buyers well worth having?	( )	( )	( )

People typically give different answers. For Question 1 perhaps 25 per cent say 'Yes', 35 per cent 'No' and 20 per cent 'Don't know/all depends' (with the remaining 20 per cent apparently not knowing that they didn't know). There is little consensus. But for Question 4 people invariably answer 'Yes, 100 per cent loyalty is a good thing'. Our own answers are clear 'Yeses' for Questions 1 – 3, but an emphatic 'No!' for Question 4. Our reasons are:

Q1 There are many different loyalty-related measures (see Technical appendix), but they all reflect or measure the same thing – loyalty.
Q2 The degree of loyalty for brands of the same size has been found to be much the same in more than 50 different product categories or services.
Q3 The loyalty measures follow regular patterns and are predictable, as we shall see.
Q4 No: 100 per cent loyal buyers are few and they buy little.

In practice, few consumers are by nature either monogamous (near 100 per cent loyal) or promiscuous. They are mostly *polygamous*. They have steady ongoing relationships with several serious partners, one usually consumed more often than others.

Only occasionally do they try out a new relationship or drop an established one. Loyalty can therefore be defined as an ongoing propensity to buy the brand, usually as one of several. This predicts all the customary brand performance measures (e.g. buying rates) without presuming any deep commitment.

Table 2.5 gives the annual penetrations and average rates of buying of the eight leading US instant coffee brands. The penetrations differ greatly, by a factor of four, from 24 per cent buying Maxwell House down to 6 per cent buying Maxim. But the buying rates differ far less (they are all about 3, from 3.6 just down to 2.6 or so). Together these two measures make up the brand's sales. Sales = penetration × average purchase rate. Market shares (sales) therefore differ mainly by how many customers you have, and hardly at all by how 'loyal' they are (unless the penetration is *very* high). This pattern has been widely found.

A single 'split-loyalty' model is named after markets. It assumes that a consumer tends to have steady propensities to buy each of a small repertoire of brands, with differing probabilities. But the model does not imply that the market *has* to be steady. It only predicts what the market is like when it *is* steady (which, in practice, it does tend to be). The predictions are also robust to departures from strict stationarity: they benchmark the regular patterns that occur and pinpoint the deviations.

To calibrate the model only three simple numerical inputs for the product category are required: (1) how many consumers bought it; (2) on average how often (e.g. 67 per cent in Table 2.5 buying any instant coffee, on average 6.7 times in a year); and (3) how many brands they bought (on average 1.7).

Additional patterns in consumers' buying behaviour which are also predicted by the Dirichlet theory include the following:

The '80:20' rule Traditionally, a brand's 50 per cent heaviest buyers are said to account for about 80 per cent of its sales, and its 50 per cent lighter ones for only

Table 2.5 Brand penetration and purchase rates

US annual	Market share percentage	Percentage buying		Average purchase per buyer	
		0	T	0	T
Any instant	100	67	—	6.7	—
Maxwell House	19	24	**27**	3.6	**3.1**
Sanka	15	21	**23**	3.3	**3.0**
Tasters Choice	14	22	**21**	2.8	**2.9**
High Point	13	22	**20**	2.6	**2.9**
Folgers	11	18	**17**	2.7	**2.8**
Nescafé	8	13	**14**	2.9	**2.7**
Brim	4	9	**7**	2.0	**2.6**
Maxim	3	6	**6**	2.6	**2.6**
Other brands	13	20	**21**	3.0	**2.9**
Average brand	11	17	**17**	2.8	**2.8**

Note
0 = observed; T = theoretical Dirichlet predictions.

Source: MRCA.

49

about 20 per cent. This occurs broadly for each of the coffee brands listed in Table 2.5 (with a double jeopardy effect of slightly more light buyers for the smaller brands). In the model even the very light buyers are, however, still loyal to the brand: they buy it again but infrequently (e.g. more than a year later).

100 per cent loyal buyers Unlike most people's expectations, 100 per cent loyal or near 100 per cent loyal buyers are *not* important to one's sales: there are few of them and they are not heavy buyers. This is predictable and rarely changes. (Many people are misled over this because in *short* time periods the proportion of 100 per cent loyal is necessarily vastly higher: in a week, say, most people would rarely buy coffee more than once and hence would buy only one brand.)

Multibrand buying Nearly all of a brand's customers are therefore multibrand buyers over a year or so. This is so even under steady market conditions. Typically, the customers of Nescafé in Table 2.5 buy *other* brands about twice as often (on average six times compared with purchases of Nescafé itself). Nescafé's 'share of customers' category requirements' (SCR) is therefore as low as about 30 per cent (3/9): 'Your customers are mostly other brands' customers who occasionally buy you.'

The theoretical model implies (and the empirical data support it), that such multibrand buyers are none the less loyal to their brands, that is, they go on buying each brand with more or less steady propensities. People may buy different brands for different end users or different end uses (e.g. mid-morning versus after-dinner coffee), or just because most brands are very much alike and they want *some* variety of choice but still find having a *small* repertoire of habitual brands convenient.

The duplication of purchase law Which specific other brands your customers buy also is predictable. With equally substitutable brands, the proportion of buyers of brand *A* who also buy brands *B*, *C* or *D* varies directly with *B*, *C* and *D*'s overall market penetrations.

In Table 2.5 far more people bought Maxwell House than Maxim (24 per cent and 6 per cent). In line with that, about four times as many customers of any *other* brand also bought Maxwell House than Maxim. However, some markets are more or less heavily 'partitioned' – for example, ground versus instant coffee, or leaded and unleaded petrol as an extreme example (Ehrenberg and Uncles, 1998). There is, then, much more switching in each such sub-market, but the Duplication of Purchase Law (and the Dirichlet model generally) still holds in each.

These results lead to five main conclusions:

1   Different loyalty-related measures mostly vary together: hence there is 'loyalty'.
2   Individual consumers generally have 'split-loyalty' portfolios of several habitual brands.
3   Loyalty levels differ little between brands of the same size.
4   Smaller brands inherently have slightly lower loyalty measures (the double jeopardy effect).
5   What distinguishes a large brand from a smaller one is therefore how many customers each has, not how often they tend to buy the product (unless penetration is already very high).

The patterns and predictive Dirichlet theory outlined here are much the same for different brands and products. This provides simple and near universal benchmarks for assessing the loyalty levels in one's market and auditing the performance of one's brands.

In the model, brands are seen as similar and substitutable: 'brands are brands'. Maxwell House, Nescafé and so on, are all coffee, not dishwashing liquid. But brands are also distinct, that is, they have their unique names and packaging (the product with a name) and very different market shares.

In practice even similar brands can and do differ in 'minor' aspects. (e.g. nuances of flavour, texture, the bottle top or the car door handle, being out of stock more often and so on). Such minor differences are usually not copied by the competition or explicitly featured in the advertising. Consumers therefore notice them (if at all) only after having tried the brand – a typical example of attitude change *following* a change in behaviour.

Overall, the main driver of market share is not variations in aspects of loyalty but large differences in market penetration – the number of customers you have. This is determined not by any single factor but by the marketing mix and how well it is applied.

Questions

1　What are the two measures making up a brand's sales?
2　What are the basic premises behind the Dirichlet model?
3　Comment on additional patterns in consumers' buying behaviour that are also predicted by the Dirichlet theory.
4　By analysing Table 2.5, what conclusions can be drawn? For example, with regard to loyalty measures, impacts on large and small brands, patterns resulting from the predictive Dirichlet theory, and effect on market share.

References and further reading

Boedeker, M. (1997) Recreational shopping: the role of basic emotional dimensions of personality, Truku, Finland: Turku School of Economics and Business Administration, Series A-9 (http: www.tukk.fi).

Chaudhuri, A. (1997) Consumption emotion and perceived risk: a macro-analytic approach, *Journal of Business Research*, 39: 81–92.

Ehrenberg and Uncles (1998) Advertising: strongly peruasive or nudging, *Journal of Advertising Research*, 37.

Hauser, J.R. and Wernesfelt, B. (1990) An evaluation cost model of consideration sets, *Journal of Consumer Research*, 16 March: 393–408.

Kahle, L.R., Beatty, S.E. and Homer, P.C. (1986) Alternative measurement approaches to consumer values: the list of values (LOV) and values and lifestyles (VALs), *Journal of Consumer Research*, 13: 405–9.

Mano, H. and Oliver, R.L. (1993) Assessing the dimensionality and structure of the consumption experience: evaluation, feeling and satisfaction, *Journal of Consumer Research*, 20: 451–66.

Mick, D.G., DeMoss, M. and Faber, R. (1992) A projective study of motivations and meanings of self-gifts: implications for retail management, *Journal of Retailing*, 68: 122–44.

Pieters, R. and van Raaij, F. (1988) Functions and management of affect: applications to economic behaviour, *Journal of Economic Psychology*, 9: 251–82.

Rokeach, M. (1973) *The Nature of Human Values*, New York: The Free Press.

Rook, D.W. and Gardner, M.P. (1993) In the mood: impulse buying's affective antecedents, *Research in Consumer Behaviour*, 6: 1–23.

Ruth, J.A. (1996) It's the feeling that counts: toward an understanding of emotion and its influence on gift-exchange processes, in Otnes, C. and Beltramini, R.F. (eds) *Gift Giving: A Research Anthology*, Bowing Green, OH: Bowling Green State University Popular Press, pp. 195–214.

Schwartz, S.H. (1994) Beyond individualism/collectivism: new cultural dimensions of values, in Kim, U., Triandis, H.C., Kagiteibasi, C., Choi, S. and Yoon, G. (eds) *Individualism and Collectivism: Theory Method and Application*, London: Sage, pp. 85–119.

Scitovsky, T. (1986) *Human Desire and Economic Satisfaction: Essays on the Frontiers of Economics*, Brighton: Wheatsheaf.

3

Marketing Research and Market Forecasting

Marketing is the process of planning and executing the conception, pricing, promotion and distribution of ideas, goods and services to create exchanges that satisfy individual and organisation objectives. The marketing concept requires that customer satisfaction rather than profit maximisation be the goal of an organisation. In other words, the organisation should be consumer-oriented and should try to understand the consumer's requirements and satisfy them quickly and efficiently, in ways that are beneficial to both the consumer and the organisation. Marketing is also often defined as providing products and services that help satisfy the needs of a particular market. To find out what the market's needs are, marketers must learn as much as they can about their customers. In fact, marketers have an insatiable desire to find out more and more about whom they sell to – so much so that it has created an enormous marketing research industry that supports the need for more information. This means that any organisation should try to obtain information on consumer needs and gather marketing intelligence to help satisfy these needs efficiently.

Marketing researcher is a critical part of such a marketing intelligence system; it helps to improve management decision-making by providing accurate, relevant and timely (ART) information. Every decision poses unique needs for information, and relevant strategies can be developed based on the information gathered through marketing research. The process of a research project includes the following: find a market issue; translate it into a marketing research project; design a survey questionnaire; collect information from a survey; conduct analyses; and report the findings and marketing implementations.

The Internet has changed the way business is conducted today. More and more businesses are going online in order to leverage the almost boundless possibilities that the Internet has to offer. The Internet boom has in turn affected the way marketing research is conducted today. Marketing research on the Web requires a thorough understanding of how consumer behaviour changes in the cyberworld.

Another part of your job as marketing manager is to prepare an estimate of current market potential and to make forecasts for the future. Estimates of potential are based on projections of the number of users and the expected purchase rate. Geographical measures of potential can be obtained by using the chain ratio, Buying Power Index (BPI) and SIC Code. Forecasts of the future may be extensions of historical data or, in the case of new products, based on judgement. Examples of subjective forecasting methods include sales forecast composite, jury or executive opinion, Delphi, customer surveys and leading indicators. When you are working with historical data, you can often improve the accuracy of your forecasts by seasonally adjusting your data.

There are a variety of numerical sales forecasting techniques available, and you need to understand how they work and where they should be employed. Detailed explanations have been presented for naïve, moving average, exponential smoothing, regression procedures, diffusion models and econometric models. Your choice among these methods, and others that are available, should be based on the length of the forecast, pattern of the data, cost accuracy and ease of understanding. Possibly the ideal forecasting procedure combines a numerical analysis of past data with your own interpretation of current developments.

(M) *Problem 3.1* The expected value of added information

Introductory comments

Some managers use subjective probability scales to help them in their decision-making process. Some of these scales measure the level of combined disagreement among executives with regard to a specific project's final decision. Agreement/disagreement levels reflect attitudes that can affect the nature of the decision-making process and final agreement will not remove conflicting objectives. Another type of scale, which can be concurrently used, is the profit consequences scale, which is intended to measure the expected monetary value in terms of the overall profitability of the project. Combining these two 5-point subjective scales (combined disagreement and profit consequences) in a summated 10-point scale will help managers in the process of choosing a decision alternative when the state of nature is not known.

When there is a situation where the management disagreement level/profit consequences scores suggest delaying a decision to obtain additional information to increase the likelihood of selecting the correct alternative, increased costs become a factor to consider. Decision delay is not without some cost; the reduction of uncertainty is not free of charge. This cost must be compared to the expected gain resulting from increasing the probability of selecting the best course of action; that is to say, the cost of such added information should not exceed its value.

If additional information is deemed necessary, how can the decision-makers determine the amount of money to be allocated to the marketing research unit that will gather it? If marketing research is the only cost associated with decision delay, the marketing manager could, in theory, allocate any amount that does not exceed the estimated profit consequences of a wrong decision. In other words, if additional research data improve the chances for a more profitable decision, then the maximum amount that should be expended for such data is the difference between the expected profit consequences of the decision taken without additional data and the expected profit consequences of the decision taken with additional data. This difference is sometimes referred to as 'the expected value of added information'.

The cost of marketing research is only one cost element in decision delay. Opportunity cost is another. For example, delaying the introduction of a new product pending the results of extensive consumer research may improve the chances of making the right decision. However, the expected benefits from such a decision should be compared with the amount of predicted sales revenue that would be lost during the testing period.

A third cost in decision delay stems from the reduction of lead time over competitive counteraction. Less and less frequently do companies enjoy long periods of competitive product advantage. A new product, even when a competitor is caught by surprise, can often be quickly duplicated, or a highly similar product soon introduced. To test a contemplated product-line addition in the marketplace over a long period of time will alert competitors. They can purchase test products, analyse them and product similar ones in quantity, while the originator is still seeking additional data for the reduction of uncertainty. Many grocery and drug manufacturers are by-passing large portions of the market-testing operation in order to increase their lead time over competitive responses. Less reliable data are being judged adequate when contrasted with the financial losses that might follow early countermoves by competitors.

Problem

Table 3.1 is a payoff table for a marketing decision on the introduction of a proposed new product by All-Juice Soft Drinks, Inc. The marketing alternatives in Table 3.1 have been evaluated in terms of the established monetary criterion, namely, expected profit. The expected profit for each alternative was obtained by multiplying the probabilities of the outcomes by the payoffs for each alternative and summing up as follows:

Alternative	Expected profit
Introduce product	$(.3) \times (£4.0) + (.7) \times (-£2.0) = -£0.2$
Do not introduce product	$(.3) \times (£0) + (.7) \times (£0) = £0$

At this point, the principal decision-maker was reluctant to pass up a chance to make £4m, and was wondering if more information should be gathered before taking action, thus incurring delay. In terms of the combined disagreement (say, level 3) and profit consequences (say, level 5) on the ten-point (combined disagreement and profit-consequences) scales used by the top management of the company, this situation 'scored' between 8 and 9.

It would thus meet the criterion for deciding to delay the marketing decision and gather more information.

Questions

1   In the context of the decision analysis framework, comment on the given payoff table regarding the marketing decision situation faced by All-Juice Soft Drinks Inc.
2   If the marketing manager authorised an expenditure of £0.2m for a market survey and the results of this survey convinced the decision-makers to revise their original estimates of the probabilities of the outcomes given in Table 3.1 to .6 for high sales and .4 for low sales, what would be the expected profit for the product introduction alternative?
3   Based upon the evaluation of the alternatives facing the company, what final decision should be taken by the top management of All-Juice Soft Drinks Inc.?

Table 3.1 Payoff table for decision on introduction of a new soft-drink product (£m)

Predicted sales	Probability of outcome	Introduce product	Do not introduce product
£40	.3	£4.0	£0
£20	.7	−£2.0	£0
Expected profit: $(.3) (£4) + (.7) (-£2) = -£0.2$			

(I) *Problem 3.2* Reliability and validity of measurements

Introductory comments

RELIABILITY OF MEASUREMENTS

In a nutshell, *reliability* is the tendency in a respondent to respond in the same or in a very similar manner to an identical or near-identical question. To state the concept of reliability somewhat differently, a measure is reliable when it elicits an identical or very similar response from the same person with successive administrations. Marketing researchers use their own jargon and say that the instrument is free from 'random response error', or, stated more simply, each person is consistent and does not respond randomly.

Reliability is a matter of degree. Some measures will exhibit perfectly consistent responses, some will show wild swings and some will generate responses that are somewhat the same. The great danger of unreliable measurements should be obvious to you. The marketing researcher cannot place any faith in them; they are just meaningless numbers. An unreliable measure will obtain different responses from respondents who have identical feelings or opinions. Precisely why the measurement is unreliable is never quite certain. Perhaps the instructions on the questionnaire are unclear. Possibly, the respondents are not motivated to pay attention. An interviewer may not have stated the question the same way each time, or the respondents may have been confused by the working of a question. Notice that researchers initially assume that the measure determines reliability. In other words, if responses are unreliable, we first look at the question, instruction, response options and so on, to see if it is at fault before looking at the respondent. At the same time, researchers realise that respondent groups differ in their abilities to 'handle' each measure. So a question that is reliable for a sample of consulting engineers with graduate degrees may not be reliable for a sample of automobile mechanics with vocational school diplomas. This fact necessitates reliability assessment for every survey performed.

There are a number of options available to the marketing researcher to assess reliability. A favourite approach is called the test–retest method. Other methods include equivalent forms and split-half. Each of the various reliability assessment methods is briefly described below.

Test–retest reliability requires that respondents be administered the identical question(s) at some later time, and that the original and retest answers be compared. Some researchers, for example, will instruct the interviewer to finish the interview with a retest section. The interviewer may say something like, 'That concludes our survey, but let me just glance back over the questions to make sure I did not skip any or forget to check your answers. Oh, yes, here's one.' He or she then repeats the question asked earlier and notes the second response. Obviously, not all questions can be repeated, so a few critical questions are selected and retested in this manner. A verification call-back is a variation of this approach. You should realise that the test–retest approach rides on the horns of a time dilemma. If the time interval between test and retest is too short, respondents may simply remember their responses, but if the time period is too long, some real changes may have occurred in the respondents' opinions. Most researchers opt for a short time interval over a long one and assume that respondents' memory is not involved.

Computer technology coupled with database management systems have opened up a new type of test–retest reliability assessment. In it, respondents are tracked over successive surveys and examined for response reliability. With this approach, a respondent's answers to identical or similar questions can be compared across studies for consistency, and inconsistent respondents can be pulled out of the database.

Equivalent forms reliability relies on the 'similar' aspect of the definition of reliability and uses equivalent forms of questions typically embedded in the same questionnaire. Here, the attempt is to make respondents think that each question is different when, in truth, they are tapping the same opinion or attitude dimension. One favourite device is to flip a question or statement. For instance, if a modified Likert form were used, one statement could be, 'Progressive Savings and Loan makes you feel like a friend.' Later on, the statement could be, 'Progressive Savings and Loan makes you feel like a stranger.' Reflective composite scales have equivalent forms reliably automatically built in as the reflective items are constructed to be highly similar to one another. The danger of this method lies in the degree of equivalence between two questions; during measure development, if respondents fail to treat them as equivalents, the usual assumption is that the measure is unreliable, not the respondents.

Split-half reliability requires that the marketing researcher separate the total sample into two groups and compare one group's responses to the other's responses. Here, the assumption is that the two groups are identical in composition, or homogeneous, and that their averages for the various scaled-response questions will be very similar. Statistical tests can be used to determine the degree of similarity. The basic complaint against this approach is its inability to reveal subgroup problems because all comparisons are done on a group-to-group basis. The following example illustrates this problem.

In a survey of college students about to graduate, we asked them to respond to the following modified five-point agree–disagree Likert statement: 'I believe I will have an exciting career.' The responses were then converted to numbers with 1 for 'strongly disagree', 2 for 'disagree' and so forth. We divided the sample into two groups and computed the averages: both groups' means were exactly 3.0. So we concluded they were equivalent and that the measure was reliable. But just to check, we looked at the two groups' responses more closely and found that in one group, all of our students responded 'neither agree nor disagree', but in the other one, 50 per cent responded 'strongly agree' and the other half responded 'strongly disagree'. These responses are not equivalent even though the comparison of means says they are. For this reason, split-half reliability is the least popular reliability assessment method.

How to develop reliable measures

Regardless of the method used, the marketing researcher has four avenues to develop and report reliable measures. First, in the instance of greatly unreliable measurements, the marketing researcher should throw out the questions completely, and they should be revamped and re-evaluated before the actual survey. You will note that reliability assessment here should occur during the development of the questionnaire, probably in the form of a series of pilot tests aimed at improving the measures. Although perhaps labourious, the development and testing of questions for acceptable reliability is a necessary step in the marketing research process.

Second, the researcher can 'collapse' scales that have too many gradations. For instance, the modified Likert responses can be collapsed into the three categories of 'agree', 'disagree' and 'no opinion', or the semantic differential responses can be collapsed into a five-point scale by combining the 1s and 2s and the 6s and 7s into single categories. Such collapsing usually increases reliability. You will note that this step takes place after the survey has been administered but while measure reliability is still a concern.

Third, as an alternative to the second step or to be performed after the second step, reliability assessment may be done on an individual basis, such as a direct comparison of each respondent's test answer with the retest or equivalent answer. It may be possible to identify those unreliable respondents and pull them out from the final analysis. But you should throw out respondents only if you are certain the measure is reliable in the first place for most respondents.

Fourth, after the first three steps have been applied, the researcher can report the reliability levels. Normally, the measurement of reliability is a coefficient analogous to a proportion in which 1.00 indicates perfect reliability. Some disagreement exists for an 'acceptable' minimum, but levels of 0.65 or 0.70 are often considered acceptable for measures that are being used for the first time, whereas higher reliability levels are expected for measures that have been used before and have undergone fine-tuning over successive administrations and improvements.

VALIDITY OF MEASUREMENTS

Validity operates on a completely different plane from reliability; it is possible to have perfectly reliable measurements that are invalid. Validity is defined as the accuracy of the measurement: it is an assessment of the exactness of the measurement relative to what actually exists. To illustrate this concept and its difference from reliability, think of a respondent who is embarrassed by a question about his income. This person makes under £12,000 per year, but he does not want to tell it to the interviewer. Consequently, he responds with the highest category – 'Over £50,000.' In a retest of the questions, the respondent persists in his lie by stipulating the highest income level again. Here, the respondent has been perfectly consistent, but he has also been completely untruthful. Of course, lying is not the only reason for invalidity. The respondent may have a faulty memory, may have a misconception, or may even be a bad guesser, which causes his responses to be inexact from reality.

How do you remember the difference between reliability and validity? Think of your wristwatch. If you set your watch incorrectly, it will save 1:00 every 12 hours (reliable), but it will be inaccurate (not valid). But how would you determine whether a person was accurate in his or her response? Naturally, you would need some means of verification. For income, an income tax form or verification from the employer would serve to determine the validity. Of course, either of these items would be very difficult to obtain, but what about an estimate of the person's income from another family member? Regardless of the source used, this example demonstrates the basic concept in validation: the identical answer must be obtained from a different source of data collection. This approach is known as convergent validation, or assessing the validity of information by using two different methods to obtain the information. Convergent validation is described more fully later in this section.

Actually, there are a number of different types of validity involved in measurement. The ones more commonly considered by marketing researchers are fact, predictive, convergent and discriminant.

Face validity is concerned with the degree to which a measurement 'looks like' it measures that which it is designed to measure. It is a judgement call by the researcher and is made as the questions are designed. Thus, as each question is developed, there is an implicit assessment of its face validity. Revisions enhance the face validity of the question until it passes the researcher's subjective evaluation. Unfortunately, this method of assessing validity is the weakest. It can be strengthened somewhat by having other researchers critique the questions.

Predictive validity pertains to the extent to which a particular measure predicts or relates to other measures. For instance, we might ask respondents to indicate their purchase intentions for onion dip on a probability scale. Those who indicate high likelihoods of purchasing the product or brand should have high incidence of actual purchasing, whereas those with low likelihoods should have a low incidence of actual onion dip purchasing. So we ask them to tell us how many onion dips they have purchased in the last month to validate their responses. You would predict that a respondent who says she dislikes purchasing onion dip would not have purchased as much onion dip as one who likes purchasing onion dip. Those with strong positive attitudes towards a brand should have good things to say about that brand and so forth. If your logical predictions are supported by the findings, predictive validity has been demonstrated for those measures.

When the researcher uses two different methods or sources of data collection for the same piece of information, *convergent validity* is being assessed. For example, field research companies often use a telephone validation technique to verify respondents who were interviewed by their interviewers in a high-street mall-intercept study. If the two different methods produce similar results, convergent validity is demonstrated.

In another example of convergent validity, a drop-off survey was delivered by college students to every tenth house in a medium-sized city. The students explained the survey and left the questionnaire with a head of the household. They returned later that day to pick up the completed questionnaires. The convergent validity was assessed by follow-up telephone calls. In the drop-off phase, 386 homeowners responded, and the average age of the home was 14.2 years. Thirty questionnaires were selected at random, and follow-up telephone calls were made to these homes. This time, the other head of the household was questioned, and the average home age was determined as 14.6 years. The closeness of the two averages (14.2 and 14.6) indicates convergent validity. (A statistical test revealed no significant difference.)

Discriminant validity means that dissimilar constructs should differ. In other words, questions that measure different objects should yield different results. When the researcher knows that real differences do exist, he or she should find that the responses differ. Otherwise, there is some doubt as to the validity of the measurements.

Discriminant validity was also assessed in the homeowners' survey just described. One question on the survey asked how concerned homeowners were about home security. They were to indicate concern using a scale from 1, meaning 'not concerned at all', to 7, meaning 'very concerned'. Another question asked about their concern about home fire safety using the same 7-point scale. The averages were found to be 4.3 and 5.6, respectively. Thus, they were more worried about fire safety than about break-ins, and this difference seems reasonable because fires can happen any time, but break-ins are more rare. These are two different constructs, and their discriminant validity was demonstrated by the difference between the averages.

How to develop valid measures

What does the marketing researcher do about validity? Face validity becomes second nature to the researcher, and it should be constantly evaluated throughout the design of the questionnaire. Unfortunately, in most cases, face validity is the only assessment used to determine the validity of research measures.

There is very good reason to be vitally concerned about reliability and validity of measurements in marketing research: if a measure is unreliable or invalid, the entire study falls apart. Consequently, we have provided a quick reference summary of the various tests discussed in this section in Table 3.2.

Problem I

In conducting a survey for the Equitable Insurance Company, Burke Marketing Research assesses reliability by selecting a small group of respondents, calling them back, and readministering five questions to them. One question asks, 'If you were going to buy life insurance sometime this year, how likely would you be to consider the Equitable Company?' Respondents indicate the likelihood on a probability scale (0–100 per cent likely). Typically, this test–retest approach finds that respondents are within 10 per cent of their initial response, that is, if a respondent indicated that he was 50 per cent likely in the initial survey, he responded in the 45–55 per cent range on the retest.

Table 3.2 Criteria for reliability and validity tests used in marketing research

Test	Criterion
Test–retest reliability	Most respondents give an identical response to the same question administered with some time interval between.
Equivalent forms reliability	Most respondents give an equivalent response to near identical questions administered at different times.
Split-half reliability	The responses of one-half of the sample are highly similar to the responses of the other half when key questions are compared.
Face validity	The researcher judges that a question 'looks like' it is measuring what it is supposed to measure.
Predictive validity	One measure that logically should predict another measure is found to do so statistically (usually correlation).
Convergent validity	Two completely different methods of measuring the same variable are found to yield similar statistical findings (usually means or correlation).
Discriminant validity	One measure that logically should not be related to another measure is found not to do so statistically (usually correlation).

Problem II

General Food Corporation includes Post, which is the maker of Fruit and Fibre cereal. The brand manager is interested in determining how many Fruit and Fibre consumers think it is helping them towards a healthier diet, but she is very concerned that respondents in a survey may not be entirely truthful about health matters. They may exaggerate what they really believe so they 'sound' more health conscious than they really are, and they may say they have healthy diets when they really do not.

The General Foods Corporation marketing research director provides a unique way to overcome the problem. She suggests that they conduct a survey of Fruit and Fibre customers in Pittsburgh, Atlanta, Dallas, London, Birmingham, Bristol and Manchester and Denver. Fifty respondents who say that Fruit and Fibre is helping them towards a healthier diet and who also say they are more health conscious than the average Briton will be selected, and General Foods will offer to 'buy' their groceries for the next month. To participate, the chosen respondents must submit their itemised weekly grocery trip receipts. By reviewing the items bought each week, General Foods can determine what they are eating and make judgements on how healthy their diets really are.

Questions

1   The survey has been going on for four weeks, and it has two more weeks before the data collection will be completed. Respondents who are retested are called back exactly one week after the initial survey. In the last week, reliability results have been very different. Now Burke Marketing Research is finding that the retest averages 20 per cent higher than the initial test. Has the scale become unreliable? If so, why has its previous good reliability changed? If not, what has happened, and how can Burke Marketing Research still claim that it has a reliable measure?
2   What is your reaction to General foods approach? Will General Foods be able to assess the validity of its survey this way? Why or why not?

(l) Problem 3.3 Computer-administered survey

Introductory comments

As our introductory example illustrates, computer technology represents a viable option with respect to survey mode, and new developments occur almost every day. Although person-administered surveys are still the industry mainstay, it is important to discuss computer-administered survey methods as we are certain that this approach will grow and become common in the foreseeable future. Computer-assisted surveys are in an evolutionary state, and they are spreading to other survey types. For instance, a computer may house questions asked by a telephone interviewer, or a questionnaire disk may be mailed to respondents for self-administration. Basically, a computer-administered survey is one in which computer technology plays an essential role in the interview work. Here, either the computer assists an interview, or it interacts directly with the respondent. In the case of Internet questionnaires, the computer acts as the medium by which potential respondents are approached, and it is the means by which respondents return their completed questionnaire. As with person-administered surveys, computer-administered surveys have their advantages and disadvantages.

ADVANTAGES OF COMPUTER-ADMINISTERED SURVEYS

At least five advantages of computer-administered surveys are evident: speed; error-free interviews; use of pictures, videos and graphics; real-time capture of data and reduction of 'interview evaluation' concern in respondents.

1   *Speed* The computer-administered approach is much faster that the human interview approach. Computers can quickly jump to questions based on specific responses, they can rapidly dial random telephone numbers, and they can easily check on answers to previous questions to modify or otherwise custom-tailor the interview to each respondent's circumstances. The speed factor translates into cost savings, and there is a claim that Internet surveys are about one-half the cost of mail or telephone surveys.

2   *Error-free interviews* Properly programmed, the computer-administered approach guarantees zero interviewer errors such as inadvertently skipping questions, asking inappropriate questions based on previous responses, misunderstanding how to pose questions, recording the wrong answer and so forth. Also, the computer neither becomes fatigued nor cheats.

3   *Use of pictures, videos and graphics* Computer graphics can be integrated into questions as they are viewed on a computer screen. So rather than having an interviewer pull out a picture of a new type of window unit air conditioner, for instance, computer graphics can show it from various perspectives. CD ROM disk capabilities allow high-quality video windows to appear so the respondent can see the product in use or can be shown a wide range of visual displays.

4   *Real-time capture of data* Because respondents are interacting with the computer and not a human who is recording their answers on a questionnaire, the information is directly entered into a computer's data storage system and can be accessed for tabulation or other analyses at any time. Once the interviews are completed, final tabulations can be completed in a matter of minutes. This feature is so beneficial that some interview companies have telephone interviewers directly linked to computer input when they conduct their interviews.

5   *Reduction of 'interview evaluation' concern in respondents* Some people, when they are involved in responding to questions in a survey, become anxious about the possible reaction of the interviewer to their answers. Questions about personal hygiene, political opinions, financial matters and even age are considered to be 'personal' by many people, and the presence of a human interviewer may deter them from answering, or they may give false answers that they believe the interviewer will accept. On the other hand, some respondents try to please the interviewer by saying what they think the interviewer wants to hear. In any case, some researchers believe that respondents will provide more truthful answers to potentially sensitive topics when interacting with a machine.

DISADVANTAGES OF COMPUTER-ADMINISTERED SURVEYS

Obviously, computer-assisted surveys must have some disadvantages; otherwise, more surveys would make use of computer technology. Although computers are relatively inexpensive at present, there are significant costs involved in computer design, programming, debugging and set-up, which must be incurred with each survey. These costs, including the time factor associated with them, often render computer-administered delivery systems for surveys unattractive relative to other data-collection options. However, set-up costs are falling rapidly with user-friendly programs such as Decisive Survey.

A disadvantage that plagues all online surveys and one that exists on a global level is privacy. Marketing Research Insight 9.1 describes how online privacy issues are moving towards legal protection of citizens in the USA and in Europe.

Problem

Mackenzie's Knife Shop is a family-owned business located in Helensburgh, Argyll and Bute, Scotland. The shop was opened in 1975 by Bill 'Skinner' Roberts whose personal knife collection had become too large to keep in his mobile home, so he decided to go into the knife trading business. For five years, Mackenzie travelled from swap meet to swap meet in his Ford pickup truck selling his knives around Argyll and in neighbouring counties. Eventually, Mackenzie, tired of travelling, decided to open up a knife store in Luss in Loch Lomond.

In the past 15 years, Mackenzie's Knife Shop has grown steadily, and now its line includes quality knife manufacturers such as Stanley Tools. Customers range from retail 'walk-in' trade, which includes hunters, fishermen, tradespersons, collectors and homemakers, to wholesale 'UPS Delivery' trade where Mackenzie's Knife Shop supplies bulk shipments to approximately 50 different hardware or sporting goods stores located in the western coast of Scotland. Mackenzie's Knife Shop also supplies special-order knives to about 200 other retailers who order in small quantities from time to time. Sales are divided 40–60 per cent, retail–wholesale.

Knife sales are seasonal or non-seasonal, depending on the type of knife. Hunting and fishing knives are in greater demand at the beginning of hunting and fishing seasons, whereas kitchen knives are fairly constant across the year. Specialty knives, such as those sold to collectors, are not seasonal.

Mackenzie is contemplating using the Internet as a selling channel. He has heard that a great deal of business can be gained by opening up an Internet homepage shop. One of Mackenzie's employees is Jason McLachlan, and Jason is a marketing student at nearby Glasgow University. Jason convinces Mackenzie that he can do marketing research as part of a marketing internship to determine the feasibility of a Mackenzie's Knife Shop homepage. Mackenzie agrees to let Jason do this as long as Jason maintains one-half of his time selling knives and doing his regular duties around the store.

Questions

1   An alternative being considered by Jason is to place a questionnaire on the Internet itself. Jason took a course in Internet programming, and he can perform a survey on the Internet. What is your reaction to this data-collection alternative?
2   Discuss some of the disadvantages related to the use of computer-assisted surveys.
3   What aspects of computer-administered surveys make them attractive to marketing researchers?
4   What are the advantages of person-administered surveys over computer-administered ones?

(A) Problem 3.4 Sample size determination for simple random sample (SRS); samples for multinomial problems

Introductory comments

We are frequently interested in obtaining estimates from multinomial populations. A multinomial population is one in which each element can be classified into one of more than two categories. All multiple-choice questions involve multinomial populations. Estimating the proportion of users of each of three or more brands of a product or the

Table 3.3 Factors for converting binomial sample size to multinomial sample size

Confidence coefficient	No. of proportions to be examined					
	3	4	5	10	15	20
95%	1.53	1.66	1.73	2.05	2.37	2.53
90%	1.71	1.84	2.04	2.44	2.76	2.91

Source: Adapted from Tortora, 1978:101. Reprinted with permission from the American Statistical Association.

proportion of viewers of each of the five UK television channels during a given 15-minute period during the day are examples in marketing research.

In such cases, if the specifications of error that can be allowed (e) and of the confidence coefficient are to apply to the estimates of proportions for each of the several categories (rather than to only two of them, as it would if it were a binomial estimation problem), a larger sample will have to be taken than if the population were a binomial one. This is because three or more proportions are being estimated simultaneously and the estimates are such that the error in one of them affects the error in one or more of the others.

The direct determination of sample size for estimates of proportions from multinomial populations involves a somewhat complicated set of calculations. Fortunately, however, a table is available that permits conversion of the sample size that would be used if the estimate were to be treated as if it were to be made from a binomial population to the one that is appropriate for the multinomial population. The method for calculating the sample size directly and the conversion table (Table 3.3) are given in Tortora (1978).

The steps in the procedure to determine the appropriate sample size are as follows:

1   Specify the allowable error (e) that is applicable to each proportion to be estimated.
2   Specify the confidence coefficient for the estimates.
3   Using prior information, estimate the population proportion for each item.
4   Calculate the sample size that would be required for the estimate of the proportion for each item if the population were treated as if it were binomial. (*Note:* If the same confidence coefficient is used for the estimate of the population proportion for each of the items, one needs to calculate only the sample size for the item whose estimated population proportion is closest to (or equal to) .50. This sample size will always be the largest because the product $\hat{P}_i(1 - \hat{P}_i)$ in the numerator becomes larger as $\hat{P}_i$ approaches .50.)
5   Multiply the largest sample size obtained in step 4 by the appropriate conversion factor from Table 3.3. The result is the proper sample size for the estimates to be made from the multinomial population.

Problem

Kleanfast Household Products Ltd wants to estimate the proportion of all users of silver-polishing products who use brand A, brand B and brand O (all other brands). Robin Jones, the company's marketing research manager, is assuming that the proportion of users of brand A, brand B and brand O are each to have an allowable error of ±.05. He is also assuming a 95 per cent level of confidence (Z = 1.96). Using prior information,

Robin was able to assume the following population proportion estimates for the brands:

Brand A	$\hat{P}_A = .30$
Brand B	$\hat{P}_B = .20$
Brand O	$\hat{P}_0 = .50$
	$\overline{1.00}$

Questions

1   Calculate the sample size that would be required for the estimate of the proportion for brand A if the population were treated as if it were binomial (ignoring the finite population correction).

2   Calculate the sample size that would be required for the estimate of the proportion for brand B using the same procedure.

3   Make the same calculations for brand O.

4   Calculate the proper sample size for the estimates to be made from the multinomial population.

(M) Problem 3.5 Sampling error

Introductory comments

Execution of a research project always introduces some error in the study. The total error in a research study is the difference between the true value (in the population) of the variable of interest and the observed value (in the sample). The total error in the study has two major components: sampling and non-sampling errors. If the difference in value (error) between the population parameter and the sample statistic is only because of sampling, then the error is known as *sampling error*. If a population is surveyed and error is observed, this error is known as a *non-sampling error*. Non-sampling errors can be observed in both a census and a sample. Some of the common sources of non-sampling errors include measurement error, data-recording error, data analysis error and non-response error.

Because of their nature, sampling errors can be minimised by increasing the sample size. However, as sample size is increased, the quality control of the research study may become more difficult. Consequently, non-sampling errors can increase (e.g. the number of non-responses can go up), thereby setting up a classic trade-off between sampling and non-sampling errors. Since non-sampling errors can occur from various sources, it is difficult to identify and control them. Therefore, more attention should be given to reducing them.

SAMPLING AND NON-SAMPLING ERRORS

Consider a situation in which the goal is to determine the average gross income of the members of a particular population. If the researcher could obtain accurate information about all members of the population, he or she could simply compute the population parameter average gross income. A *population parameter* is a value that defines a true characteristic of a total population. Assume that μ (the population parameter average gross income) is £30,210. As already noted, it is almost always impossible to measure an entire population (take a census). Instead, the researcher selects a sample and makes inferences about population parameters from sample results. In this case, the researcher might take a sample of 400 from a population of 250,000. An estimate of the average age of the members of the population ($\bar{X}$) would be calculated from the sample values. Assume that the average gross income of the sample members is £29,300. A second random sample of 400 might be drawn from the same population, and the average again computed. In the second case, the average might be £43,400. Additional samples might be chosen, and a mean calculated for each sample. The researcher would find that the means computed for the various samples would be fairly close but not identical to the true population value in most cases.

The accuracy of sample results is affected by two general types of error: sampling error and non-sampling (measurement) error. The following formula represents the effects of these two types of error on estimating a population mean:

$$\bar{X} = \mu \pm \varepsilon_s \pm \varepsilon_{ns}$$

where $\bar{X}$ = sample mean; μ = true population mean; ε_s = sampling error; ε_{ns} = non-sampling, or measurement, error.

Sampling error results when the sample selected is not perfectly representative of the population. There are two types of sampling error: administrative and random. *Administrative error* relates to the problems in the execution of the sample – that is, flaws in the design or execution of the sample that cause it to not be representative of the population. These types of error can be avoided or minimised by careful attention to the design and execution of the sample. Random sampling error is due to chance and cannot be avoided. This type of error can be reduced, but never totally eliminated, by increasing the sample size. *Non-sampling*, or *measurement error*, includes all factors other than sampling error that may cause inaccuracy and bias in the survey results.

X is a sample characteristic, it will change if a new sample is obtained. The sample mean $\bar{X}$ is used to estimate the unknown population mean (μ).

SAMPLE RELIABILITY

All samples will not generate the same value of $\bar{X}$ (or s). If another simple random sample of size 10 were taken from the population, $\bar{X}$ might be 0.3 or 1.2 or 0.4, or whatever. The point is that $\bar{X}$ will vary from sample to sample.

Intuitively, it is reasonable to believe that the variation in $|\bar{X}|$ will be larger as the variance in the population σ^2 is larger. At one extreme, if there is no variation in the population, there will be no variation in $\bar{X}$. It is also reasonable to believe that as the size of the sample increases, the variation in $|\bar{X}|$ will decrease. When the sample is small, it takes only one or two extreme scores to substantially affect the sample mean, thus generating a relatively large or small $\bar{X}$. As the sample size increases, these extreme values will have less impact when they do appear because they will be averaged with more values. The variation in $\bar{X}$ is measured by its *standard error*, which is

$$\sigma_{\bar{x}} = \text{standard error of } \bar{X} = \sigma_x / \sqrt{n} = 1.49 / \sqrt{10} = 0.47$$

(σ_x can be written simply as σ). Note that the standard error of $\bar{X}$ depends on n, the sample size. If n is altered, the standard error will change accordingly, as Table 3.4 shows.

The variable X has a probability distribution, as reflected in Figure 3.1. The sample mean, $|\bar{X}|$, also has a probability distribution. It is customary to assume that the variation

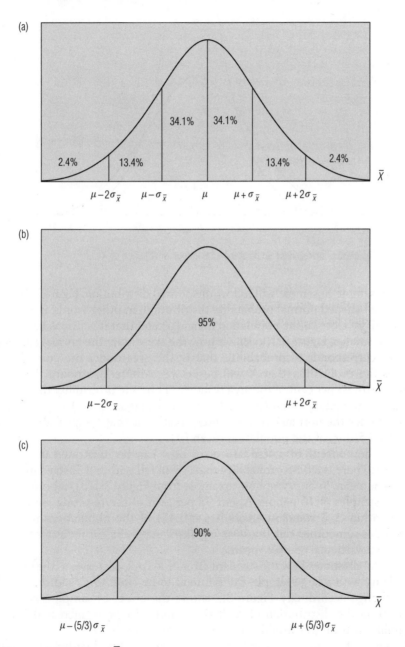

Figure 3.1 The normal distribution of $\bar{X}$.

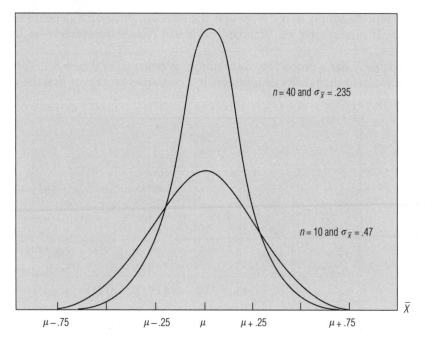

$n = 40$ and $\sigma_{\bar{x}} = .235$

$n = 10$ and $\sigma_{\bar{x}} = .47$

$\bar{X}$

$\mu - .75$ $\mu - .25$ μ $\mu + .25$ $\mu + .75$

Figure 3.2 The effect of increasing sample size on the normal distribution of $\bar{X}$.

of $\bar{X}$ from sample to sample will follow the normal distribution. Figure 3.1(a) shows the familiar bell-shaped normal probability distribution. In other words, it indicates that $\bar{X}$ usually will be close to the population mean (μ) and that it is just as likely to be larger than $|\mu|$ as smaller. Figure 3.1(a) shows how the area under the normal curve is divided. The area corresponds to probability, that is, the area under the curve between two points is the probability that $\bar{X}$ will be between those two points. For example, in Figure 3.1(b), 95 per cent of the area is shown. Thus, the probability that $|\bar{X}|$ lies within $2\sigma_{\bar{x}}$ of the population mean (μ) is 0.95. Similarly, Figure 3.1(c) shows 90 per cent of the area under the normal curve. Its interpretation is that the probability is 0.90 that $\bar{X}$ is within 5/3 $\sigma_{\bar{x}}$ of the population mean (μ).

Thus, the concept of a standard error now can be illustrated in the context of Figure 3.1. There is a 0.95 probability that $\bar{X}$ will fall within $\pm$ 2 standard errors of the population mean. In our symphony example from Figure 3.1(b), suppose we drew 100 different samples of 10 people. About 95 per cent of the resulting sample means ($\bar{X}$) will be within $\pm$ 2 standard errors ($\sigma_{\bar{x}} = 0.47$) of the population mean ($\mu = 0.3$). Figure 3.2 is sometimes called a *sampling distribution*, since it indicates the probability of getting a particular sample mean.

Table 3.4 illustrates how the standard error of $\bar{X}$, ($\sigma_{\bar{x}}$), decreases as the sample size gets larger. Thus, with a large sample, $|\bar{X}|$ will tend to be close to μ, and the distribution of $\bar{X}$ will change accordingly. Figure 3.2 shows the effect of sample size change from 10 to 40 on the distribution of $\bar{X}$. If the sample size were increased further, the $\bar{X}$ probability distribution would get taller and narrower.

A source of confusion is the fact that two probability distributions are being discussed. It is very important to keep them separate. The first is the distribution of

Table 3.4 Increasing sample size

Sample size	σ_x	$\sigma_{\bar{x}} = \sigma_x/\sqrt{n}$
10	1.49	0.470
40	1.49	0.235
100	1.49	0.149
500	1.49	0.067

response over the population, as illustrated by Figure 3.2. The population standard deviation, σ, reflects the dispersion of this distribution. The second is the distribution of $\bar{X}$, illustrated by Figure 3.2 (the dispersion of which is reflected by $\sigma_{\bar{x}}$). To conceptualise the X distribution (distribution of the sample), it is necessary to conceive many replications of the sample.

INTERVAL ESTIMATION

The sample mean, $\bar{X}$, is used to estimate the unknown population mean (μ). Because $\bar{X}$ varies from sample to sample, it is not, of course, equal to the population (μ). There is a sampling error. It is useful to provide an interval estimate around $\bar{X}$ that reflects our judgement of the extent of this sampling error:

$\bar{X} \pm$ sampling error = the interval estimate of μ

The size of the interval will depend on the confidence level. If it were necessary to have a 95 per cent confidence level, the interval estimate containing the true population mean would be

$\bar{X} \pm 2\sigma_{\bar{x}} = \bar{X} \pm 2\sigma_x / \sqrt{n} = 95\%$ interval estimate of μ

(recall that $\sigma_{\bar{x}} = \sigma_x / \sqrt{n}$). The interval size is based on $2\sigma_{\bar{x}}$ because, as Figure 3.1 shows, the probability that X will be within $2\sigma_{\bar{x}}$ of the population mean is 0.95. In our example, the interval would be

$\bar{X} \pm 2\sigma_{\bar{x}} = 0.5 \pm 2 \times 0.47 = 0.5 \pm 0.94$

since $\sigma_{\bar{x}} = \sigma_x / \sqrt{n} = 0.47$. Note that this interval includes the true population mean (recall from Figure 3.1 that $\mu = 0.3$). About 95 per cent of samples will generate an interval estimate that will include the true population mean.

If the desire were to have a 90 per cent confidence level, then the interval estimate containing the true population mean would be

$\bar{X} \pm 5/3(\sigma_{\bar{x}}) = \bar{X} \pm 5/3(\sigma_x) / \sqrt{n} = 90\%$ interval estimate of μ

Again, the interval is based on 5/3 ($\sigma_{\bar{x}}$) because, as shown in Figure 3.2, there is a 0.90 probability that $\bar{X}$ is within 5/3 ($\sigma_{\bar{x}}$) of the true population mean μ. In our example, the 90 per cent interval estimate is

$$\bar{X} \pm 5/3(\sigma_{\bar{x}}) = 0.5 \pm 5/3(0.47) = 0.5 \pm 0.78$$

Note that the interval is smaller, but that we are less confident that it would include the true population mean.

If the population standard deviation $(\sigma_x = \sigma)$ is not known, it is necessary to estimate it with the sample standard deviation. Thus, the 95 per cent interval estimate would be

$$\bar{X} \pm 2s/\sqrt{n} = 95\% \text{ interval estimate with } \sigma \text{ unknown}$$

In our example, it would be

$$0.5 \pm 2(1.27/\sqrt{10}) = 0.5 \pm 0.80$$

Since, from Figure 3.2, s was determined to be 1.27.

To summarise, the interval estimate of the population mean, μ, can be written as

$$\bar{X} \pm \text{sampling error, or } \bar{X} \pm z\sigma_x/\sqrt{n}$$

where $z = 2$ for a 95 per cent confidence level; $z = 5/3$ for a 90 per cent confidence level; σ_x = population standard deviation (s is used if σ_x is unknown); n = the sample size.

Thus, the size of the interval estimate will depend on three factors. The first is the confidence level. If we are willing to have a lower confidence level of the interval estimate to include the true unknown population mean, then the interval will be smaller. The second factor is the population standard deviation. If there is little variation in the population, then the interval estimate of the population mean will be smaller. The third is the sample size. As the sample size gets larger, the sampling error is reduced and the interval gets smaller.

Question

Now we are finally ready to use these concepts to help determine sample size. To proceed, the analyst must specify:

1 The size of the sampling error that is desired.
2 The confidence level, for example, the 95 per cent confidence level.

This specification will depend on a trade-off between the value of more accurate information and the cost of an increased sample size. For a given confidence level, a smaller sampling error will 'cost' in terms of a larger sample size. Similarly, for a given sampling error, a higher confidence level will 'cost' in terms of a larger sample size. These statements will become more tangible in the context of some examples.

Using the general formula for the interval estimate (recall that σ and σ_x are the same),

$$\bar{X} \pm \text{ sampling error, or } \bar{X} \pm z\sigma_x/\sqrt{n}$$

We know that

$$\text{Sampling error} = z\sigma/\sqrt{n}$$

Dividing through by the sampling error and multiplying by $\sqrt{n}$

$$\sqrt{n} = z\sigma/(\text{sampling error})$$

and squaring both sides, we get an expression for sample size:

$$n = z^2\sigma^2/(\text{sampling error})^2$$

Thus, if we know the required confidence level, and therefore z, and also know the allowed sampling error, then the needed sample size is specified by the formula.

Let us assume that we need to have a 95 per cent confidence level so that our sampling error in estimating the population mean does not exceed 0.3. In this case, sampling error = 0.3, and, since the confidence level is 95 per cent, $z = 2$. In our example from Figure 3.2, the population standard deviation is 1.49, so the sample size should be

$$n = 2^2(1.49)^2/(0.3)^2 = 98.7 \approx 99$$

Changing the confidence level If the confidence level is changed from 95 per cent to 90 per cent, the sample size can be reduced, because we do not have to be as certain of the resulting estimate. The z term is then 5/3 and the sample size is

$$n = (z\sigma)^2/(\text{sampling error})^2 = (5/3)^2(1.49)^2/(0.3)^2 = 68.5 \approx 69$$

Changing the allowed error If the allowed error is increased, the sample size will also decrease, even if a 95 per cent confidence level is retained. In our example, if the allowed error is increased to 0.5, then the sample size is

$$n = (z\sigma)^2/(\text{sampling error})^2 = 4(1.49)^2/(0.5)^2 = 35.5 \approx 36$$

Population size It should be noted that the sample size calculation is independent of the size of the population. A common misconception is that a 'good' sample should include a relatively high percentage of the sampling frame. Actually, the size of the sample will be determined in the same manner, whether the population is 1,000 or 1,000,000. There should be no concern that the sample contain a reasonable percentage of the population. Of course, if the population is small, the sample size can be reduced. Obviously, the sample size should not exceed the population.

Problem

A researcher knows from experience the average costs of various data collection alternatives:

Data collection method	Cost/respondent
Personal interview	£15.00
Telephone interview	£3.20
Mail survey	£0.50 (per mail out)

Question

If £2,500 is allocated in the research budget for datacollection, what are the levels of accuracy for the sample sizes allowable for each data-collection method? Based on your findings, comment on the inappropriateness of using cost as the only means of determining sample size.

(I) *Problem 3.6* Estimation of market potential

Introductory comments

All companies are concerned with: (1) defining sales territories; (2) allocating marketing budgets; (3) setting sales targets; and (4) evaluating performance. Sound market potential estimates are needed as the basis for each of these aspects of managing the marketing of products and services.

The terms *market potential* and *industry sales forecast* are not necessarily the same, although they are often used in that way. The word *potential* implies existing in possibility or capable of being developed although not existing at the moment. For some purposes it is useful to define market potential as the industry sales that would result from the optimum development of the market. This is the case when one is investigating a potential new product that has no well-defined product class. The electronic computer in the late 1940s is an example. It is also true when new markets and/or new uses for existing products suddenly open up so that present industry sales are not a valid measure of the potential that exists. The use of Teflon in cooking ware – it had previously been used as an insulating material in electrical equipment – is an example of a new market for a product that resulted in large increases in industry sales.

To avoid confusion, whenever we refer to market potential it is in the sense of the potential sales for the product class with optimum market development. Industry sales, or an industry forecast, is referred to as such.

Four major methods are available for estimating market potential: (1) adjusted industry sales; (2) purchase proportion; (3) correlative indexes; and (4) surveys of users.

Adjusted industry sales method Industry sales data are compiled for many industries by trade associations and by governmental agencies. The National Electrical Manufacturers, Association, for example, collects and reports data on shipments of television sets to retailers by area. The Air Transport Association provides detailed data on passenger and cargo traffic for domestic airplanes. The Bureau of the Census publishes the *Survey of Manufacturers* annually and the *Census of Manufacturers* every five years. Each work contains sales data for more than 500 industries.

Market potential is a measure of what *could be* rather than what *is*. Therefore, when industry sales data are available, estimates of market potential can be made using the industry sales figure as a base and making suitable adjustments. If one were interested in estimating the market potential for margarine, for example, one might reasonably view it as being the sum of margarine and butter sales for the preceding period adjusted for expected growth (or decline) in the coming period. Similarly, an estimate of the potential for ton-miles of freight in an area served by a trucking concern could be prepared by aggregating data on all area intercity freight traffic by the various types of carrier (rail, air, road and water) and adjusting the aggregate for growth.

Purchase proportion Industry sales data are not always available for the territories of interest. In such cases it becomes necessary to estimate industry sales before adjusting them to obtain the market potential estimate.

Data from the *Census of Manufacturers* permits estimates of sales of industrial products to be made by Standard Industrial Classification (SIC) code by using industry by county and by SMSA. It involves calculating and applying a purchase proportion. There is evidence that this method of estimating market potential is widely used. There is also evidence that sizeable errors result in the estimates of market potentials for some products. One should therefore use it with caution and, if possible, in conjunction with other methods, so that there can be intra-method comparisons of estimates.

Correlative indexes Indexes are useful primarily as indicators of the *relative* market potential between geographic territories. The principle underlying their use is that when one series is highly correlated with another one, the first series may be used to predict the second. The number of births during the past three years in an area is highly correlated with sales of baby foods, for example. Thus, an index of births by geographic area of the type

$$MP_i = (b_i / b_t)100$$

where MP_i = measure of relative market potential for baby foods in territory i; b_i = number of births in the area; b_t = total number of births in all geographic areas, is a good indicator of the relative market potential for baby foods by area.

An index may be *single* or *multiple factor* in nature. The example cited is of a single-factor index. As is evident from inspection of the formula, single-factor index numbers are simply the percentages of each of a set of variates to some quantity selected as a base. The relative market potential for baby food in area i is the proportion represented by the percentage of births in area i of the total of all births in the marketing areas of the company.

For most products, a single factor is not a satisfactory indicator of market potential. For consumer products other than low-priced staples, some measure of *number* of consumers and of *income* is usually necessary for making estimates of potential of the accuracy required. Other factors also may be required; a furniture manufacturer may find it necessary to add a measure of marriages by area, for example, and an ethical drug manufacturer may need to add the number of pharmacists by area to obtain the accuracy desired.

Multiple-factor indexes usually take the form

$$RMP_i = \frac{f_{1,i}W_1}{f_{1,t}} + \frac{f_{2,i}W_2}{f_{2,t}} + \cdots + \frac{f_{n,i}W_n}{f_{n,t}}$$

where RMP_i is the market potential in area i relative to that for the total marketing area of the company; $f_{1,i}$ is a measure of factor 1 in area i; $f_{1,t}$ is a measure of factor 1 for the total marketing area of the company and W_1 is the weight assigned factor 1.

The critical data requirement for applying the statistical procedures for determining the factors to use and the weight to assign to each is a satisfactory substitute for industry sales for the individual marketing areas for which an index of market potential is desired. Direct data on industry sales by such a territorial breakdown will not be available: if they were, there would be no need to resort to a correlative index as an indicator of market potential. Data for each of the factors to be considered for inclusion in the index have to be available for each of the territories or else they are of no value for the index.

If a satisfactory substitute for industry sales data by the territorial breakdown desired is available, a *multiple correlation analysis* can be run on the candidate factors to help select those that should be included in the index. Once the factors are selected, one may run a multiple-regression analysis on the industry sales data. The coefficients for the factors in the resulting regression equation can then be used to determine the factor weights.

The question that remains is: What kinds of data are available to be used as substitutes for industry sales data? The answer is that generally they are data series for a *related industry*, a *different time* or a *different set of geographic areas* than desired. In the case of the furniture manufacturer, for example, monthly data on department store sales are available by region and selected SMSAs. These data could be used in lieu of furniture industry sales in selecting the factors and determining the weights for the index. An alternative would be to use the sales data on 'furniture, home furnishings and equipment' by county that are collected and published every five years in the *Census of Business*. Still another alternative would be to use the annual estimate of retail sales of 'furniture and home furnishings' by state published by *Sales Management* in the annual *Survey of Buying Power* issue.

Perhaps the best-known general index used for setting market potentials is the annual *Sales Management Buying Power Index*. The factors used in this index are population, net income and retail sales. The weights assigned to each are, respectively, .2, .5 and .3. This index is best suited for estimating potentials for low-priced products that are mass marketed and is given by county and city for each state.

Surveys of users One of the major producers of coal chemicals (chemicals that are produced as a by-product of the coking of coal) conducts an annual survey of all known present and potential users of the chemicals the company produces. The purpose of the survey is to obtain an estimate from the responding companies of how much of each chemical they will use during the coming year. The market potential for each of their products by geographic area is then determined as the sum of the requirements of the individual firms in that area for that chemical. Potentials can also be determined by end use (the amount of benzene required for automobile and truck tyres, solvent for paint and the like) from survey data.

In the example just cited, a *census* was taken of all known present and potential users of a group of industrial products. In this case, a census was used instead of a sample because the total population of users was reasonably small and the purposes of the survey included generating sales leads as well as developing estimates of potentials. If the population of users is large, however, a census may be too costly. In that case a sample may be warranted.

The sample results will, of course, have to be inflated to obtain overall estimates of potential. The usual method of projecting sampling totals to population totals requires that information on both SIC industry and number of employees, as well as the anticipated amount of the product to be purchased, be obtained from the firms in the sample. An estimate of expected usage per employee per SIC industry represented in the sample can then be developed. These estimates can be projected to SIC industry totals by geographic area by multiplying by the number of employees in that industry in that area (obtained from the latest *Census of Manufacturers* or the current *Annual Survey of Manufacturers*, whichever is appropriate). Summing the using industry totals by an area then gives the estimate of overall market potential for that area.

A similar procedure is employed to obtain overall estimates of potential for a consumer good from a survey of a sample of consumers. Data on the usage of the product and on the income of the responding family can be obtained in the survey. Estimates of average usage amounts by income level can then be developed. Because family income data are available at the county (and SMSA) level, estimates of potential by income level can be obtained by county by multiplying the average usage per family for each income level by the number of families in that income level in each county. The overall potential for each county is then found by summing the potentials across income levels.

Problem

An analyst for a furniture manufacturer, for example, might conclude that a multiple-factor index by area using income (I), population (N) and number of marriages (M) is needed as an indicator of relative market potential. It might be further concluded that the factor weights should be such that income and population should be weighted equally and each have one-half the weight assigned to the number of marriages.

Questions

1   How would you determine the index number for each area?
2   Analyse and discuss some of the pitfalls and disadvantages associated with this particular forecasting method.
3   What kinds of data are available to be used as substitutes for industry sales data?

(M) *Problem 3.7* Extrapolation

Introductory comments

Mention of the term 'forecasting' brings forth a myriad of images, including complex computerised models, planning and bad guesses. To some people, 'forecasting' and 'marketing research' are nearly synonymous. However, the diversity of associations that the term 'forecasting' brings to mind immediately suggests that forecasting encompasses many different problems and approaches. The purpose of this problem is to briefly suggest what marketing forecasting is and how one might go about producing forecasts.

One general point about forecasting is very important. When asking for a forecast, most people want a single number. Providing a best-guess number is important. However, it is also important to provide a range of likely outcomes. In many cases the range may be at least as important as the best guess. The range gives the user of the forecast a notion of how tightly he or she can plan. For example, if a sales forecast range is provided, the user can count on needing production capacity for meeting the low end of the range and can develop contingency plans for meeting demand up to the higher end of the range.

EXTRAPOLATION: QUALITATIVE

As a starting point for, or an alternative to, expert judgement, a variety of extrapolation procedures exist. Two of these are essentially qualitative/judgemental in nature: last period + X per cent and graphical eyeball.

Last period + X per cent One of the most common approaches to forecasting is to estimate the percentage change expected in the variable to be forecast. This is especially common in deriving annual sales forecast for major product breakdowns. For example, we may forecast dishwater sales in pounds at the past year's rate plus 6 per cent.

Graphical eyeball Similar to the last period + X per cent method, the graphical eyeball approach requires that past data be plotted. Then the next value is eyeball to match the past pattern. As should be obvious, this method does by graph what many quantitative techniques do by number-crunching.

EXTRAPOLATION: QUANTITATIVE

A variety of quantitative extrapolation procedures are also available. Some of the most commonly used are discussed below.

Moving average Moving averages, an old forecasting standby, are widely used as a means of reducing the noise in data to uncover the underlying pattern. In doing so, it is important to recognise that past data have at least four major components:

1   base value;
2   trend;
3   cycles (seasonality);
4   random.

What moving averages essentially do is smooth out random variation to make the pattern (trends and cycles) more obvious.

Complex moving-average models are available for estimating trends and cycles. For purposes of introduction, however, we will consider only the simple moving-average approach. A three-period moving average of sales at time t is given by

$$\hat{S}_t = \frac{S_{t-1} + S_t + S_{t+1}}{3}$$

Note that this implies that (i) each data point used is weighted equally and (ii) no trend or cycle is accounted for. Recently, regression analysis has begun to replace moving averages as a forecasting tool for all but the simple situations.

Exponential smoothing A second major approach to extrapolation is exponential smoothing. As in the case of moving averages, this approach literally smoothes out the random variation in period-to-period value. Also like moving averages, trends and cycles must be estimated (smoothed) separately. The simplest form of exponential smoothing produces a forecast which is a weighted combination of last period's results and last period's forecast. The formula for this is:

$$\hat{S}_{t+1} = \alpha S_t + (1 - \alpha)\hat{S}_t$$

where the smoothing constant α = weight of last period sales and $(1 - \alpha)$ = weight of the last forecast. Notice that when α equals 1, we are simply using last period's results as a forecast. When $\alpha = 0$, on the other hand, we are completely ignoring last period's sales and keeping the forecast constant. Typically, the 'right' value of α is somewhere in between.

Note: The term *exponential smoothing* comes from the property of this method which weights the most recent period most heavily, the next most recent period next most heavily and so forth in an exponential manner. This property can be seen by examining the simple model:

$$\hat{S}_{t+1} = \alpha S_t + (1 - \alpha)\hat{S}_t$$

But

$$\hat{S}_t = \alpha S_{t-1} + (1 - \alpha)\hat{S}_{t-1}$$

Therefore

$$\hat{S}_{t+1} = \alpha S_t + (1 - \alpha)[\alpha S_{t-1} + (1 - \alpha)\hat{S}_{t-1}]$$

$$= \alpha S_t + \alpha(1 - \alpha)S_{t-1} + (1 - \alpha)^2 \hat{S}_{t-1}$$

Similarly, we can substitute for $\hat{S}_{t-1}$ and get

$$\hat{S}_{t+1} = \alpha S_t + (1 - \alpha)S_{t-1} + \alpha(1 - \alpha)^2 S_{t-2} + (1 - \alpha)^3 \hat{S}_{t-2}$$

By extension this becomes

$$\hat{S}_{t+1} = \alpha S_t + \alpha(1 - \alpha)S_{t-1} + \alpha(1 - \alpha)^2 S_{t-2}$$

$$+ (1 - \alpha)^3 S_{t-3} + \cdots + \alpha(1 - \alpha)^n S_{t-n} + \cdots$$

Hence, the data points are weighted exponentially where the exponent indicates the age of the data.

Searching for the right α is really a trial-and-error process. To account for both trend and seasonality by means of exponential smoothing requires a more complex model:

$$\hat{S}_{t+1} = \frac{\alpha S_t}{F_{t-L}} + (1 - \alpha)(\hat{S}_t + R_{t-1})$$

where the seasonality is given by

$$F_t = \beta \frac{S_t}{\hat{S}_{t+1}} + (1 - \beta)F_{t-L}$$

where L is the periodicity (length) of the seasonal pattern and the trend is obtained from

$$R_{t+1} = \gamma(S_{t+1} - S_t) + (1 - \gamma)R_t$$

and α, β and γ are three separately estimated smoothing constants. Generally, data involving cycles and trends are handled by means of regression analysis rather than by exponential smoothing.

Time-series regression A third way to extrapolate data is by using regression analysis with time (period) as the independent variable. Time-series regression produces estimates of the base level (intercept) and trend (slope). Seasonal patterns can be handled outside the regression (i.e. by removing the estimated seasonal component from the value of the dependent variable before performing the regression) or by various 'tricks' within the regression (e.g. using dummy variables).

Actually, all three methods (moving average, exponential smoothing and time-series regression) are very similar. They do weight data differently: moving average weights some of the data points equally, exponential smoothing weights all the data points unequally, and regression typically weights all the points equally, although unequal weights can be used. Choice among the three is therefore a matter of taste, availability and experience. Since the reader is presumably already familiar with regression at this point, he or she might be well advised to use time-series regression when the choice arises.

Box-Jenkins The Box-Jenkins methodology is a complicated statistical procedure for extrapolating time-series data. The basic approach is to assume that sales in the current period are based on a combination of random shocks (called white noise) and past sales. It encompasses several different approaches:

1   AR (auto-regressive), where the variable to be forecast can be written as a linear combination of previous values of the variable:

$$S(t) = \alpha_1 S(t-1) + \alpha_2 S(t-2) + \cdots + \alpha_k S(t-k)$$

2   MA (moving average), where the variable to be forecast can be written as a linear combination of previous random shocks:

$$S(t) = b_1 e(t-1) + b_2 e(t-2) + \cdots + b_p e(t-p)$$

3   ARMA (auto-regressive moving average), where the variable to be forecast can be expressed as a combination of equations x and x.
4   ARIMA (auto-regressive integrated moving average), where the variable to be forecast is expressed as differences in equations x and x to make the series stationary (i.e. a fixed mean).

The whole forecasting process can be viewed as a three-stage trial-and-error process. First, a tentative model is identified; second, that model is estimated; and third, some diagnostic checking is performed. If a model performs adequately, it can be used for forecasting; if it does not perform well, a new model is then tested. The advantage of the model is that it is often an accurate predictor in stable environments. The disadvantages are that it requires many periods of data to be estimated, and that the choice

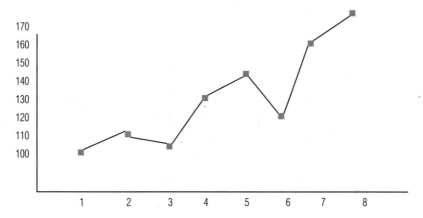

Figure 3.3 Hypothetical sales patterns over time.

Table 3.5 Zamir Inc.

Period	Sales	Three-month moving average	Trend	Three-period average of the trend
1	100			
2	110	105	+10	
3	105	115	−5	+10
4	130	125	+25	+10
5	140	130	+10	+5
6	120	140	−20	+10
7	160	152	+40	+11.67
8	175		+15	

of the appropriate model requires considerable expertise. Put differently, it is not a tool for uninitiated.

Additive versus multiplicative model One final point is important in considering extrapolation procedures. In building a model of sales as a function of base values, trends and cycles, these components may be combined in more than one way. The best way to decide how to combine them is to look at a graph of the data, such as Figure 3.3. In case A, the cycle explodes, and therefore a multiplicative model is appropriate:

Sales = (base)(trend)(seasonality)

In case B, on the other hand, the spread of the cycle is constant, indicating a linear model:

Sales = base + trend + seasonality

Generally, an additive type model will suffice.

Problem – example

Consider the three-month moving average for the eight periods of data in Table 3.5. As can be seen readily, the fluctuation in values is much less in the moving averages

Table 3.6 Exponential smoothing

Sales	$\alpha = .2$			$\alpha = .8$		
	$\hat{S}_t$	$.2S_t$	$.8S_t$	$\hat{S}_t$	$.8\hat{S}_t$	$.2\hat{S}_{t-1}$
100	100	20	80	100	80	20
110	100	22	80	100	88	20
105	102	21	81.6	108	84	21.6
130	102.6	26	82.1	105.6	104	21.1
140	108.1	28	86.5	125.1	112	25.0
120	114.5	24	91.6	137.0	96	27.4
160	115.6	32	92.5	123.4	128	25.7
175	124.6	35	99.6	153.7	140	30.7
	134.6			170.7		

than in the raw data, and a consistent trend of increase of about 10 units per period becomes quite apparent. Forecasts would now be based on the pattern of the moving averages, rather than the raw data.

Moving-average methods can be extended to track trends and seasonal patterns as well. As we can see in Table 3.5, a three-period average of the trend indicates approximately a 10-unit increase per period.

Using the eight-period example of Table 3.6, we can see how a small α (.2) produces a slowly changing forecast, while a large α (.8) tracks last-period sales much more closely. In both cases, a value of 100 was arbitrarily used for the first forecast. (The effect of this value on the forecast gradually decreases as more periods are included). For $\alpha = .2$, the forecast for the second period becomes:

$$\hat{S}_2 = .2(S_1) + .8(\hat{S}_1)$$
$$= .2(100) + .8(100) = 100$$

Similarly, the third-period forecast becomes:

$$\hat{S}_3 = .2(S_2) + .8(\hat{S}_2)$$
$$= 2(110) + .8(100) = 102$$

Notice that both sets of forecasts lag behind actual sales. The reason for this is that the trend was ignored.

Questions

1 Comment on the fluctuation of values presented in Table 3.5 relating to Zamir Inc.'s sales figures.
2 Is there a consistent trend?
3 Can moving-average methods be also used to track trends and seasonal patterns?
4 For the same eight-period example depicting Zamir Inc.'s sales, apply time-series regression and calculate the forecast for periods 1–10.

(A) *Problem 3.8* Cross-impact analysis

Introductory comments

Cross-impact analysis is a technique used for examining the impacts of potential future events upon each other. It indicates the relative importance of specific events, identifies groups of reinforcing or inhibiting events and unfolds relationships between events that appear unrelated. In brief, cross-impact analysis provides a future forecast, making due allowance for the effect of interacting forces on the shape of things to come.

Essentially, this technique consists of selecting a group of five to ten people to serve as project participants. They are asked to specify critical events having any relationship with the subject of the project. For example, in a marketing project the events may fall into any of the following categories:

1   corporate objectives and goals;
2   corporate strategy;
3   markets or customers (potential volume, market share, possible strategies of key customers, etc.);
4   competitors (product, price, promotion and distribution strategies);
5   overall competitive strategic posture, whether aggressive or defensive;
6   internally or externally developed strategies that might affect the project;
7   legal or regulatory activities having favourable or unfavourable effects;
8   other social, demographic or economic events.

The initial attempt presumably will generate a long list of alternatives, which should be consolidated into a manageable size (e.g. 25–30 events) by means of group discussion, concentrated thinking, elimination of duplications and refinement of the essence of the problem. It is desirable for each event to contain one and only one variable, thus avoiding the double counting of impacts. The selected events are represented in an '$n \times n$' matrix for developing the estimated impact of each event on every other event. This is done by assuming for each specific event that it has already occurred and will have an enhancing, an inhibiting or no effect on other events. If desired, the impacts may be weighted. The project coordinator seeks the impact estimates from each project participant individually and displays the estimates in the matrix in a consolidated form. The individual results, in summary form, are then presented to the group. The project participants vote on the impact of each event. If the spread of the votes is too wide, the coordinator will ask those voting at the extremes to justify their positions. The participants are encouraged to discuss differences in the hope of clarifying the problem. Another round of voting takes place. During this second round the opinions usually converge and the median value of the votes is entered in the appropriate cell in the matrix. This procedure is repeated until the entire matrix is complete.

In the process of matrix completion, the review of occurrences and interactions identifies those events that are strong actors and significant reactors, and provides a subjective opinion on their relative strengths. This information then serves as an important input in formulating strategy.

Problem

G&W Foods plc is a large and growing company that recognises that continued growth and profitability in the future stems from current strategic planning. Faced with increased domestic competition, decreased consumption of confectionery and a continual dependence upon suppliers, G&W's strategic alternatives clearly point to increased emphasis upon products and markets not traditionally associated with G&W's well-known confectionery operations. Diversification efforts have launched G&W into several food-related businesses, including restaurant and ice-cream parlour operations, coffee service, pasta production and distribution and, most recently, international operations. G&W must determine the best strategic plan that will lower the company's risk posture while, at the same time, take advantage of the company's financial, operating and R&D strengths to ensure the company's optimal growth and profitability in the future.

G&W's financial situation might best be described in one word as 'solid'. Their sales have climbed steadily upwards and net income has kept pace while keeping costs of goods sold and operating expenses under control. Relative to the competition, market share for G&W confectionery products has slipped during the past decade or so. In 1989, G&W's confectionery-bar market share stood at 27 per cent compared with 36 per cent for its primary competitor.

The company has decided to use cross-impact analysis in order to enable its managers to map out a strategic plan. In addition to competition, G&W was concerned with the analysis of four main environmental factors (events):

1 trend towards decreased confectionery consumption (a 25 per cent per-capita decrease in ten years);
2 the extremely high dependency upon suppliers;
3 prices of raw materials (sugar, coffee, cocoa beans, almonds and wheat) seem out of G&W's control;

If this event were to occur	Then the impact upon this event would be			
	A	B	C	D
A Trend towards decreased confectionery consumption (a 25 per sent per-capita decrease in ten years)	✕	↓	↓	↑
B The extremely high dependency upon suppliers	–	✕	↑	↑
C Prices of raw materials (sugar, coffee, cocoa beans, almonds and wheat) seem out of G and W's control	↑	↑	✕	↑
D The trend towards the development of substitutes for sugar, cocoa beans and other ingredients, as well as towards backward integration efforts	↑	↑	↑	✕

Key: ↑ = enhancing; – = no effect; ↓ = inhibiting;

Figure 3.4 Basic format for G&W cross-impact matrix.

4   the trend towards the development of substitutes for sugar, cocoa beans and other ingredients, as well as towards backward integration efforts.

These events are arranged in matrix form as shown in Figure 3.4. The arrows show the direction of the analysis. For example, the occurrence of event D (the development of raw material substitutes) would be likely to bring a price decrease in the commodities market. The extremely high dependency upon suppliers (event B) is likely to raise the prices of raw materials (event C). Therefore, an inhibiting arrow is placed in the cell where row B and column C intersect. It is not expected that the occurrence of event B would have any effect on event A, so a horizontal line is placed in this cell. It is judged that the occurrence of event A would make event B less likely to occur, and an inhibiting arrow is placed in this cell. The cells are completed in accordance with these judgements. The completed matrix shows the direction of impact of rows (actors) upon columns (reactors). If the interest is primarily in event D, column D should be studied for actor events. Then each of those actor events should be examined to determine what degree of influence, if any, it is possible to have on these actors in order to bring about event D.

Next, the impacts should be quantified to show linkage strengths (i.e. to determine how strongly the occurrence or non-occurrence of one event would influence the occurrence of each of the other events). To assist in quantifying the interactions, a subjective rating scale such as the one shown in Table 3.7 may be used. There are a number of variations in the quantification techniques. For example, the subjective scale could be 0 to 10, rather than −8 to +8, as shown in Table 3.7.

Another technique involves the use of probabilities of occurrence. If the probability of occurrence of each event is assessed before the construction of the matrix, then the change in that probability can be assessed for each interaction. The probabilities of occurrence can be entered in an information column preceding the matrix. Next, the matrix is constructed in the conventional manner.

Often, influences that bring about the desired results at the critical moment are secondary, tertiary or beyond. In many instances the degree of impact is not the only important information to be gathered from a consideration of interactions. The time relationships are often very important and can be shown in a number of ways. For

Table 3.7 Subjective rating scale

Voting scale		Subjective scale	
+8	Critical	Essential for success	Enhancing
+6	Major	Major item for success	
+4	Significant	Positive, helpful, but not essential	
+2	Slight	Noticeable enhancing effect	
0	No effect		
−2	Slight	Noticeable enhancing effect	Inhibiting
−4	Significant	Retarding effect	
−6	Major	Major obstacle to success	
−8	Critical	Almost insurmountable hurdle	

example, time information can be added (within parentheses) to each probability of occurrence within each cell of the matrix.

Questions

1   Quantify the cross-impact matrix developed by G&W by using a subjective rating scale.
2   Apply interactive probabilities of occurrence and their time relationships to G&W's cross-impact matrix.

(A) *Problem 3.9* Model building and scenario planning

Introductory comments

'Objective' and 'analytical' forecasting methods are the most advanced methods, scientifically speaking. They are based upon the construction of *explicative mathematical models*, which allow the simulation of market situations in alternative scenarios. In its basic philosophy, mathematical modelling is very similar to the expert approach: identifying a causal structure, constructing one or several scenarios and deducting the probable level of demand in each of them. The difference comes from the fact that *the causal structure was established and validated experimentally in objectively observable and measurable conditions.*

IDENTIFICATION OF THE CAUSAL STRUCTURE

The identification of the causal structure of the phenomenon under study is the starting point for any model-building exercise. Let us take as an example the case of a distributor who wishes to increase the loyalty rate of his customers and who is trying to identify the best means of reaching this result. The questions to be asked are:

- What are the determining factors behind the *image* of a distributor?
- How does this image influence the *visit frequency* of stores?
- What other factors explain customer *satisfaction*?
- To what extent does the level of satisfaction generate long-term customer store *loyalty*?

Rather typically, we are faced here with successive causal relationships where the first dependent variable (*image*) becomes the explanatory variable of a second dependent variable (*visit frequency* and *satisfaction*), which then explains *loyalty*. This is obviously a set of hypotheses based on the observation of buyer behaviour and on assumptions or reasoning suggested by behavioural theory. These hypotheses should be verified (or disproved) on the basis of empirical data gathered by the market analyst. If confirmed, the model could then be used to guide the distributor's decisions.

THE SCENARIO PLANNING APPROACH

The examination of the different possible forecasting approaches has shown the advantages and limitations of each. In reality, the approaches are very complementary and a good forecasting system should be able to make use of all of them.

In a turbulent environment, it is clear that intuition and imagination can be precious instruments of perception of reality and complementary to quantitative approaches which, by definition, rely solely on observed facts. In addition, a purely qualitative approach runs certain risks, and as much as possible intuitions and visions should be analysed in the light of the facts available. What is important is thus the confrontation of these two approaches. The integration of the different methods evoked by the scenarios method is a good manner in which to approach a forecasting problem.

DESCRIPTION OF SCENARIO PLANNING

A *scenario* can be defined as follows:

A presentation of the key explanatory factors to be taken into consideration, and a description of the manner(s) in which these factors could affect demand.

A scenario is thus different from a forecast. A forecast is more a judgement which tends to predict a specific situation and which is to be taken or left on its own value. A scenario, on the other hand, is an instrument which is conceived for analysis and reflection. It aims to:

- give a better understanding of a market's situation and its past evolution;
- sensitise the company to its interactions with the environment;
- evaluate its vulnerability to threats;
- identify possible lines of action.

Scenario planning avoids the danger of a single-point forecast by allowing users to explore the implications of several alternative futures. By surfacing, challenging and altering beliefs, managers are able to test their assumptions in a non-threatening environment. Having examined the full range of possible futures, the company is well positioned to modify its strategic direction as actual events unfold. Thanks to this sensitisation, the method allows the company to improve its anticipation capability and to develop its flexibility and adaptability. A scenario should be regarded together with others: one basic scenario and other alternatives based on key factors, as illustrated in Figure 3.5.

METHODOLOGY OF SCENARIO PLANNING

The key steps in the scenario planning process are the following:

- determine the model's scope and time frame;
- identify the current assumptions and mental models of the individuals who influence these decisions;
- create divergent, yet plausible, scenarios of how the future might evolve, along with underlying assumptions;
- test the impact of key variables in each scenario;
- develop action plans based on either the most robust solutions that play well across scenarios, or the most desirable outcome towards which a company can direct its efforts;
- monitor events as they unfold to test the corporate direction and be prepared to modify it as required (Shoemaker, 1995).

This approach, which is based upon the conviction that the future can never be completely measured and controlled, presents several advantages for management. First, it sensitises the company to the uncertainties which characterise any market situation; in a turbulent environment, sound management implies the *ability to anticipate* the

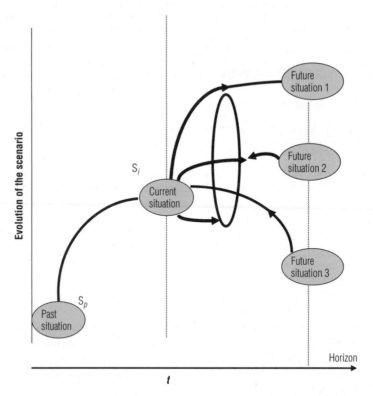

Figure 3.5 Scenario analysis: extrapolation + normative forecast.

Source: de Boisanger (1988).

evolution of the environment. Second, the scenario method facilitates *integration of the different forecasting approaches*, qualitative or quantitative. Third, the practice of this approach introduces more flexibility in management and induces the company to develop alternative plans and a system of *contingency planning*.

The spectacular development of information technology has largely facilitated the application of this method, notably in allowing its decentralisation within the company.

INDUSTRY FORESIGHT

A somewhat related methodology to scenario planning, which is gaining popularity, is industry foresight. According to Hamel and Prahalad: 'Industry foresight is based on deep insights into the trend in technology, demographics, regulation, and lifestyles that can be harnessed to rewrite industry rules and create new competitive space' (Hamel and Prahalad, 1994: 76). Industry foresight helps managers to understand and influence the forces shaping the future of the industry. Developing industry foresight requires more than good scenario planning or technology forecasting: 'Scenario planning typically starts with what is, and then projects forward to what might happen. The quest for industry foresight often starts with what could be, and then works back to what must happen for that future to come about' (Hamel and Prahalad, 1994: 82). Also, industry foresight is the product of many people's visions.

Problem – example

DYNAMIC MODELLING

Peeters (1992) has developed a dynamic model for estimating the demand for lorries on different European markets. The demand function adopted is:

Demand = F(production, interest rates, prices, error term)

where demand = monthly registrations of lorries weighing 15 tonnes and more; production = monthly index of industrial production; interest = monthly interest rate of state guaranteed bonds and price = index of fuel prices.

Data are deseasonalised and expressed as logarithms. The mathematical model used is a dynamic model which describes the structure of the market response. Thus:

- the *production* variable is introduced under a distributed lag model taking the shape of a decreasing geometric progression *from t to t − k* with a rate of 0.4557 (Koyck model);
- the *interest rate variable* comes into the model with an 8-month lag, which means that the time lag of a change in the interest rate on demand is 8 months; this lag was identified through an iteration procedure;
- the *price* variable is also introduced with an 8-month lag;
- the *error term* also has a dynamic structure as it is composed of a weighted sum of the preceding error terms (U) and of a random term (e).

The demand equation, estimated through a numerical method of maximum likelihood, is

$$Q_t = 5.503 + 1.7479 \cdot \text{Prod}_t + 0.7960 \cdot \text{Prod}_{t-1} + 0.3630 \cdot \text{Prod}_{t-2} + \cdots$$
$$- 0.1899 \cdot \text{Interest}_{t-8} - 0.4767 \cdot \text{Price}_{t-8}$$
$$+ 0.2463 \cdot U_{t-1} + 0.1389 \cdot U_{t-2} + 0.2602 \cdot U_t - 3 + e_t$$
$$N = 86 \; DW = 1.989 \; R^2 = 0.865$$

The quality of the statistical fit is measured by the usual statistical indicators. The determination coefficient here is 0.865. The *t-tests* measuring the precision of the individual coefficients are also statistically significant at the 5 per cent level or higher. The interpretation of the coefficients is straightforward as they are elasticities. Thus, as an example:

- the cumulative total effect (sum of effect for all lags) of the industrial production variable is 2.907, which means that a 1 per cent increase of the industrial production index generates an increase of 2.9 per cent of truck registrations;
- a decrease in the interest rate of 10 per cent causes, eight months later, an increase of 1.9 per cent of the demand for trucks;
- a 10 per cent increase in the price of fuel causes, eight months later, a decrease of 4.8 per cent in the demand for trucks.

The comparison of the observed and calculated sales via the model for the past ten months confirmed the goodness of fit.

Questions

1 Comment and discuss the strengths and limitations associated with mathematical model building.
2 Name and analyse the sequence of key steps involved in the application of the scenario planning technique.

References and further reading

de Boisanger, P. (1988) Reduire l'imprevu a l'imprevisible, *Futuribles*, March: 59–67.

Eiglier, P. and Langeard, E. (1987) *Servuction*, Paris: Ediscience International.

Hamel, G. and Prahalad, C.K. (1994) *Competing for the Future*, Boston, MA: Harvard Business School Press.

Levitt, T. (1965) *L'Imagination au Service du Marketing*, Paris: Economica.

Peeters, R. (1992) *Total Truck Demand in Europe: A Case Study*, IAG, Louvain-la-Neuve: Universite Catholique de Louvain.

Shoemaker, P.J.H. (1995) Scenario planning: a tool for strategic thinking, *Sloan Management Review*, Winter: 25–40.

Tortora, R.D. (1978) A note of the sample size estimation for multinomial problems, *The American Statistician*, August: 100–2.

4

Strategic Marketing

The strategic planning process and the marketing process are closely related, as marketing management decisions must be consistent with a firm's overall business strategy. Although strategic market planning can occur throughout the marketing organisation ecocycle, it is most noticeable in the growth phase, where conscious, rational decisions are made to guide the direction of the company.

Strategic decisions are related to an understanding of customer's needs, competitors' activities, and the financial implications of each decision. In turn, tactical marketing plans are based on a clear vision of the firm's overall business strategy and an understanding of its marketing strategies. Both strategic and tactical planning must be responsive to changes in the marketplace. For example, PowerCerv, a client-server application company (creating database and end-user software for industry use), enjoyed rapid growth from 1992 to 1993. In 1993, PowerCerv launched one of its own software applications, PowerTOOL, as a separate product for sale only to its current customers. By the end of 1994, the rapid growth of client-server technology and the initial success of PowerTOOL caused the company to reconsider its original strategic vision, and PowerCerv repositioned itself with a differentiation strategy that focused on services built around its own software products.

The term *strategy* is used interchangeably with *competitive strategy* or *business strategy*. Strategy embodies a firm's objectives and reasons for being in business. It includes corporate policies, resource allocations, customer markets and the competitive environment in which it chooses to operate. A firm's strategy is its vision of its future. It is an explicit statement that provides direction for coordinated business decisions in marketing and other functional areas.

Regardless of the size or scope of an organisation, strategic planning generally occurs at several levels: corporate, division or strategic business unit, and functional or operating level. Managers at these levels are responsible for making a group of interdependent decisions that vary somewhat at each level. At the corporate level, managers have a primary responsibility for satisfying customers and for the financial performance of the entire company over the long term. They also are responsible for the relationships among divisions of the company and the organisation's culture and values in the greater society. Corporate-level tactics become the strategy that drives decisions at the next lower level, the division or strategic business unit (SBU).

The strategic planning process involves a number of fundamental steps, although managers may differ somewhat as to the exact nature or order of each step. In fact, strategic planning generally follows an iterative process, rather than following a specified sequence, as new information is made available that may affect decisions made in a preceding step.

The process starts with a clear understanding of the firm's mission and philosophy, because long- and short-range plans must be consistent with the firm's reason for being in business. Both an external environmental analysis (i.e. customers, competitors and market) and an internal self-analysis must be performed to make informed strategic decisions. Based on the firm's corporate mission and performance objectives and the results of the environmental analyses, the next step is to determine strategic objectives and define the broad strategy to achieve those objectives. This step is followed by a plan for implementation and tactics (marketing mix strategy), execution of the plan, and evaluation and control measures.

(I) *Problem 4.1* The marketing planning process

Introductory comments

THE PROCESS

Figure 4.1 depicts the relationship between the marketing planning process and the output – the strategic and tactical marketing plans. This process can also be drawn as a circular process, indicating the ongoing nature of the marketing planning process and the link between strategic and tactical marketing plans.

MARKETING PLANNING SYSTEMS

The degree to which organisations need formalised systems for marketing planning depends on their size and complexity. In small companies, top management tends to have an in-depth knowledge of the market, and a clear view of comparative strengths and weaknesses. Often, there is also a shared understanding between top and middle management of the logical framework of ideas within which they are all working. In large organisations and in those operating in complex product and market situations, a more formalised approach via operating manuals, procedures and processes is necessary because of the sheer size and complexity. 'Increasingly firms are using more sophisticated decision models, where both the criteria and the weights used are based on actual research-based evidence.' Research, however, has shown that the process is universally applicable, with the degree of formality of the systematisation being the variant (please refer to Figure 4.2).

BARRIERS TO EFFECTIVE MARKETING PLANNING

It has been pointed out that, in environmental and competitive circumstances that are directly comparable, companies with complete marketing planning systems will be more successful than those without. However, there is a significant gap between theory and practice, in that few companies seem to implement marketing planning successfully. Thus, some obvious contradictions are apparent, and it is clear that there are many barriers to the implementation of effective marketing planning. Notwithstanding the importance of marketing planning and its universal acceptance by scholars as being central to the profit-making process, little research has been carried out to find out why it appears to be poorly understood and badly executed by a large number of companies on both sides of the Atlantic.

Table 4.1 summarises what little research has been carried out in this domain. There seems to be wide agreement in the literature that the two biggest barriers are:

- *cultural/political*: lack of a belief in marketing planning and/or the need to change;
- *cognitive*: lack of knowledge and skills.

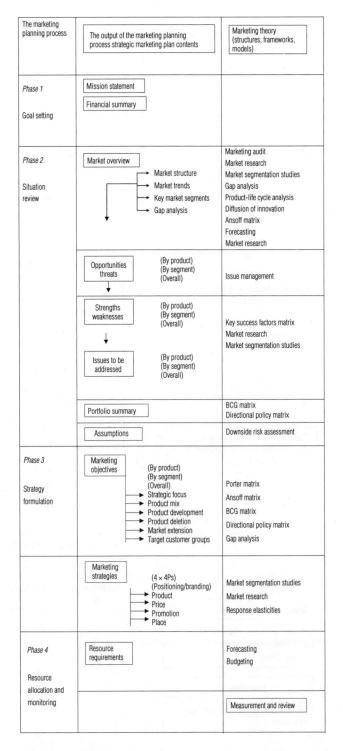

Figure 4.1 The marketing planning process.

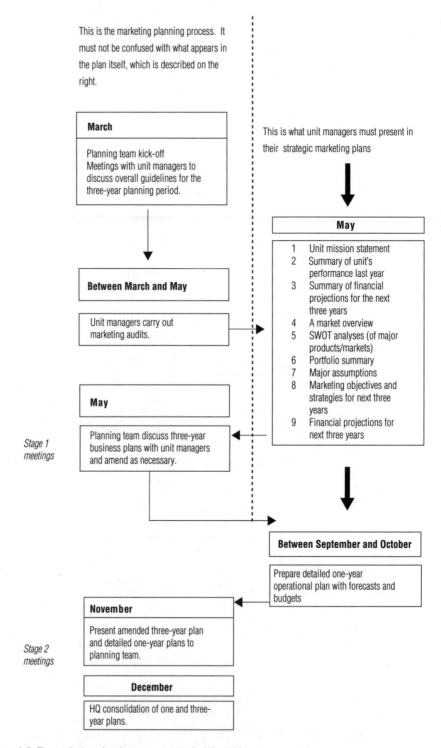

This is the marketing planning process. It must not be confused with what appears in the plan itself, which is described on the right.

March

Planning team kick-off
Meetings with unit managers to discuss overall guidelines for the three-year planning period.

This is what unit managers must present in their strategic marketing plans

May

1   Unit mission statement
2   Summary of unit's performance last year
3   Summary of financial projections for the next three years
4   A market overview
5   SWOT analyses (of major products/markets)
6   Portfolio summary
7   Major assumptions
8   Marketing objectives and strategies for next three years
9   Financial projections for next three years

Between March and May

Unit managers carry out marketing audits.

May

Stage 1 meetings

Planning team discuss three-year business plans with unit managers and amend as necessary.

Between September and October

Prepare detailed one-year operational plan with forecasts and budgets

November

Stage 2 meetings

Present amended three-year plan and detailed one-year plans to planning team.

December

HQ consolidation of one and three-year plans.

Figure 4.2 The marketing planning process: a typical timetable.

Table 4.1 Marketing planning barriers

Barriers	Research studies										
	1	2	3	4	5	6	7	8	9	10	11
Roles people play											
B1 Lack of chief executive/senior management involvement	*	*	*	*	—	—	*	*	*	—	—
B2 Lack of cross-functional involvement	*	*	*	*	—	—	*	*	*	*	—
B3 Lack of top management support	*	*	—	—	—	—	*	*	*	—	—
Cognitive											
B4 Knowledge and skills	*	—	—	—	—	*	*	—	—	—	—
B5 Lack of innovation/non-recognition of alternatives	—	*	*	—	—	—	*	—	—	*	—
Systems and procedures											
B6 Lack of care in marketing planning introduction	*	—	—	—	*	—	—	—	—	*	—
B7 Forecasts without documentation of intervention	*	—	*	—	—	—	*	—	—	—	—
B8 Inflexible application of textbook process	*	—	*	—	—	*	—	—	—	*	—
B9 Lack of follow-through to tactics	*	—	*	—	—	—	—	—	—	—	—
B10 Too much detail	*	—	*	—	—	—	*	—	*	—	—
Resources											
B11 Lack of time (elapsed and/or effort)	*	*	—	—	—	—	—	—	*	*	—
B12 Lack of money (for market research, etc.)	*	—	—	—	—	—	—	—	—	*	—
Organisational environment/culture											
B13 Organisational structure inappropriate	*	—	*	—	—	*	*	*	—	—	—
B14 Stage of organisational development	—	—	—	—	*	—	—	—	—	—	—
B15 Corporate politics	—	*	*	—	—	—	*	*	—	—	—
B16 Short-term-oriented reward systems	*	—	—	—	—	—	—	—	—	—	—
B17 Culture-stifling idea generation/openness	—	—	*	*	*	—	—	—	—	*	—
Data											
B18 Lack of Environmental information	*	*	*	*	—	*	—	—	*	—	—
B19 Difficulty of forecasting in times of turbulence and inflation	—	*	—	—	—	—	—	—	—	—	—

Note
* The study explicitly claims to have derived the barrier from empirical data with a clearly described and plausible research method. The research sources, studies used are as follows: 1. McDonald (1982); 2. Hopkins (1981); 3. Ames (1968); 4. Stasch and Lanktree (1980); 5. Leppard (1987); 6. Hooley (1984); 7. Liander (1967); 8. Saddick (1966); 9. Ringbakk (1971); 10. Camillus (1975); 11.Weichmann and Pringle (1979). Dashed are null entries.

At the end of the 1990s, much attention was paid to these two factors as key determinants of strategic marketing planning success, and it is clear that, for marketing planning to be effective, the following conditions have to be met:

• The process must be driven from the top down by the board.
• Marketing planning should be a cross-functional team process.
• There should be no confusion between the strategic marketing planning process and the tactical, one-year operational plan.

- The necessary marketing skills must be acquired by relevant marketing staff.
- There have to be well-understood processes in place for marketing planning.
- Appropriate resources have to be made available.
- The organisational culture must be supportive of marketing planning.
- Measurement and reward systems must be linked to the critical success factors identified in the marketing plan.
- It has to be a creative/innovative process.

THE FUTURE

The process of marketing planning will remain the same as it has always been because, given the multicultural, multi-market, multi-sector, multi-segment, multifunctional, multi-product nature of commerce, some kind of rational process has to be used to cope with the complexity. The complexity itself, however, will increase, as the world becomes more international in scope and as customers gain more power and choice in an oversupplied world. Furthermore, this level of turbulence will increase with the acceleration of technological advances, which continue to reduce the window of opportunity for the commercialisation of innovation.

Customer power has also thrown into sharp relief the pivotal importance of key account planning, as fewer customers account for a larger proportion of total sales. With a growing number of truly international customers, strategic marketing planning will only be as good as the strategic planning that occurs at the individual customer level. This, in turn, will make strategic marketing planning more international, as global key accounts demand seamless service internationally.

Finally, the complexity of strategic marketing planning will intensify as the trend towards supply-chain management grows.

A problem that was endemic to most industries at the end of the 1990s was that of correct market definition. The days of neat markets, constrained by Standard Industrial Classification (SIC) codes, had all but disappeared. A typical example of this is the automotive industry and its impact on all associated value chains. The industry is being driven by more complex technology, stricter environmental legislation, mature markets, more sophisticated customers and globalisation. This has led to the need to become less vertically integrated in order to become leaner, leading in turn to partnerships with a small number of tier-one suppliers. These tier-one suppliers are no longer just component manufacturers, but are truly systems and integrated module suppliers, servicing their clients seamlessly on a global basis through alliances, joint ventures and acquisitions.

This leaves a massive question mark over the future direction of major corporations such as SKF. Does an organisation as this become a tier-two, or even a tier-three supplier? The same issues face organisations like British Telecom, for the trends indicate the possibility of their becoming a second-tier supplier to service organisations capable of forming alliances in the value chain to deal with the totality of the communications problems of major companies.

Everywhere one looks, one sees such massive challenges spilling over into relatively placid domains such as key account management. There is little doubt that all of the above will make strategic marketing planning even more important to organisational success. Let us stress once again, however, that the processes outlined in this chapter will remain essentially unchanged.

Problem – example

SUPPORT FROM THE TOP

A well-known global energy company introduced strategic marketing planning via a series of workshops across Europe during 1993 and 1994. Marketing planning manuals were designed and distributed but, in spite of all the goodwill generated by the process, very few benefits were delivered. This was because the directors were still driven by financial husbandry and were blocking the new market-driven initiatives.

Then, in 1996, the European Board was introduced to strategic marketing planning at a day-long seminar. After that, marketing planning became the main driving force in the organisation. More progress was made in three months with the understanding, support and participation of the directors than had been made in three years. Profits are the best in the industry and morale is high. This is now a market-driven organisation.

Questions

1   Explain the components involved in the 'strategy formulation' stage (phase 3) of the marketing planning process.
2   What are some of the basic conditions that need to be met in order for the marketing planning process to be effective?
3   Discuss the relationship between customer power and the process of marketing planning.

(A) *Problem 4.2* Marketing information systems and the marketing process

Introductory comments

Companies need a marketing information system to enable them to define and measure opportunities. Information must be obtained from consumers, competitors and internal company records to obtain a reliable measure of past performance and future market opportunities. A marketing information system (MKIS) is a set of interacting facilities and procedures designed to provide management with reliable information for defining opportunities and developing marketing plans. The collection and dissemination of information by an MKIS facility should be systematic and ongoing, meaning that management should receive information on marketing performance and environmental trends regularly. Information should also be as reliable as possible, meaning that marketing action can be taken on the basis of the information. The consumer is the primary source of marketing information. Information on consumer needs, brand awareness, brand attitudes, advertising awareness, demographic and lifestyle characteristics and buying intentions is determined by consumer surveys. Marketing research is the primary means of collecting consumer information and is the central component of the marketing information system. Marketing research provides the basic input to enable management to develop marketing plans and formulate marketing strategies.

Marketing information comes from diverse sources – marketing research studies, internal company data, government agencies, syndicated research services and marketing intelligence data. Management must combine these sources into an integrated information system capable of providing meaningful and timely data. Figure 4.3 details

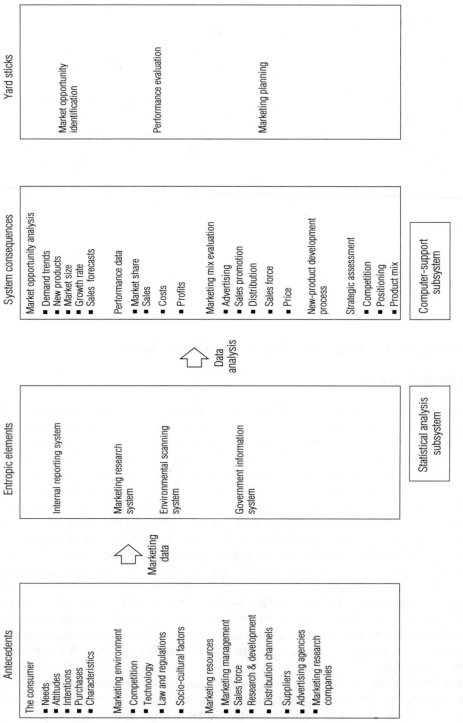

Figure 4.3 Components of a marketing information system (Adapted from Assael, 1985).

the components of a marketing information system using data from three sources: the environment, the company and the consumer. Information is collected from these sources and is fed into four MKIS components: an internal reporting system, a marketing research system, an environmental scanning system and a government information system. Data are then analysed to provide information in one or more of the output areas listed. Analysis requires the application of computer facilities and statistical programs as support. Information output deals with marketing opportunity analysis, performance data (profitability, sales, marketing costs), product-mix evaluation and marketing-mix evaluation (advertising, sales, promotion, price, personal selling activity and distribution).

Information is also provided on overall corporate strategies (product-mix evaluation, assessment of acquisitions, portfolio analysis, resource allocation, etc.). Information is then presented to management in report form for defining opportunity, evaluating performance and developing marketing plans.

Problem

Reilly Confectionery Ltd planned to introduce TARA, an ice-cream cake mix, nationally. This was its first entry into the dairy category market. The mix is composed of milk, sugar, butterfat and fresh eggs, all of which are mixed and freeze dried. The units are encased in a cone-shaped capsule with a candy shell for protection and stability. In 20 minutes each unit freezes into an ice-cream cake. The mix comes in chocolate, lemon, vanilla and coffee, but the consumer can add other flavours when mixing.

Ice-cream cake mix is a new product, with an expected growth rate of 1.5% a year in units consumed. Housewives are the prime purchasers, and the product is consumed in all socioeconomic groups.

Supermarkets sell 63% of all cake mixes and are the dominant channel of distribution. TARA comes in an innovative package that can be used to freeze the ice-cream component. Eight units are packaged in each container. A case of 12 containers sells to the retailer for £6.25. The suggested retail price is £0.80 per container. Costs as a percentage of factory sales were estimated as follows: fixed costs, 38%, variable costs, 12%, media/production costs, 15%, sampling/couponing, 4%, trade allowance, 4%, other promotion, 2%, sales force, 6%, distribution costs, 4%, and administration and market research, 2%. Sales are forecast at 1.6 million cases.

The TARA product manager is required to present an annual marketing plan to the group product manager. Reilly Confectionery Ltd uses a standardised format containing the following items: (1) brand's current (expected) performance; (2) recommendations; (3) effect of the recommendations on income; (4) situation analysis; (5) opportunities and problems; (6) marketing strategies; and (7) tests and marketing research.

A sophisticated marketing planner must be able to ask the right questions and must know where to get valid and reliable information to help answer those questions. These planning questions must be related to the problem of building a marketing information system. An information system is based on the answers to five questions:

1   What information is required?
2   How frequently will we need the information?
3   What are the sources of information?

4   How are the resulting data analysed?
5   Is the information worth the cost?

This short case takes the marketing planner's viewpoint towards marketing research not that of the marketing researcher. The goal is to make the product manager a sophisticated user and contractor of research. The product manager should know his or her needs and the limitations of research. An understanding of the roles and limitations of research will enable a marketing manager to work more effectively with researchers.

Peter Morgan, the product manager in charge of TARA, knew some of the questions that must be asked at each stage of the planning process. He was concerned, though, about the frequency for reviewing these planning questions, which in turn would indicate how frequently the marketing information system must supply data at each stage of the marketing planning process. He was also wondering about the sources of information and the methods of analysis that should be used. Of course, the informational needs of planners and the sources of data vary so widely across products, services and industries that generalisations are impossible.

At this point, Peter has decided to prepare the following list of planning stages with some critical questions that needed to be answered.

Planning stage	Example of critical questions
Environmental analysis, organisation values, objectives and policies	• What are the values and objectives of those persons who are in control?
Marketing organisation	• How are resources, responsibility and authority organised?
Situation analysis	• What are the unmet needs of the market?
	• What are the profiles of users and nonusers?
	• What are the segments for the product type?
	• What are the trends with regard to competitors?
	• What are our brand benefits?
	• What are the industry success factors, capacities and competitive structures?
Competition	• What are our strengths and weaknesses?
Public policy	• How do environmental concerns affect our strategies?
Strategy worksheet	
Marketing-mix strategies	
Product	• Can costs be reduced?
	• Does it meet needs adequately?
Price	• What is the price elasticity?
	• What price must we charge to break even?
	• For a given ROI?
	• What are competitor's costs and prices?
Channels of distribution	• Which channels are the most productive?
Advertising	• What copy theme should be used?
	• Which media should we use? How frequently?
Personal selling	• How should we recruit, train, motivate and compensate the sales force?
	• How should sales territories be determined?
Marketing research	• Are the data worth the cost of research?
Profit plan	• What are our forecast sales and costs?
	• Do learning and experience curves apply?
	• What is the payback period?
Evaluation	• Are we achieving our corporate strategic objectives?
	• Are we achieving our marketing tactical goals?
Control	• How do we implement and control the performance of the marketing plan?

Questions

1 What other planning questions should the TARA product manager consider as his most important informational needs for the marketing planning process?
2 Define the appropriate frequency of review that Peter Morgan should consider for each critical planning question.
3 Describe the most appropriate sources of information to be used for each planning question.
4 What methods of data analysis should the product manager apply in order to answer each marketing planning question?

(I) *Problem 4.3* Strategies for market leaders

Introductory comments

Although a position of market leadership has undoubted attractions both in terms of the scope that often exists to influence others and a possibly higher return on investment, leaders have all too often in the past proved to be vulnerable in the face of an attack from a challenger or when faced with the need for a major technological change. If therefore a market leader is to remain as the dominant company, it needs to defend its position constantly. In doing this, there are three major areas to which the marketing strategist needs to pay attention:

1 how best to expand the total market;
2 how to protect the organisation's current share of the market;
3 how to increase market share.

A summary of the ways in which leaders might do this appears in Figure 4.4.

Of these, it is an *expansion of the overall market* from which the market leader typically stands to gain the most. It follows from this that the strategist needs to search for new users, new uses and greater usage levels of his or her firm's products. This can be done in a variety of ways. For example, Honda increased its sales by targeting groups that traditionally had not bought motorcycles. These groups, which included commuters and women, were seen to offer enormous untapped potential. The company unlocked this by developing a range of small, economic and lightweight machines which they then backed with a series of advertising campaigns giving emphasis to their convenience and style. The strategy began to change yet again as the company recognised the potential for selling motorcycles almost as an adjunct to fashion. Styling therefore became far more important. This repositioning was then taken several steps further as Honda, along with other manufacturers, began targeting the middle-aged executive market with a series of larger motorcycles that were supported by advertising campaigns giving emphasis to the re-creation of youthful values.

As a second stage the strategist might search for *new uses* for the product. Perhaps the most successful example is Du Pont's Nylon which was first used as a synthetic fibre for parachutes and then subsequently for stockings, shirts, tyres, upholstery and carpets.

The third approach to market expansion involves encouraging *existing users* of the product to *increase their usage rates*, a strategy pursued with considerable success by Proctor & Gamble with its Head & Shoulders brand of shampoo which was promoted on the basis that two applications were more effective than one.

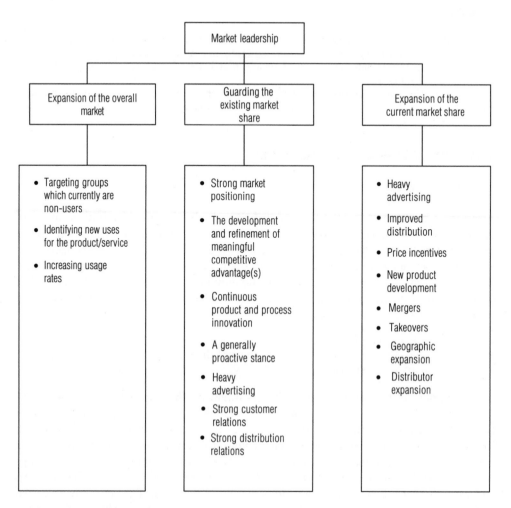

Figure 4.4 Strategies for market leaders.

At the same time as trying to expand the total market, the market leader should not lose sight of the need to *defend its market share*. It has long been recognised that leaders represent a convenient target as, because of their size, they are often vulnerable to attack. Whether the attack is successful is often determined largely by the leader's ability to recognise its vulnerability and position itself in such a way that the challenger's chances of success are minimised. The need for this is illustrated by examples from many industries including photography (Kodak having been attacked in the film market by Fuji and in the camera market by Polaroid, Minolta, Nikon and Pentax); soft drinks (Pepsi Cola attacking Coca-Cola); car hire (Avis against Hertz); potato crisps (Golden Wonder attacking Smiths, and then subsequently both companies being attacked by Walker's); razors (Bic and Wilkinson Sword attacking Gillette); and computers (IBM being attacked by, among others, Apple and Amstrad).

Although there are obvious dangers in generalising, the most successful strategy for a leader intent on fighting off attacks such as these lies in the area of continuous innovation. This, Kotler (2000: 235) argues, involves the leader refusing

to be content with the way things are and leading the industry in new-product ideas, customer services, distribution effectiveness, and cost cutting. It keeps increasing its competitive effectiveness and value to customer. The leader applies the 'military principle of the offensive': the commander exercises initiative, sets the pace, and exploits enemy weaknesses. The best defence is a good offence. The dominant firm even when it does not launch offensives, must at least guard all of its fronts and not leave any exposed flanks. It must keep its costs down, and its prices much be consonant with the value customers see in the brand. The leader must 'plug holes' so that attackers do not jump in.

Among the ways in which this can be done in the consumer goods sector at least is by producing a product in several forms (e.g. liquid soap as well as bars of soap) and in various sizes (small, medium, large and economy) to tie up as much shelf space as possible.

Although the cost of 'plugging holes' in this way is often high, the cost of failing to do so and being forced out of a product or market segment can often be infinitely higher. As an example of this, Kotler cites the camera market and the way in which Kodak withdrew from the 35 mm sector because its product was losing money. The Japanese subsequently found a way of making 35 mm cameras profitably at a low price and took share away from Kodak's cheaper cameras.

The third course of action open to market leaders intent on remaining leaders involves *expanding market share*. This can typically be done in a variety of ways including by means of heavier advertising, improved distribution, price incentives and new products.

It should be apparent from what has been said so far that leadership involves the development and pursuit of a consistently proactive strategy.

THE PIMS STUDY AND THE PURSUIT OF MARKET SHARE

The significance of market share, and in particular its influence upon return on investment, has long been recognised, and has been pointed to by a variety of studies over the past 30 years, the best known of which is the profit impact of market strategy (PIMS) research.

The aim of the PIMS programme, which now has a database of more than 3,560 businesses, has been to identify the most significant determinants of profitability. The factors that have shown themselves to be persistently the most influential are:

1   *competitive position* (including market share and relative product quality);
2   *production structure* (including investment intensity and the productivity of operations);
3   the *attractiveness of the served market* (as shown by its growth rate and customers' characteristics).

Taken together, these factors explain 65–70 per cent of the variability in profitability among the firms in the PIMS database. By examining the determinants of profitability it is possible to address a series of strategic questions such as:

*   What rate of profit and cash flow is normal for this type of business?
*   What profit and cash flow outcomes can be expected if the business continues with its present strategy?
*   How will future performance be affected by a change in strategy?

One of the key notions underlying strategic marketing management is, as we have already emphasised, that of the relative position of affirm among its competitors, particularly with regard to unit costs, profitability and market share. This is reflected in the PIMS approach which is illustrated in Figures 4.5 and 4.6.

The respective contribution of each of the variables in Figure 4.6 to overall profitability is estimated by means of a multiple regression model. This allows the impact of weak variable to be offset by strong variables; a low market share might for example, be offset by high product quality. Once the model has been applied to a given company, it can then be used to assess the relative strengths and weaknesses of competitors in order to identify the best source of competitive advantage. From the viewpoint of the marketing strategist, this has most typically been seen in terms of the organisation's relative market share, a factor which has been given considerable emphasis by successive PIMS reports: 'The average ROI for businesses with under 10 per cent market share was about 9 per cent...On the average, a difference of 10 percentage points in market share is accompanied by a difference of about 5 points in pretax ROI.' The study has also shown that businesses with a market share of more than 40 per cent achieve ROIs of 30 per cent, or three times that of firms with shares under 10 per cent.

In the light of these findings, it is not at all surprising that many organisations have pursued a goal of share increases, as it should lead not just to greater profits but also to greater profitability (i.e. return on investment).

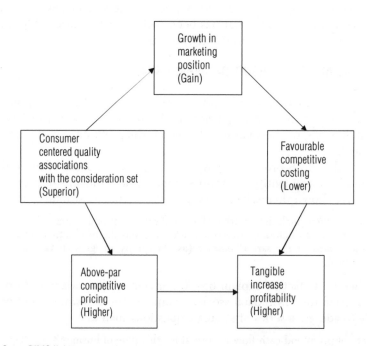

Figure 4.5 Some PIMS linkages.

Source: Adapted from Buzzell and Gale (1987: 81).

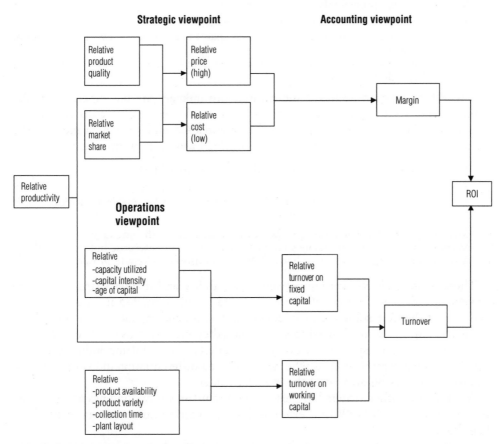

Figure 4.6 The determinants of profitability.

Source: Day (1986: 120).

Although the findings and conclusions of the PIMS study have an initial and pragmatic appeal, the general approach has been subjected to an increasing amount of critical comment in recent years. In particular, critics have highlighted:

- measurement errors;
- apparent deficiencies in the model;
- the interpretations of the findings.

Perhaps the main concern, however, is over the practice of deriving prescriptions about strategy from unsupported causal inferences. It is therefore important in using PIMS data to understand the limitations of the approach. When used in this way the PIMS programme can, its defenders argue, provide valuable insights to effective marketing and corporate strategy. In particular, they point to some of the broad conclusions from the programme which can be summarised as:

1   In the long-run, the single most important factor affecting performance is the quality of an enterprise's products/services relative to those of its competitors.

2   Market share and profitability are strongly related:
   - ROI increases steadily as market share increases;
   - Enterprises having relatively large market shares tend to have above-average rates of investment turnover;
   - The ratio of marketing expenses to sales revenue tends to be lower for enterprises having high market shares.

The PIMS programme has demonstrated the linkages among superior relative quality, higher relative prices, gains in market share, lower relative costs and higher profitability. These linkages are portrayed in Figures 4.5 and 4.6 which indicate the causal role that relative quality plays in influencing business performance.

3   High investment intensity acts as a powerful drag on profitability:
   - the higher the ratio of investment to sales, the lower the ROI;
   - enterprises having high investment intensity tend to be unable to achieve profit margins sufficient to sustain growth.

4   Many dog and wildcat activities generate cash, while many cash cows do not.
5   Vertical integration is a profitable strategy for some kinds of enterprise but not for others.
6   Most of the strategic factors that boost ROI also contribute to long-term value.

There is no *single relationship* between profitability and market share, unless one conveniently defines the market so that focused or differentiated firms are assigned high market shares in some narrowly defined industries and the industry definitions of cost leadership firms are allowed to stay broad (they must because cost leaders often do not have the largest share in every sub-market). Even shifting industry cannot explain the high returns of firms who have achieved differentiation industry wide and held market shares below that of the industry leader.

A number of other writers have also argued that the study's findings are generally spurious. Hamermesh (1996) for example, have pointed to numerous successful low-share businesses.

Findings such as these suggest the existence not of a linear relationship between market share and profitability but, in some industries at least, of a V-shaped relationship. This is illustrated in Figure 4.7.

In such an industry there will be one or two highly profitable market leaders, several profitable low-share firms, and a number of medium-share, poorly focused and far less profitable organisations.

Perhaps the most important point to come from this sort of observation is that the marketing strategist should not blindly pursue market share in the expectation that it will automatically improve profitability. Rather it is the case that the return will depend upon the *type* of strategy pursued. In some cases, for example, the cost of achieving a share gain may far exceed the returns that are possible. There are therefore twelve factors which need to be taken into account in deciding whether to pursue a share gaining strategy:

1   The cost of gaining share and whether this will be higher than the returns that will follow. This is likely to occur in various situations, but most obviously when the market is in or near maturity, since in these circumstances sales (and hence share) can only be gained on the basis of what would typically be a zero sum game (this would in effect lead to a pyrrhic victory in which the benefits of victory are outweighed by the costs of achieving that victory). In other words, the only way in which a company can gain sales is at the expense

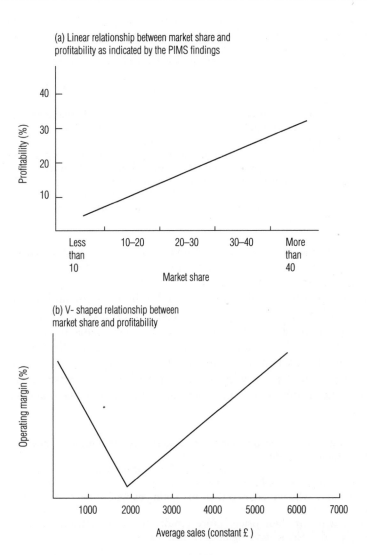

Figure 4.7 The relationship between market share and profitability.

of someone else in the market. By contrast, when the market is in growth stage, sales can be gained without the need to pursue a confrontational strategy.

2   When the implication of gaining extra share has a knock-on effect to another part of the organisation. This might happen when a firm is already operating at full capacity and any increase would involve a heavy investment in new capacity and the likelihood of achieving a positive ROI is then small.

3   There is already a high degree of loyalty to competitors' products among the customer base and this loyalty can only be broken down at a disproportionately high cost.

4   The company intent on gaining share has few obvious or sustainable competitive advantages and hence a weak selling proposition.

5   The future life cycle of the product or market is likely to be short.

6   An increase in share is likely to lead to the firm running foul of anti-monopoly legislation.

7   The increase in share can only be gained by moving into less appealing and less profitable segments.

8   The pursuit of higher share is likely to spark off a major – and potentially unmanageable – competitive fight.

9   It is unlikely that any gain in share can be maintained for anything other than the short term.

10   By increasing share, a larger competitor begins to perceive the organisation as an emerging threat and decides to respond in a way in which, assuming the organisation had not decided to grow, the two would have co-existed peacefully.

11   The organisation has developed a reputation as a specialist or niche operator and any move away from this would compromise brand values and the brand equity.

12   By growing, the organisation would fall into a strategic 'no-man's land' in which the firm is too big to be small (in other words, it would no longer be a niche operator), but too small to be big enough to fight off the large players in the market on an equal footing; this is illustrated in Figure 4.7.

In addition, of course, share gaining strategies can also be argued against when the management team has neither the ability nor the *fundamental* willingness to develop and sustain an appropriate and offensive strategy.

These sorts of points have also been referred to by Jacobson and Aaker (1985) who in an article entitled 'Is market share all that it's cracked up to be?' raised a series of fundamental questions about the value of chasing share gains. It is, however, possible to identify the two conditions under which higher share generally does lead to higher profits. There are, first, when the company offers a superior quality product which is then sold at a premium price which more than offsets the extra costs of achieving higher quality, and second, when unit costs fall significantly as sales and share increase.

Thus

1   the successful share gainers developed and added a greater number of new products to their range than their competitors;

2   companies that increased their relative product quality achieved greater share gains than those whose quality stayed constant or declined;

3   those companies which increased their marketing expenditures more rapidly than the rate of market growth gained share;

4   companies that cut their prices more rapidly than competitors rarely – and perhaps surprisingly – did not achieve significant share gains.

Problem – example

CHANGE, TRANSFORMATION AND A MARKET FOCUS: REASSERTING MARKET LEADERSHIP

Three of the best-known and most successful organisational change programmes over the past decade have taken place at British Airways ('from Bloody awful to bloody awesome'), Grand Met and SmithKline Beecham. In each case, a slow-moving and increasingly unsuccessful organisation has been refocused and transformed into a marketing leader. However, the problems of achieving transformation *and maintaining* a successful profile are highlighted by the way in which only five years after the publication of Peters and Watema's 1982 bestseller *In Search of Excellence*, all but 14 of its 43 'excellent' companies had either grown weaker or were declining rapidly.

In commenting on this, Richard Pascale (1990) argues that too few managers really understand what is involved in transforming an organisation. To him, transformation involves not only a discontinuous shift in an organisation's capability, but also the much more difficult task of sustaining that shift. Faced with the need for change, he suggests, companies come to a fork in the road. About 80 per cent take the easy route, stripping themselves 'back to basics', searching for the latest tools and techniques and going on to risk stagnation or decline. Only a fifth of companies take the much tougher, alternative route. This involves three big steps: the first he refers to as 'inquiring into their underlying paradigm' (i.e. questioning the way they do everything, including how managers think); attacking the problems systematically on all fronts, notably strategy, operations, organisation and culture; and 'reinventing' themselves in such a way that the transformation becomes self-sustaining. It is only in this way that truly intellectual learning is matched by the emotional learning that is needed and transformation truly becomes embedded in the organisation.

WILLIAM HOLDINGS AND ITS PURSUIT OF MARKET LEADERSHIP

In just eight years, Williams Holdings plc, under the chairmanship of Nigel Rudd, grew from an annual turnover of £6 million to more than £1,000 million. This was achieved by aggressive management of the firm's portfolio and a series of carefully targeted acquisitions.

The company, which now operates throughout Europe and the USA, has relentlessly pursued an objective of growth by focusing much of its efforts on 'businesses which are pre-eminent in their sphere of operations'. The company's publicly stated policies include:

* owning businesses which have significant shares in their relevant markets;
* generating above-average margins and cash flow to enable the companies to market their products and services aggressively;
* to invest capital consistently to create the position of lowest cost producer.

Questions

1 Define and discuss a number of market leadership strategies linked with (i) the expansion of the overall market; (ii) guarding the existing market share; and (iii) the expansion of the current market share.
2 According to the PIMS programme, which are the three most significant determinants of profitability? By examining these same key determinants, what strategic questions can be raised?
3 Discuss the rationale behind a V-shaped relationship between market share and profitability.

(M) Problem 4.4 Criteria for marketing effort allocation

Introductory comments

The decision to increase or decrease the level of marketing expenditures in a particular market is based on an evaluation of past performance and future aspirations. Factors to consider include market potential, competition, sales, costs and profits, and these can be brought together in a number of useful ways. Consider the following criteria, which might be used for allocating marketing expenditures.

MARKET POTENTIAL

Market potential is the limit approached by market demand as industry marketing expenditures approach infinity, for a given environment. The potential in a market can be an appropriate guide to effort allocation when a company does not have adequate information on profits, costs and competition in that market. Furthermore, sales will not be an acceptable guide to effort allocation if the company has not been selling in the market, or if it has not sufficiently penetrated the market to the extent that sales adequately reflect potential. Thus when the company's sales, profits, costs and competitive information inadequately reflect market conditions, market potential may be the only useful effort allocation measure available to the company. In such cases, the following ratio might be used when allocating effort to individual markets:

$$\frac{\text{Percentage of company's total market potential}}{\text{Percentage of company's total marketing expenditures}}$$

with the following actions taken for various values of the ratio:

Ratio value	Recommended action
Greater than one	Increase effort
Equal to one	Make no change
Less than one	Decrease effort

MARKET POTENTIAL ADJUSTED FOR COMPETITION

Potential adjusted for competition is a better guide to marketing effort allocation than that discussed above because it more realistically reflects market conditions and profit opportunities. Potential is useful as a criterion primarily when no additional information is available. As activity has been poorly estimated, the level of sales realised in a market may not even closely resemble the level of sales the company could reasonably expect to enjoy in that market. Consequently, profits tend to be a poor criterion for allocating sales effort if accurate potential, competition, sales and cost information has not been gathered previously. Once this information is available in accurate form, the ratio of

$$\frac{\text{Percentage of company's profits}}{\text{Percentage of company's total marketing expenditures}}$$

can be used to guide the allocation of the company's marketing efforts towards those markets that are contributing more to the company's profits.

A little reflection on the foregoing four criteria suggests that (1) they form a hierarchy; and (2) they should be used in conjunction with one another, rather than separately. Consider the following inadequacies:

1   Potential does not take into consideration competition, realisable sales or profits.
2   Potential adjusted for competition may bear little relationship to a market's profitability.
3   Actual sales may not adequately reflect sales and profit potential in those markets that have been poorly exploited or completely ignored by the company.
4   Profits are a useful criterion only after the company has ascertained that marketing effort allocation has not ignored potential and competition, and only after the company has ascertained that sales adequately reflect realisable potential.

If these four statements are valid, they suggest that the criteria should be used together in some way. Individually, they all demonstrate certain weaknesses, which can be overcome if they are used in conjunction with one or more of the other criteria.

It should be noted that the four criteria discussed above apply principally to short-term situations. Occasionally, management may choose to invest in a market because of its future potential. Such a situation falls primarily under the market-potential criterion discussed above. That is, using some measure of future potential, management foresees a figure large enough to justify a long-term investment in that market. To a lesser extent, potential adjusted for competition may also apply to such a situation. However, the sales and profit criteria would not. Hence, for those markets where future potential justifies a present investment in that market, the marketing-effort allocation decision should be based primarily on the first criterion, and to a much lesser extent on the second, third and fourth criteria.

Problem

Schwartz Inc. is a medium-sized manufacturer of leisure equipment and sporting goods. The company is at present trying to penetrate and increase market share in five different geographic markets. Schwartz has been experiencing some pressure from three major competitors marketing a very similar product mix. John Montgomery, the company's marketing manager, is in the process of preparing next year's marketing plan and he is considering and testing different criteria for allocating marketing expenditures. Table 4.2 illustrates the use of the market-potential criterion.

Table 4.2 Market-potential criteria for allocation of marketing expenditures – Schwartz Inc.

Market	Potential		Current effort allocation	
	(000s) (Units)	(%)	(000s) (£)	(%)
1	100	20	100	20
2	100	20	100	20
3	100	20	80	16
4	100	20	120	24
5	100	20	100	20
		100		100

Table 4.3 illustrates the marketing-effort allocation changes as suggested by the use of the adjusted market-potential criterion if effort had previously been allocated in proportion to potential. The adjusted potential shown in the fourth column is simply potential divided by the number of competitors plus one.

Table 4.4 illustrates the marketing-effort allocation changes as suggested by the use of the sales criteria if effort had previously been allocated in proportion to 'potential adjusted for competition'. Table 4.5 illustrates the marketing-effort allocation changes

Table 4.3 Adjusted market-potential criteria for allocation of marketing expenditures – Schwartz Inc.

Market	Potential (000s) (Units)	Competitors	Adjusted potential		Effort allocation	
			(000) (Units)	(%)	(000s) (£)	(%)
1	100	1	50	25.0	100	20
2	100	3	25	12.5	100	20
3	100	3	25	12.5	100	20
4	100	1	50	25.0	100	20
5	100	1	50	25.0	100	20
				100.0		100

Table 4.4 Sales criteria for allocation of marketing expenditures – Schwartz Inc.

Market	Sales		Effort allocation*	
	(000s) (Units)	(%)	(000s) (£)	(%)
1	40	18.2	125.0	25.0
2	20	9.1	62.5	12.5
3	30	13.6	62.5	12.5
4	60	27.3	125.0	25.0
5	70	31.8	125.0	25.0
		100.0		100.0

Note
* See Table 4.3.

Table 4.5 Profit criteria for allocation of marketing expenditures – Schwartz Inc.

Market	Sales		Effort allocation*	
	(000s) (£)	(%)	(000s) (£)	(%)
1	275.0	16.2	91.0	18.2
2	137.5	8.1	46.0	9.2
3	237.5	14.0	68.0	13.6
4	475.0	28.0	137.0	27.4
5	575.0	33.7	158.0	31.6
		100.0		100.0

Note
* See Table 4.4.

as suggested by the use of the profit criteria if effort had previously been allocated in proportion to sales.

Questions

1. Regarding the use of the market-potential criteria for allocation of marketing expenditures, calculate the values of the ratio and recommend a final decision for each of the five markets.
2. Regarding the use of the adjusted market-potential criteria for allocation of marketing expenditures, calculate the values of the ratio and recommend a final decision for each of the five markets.
3. Regarding the use of the sales criteria for allocation of marketing expenditures, calculate the values of the ratio and recommend a final decision for each of the five markets.
4. Finally, regarding the use of the profit criteria for allocation of marketing expenditures, calculate the values of the ratio and recommend a final decision for each of the five markets.

(M) *Problem 4.5* Allocating resources using sales response functions

Introductory comments

Marketing managers search continuously to find a competitive advantage – a strength relative to their competitors in some market niche – in the markets they serve and the products they offer. Having identified this competitive advantage, they must allocate their company's resources to exploit it.

A sales response function relates the expense of marketing effort to the marketing results obtained, such as sales revenue profit, units sold or level of awareness. For simplicity in the analytical problem that follows, only the effects of marketing effort on sales revenue will be analysed, but the concept applies to other measures of marketing success as well.

MAXIMISING INCREMENTAL REVENUE MINUS INCREMENTAL COST

At a theoretical level, optimal resource allocation for a manager is simple: allocate the company's marketing, production and financial resources to the markets and products where the excess of incremental revenues over incremental costs is greatest. This parallels the marginal revenues – marginal cost analysis.

The sales-response function forecasts the likely sales revenue/sales volume during a specified time period associated with different possible levels of marketing effort or of a marketing-mix element effort, holding constant the other marketing-mix elements. To the extent that marketing managers have a good intuition for the relevant sales-response functions, they are in a position to formulate more effective marketing plans.

There are four possible functional relationships between sales revenue/sales volume and marketing expenditures. The first states that sales revenue/sales volume is not affected by the level of marketing expenditures. The second states that sales revenue/sales volume grows linearly with marketing expenditures. The third states that marketing-expenditure function is a concave function showing sales revenue/sales volume increasing throughout at a decreasing rate. Finally, the fourth states that marketing-expenditure function is an S-shaped function showing sales volume initially increasing at an increasing rate and then increasing at a decreasing rate. The occurrence

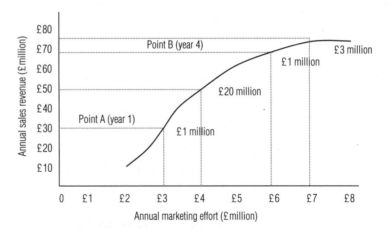

Figure 4.8 Sales-response function showing the situation for two different years.

of eventually diminishing returns to increases in marketing expenditures is plausible for the following reasons. First, there is an upper limit to the total potential demand for any particular product. As the upper limit is approached, it becomes increasingly expensive to attract the remaining buyers. And second, as a company steps up its marketing effort, its competitors are likely to do the same, with the net result that each company experiences increasing sales resistance.

Problem

Figure 4.8 illustrates the resource-allocation principles explained above. The company's annual marketing effort, such as sales and advertising expenses, is plotted on the horizontal axis. As this annual marketing effort increases, so does the resulting annual sales revenue! The relationship is assumed to be S-shaped, showing that £1 million of marketing effort results in far greater increases of sales revenue in the mid-range (such as £4 million) than at either end (such as £2 or £7 million).

Suppose Figure 4.8 shows the situation for a new herbal-essence shampoo developed by Bernd Geyer Co. of Hamburg. Also assume the sales-revenue response function does not change through time. Point A shows the position of the company in year 1 and point B shows it three years later in year 4. Marketing effort in the form of advertising and other promotions has increased from £3 to £6 million a year, while sales revenue has increased from £30 to £70 million a year.

Questions

1 Let's look at the major resource-allocation question: what are the probable increases in sales revenue in years 1 and 4 for an extra £1 million of marketing effort?
2 What are the ratios of incremental sales revenue to marketing effort in the years 1 and 4?
3 Based on your analysis of the findings, make specific recommendations to the company regarding a future effective resource-allocation strategy.

Table 4.6 Competitive reaction matrix (Lambin, 1976: P24)

Brand A actions	Competing brand B's reactions		
	Price (p)	Advertising (a)	Quality (x)
Price	$\varepsilon_{p,p}$	$\varepsilon_{p,a}$	$\varepsilon_{p,x}$
Advertising	$\varepsilon_{a,p}$	$\varepsilon_{a,a}$	$\varepsilon_{a,x}$
Quality	$\varepsilon_{x,p}$	$\varepsilon_{x,a}$	$\varepsilon_{x,x}$

Note: In columns 2–4, the first subscript is for the brand initiating the move; the second is for the rival's response.

(A) *Problem 4.6* Competitive reaction matrix and measuring market power

Introductory comments

Firms compete with one another by emphasising different elements of the marketing mix and by insisting differently on each component of the mix. The competitive reaction matrix presented in Table 4.6 is a useful instrument for analysing alternative action–reaction patterns among two competing companies (Lambin, 1993: 22–7). The matrix might include two brands, the studied brand and its priority competitor, and three or four components of the marketing mix, such as price, media advertising, promotion or product quality.

In Table 4.6 the horizontal rows designate the actions initiated by our brand A. The alternative actions might be to cut price, increase advertising or improve quality. The responses of brand B, the direct competitor, are represented by the vertical columns. The coefficients in the matrix are the reaction elasticities or the probabilities of brand B reacting to brand A's move.

On the diagonal we have the *direct reaction elasticities*, or the likelihood of brand B responding to a move of brand A with the same marketing instrument, that is meeting a price cut with a price cut. Off diagonal, we have the *indirect reaction elasticities*, or the probabilities of brand B responding to brand A with another marketing instrument, for example, meeting a price cut with increased advertising. These reaction elasticities can be estimated by reference to past behaviour or by seeking management's judgement concerning the strengths and weaknesses of competition. Once the matrix is developed, management can review each potential marketing action in the light of probable competitor reactions.

The entries of the matrix can also be probabilities. In this case, their horizontal sum must be equal to one.

For example, if management considers that there is a 70 per cent chance that competition will meet our price cut, but only a 20 per cent chance that it will meet a quality increase, it might consider that a quality increase programme will help more to develop a unique marketing approach than the price cut, as it is less likely to be imitated.

The competitive matrix is useful in helping to develop a distinctive marketing approach to the market and to anticipate competitors' reactions. More columns can be added representing other marketing instruments. Delayed responses can also be analysed.

CONDITIONS FOR SUCCESSFUL DIFFERENTIATION

For a differentiation strategy to be successful, a number of conditions need to be present:

- Differentiation of any kind must represent some *value* to buyers.
- This value can either represent a better *performance* (higher satisfaction) or reduced *cost*.
- The value to buyers must be high enough for them to be prepared to pay a *price premium* to benefit from it.
- The element of differentiation must be *sustainable*; in other words, other rivals should not be able to imitate it immediately.
- The price premium paid by buyers must exceed the *cost supplement* borne by the firm to produce and maintain the element of differentiation.
- Finally, in so far as the element of differentiation is not very apparent and is unknown by the market, the firm must produce *signals* to make it known.

The effect of differentiation is to give the firm some degree of *market power*, because it generates preferences, customer loyalty and weaker price sensitivity. The buyer's bargaining power is thus partially neutralised. Differentiation also protects the firm from rival attacks, given that as a result of the element of differentiation, substitution between products is reduced. The monopolistic firm is relatively independent in its actions vis-à-vis its rivals. Finally, it also helps the firm to defend itself better against suppliers and substitute products. *This is the typical competitive situation that strategic marketing seeks to create.*

MEASURING MARKET POWER

The degree of market power is measured by the firm's ability to dictate a price above that of its priority competitors. One measure of this sensitivity is the price elasticity of the firm's or differentiated product's selective demand. The lower this demand elasticity, the less volatile or sensitive will market share be to a price increase.

If brand A has price elasticity equal to −1.5 and brand B an elasticity of −3.0, the same price increase of 5 per cent will lower demand for A by 7.5 per cent and demand for B by 15 per cent.

Therefore, a firm or brand with market power has a less elastic demand than a poorly differentiated product. As a result, it is in a position to make the group of buyers or consumers who are sensitive to the element of differentiation accept a higher price. In fact, economic theory shows that the less elastic (in absolute value) the demand for a product, the higher is the optimal price, that is the price that maximises profits. If we know the elasticity, the optimal price can be calculated as follows:

$$P(\text{opt}) = C \times \varepsilon/(1 - \varepsilon)$$

or

Optimal price = unit direct cost × cost mark-up

where

Cost mark-up = price elasticity/(1 − price elasticity)

Table 4.7 Optimal cost mark-up as a function of price elasticity

Price elasticity ε_{qp}	Optimal cost mark-up $\varepsilon_{qp}/(1-\varepsilon_{qp})$	Price elasticity ε_{qp}	Optimal cost mark-up $\varepsilon_{qp}/(1-\varepsilon_{qp})$
1.0	—	2.4	1.71
1.2	6.00	2.6	1
1.4	3.50	—	—
1.6	2.67	3.0	1.50
1.8	2.22	4.0	1.33
2.0	2.00	5.0	1.25
2.2	1.83	—	—
—	—	15.0	1.07

Thus, the optimal price is obtained by multiplying unit variable cost (marginal cost) by a percentage which depends on price elasticity and is independent of costs. The derivation of this optimisation rule is presented here.

As Table 4.7 shows, the optimal cost mark-up is higher when price elasticity is lower in absolute value, that is closer to unity. When price elasticity is high, which is the case in highly competitive markets of undifferentiated products, mark-up is close to unity; the firm's market power is weak and the price accepted by the market is close to unit costs. Conversely, the closer elasticity is to unity, the higher is the price acceptable by the market.

ACHIEVING COMPETITIVE ADVANTAGE THROUGH COST DOMINATION

Gaining market power through successful product differentiation is one way to get a competitive advantage. Another way is to achieve cost domination vis-à-vis competition through better productivity and cost controls. Cost reductions can be achieved in many ways. In many industries, where the value added to the product accounts for a large percentage of the total cost, it has been observed that there is an opportunity to lower costs as a firm gains experience in producing a product. Seven sources of experience effects:

- *Labour efficiency* As workers repeat a particular task, they become more dextrous and learn improvements and short-cuts which increase their efficiency.
- *Work specialisation and methods improvements* Specialisation increases worker proficiency at a given task.
- *New production processes* Process innovations and improvements can be an important source of cost reductions, such as the introduction of robotics or of computer-assisted systems.
- *Better performance from production equipment* When first designed, a piece of production equipment may have a conservatively rated output. Experience may reveal innovative ways of increasing its output.
- *Changes in the resource mix* As experience accumulates, a producer can often incorporate different or less expensive resources in the operation. For instance, less skilled workers can replace skilled workers, or automation can replace labour.
- *Product standardisation* Standardisation allows the replication of tasks necessary for worker learning. Even when flexibility and/or wider product line are important marketing factors, standardisation can be achieved by modularisation.

- *Product redesign* Once the firm has a clear understanding of the performance requirements, a product can be redesigned to incorporate less costly materials and resources.

DERIVATION OF THE PRICE OPTIMISATION RULE

We have the following demand function:

$$Q = Q\ (P/M, E)$$

where Q denotes quantity, P the selling price, M other marketing variable and E environmental factors. Assuming M and E are constant, the problem is to derive the optimum price.

The profit function is as follows:

$$\pi = (P - C)Q - F$$

where π is gross profit, C the direct unit cost and F the fixed costs specific to the activity considered.

To identify the optimum price, let us calculate the first derivative of π with respect to price and set the derivative equal to zero.

$$\frac{\delta \pi}{\delta P} = (P - C)\frac{\delta Q}{\delta P} + Q = 0$$

Multiplying each term by the ratio P/Q and rearranging terms we have

$$P(1 + \varepsilon_{qp}) = C\varepsilon_{qp}$$

which is the *marginal revenue-marginal cost equality rule* expressed by reference to price elasticity. Solving for P^*, the optimum price, we have

$$P^* = C\left(\frac{\varepsilon_{qp}}{1 - \varepsilon_{qp}}\right)$$

The *second-order condition* stipulates that the price elasticity in absolute value should be larger than one.

Problem – example

To illustrate, Table 4.8 presents estimated price elasticities for six brands of a feminine hygiene product, as well as the mark-up on unit costs that each brand could adopt when calculating the optimal price. A measure of market power is obtained by calculating the ratio of the brand's mark-up to the average mark-up observed in the market.

Questions

1 How would you describe the different types of elasticity contained in the competitive reaction matrix?
2 What are the basic conditions for successful differentiation?

Table 4.8 Measuring brand market power: the market for feminine hygiene products (Lambin, 1993)

Brands	Estimated price elasticity	Implied optimal cost mark-up	Indicator of market power
Brand A	−1.351	3.849	1.334
Brand B	−1.849	2.178	0.755
Brand C	−1.715	2.399	0.832
Brand D	−1.624	2.603	0.902
Brand E	−1.326	4.067	1.410
Brand F	−1.825	2.212	0.767
Average	−1.615	2.885	1.000

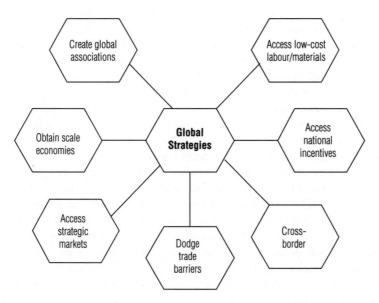

Figure 4.9 Motivations for global strategies.

3   If a marketing manager has information about elasticity, how can he/she calculate the optimal price?

4   By way of illustration, if $\varepsilon = -2.1$ and C = 105, calculate the optimum price as well as the optimal cost mark-up.

(I) *Problem 4.7* Global strategies

Introductory comments

A global strategy can result from several motivations in addition to simply wanting to invest in attractive foreign markets. The diagram of these motivations shown in Figure 4.9 provides a summary of the scope and character of global strategies.

OBTAINING SCALE ECONOMIES

Scale economies can occur from product standardisation. The Ford world-car concept, for example, allows product design, tooling, parts production and product testing to be spread over a much larger sales base. However, standardisation of the development and execution of a marketing programme can also be an important source of scale economies. Consider Coca-Cola, which since the 1950s has employed a marketing strategy – the brand name, concentrate formula, positioning and advertising theme – that has been virtually the same throughout the world. Only the artificial sweetener and packaging differ across countries. McCann-Erickson claims to have saved £90 million in advertising production costs over 20 years by producing worldwide Coca-Cola campaigns such as 'It's the real thing' and 'Can't beat the feeling'.

Several influential observers have suggested that the SCAs emerging from worldwide scale economies are becoming more important and that in many industries they are becoming a necessary aspect of competition. Thedore Levitt, in a visible article on the globalisation of markets, posits that worldwide communications have caused demand and fashion patterns to be similar across the world, even in less developed countries. Kenichi Ohmae, long-time head of McKinsey in Japan, cites a litany of products that are virtually identical in Japan, Europe and the USA, including Nike footwear, Pampers diapers, Band-Aid bandages, Cheer detergent, Nestlé coffee, Kodak film, Revlon cosmetics and Contac paper. He notes that people from different countries, from youth to businesspeople, wear the same fashions.

Ohmae also suggests that the long-accepted waterfall model of international trade is now obsolete. In the waterfall model, a firm first established itself in a domestic market. It then penetrates the markets of other advanced countries before moving into less-developed countries. The experience of Honda in motorcycles is representative. After creating a dominant position in Japan with considerable scale economies, it entered the US market by convincing people that it was 'fun' to ride its small, simple motorcycle and by investing in a 2,000-dealer network. With its scale economies thus increased, Honda expanded its line to include larger cycles and then moved into the European market.

The new model, according to Ohmae, is that of a 'sprinkler', where a product is exposed all over the globe at once. He points to products such as the Sony Walkman, Canon's AE-1 and the Mintola A-7000, which exploded onto the worldwide market in a matter of months. The Walkman actually first took off in California. Under the sprinkler model, a firm introducing a new product does not have the time to develop a presence and distribution channel in a foreign market. Instead, it forms a consortium with other firms that have already established distribution in other countries. This allows the new product to go global immediately. The resulting economies of scale can allow lower prices, often a key to creating markets and a barrier to competitors.

In order to achieve maximum scale economies, a manufacturer would need to make all units in its home country. Yet, for many reasons, companies spread component production and final assembly throughout the world. Matsushita, which has 150 plants in 38 countries, has developed 'export centres' as a way to gain the advantages of politically hospitable, low-cost host countries close to regional markets that will support substantial economies of scale. The export centre does more than simply manufacture a product. It controls the product from the drawing board to the loading dock. The Malaysian export centre, one of the first, produces one quarter of Matsushita's air conditioner and TV volume.

DESIRABLE GLOBAL BRAND ASSOCIATIONS

Brand names linked to global strategies can have useful associations. For customers and competitors, a global presence automatically symbolises strength, staying power and the ability to generate competitive products. Such an image can be particularly important to buyers of expensive industrial products or consumer durables such as cars or computers because it can lessen concern that the products may be unreliable or rendered obsolete by technological advances. Japanese firms such as Yamaha, Sony, Canon and Honda operate in markets where technology and product quality are important, and they have benefited from a global brand association.

ACCESS TO LOW-COST LABOUR OR MATERIALS

Another motivation for a global strategy is the cost reduction that results from access to the resources of many countries. Substantial cost differences can arise with respect to raw materials, R&D talent, assembly labour and component supply. Thus, a computer manufacturer may purchase components from Korea and Singapore, obtain raw materials from South America, and assemble in Mexico and five other countries throughout the world in order to reduce labour and transportation costs. Access to low-cost labour and materials can be a sustainable competitive advantage (SCA), especially when it is accompanied by the skill and flexibility to change when one supply is threatened or a more attractive alternative emerges.

ACCESS TO NATIONAL INVESTMENT INCENTIVES

Another way to obtain a cost advantage is to access national investment incentives which countries use to achieve economic objectives for target industries or depressed areas. Unlike other means to achieve changes in trade, such as tariffs and quotas, incentives are much less visible and objectionable to trading partners. Thus, the British government has offered Japanese car manufacturers a cash bonus to locate a plant in Britain. Ireland, Brazil and a host of other governments offer cash, tax breaks, land and buildings to entice factories to locate in their particular country.

CROSS-SUBSIDISATION

A global presence allows a firm to cross-subsidise, to use the resources accumulated in one part of the world to fight a competitive battle in another. Consider the following: one firm uses the cash flow generated in its home market to attack a domestically oriented competitor. For example, in the early 1970s Michelin used its European home profit base to attack Goodyear's US market. The defensive competitor (i.e. Goodyear) can reduce prices or increase advertising in the USA to counter, but by doing so, it will sacrifice margins in its largest markets. An alternative is to attack the aggressor in its home market where it has the most to lose. Thus, Goodyear carried the fight to Europe to make a dent in Michelin's profit base.

The cross-subsidisation concept leads to two strategic considerations:

- To influence an existing or potential foreign competitor, it is useful to maintain a presence in its country. The presence should be large enough to make the threat of retaliation meaningful. If the share is only 2 per cent or so, the competitor may be willing to ignore it.
- A home market may be vulnerable even if a firm apparently controls it with a large market share. A high market share, especially if it is used to support high prices and profits, can attract foreign firms that realise the domestic firm has little freedom for retaliation. A major reason for the demise of the US consumer electronics industry was that US firms were placed at a substantial disadvantage compared with global competitors that had the option to cross-subsidise.

DODGE TRADE BARRIERS

Strategic location of component and assembly plants can help gain access to markets by penetrating trade barriers and fostering goodwill. Peugeot, for example, has plants in 26 countries from Argentina to Zimbabwe. Locating final assembly plants in a host country is a good way to achieve favourable trade treatment and goodwill because it provides a visible presence and generates savings in transportation and storage of the final product. Thus, Caterpillar operates assembly plants in each of its major markets, including Europe, Japan, Brazil and Australia, in part to bypass trade barriers. An important element of the Toyota strategy is to source a significant portion of its car cost in the USA and Europe to deflect sentiment against foreign domination.

ACCESS TO STRATEGICALLY IMPORTANT MARKETS

Some markets are strategically important because of their market size or potential or because of their raw material supply, labour cost structure or technology. It can be important to have a presence in these markets even if such a presence is not profitable. Because of its size, the US market is critical to those industries in which scale economies are important, such as automobiles or consumer electronics.

Sometimes a country is important because it is the locus of new trends and developments in an industry. A firm in the fashion industry may benefit from a presence in countries that have historically led the way in fashion. Or a high-tech firm may want to have operations in a country that is in the forefront of the relevant field. For example, an electronics firm without a Silicon Valley presence will find it difficult to keep abreast of technology developments and competitor strategies. Sometimes adequate information can be obtained by observers, but those with design and manufacturing groups on location will tend to have a more intimate knowledge of trends and events.

STANDARDISATION VERSUS CUSTOMISATION

A key issue in the development of a global strategy is the extent to which the strategy, particularly the marketing strategy, will be standardised across countries. The prime motivation for standardisation is economics. The more the standardisation, the more potential there is for scale economies. The vision of a single global product sharing not only R&D and manufacturing but also a common name, position, package and advertising drives some people's version of the ultimate global strategy. The

Table 4.9 Marketing strategy – customisation versus standardisation

Standardisation provides	Customisation provides

Scale economies in the development of advertising, packaging, promotion, etc.
Exploitation of
   media overlap
   exposure to customers who travel
Associations of
   global presence
   the 'home' country
	Names, associations and advertising that can be:
	   developed locally
	   tailored to local market
	   selected without the constraints of standardisation
	Reduced risk from 'buy local' sentiments

assumption is that it will lead to decisive efficiencies and scale economies because the cost of developing product and marketing programmes will be spread over a larger sales base.

A second motivation for globalisation is to create impact for the marketing programme outside the main country through media spillover and international customer travel. Brand awareness, and awareness of packaging and visual imagery in particular, can benefit from the exposure of a brand in a different country when customers travel between countries. When media coverage overlaps regions, a global brand can buy exposure of a brand in a different country when customers travel between countries. When media coverage overlaps regions, a global brand can buy exposures much more efficiently. As the European common market matures, there is likely to be more and more medial overlap and customer crossover and thus more payoff for a global brand strategy.

A third motivation for a standardised global marketing strategy is the associations that can result. The image of a global player such as that achieved by IBM, Ford and Canon can provide prestige and reassurance to customers. In other contexts, a 'home' country association can be the essence of a brand's positioning. For example, Levi's are US jeans, Chanel is French perfume, Dewar's is Scottish whiskey and Bertolli is Italian olive oil. In each case, the brand is established in its home country and the country itself is central to the image of the brand. In such a context, a standardised strategy may pay off. Table 4.9 summarises the advantages of standardisation.

The reality is that a standardised global product and marketing effort is not always sdesirable or even possible. In general, each element of a marketing programme needs to be analysed to determine whether the advantages of standardisation outweigh the effectiveness of tailoring the programme to local markets. There are times when standardisation is not the answer, and it makes sense to tailor the product and marketing programme to a particular country.

THE CUSTOMISATION OPTION

Achieving standardisation in some aspects of a strategy can be difficult because of differences between countries and little potential for scale economies. For example, Kentucky Fried Chicken has been successful in Japan, but only after the firm realised that the US, model of free-standing units would not work in land-scarce Japanese cities.

It also changed its menu (fries replaced mashed potatoes and slaw became less sweet) and adopted Japanese training methods. Insisting on a US clone in Japan would have saved little money and guaranteed failure.

Distribution and personal selling are two elements that usually need to be adapted to the realities of a country. Hitotsubashi University's Hiro Takeuchi and Harvard's Michael Porter studied 7 major Japanese firms and 46 different product categories. Research revealed that while brand name and advertising are often the same across countris, distribution and sales organisations tend not to be standardised – there are simply too few economies of scale involved, and there was often a substantial fit problem.

Recognising the need to customise distribution can be a key to success. Firms willing to make an investment and commitment to a different distribution/selling system in Japan, for example, have been able to attack or create competitive barriers. Coca-Cola developed an in-house delivery system that has become an important advantage, leading to its domination of the Japanese soft-drink market. Kodak in 1985 broke the Fuji lock on the Japanese market only when it built its own distribution network. The Kodak approach not only gave the firm access to markets but also direct contact with customers, providing better information on customer needs.

Even the use of a common brand name is not always desirable or even feasible. Some names with useful associations in one language will have a damaging meaning in other countries.

A local association can be a useful point of differentiation and a basis for customer loyalty. Further, a global brand can have negative associations locally if it has an undesirable meaning in some countries or if it is tied to a country's politics and thus is subject to the ups and downs of international events.

A worldwide advertising theme may simply not be appropriate in some countries because of the competitive context. A British Airways globalisation effort involved the centralisation of advertising, which resulted in the 'world's favourite airline' theme. It featured a 90-second commercial that showed the Manhattan skyline rotating slowly through the sky. Even in the USA, where the campaign originated, managers wondered if the replaced campaign (which emphasised traditional British values with the theme 'we'll take good care of you') was not more effective.

Indicators that strategies should be global

- Major competitors in important markets are not domestic and have a presence in several countries.
- Standardisation of some elements of the product or marketing strategy provides opportunities for scale economies.
- Costs can be reduced and effectiveness increased by locating value-added activities in different countries.
- Competitors have the potential to use the volume and profits from one market to subsidise gaining a position in another.
- Trade barriers inhibit access to worthwhile markets.
- A global name can be an advantage and the name is available worldwide.
- A brand position and its supporting advertising will work across countries and has not been pre-empted.
- Local markets do not require products or service for which a local operation would have an advantage.

In countries where British Airways was an also-ran, the claim did not make much sense. Furthermore, there were operational problems. For example, 90-second ads could not be used in South Africa.

A decentralised approach to the development of marketing programmes can generate a product or advertising campaign that can be used globally. Level Strauss got its successful Dockers pants from a product development effort in its Brazilian operation. When Polaroid was repositioning from a 'party camera' platform to a more serious, utilitarian one, a campaign that was developed in Switzerland was the most effective. It promoted the functional use of instant photography as a way to communicate with family and friends – the 'learn to speak Polaroid' campaign. If local units had not been free to generate their own campaigns, this superior campaign would not have surfaced.

Problem – example

Parker Pen: a global strategy that failed

In 1985, Parker Pen launched a global business strategy to combat Cross from above and the Japanese from below. The centrepiece of the strategy was a rolled-ball pen called the Victor. Victor was to be priced throughout the world at a low (for Parker) £2.98 and made at a new automated production facility for £0.29. The common advertising campaign used the theme, 'It's wrought from pure silver and writes like pure silk,' and the slogan, 'Make your mark with a Parker.' The effort was a disaster. In many of Parker's 150 markets, local units resisted pressures to adopt the product. A Parker executive was quoted shouting at a meeting of the London agency branch, 'Yours is not to reason why, yours is to implement.'

The common pricing was one problem, especially for the countries which had established a position either above or below the new price. The selected name did not have relevant associations in all countries. The advertising and resulting associations were judged by many to be bland and ineffective. Furthermore, there were manufacturing problems which affected Parker's ability to deliver its product.

Among the casualties of the global branding strategy were some effective local branding efforts. For example, an offbeat English advertising agency, one of 40 agencies used by Parker prior to globalisation, had developed a particular successful campaign. It associated the brand with people who had the élan to deliver a well-crafted insult written with a Parker. One such insult was a note to an airline reading, 'You had delusions of adequacy?' The campaign's humour was very British and would not have worked elsewhere.

Questions

1 Explain the fundamentals behind a 'cross-subsidisation' global strategy.
2 Discuss the critical benefits that can be provided to a company when implementing either a standardised marketing strategy or a customised marketing strategy.
3 Provide some indicators which would lead companies to embark on the pursuit of global strategies.

(M) *Problem 4.8* Choice and evaluation of strategy

Introductory comments

Once the position of the SBU is located on the industry maturity/competitive position matrix, the guide shown in Table 4.10 may be used to determine what strategy the

Table 4.10 Guide to strategic thrust options

Stages of industry maturity

Competitive position	Embryonic	Growth	Mature	Ageing
Dominant	Grow fast Start up	Grow fast Attain cost leadership Renew Defend position	Defend position Focus Renew Grow fast	Defend position Renew Grow into maturity
Strong	Start up Differentiate Grow fast	Grow fast Catch up Attain cost leadership Differentiate	Attain cost leadership Renew, focus Differentiate Grow with industry	Find niche Hold niche Hang in Grow with industry Harvest
Favourable	Start up Differentiate Catch up Focus Grow fast	Differentiate, focus Find niche, hold niche Grow with industry	Harvest, hang in Turn around Renew, turn around Differentiate, focus Grow with industry	Retrench
Tenable	Start up Grow with industry Focus	Harvest, catch up Hold niche, hang in Find niche Turn around Focus Grow with industry	Harvest Turn around Find niche Retrench	Divest Retrench
Weak	Find niche Catch up Grow with industry	Turn around Retrench	Withdraw Divest	Withdraw

SBU should pursue. Actually, the strategies shown in the exhibit are guides to strategic thrust rather than strategies per se. They show the normal strategic path a business unit may adopt, given its industry maturity and competitive position.

To bridge the gap between broad guidelines and specific strategies for implementation, further analysis is required. A three-stage process is suggested here. First, using broad guidelines, the SBU management may be asked to state strategies pursued during previous years. Second, these strategies may be reviewed by using selected performance ratios to analyse the extent to which strategies were successfully implemented. Similarly, current strategies may be identified and their link to past strategies established. Third, having identified and analysed past and current strategy with the help of strategic guidelines, the management, using the same guidelines, selects the strategy it proposes to pursue in the future. The future perspective may call for the continuation of current strategies or the development of new ones. Before accepting the future strategic course, however, it is desirable to measure its cash consequences or internal deployment (i.e. percentage of funds generated that are reinvested). Figure 4.10 illustrates an SBU earning 22 per cent on assets with an internal deployment of 80 per cent. Such an SBU would normally be considered in the mature stage. However, if the previous analysis showed that the SBU was in fact operating in a growth industry, the corporation would need to rethink its investment policy. All quantitative information pertaining to an SBU may be summarised on one form, as shown in Figure 4.11.

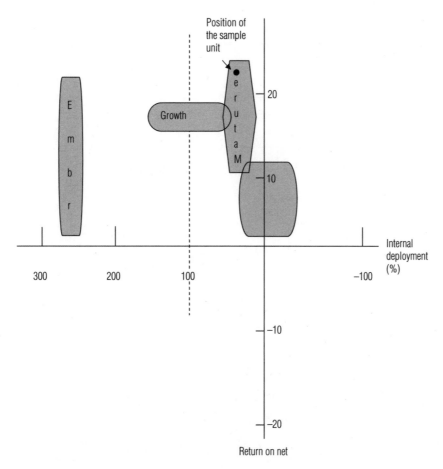

Figure 4.10 Profitability and cash position of a business.

Different product/market plans are reviewed at the SBU level. The purpose of this review is twofold: (a) to consider product/market strategies in finalising SBU strategies and (b) to approve product/market strategies. The underlying criterion for evaluation is a balanced achievement of SBU goals, which may be specified in terms of profitability and cash consequences. If there is a conflict of interest between two product/market groups in the way the strategy is either articulated or implemented, the conflict should be resolved so that SBU goals are maximised.

Assume that both product/market groups seek additional investments during the next two years. Of these, the first product/market will start delivering positive cash flow in the third year. The second one is not likely to generate positive cash flow until the fourth year, but it will provide a higher overall return on capital. If the SBU's need for cash is urgent and if it desires additional cash for its goals during the third year, the first product/market group will appear more attractive. Thus, despite higher profit expectations from the second product/market group, the SBU may approve

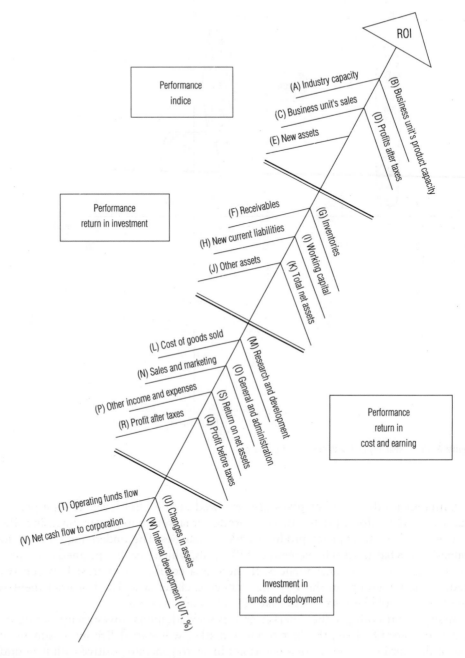

Figure 4.11 Source of competitive information.

Source: Adapted from Arthur D. Little, Inc.

investment in the first product/market group with a view to maximising the realisation of its own goals.

At times, the SBU may require a product/market group to make additional changes in its strategic perspective before giving its final approval. On the other hand, a product/market plan may be totally rejected and the group instructed to pursue its current perspective.

Industry maturity and competitive position analysis may also be used in further refining the SBU itself. In other words, after an SBU has been created and is analysed for industry maturity and competitive position, it may be found that it has not been properly constituted. This would require redefining the SBU and undertaking the analysis again.

STRATEGY EVALUATION

'The time required to develop resources is so extended, and the timescale of opportunities is so brief and fleeting, that a company which has not carefully delineated and appraised its strategy is adrift in white water.' This quotation from an article by Seymour Tilles underlines the importance of strategy evaluation. The adequacy of a strategy may be evaluated using the following criteria:

1   *Suitability* – Is there a sustainable advantage?
2   *Validity* – Are the assumptions realistic?
3   *Feasibility* – Do we have the skills, resources and commitments?
4   *Internal consistency* – Does the strategy hang together?
5   *Vulnerability* – What are the risks and contingencies?
6   *Workability* – Can we retain our flexibility?
7   *Appropriate time horizon* – Do we have enough timeframe to implement?

Suitability

Strategy should offer some sort of competitive advantage. In other words, strategy should lead to a future advantage or an adaptation to forces eroding current competitive advantage. The following steps may be followed to judge the competitive advantage a strategy may provide: (a) review the potential threats and opportunities to the business, (b) assess each option in light of the capabilities of the business, (c) anticipate the likely competitive response to each option and (d) modify or eliminate unsuitable options.

Validity (consistency with the environment)

Strategy should be consistent with the assumptions about the external product/market environment. At a time when more and more women are seeking jobs, a strategy assuming traditional roles for women (i.e. raising children and staying home) would be inconsistent with the environment.

Feasibility (appropriateness in light of available resources)

Money, competence and physical facilities are the critical resources a manager should be aware of in finalising strategy. A resource may be examined in two different ways: as a constraint limiting the achievement of goals and as an opportunity to be exploited as the basis for strategy. It is desirable for a strategist to make correct estimates of resources available without being excessively optimistic about them. Further, even if resources are available in the corporation, a particular product/market group may not be able to lay claim to them. Alternatively, resources currently available to a product/ market group may be transferred to another group if the SBU strategy deems it necessary.

Internal consistency

Strategy should be in tune with the different policies of the corporation, the SBU and the product/market arena. For example, if the corporation decided to limit the government business of any unit to 40 per cent of total sales, a product/market strategy emphasising greater than 40 per cent reliance on the government market would be internally inconsistent.

Vulnerability (satisfactory degree of risk)

The degree of risk may be determined on the basis of the perspectives of the strategy and available resources. A pertinent question here is: will the resources be available as planned in appropriate quantities and for as long as it is necessary to implement the strategy. The overall proportion of resources committed to a venture becomes a factor to be reckoned with: the greater these quantities, the greater the degree of risk.

Workability

The workability of a strategy should be realistically evaluated with quantitative data. Sometimes, however, it may be difficult to undertake such objective analysis. In that case, other indications may be used to assess the contributions of a strategy. One such indication could be the degree of consensus among key executives about the viability of the strategy. Identifying ahead of time alternative strategies for achieving the goal is another indication of the workability of a strategy. Finally, establishing resource requirements in advance, which eliminates the need to institute crash programmes of cost reduction or to seek reduction in planned programmes, also substantiates the workability of the strategy.

Appropriate time horizon

A viable strategy has a time frame for its realisation. The time horizon of a strategy should allow implementation without creating havoc in the organisation or missing market availability. For example, in introducing a new product to the market, enough time should be allotted for market testing, training of salespeople and so on. But the time frame should not be so long that a competitor can enter the market first and skim the cream off the top.

Problem – example

Drawing an example from the car radio industry, considerable differences in industry maturity may become apparent between car radios with built-in cassette players and traditional car radios. Differences in industry maturity or competitive position may also exist with regard to regional markets, consumer groups and distribution channels. For example, the market for cheap car radios sold by discount stores to end users doing their own installations may be growing faster than the market served by speciality retail stores providing installation services. Such revelations may require further refinement in formulating SBUs. This may continue until the SBUs represent the highest possible level of aggregation consistent with the need for clear-cut analyses of industry maturity and competitive position.

NEW INTERNET-BASED MARKETING SYSTEMS

It is one reason why Proctor & Gamble (P&G) spends 25 per cent of sales on marketing alone; why it has cause for celebration when Johnson & Johnson brings down its sales, marketing and administration expenses by two points from 37 per cent of sales to 35 per cent. It is also why large multinational companies are desperate to find ways to unclog bureaucracy, fine-tune coordination, automate, speed up and upgrade the way their marketing department work.

If P&G is proved right, a new breed of internet-based enterprise marketing management systems is just the magic bullet they need, and it intends to help provide it. Via a joint venture, with software partner Magnifi, called Emmperative, it is offering (at a hefty price), a new marketing management system. This includes an online knowledge bank (so that novices can access 'best practice' at the click of a mouse); work-tracking systems so that teams can communicate instantly online and ensure everyone is up to speed with what's going on (and things should not grind to a halt if key personnel depart); work-flow organising systems (so that senior personnel are automatically warned if an important deadline is under threat); and sign-off mechanisms that force you to enter learning on projects (whether they succeed or fail) before you close the file.

There are three interesting things about this initiative. First, many existing software products tackle parts of the marketing management challenge, but this is the first attempt to truly integrate them into a single solution.

Sharing proprietary information

Second, the traditionally secretive P&G is making its proprietary marketing know-how publicly available, by embedding it within the system. One reason for changing track is the sheer cost of developing it: Emmperative effectively turns a sunk cost into a revenue earner. Besides, as Peter Bates, vice-president of global customer solutions at Emmperative points out, it is rather like Tiger Woods selling 'improve your golf' videos. It opens up a new revenue stream for Woods and helps other players improve – but not enough to threaten his prize money.

The third attention-grabbing item is the astonishing results claimed for the system. P&G's first live test suggests speed-to-market and event lead times slashed by up to 50 per cent and overheads cut by 10–30 per cent (along a variety of sub-heads including travel, training, couriers and reduced staff numbers). Meanwhile, by spreading best practice and state-of-the-art tools better and faster, P&G also claims to have improved marketing spend efficiency by 10–20 per cent. Not surprisingly, a wide range of companies including Coca-Cola, Campbell's Soup and Philips have already signed up.

Will hoped-for benefits always materialise? Of course not. When it comes to over claiming, software salesmen are in a league of their own. Nevertheless, the main message is undeniable. The way we organise and manage marketing has not changed much in decades. It is ripe for reform. Now new technologies are providing us with a chance to overhaul and streamline. And the race to seize these opportunities is under way.

Questions

1   Assuming that the competitive position of a particular company is perceived as favourable, provide some key strategic thrust options for both the embryonic and mature stages of 'industry maturity'.
2   Provide example of sources of competitive information in terms of (a) indices of performance and (b) return of investment.
3   Discuss how strategy evaluation criteria may be employed to review the strategy of (a) an industrial goods manufacturer and (b) Procter & Gamble as reported in the 'Problem – examples' section.
4   Comment in detail on the issues behind the intention of 'workability' within the strategy evaluation framework.

References and further reading

Aaker, D.A. (1995) *Strategic Market Management*, NY: John Wiley and Sons, Inc.

Blois, K. (2000) *The Oxford Textbook of Marketing*, Oxford: Oxford University Press.

George S. Day, Tough questions for developing strategies, *Journal of Business* (Winter 1986): 60–8.

Hamermesh von Ours (1996) "Turnover and Labor Turnover: A Taxonomy of Employment Dynamics?" *Annales d'économie et de Statistique*, 41–42 (January): 21–40.

Jacobson, R. and Aaker, D. (1985) "Is Market Share All that it's Cracked up to Be?" *Journal of Marketing*, vol. 49, no. 4 (Autumn): 11–22.

Jacobson, R. and Aaker, D.A. (1987) Strategic role of product quality, *Journal of Marketing*, vol. 51, no. 4, p. 31–44.

Jain, S.C. (1997) *Marketing Planning and Strategy*, Cincinnati, OH: South-Western College Publishing.

Kotler, Philip (2000) *Marketing Management*, New Jersey: Prentice Hall.

Lambin, J.J. (1976) *Advertising, Competition and Market Conduct in Oligopoly Over Time*, Amsterdam: North Holland Publishing, Co.

Lambin, J. (1993) *Strategic Marketing*, London: McGraw-Hill.

Mitchell, A. (2002) P&G's tips, *Marketing Business*, December/January.

Richard Pascale (1990) *Managing on the Edge: How the Smartest Companies Use Conflict to Stay Ahead*, New York: Simon and Schuster.

Seymour Tilles, How to evaluate corporate strategy, *Harvard Business Review* (July–August 1963): 111–21.

Wilson, R. and Gilligan, C. (1997) *Strategic Marketing Management – Planning, Implementation*, Oxford, England: Butterworth Heinemann.

5

Positioning, Product and Pricing

Product strategies specify market needs that may be served by different product offerings. It is a company's product strategies, duly related to market strategies, that eventually come to dominate both overall strategy and the spirit of the company. Product strategies deal with such matters as number and diversity of products, product innovations, product scope and product design.

The implementation of product strategies requires cooperation among different groups: finance, research and development, the corporate staff, and marketing. This level of integration makes product strategies difficult to develop and implement. In many companies, to achieve proper coordination among diverse business units, product strategy decisions are made by top management.

In some companies, the overall scope of product strategy is laid out at the corporate level, whereas actual design is left to business units. These companies contend that this alternative is more desirable than other arrangements because it is difficult for top management to deal with the details of product strategy in a diverse company.

Each strategy is examined from the point of view of an SBU. The term *positioning* refers to placing a brand in that part of the market where it will receive a favourable reception compared with competing products. Because the market is heterogeneous, one brand cannot make an impact on the entire market. As a matter of strategy, therefore, a product should be positioned so that it stands apart from competing brands. Positioning tells what the product stands for, what it is, and how customers should evaluate it.

Positioning is achieved by using marketing mix variables, especially design and communication. Although differentiation through positioning is more visible in consumer goods, it is equally true of industrial goods. With some products, positioning can be achieved on the basis of tangible differences (e.g. product features); with many others, intangibles are used to differentiate and position products.

New-product development is an essential activity for companies seeking growth. By adopting the new-product strategy as their posture, companies are better able to sustain competitive pressures on their existing products and make headway. The implementation of this strategy has become easier because of technological innovations and the willingness of customers to accept new ways of doing things.

Despite their importance in strategy determination, however, implementation of new-product programmes is far from easy. Too many products never make it in the marketplace. The risks and penalties of product failure require that companies move judiciously in adopting new-product strategies.

Top management can affect the implementation of new-product strategy; first, by establishing policies and broad strategic directions for the kinds of new products the company should seek; second, by providing the kind of leadership that creates the environmental climate needed to stimulate innovation in the organisation; and third, by instituting review and monitoring procedures so that managers are involved at the right decision point and can know whether work schedules are being met in ways that are consistent with broad policy directions.

Product-innovation strategy includes introducing a new product to replace an existing product in order to satisfy a need in an entirely different way or to provide a new approach to satisfy an existing or latent need. This strategy suggests that the entrant is the first firm to develop and introduce the product.

Product innovation, however, does not come easy. Besides involving major financial commitments, it requires heavy doses of managerial time to cut across organisational lines. And still the innovation may fail to make a mark in the market. A number of companies have discovered the risks of this game.

In essence, innovation flourishes where divisions are kept small (permitting better interaction among managers and staffers), where there is willingness to tolerate failure (encouraging plenty of experimentation and risk taking), where champions are motivated (through encouragement, salaries and promotions), where close liaison is maintained with the customer (visiting customers routinely; inviting them to brainstorm product ideas), where technology is shared corporatewide (technology, wherever it is developed, belongs to everyone), and where projects are sustained, even if initial results are discouraging.

(A) *Problem 5.1* Positioning services

Introductory comments

The key to strategic positioning is an understanding of how the company/organisation is perceived in relation to its competitors along those factors that underlie consumers' decisions about the product/service. This type of analysis is an application of attitude and image research, commonly called *perceptual mapping*. The perceptual map is a graphic representation of the perceived characteristics from which demand for products/services is produced.

Several quantitative methodologies, from the very simple to the complex, may be used to develop perceptual maps for use in positioning. However, the first requirement is to determine the relevant product/service characteristics used by customers in a particular market segment in selecting a source for the product/service being positioned (see Table 5.1). The concept of positioning provides a framework for viewing the company and its products/services and competitors in the marketplace.

Problem: The case of positioning financial competitors

There are a number of published studies of bank selection, which may be used as a basis for developing the perceptual criteria underlying bank and product/service selection. It is important to realise that these criteria can vary radically from market to market. A variety of perception characteristics are thought to place and product/service-use decisions. The relevant set of criteria will vary depending on the competing banks or other financial institutions in a particular market, current economic conditions and other factors. Managerial evaluation and a sound knowledge of market and competitive factors must be applied to develop an initial set of perceptual decision criteria on which to base the perceptual mapping.

Table 5.1 Steps in positioning

1 What is to be analysed:
      products/services?
      competition (firms)?
2 Identify decision criteria of customers.
3 Determine group whose perceptions are to be examined.
4 Select mapping methodology.
5 Develop data-collection instrument.
6 Apply mapping techniques.
7 Analyse market positions.
8 Determine strategy:
      solidify and hold position.
      reposition.

A two-dimensional presentation can be generated by using the mean values of the responses to a consumer attitude survey, with the questions scaled, for example, from minus three to plus three. It should be noted that the development of such maps using simple statistics assumes that the two criteria used to develop the map are not correlated. The most important consideration is the determination that these are the most important criteria used by the consumer in the evaluation of competing financial institutions.

MULTIDIMENSIONAL MAPPING TECHNIQUES

For most situations it is desirable to use more sophisticated analytical techniques, such as one of the many multidimensional scaling methodologies, canonical discriminant analysis or factor analysis to produce composite representations of the perceptual positions of the companies or product/service. These techniques allow analysis under more realistic conditions in which more than two attributes are evaluated. These statistics also provide the pictorial representation of characteristics that may have related responses. Data for these methods of analysis are collected in the same manner as mentioned earlier and through the use of similarities input for multidimensional scaling consists of an evaluation of how similar each of the items (banks and building societies in our example) are to each other.

A perceptual positioning map for the financial companies is shown in Figure 5.1, with the financial institutions mapped into the same perceptual space as the attributes along which they are evaluated. This analysis indicates that several criteria are statistically related to the survey respondents' perceptions of the competing banks and the building societies. The placement of the banks in relation to each other and to the attributes provides the manager with a visual representation of the consumers' view of the marketplace. This placement is also the basis for understanding the bank's position and repositioning when desirable and necessary.

The seven attributes determined to be related to respondent perceptions of the bank are 'friendly tellers', 'first with new services', 'best bank for the individual', 'best bank for business', 'convenient locations', 'low loan rates', 'best savings rates'. Remember that the relevant criteria in the study will depend on the competitive environment the strategic planner is facing in the bank's market area. The map shows

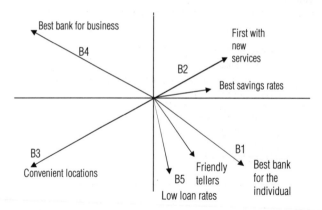

Figure 5.1 Perceptual map of five financial competitors and attributes.

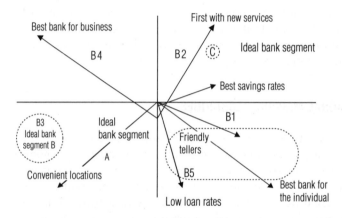

Figure 5.2 Perceptual map of five financial competitors and attributes: ideal points.

bank 1 lies close to the 'friendly tellers' attribute line but is half the length of the line from the origin to the plot. The mapping approach used in this figure places the length of the attribute position lines equal to the strength of association between the attributes and the perceptual configurations. However, this is not the case with all the techniques that may be applied to produce perceptual maps. 'Best bank for the individual' and 'first with new services' are very close together in the map. This indicates that the responses to services are very close together in the map. This indicates that the responses to these questions were correlated and that both would not have been included if only a simple plot had been used to map the perceptual positions of the financial companies. Bank 4 is perceived as being quite different from the other firms and as being more of a business than an individual-oriented financial company. This map was generated from a random sample of possible bank customers in a market area and within this market we expect to find several market segments with differing banking needs. Figure 5.2 presents this same perceptual map with the location of the respondents' ideal banks shown as large circles.

This step in the positioning–mapping methodology was conducted by using a computer technique called *cluster analysis* to determine groups of respondents with similar 'ideal' financial institutions. The mean ideal locations were then plotted onto the perceptual map. The size of the circle indicates the relative size of the market segment preferring each ideal institution. Bank 1 lies very close to the largest ideal bank position. This was expected, as bank 1 was the dominant bank in the market area.

Further, the largest ideal segment lies directly on the 'friendly tellers' attribute line, again indicative of this bank feature in the small town in which the study was conducted. The study was conducted as a survey of consumer, not business, banking, which resulted in the lack of an ideal group near the position of bank 4 and the business orientation. The position of bank 3 and the ideal segment B is very interesting. The bank is very close to a group that appears to desire convenient locations above all other features. This bank had recently added a new branch and several automatic-teller locations and promoted its convenience heavily in the market.

It should be emphasised that the concept of positioning the company in the market-place relevant to its competition involving the entire marketing mix. Many financial companies have responded to competition involving the entire marketing mix. Many financial companies have responded to competition from non-banks to new bank products by attempting to position themselves as multi-service providers by simply changing their logos and their names. Other companies have added non-bank services without addressing the impact of these changes on their competitive position. A simple name change to some broad financial term does nothing to reposition the bank in the marketplace without the other elements of the marketing mix. Simlarly, decisions to add services or to reposition should not be taken lightly, as change can cost current customers. For example, banks considering expanding to include non-bank products, such as insurance and real estate as a means of positioning themselves to capture related business, should consider how existing customers in these business areas might perceive such change.

Overall, the position of the bank is one of the major elements in relating the bank and its strategy to the marketplace. Bank management needs to realise how it is perceived in the marketplace and to have a consistent strategy in keeping with its desired position.

Question

The positioning map may be used as a basis for the development of strategies to reposition the company within the perceptual marketplace to a more advantageous position. The described consumer study has been commissioned by the First United Bank (bank 2) as its management wants to develop new strategies to reposition the institution within this particular market area. Therefore, and according to the analysis of the perceptual maps, recommend alternative repositioning strategies that could be implemented by the First United Bank.

(M) *Problem 5.2* Make-or-buy analysis

Introductory comments

Some parts, components, sub-assemblies and services can be purchased from suppliers at lower costs than if they were produced in-house. A question fundamental to product policy and process planning is: should we produce it or should we buy it? Make-or-buy analysis provides product-process planners with economic comparisons of these alternatives. Managers typically evaluate these make-or-buy decisions by taking into account the following managerial information and stages:

1 Develop the following estimates:

	Alternatives		
	Make (process A)	Make (process B)	Buy
Annual volume	—	—	—
Fixed cost/year	—	—	—
Variable cost/unit	—	—	—

2 Develop the annual cost of each alternative:

Total annual costs = Fixed cost + volume (variable cost)

3 Calculate at what annual volume should the company switch from buying to making the product on process A. Total annual cost using process A = total annual cost of buying.

4 Calculate at what volume should the company switch from process A to process B (TC = total annual costs):

$$TC_A = TC_B$$

When outside suppliers specialise in particular processes, they can often produce products/services at lower costs than other organisations that must gear up technologically. A number of factors other than cost are also important in make-or-buy decisions. Can suppliers give us the needed volume and quality? Volume and quality may be as important as cost in make-or-buy decisions. Production and Operations Management (POM) teams usually visit candidate suppliers to assure themselves that these outside suppliers can measure up to volume and quality requirements. If a supplier is selected, it can expect periodic visits from customers' engineers regarding delivery and quality performance.

Problem

Orlicky, a medium-sized manufacturer of oilfield pumps, is located in Halifax, West Yorkshire. The company has developed a new model of its high-pressure secondary-recovery purge pump with improved performance. Neil Taylor, manager of process engineering and Alastair Davies, marketing manager, are trying to decide whether Orlicky should make or buy the electronically controlled input valve for the new pump.

Together, they have developed the following estimates:

	Make (process A)	Make (process B)	Buy
Annual volume	10,000 units	10,000 units	10,000 units
Fixed cost/year	£100,000	£300,000	–
Variable cost/unit	£75	£70	£80
Total	£850,000	£1,000,000	£800,000

Questions

1   Should Orlicky make the valve using process A, make the valve using process B or buy the valve?
2   At what annual volume should Orlicky switch from buying to making the valve on process A?
3   At what annual volume should Orlicky switch from process A to process B?

(I) *Problem 5.3* Product replacement strategies

Introductory comments

As we found at the start of this chapter product replacement is the most common form of new product introduction. A study of the marketing strategies used to position product replacements in the marketplace found eight approaches based upon a combination of product change, and other marketing modifications (i.e. marketing mix and target market changes). Figure 5.3 shows the eight replacement strategies used by companies.

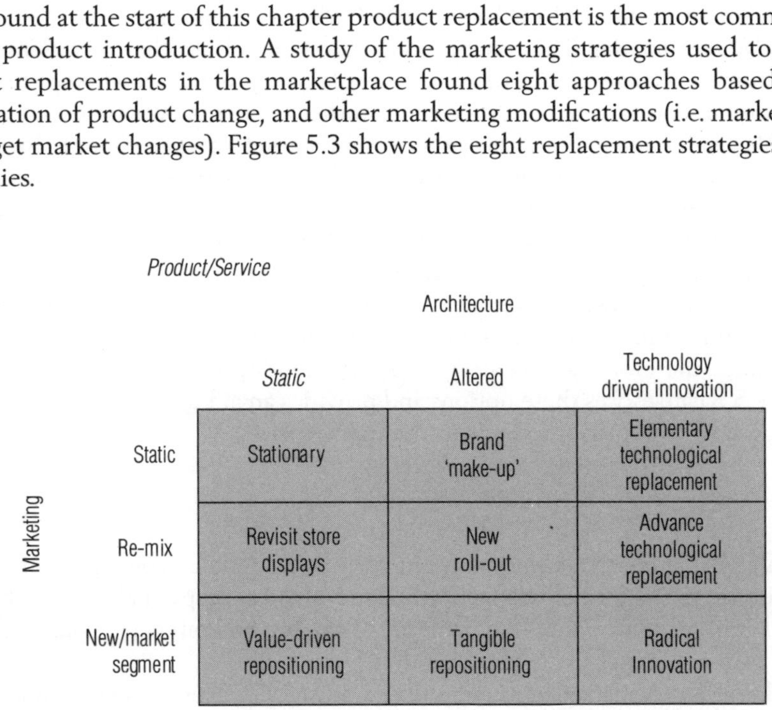

Marketing / Product/Service Architecture	Static	Altered	Technology driven innovation
Static	Stationary	Brand 'make-up'	Elementary technological replacement
Re-mix	Revisit store displays	New roll-out	Advance technological replacement
New/market segment	Value-driven repositioning	Tangible repositioning	Radical Innovation

Figure 5.3 Product/service replacement strategies.

Source: Adapted from Saunders, J. and Jobber, D. (1994) Strategies for product launch and deletion, in Saunders, J (ed.) *The Marketing Initiative*, Hemel Hempstead: Prentice-Hall, p. 227.

Facelift Minor product change with little or no change to the rest of the marketing mix or target market. Cars often undergo facelifts midway through their life cycle by undergoing minor styling alterations, for example. Japanese companies constantly facelift current electronic products such as video recorders and camcorders by changing product features, a process known as *product churning*.

Inconspicuous technological substitution A major technological change with little or no alteration of the other elements of the marketing mix. The technological change is not brought to the consumer's attention. For example, brand loyalty to instant mashed potatoes was retained through major technological process and product changed (powder to granules to flakes) with little attempt to highlight these changes through advertising.

Remerchandising A modification of name, promotion, price, packaging and/or distribution while maintaining the basic product. For example, an unsuccessful men's deodorant was successfully remerchandised by repackaging, heavier advertising, a higher price and new brand name 'Brut'.

Relaunch Both the product and other marketing-mix elements are changed. Relaunches are common in the car industry when every four to five years a model is replaced with an upgraded version. The replacement of the Ford Sierra with the Mondeo is an example.

Conspicuous technological substitution A major technological change is accompanied by heavy promotional (and other mix changes) to stimulate awareness and trial. The replacement of the IBM PC by the IBM PS/2 is an example.

Intangible repositioning The basic product is retained but other mix elements and target customers change. Lucozade is an example of a product which kept its original formulation but was targeted at different customer segments over time.

Tangible repositioning Both the product and target market change. In the UK, Kendalls – a down-market women's accessories chain – was repositioned as next, a more up-market women's clothing store.

Neo-innovation A fundamental technology change accompanied by target market and mix changes. For example, Compaq became a market leader in computers for a time by replacing its down-market inexpensive IBM PC compatible machines with up-market premium-priced computers based on the 286 chip.

Companies, therefore, face an array of replacement options with varying degrees of risk. Figure 5.3 categorises these options and provides an aid to strategic thinking when considering how to replace products in the marketplace.

Problem

Volvo is a global name that is successful in its chosen markets. Volvo pays much more than lip service to the idea of change. Although Volvo is exceptionally well established in its market, it recognises that they will stay at the top by embracing constant change.

Second, Volvo sees marketing as more than a technical function confined to a specialist department. Volvo Car UK, marketing pervades the whole company. Managers at all levels are involved and recognise that they have a role to play in the company's success.

Volvo has set itself the ambition of becoming the 'most desired and successful speciality car brand and the most customer-focused organisation in the world, achieving exemplary standards and support which will match or exceed customer expectations'. But when it speaks of being customer-focused who, exactly, is the customer?

At one level, it is the dealer network. At another, it is Volvo's corporate customers. Regardless of how a car is purchased, the customers who matter most are those at the end of the chain – the people who drive the cars. Ultimately, it is they who decide whether Volvo achieves its objectives. Clearly there would be no point in Volvo developing successful business-to-business relationships if the employees of corporate customers did not want to choose Volvos as their company car.

To tackle this issue, Volvo has two programmes. The first is corporate account relationship experience (Care). This is a corporate account programme aimed both internally and at selected dealers. It has 'the specific purpose of ensuring that everyone involved with our corporate customers delivers a level of service and professionalism consistent with our global ambitions'.

The second is 'one customer one relationship' (Oncore). This is a dealer programme designed to satisfy the end customer. Volvo describes it as 'the creation of a differentiated customer experience, an experience that will match the new products and services that Volvo will launch over the coming years'.

These two programmes work together to satisfy both the business needs of the corporate customer and the human needs of the driver. They reflect the fact that looking after corporate customers is a shared responsibility for Volvo and its dealers, the common factors being drivers, their spouses and families. Both programmes concentrate on developing the skills of all those people who touch the customer, whether they are employed by Volvo or a dealer. The two programmes dovetail together. Care is the business-to-business management process. When a car is delivered or a driver calls in at a dealership, Oncore takes over.

Volvo deals directly with its largest customers. Dealers have involved pre- and/or post-sales with all organisations that have company Volvos. The larger dealers have a business centre with a business sales manager, trained in all aspects of fleet customer requirements.

This manager's main role is to develop business-to-business relationships not handled directly by Volvo. Dealer business centres are typically in main towns and cities. They are responsible for most of Volvo's sales. But the company has wide geographic representation and service cover.

One of the interesting features of the way Volvo develops customer relationships is how it uses multiple relationships. For example, a person who drives a company Volvo is involved in as many as six relationships. Significantly, Volvo has a direct impact on every one of these relationships.

- *Volvo and its corporate customers* Relationships between Volvo and its corporate customers govern Volvo's inclusion in entitlement lists.
- *Corporate customers and their employees* The agreements reached affect which models are available to employees.
- *Corporate customers and Volvo dealers* The local dealer usually delivers and then services the cars, however they are acquired.
- *Volvo and Volvo drivers* Volvo maintains a direct marketing relationship with all drivers of its cars.
- *Volvo and its dealers* (some of which it owns) Volvo works hard with its dealer network to maintain and improve its standards.
- *Volvo dealers and Volvo drivers* Volvo dealers are the front line of meeting the drivers' expectations.

The Oncore and Care programmes are designed to ensure systematic approaches and consistent treatment across all these relationships. Volvo is seeing the benefits of its programmes. Its combined direct and dealer focus, coupled with its deliberate, near dramatic, image shift over recent years has lifted UK business purchases to 70 per cent of sales – behind competitors such as BMW and Mercedes, but still growing.

Of course, all high-engineering products are different and so are their markets and potential customers. But both British Aerospace and Volvo demonstrate that a willingness to change and develop multi-layered relationships with customers are key ingredients of success.

Questions

1 Out of nine product replacement strategies discussed, which do you feel applies more directly to the Volvo example?
2 What is the thinking behind the 'facelift' and 'relaunch' product replacement strategies?
3 Give examples of companies that have utilised a 'no change', an 'intangible repositioning' and a 're-merchandising' product replacement strategies.

(I) *Problem 5.4* Brand stretching (extension)

Introductory comments

The process of developing a range of products under the banner of one brand name is called *brand stretching*. There are certain advantages in this approach to new product launches. First and foremost, brand stretching enables a new product to take advantage of the already established functional attributes and symbolic values that make up the personality of the parent brand, whether that be product specific or corporate. Clearly, the intended personality of the parent brand should be appropriate to the new product. Second, brand stretching can, if done successfully, enhance the reputation and sales of the parent brand. An example of this is provided by the toiletries brand Nivea (see problem).

Brand stretching is, however, not without its critics. It is sometimes argued that stretching a brand can adversely affect its health (Aaker, 1991). Brand stretching the original brand proposition can result in cannibalisation of the original product's sales by the brand extension(s). It can also dilute the brand proposition such that consumers are confused by what becomes a more complex personality. However, there are probably as many examples of brand-stretching successes as there are failures. The important point is to ensure that the original brand is nurtured. This means, as we have said, periodic reviews of its saliency and relevance to the marketplace. Brands can quickly become old-fashioned and lose their sparkle.

If the existing brand is well-known and brings positive associations to mind, its fame and associations can be carried over to the new product. Three factors determine what associations will carry over into a new context:

1 *The strength of the attribute or quality associations in the existing context.* If these associations are weak to begin with, they will be weaker in the new context.
2 *The fit of a brand into the new context.* There needs to be a link such as a common use situation (hair care), user type (glamorous, upscale), functional benefits (speedy delivery) or attribute (salty). Vuarnet sunglasses are associated with skiing and fashion, and thus

a skiwear line as a brand extension would make sense, because it would share a common use context and involve the fashion attribute.

3   *Whether it is plausible to consider the brand in the new context.* Would the makers of the brand be perceived as having the expertise to make the new product class? Thus, a 'fashion-driven firm' like Vuarnet would probably be able to make skiwear, because a fashion touch is the key. A movement by Vuarnet into skis might be stretching it, however. To the extent that the new brand context is implausible, the positive attribute and quality associations will be weak and negative associations may emerge.

Developing brand extension options can start by finding out on what products a brand name would fit and what associations it would bring to the new product class. For example, when Bausch & Lomb found that many associated the firm with precision German engineering and that Bausch & Lomb hearing aids would be attractive, it bought Miracle Ear, a manufacturer with a thousand franchise outlets. When it found that customer trust could be transferred, Bausch & Lomb also decided to leverage its Sensitive Eyes name to start a lotion and cream business.

A brand extension can provide substantial support for a brand name by increasing its awareness level and by reinforcing its associations. For example, the Sunkist associations with oranges, health and vitality are reinforced by the promotion of Sunkist juice bars and Sunkist vitamin C tablets. However, extensions also have the potential to damage a core brand by creating undesirable attribute associations or weakening those that exist. Thus, the Sunkist health image may be weakened by Sunkist fruit rolls. The strong product-class associations of Kleenex and A-1 might be hurt if they were extended.

Perhaps the worst potential result of an extension is a foregone opportunity to create a new brand equity. Consider where P&G would be without Ivory, Camay, Dreft, Tide, Cheer, Joy, Pampers, Crest, Secret, Sure, Folger's, and Pringles, and its other 70 or so brands. P&G detergent, P&G toothpaste, P&G deodorant, P&G coffee, and P&G potato chips do not have the same impact.

There must be a certain logic for the brand extension to be successful. In this respect, the consumer-oriented approach can be distinguished from the manufacturer-oriented approach. In the manufacturer-oriented approach, the success of potential brand expansions is judged by the degree of production transfer, marketing transfer, substitutability and transfer of the brand image or brand concept. For example, Mars caramel sweets could benefit from production transfer, Mars chewing gum could benefit from production transfer and substitutability and Mars sports drink could benefit from image transfer. In the consumer-oriented approach, the logic follows from the meaning structure of goods and services. Table 5.2 shows three levels of brand extension. Incidentally, brand extension can occur on more than one level simultaneously. For example, products in a line extension may also possess the same benefits.

Characteristics level

At the characteristics level, brand extensions extend into variants of taste, colour, shape, etc. Classic Coke, Cherry Coke and Coca-Cola Light exist besides the normal Coke. Danone has yoghurt in different flavours. Besides normal Ariel, there is Ariel Ultra and next to Carlsberg, there is Carlsberg Light. There are Pampers nappies for boys and girls of different ages. The different colours, flavours and variants are substitutes for each other. The choice set of consumers becomes more extensive. The product is

Table 5.2 Levels of brand extension

Type of brand extension	Meaning structure	Marketing technical elements
Line extension, technical substitute	Characteristics level	Production transfer
Similar or complementary consequences, usage in similar situations	Consequences level	Marketing transfer, substitutability
Similar target group or lifestyle	Value level	Brand image transfer, brand concept transfer

differentiated and offered to different target groups. This form of brand extension is called *line extension*. This type of brand extension requires little change of the brand schema, that is assimilation. In the manufacturer approach, it is assumed that the extension will be successful because consumers think that the characteristics of the extension will have the same quality as the parent brand.

Consequences level

At the consequences level, brand extension is based on the same function, the same consequence or the same 'benefit' for the consumer. Under the name Lean Cuisine, different products that contain few calories and are good for slimming, are brought into the market. So there is Lean Cuisine margarine, cheese, pâté, cream milk and smoked sausage. These products all share the common characteristic that they are less fattening than other products. Lean Cuisine also is associated with a certain lifestyle: if you take good care of yourself and your figure, you will have more self-confidence and be happier. In the manufacturer approach, the expected success of these extensions is attributable to the transfer of marketing expertise, that is using the same marketing knowledge for similar products, and substitutability, that is substitutes have similar consequences.

Lifestyle and values

Brand extensions can also be based on the same lifestyle and values. Dunhill was originally a cigarette brand, but the brand Dunhill is now also used for completely different products such as expensive lighters, jewellery and watches. Ray Ban was originally a brand of sunglasses, but now this brand is also seen on skis and ski clothing. There are brand Porsche sunglasses. Swatch is planning to release artistic and lively coloured city cars under the brand Smart, produced by Mercedes. These brand extensions appeal to a certain target group striving for certain values and a certain lifestyle and who use these brands to express their identity. From the manufacturer's viewpoint, these extensions are expected to benefit from the transfer of brand image.

Extending brands successfully

Brand extensions are not always successful. A good brand extension must adhere to certain conditions.

* *Favourable existing schema* There must be a positive schema concerning the formal category of the original brand. In this case, positive associations can be conveyed. An Apple PC is seen as a user-friendly PC of high quality.

- *Favourable forward transfer* A positive schema should be generalisable to the new product. The new product receives the existing brand schema (transfer) plus a label with new product attributes. It is a formal categorisation with some functional labels. For example, Apple copiers may also be seen as user-friendly and of a high quality, according to some customers.
- *Favourable backward transfer* Negative schemas should not be transferred, from the existing product to the new one, or from the new product to the existing one. If photocopiers are seen as frequently defective products, a negative schema may be carried over to Apple Macs. Kleenex toilet paper might convey negative associations to Kleenex tissues. Miller Light beer had a negative effect on Miller High Life because of the schema ('almost water') of light beer. The new product under the same brand name is then created at the expense of the existing product (cannibalism).

It is not advisable to place a famous brand name of complex products on a trivial product, an IBM stapler for example or a Philips bathroom wash basin. This is called *trivialising*. The new product then detracts from the reputation of the famous brand and from the quality and complexity of the existing products brought out under that brand. It is a case of undesirable backward transfer. It is just as unadvisable to use a famous brand name of a simple product for a complex product, for example, 'Heineken computers'. The brand name then does not achieve the association of complexity and durability that is needed for the new product.

In general, an existing brand name must not be used for products with entirely different associations. With these conditions in mind, it is interesting to examine whether the following brand extensions are favourable or unfavourable to the new and to the existing product under the same brand: McDonald's theme parks, McDonald's photo printing service, Heineken soda water, Swatch city cars, Akzo Nobel contraceptive pill and Heinz peanut butter. Which levels do these brand extensions have? Are these brand extensions likely to evoke positive associations for the consumer? Which of these brand extensions would have a chance of success?

Problem

NIVEA – THE SKINCARE BRAND

Nivea, the largest toiletries brand in the world, began life in Germany as a soap manufacturer in 1906. For a long time, however, its reputation, in the rest of Europe in particular, was based upon the skin formulation, Nivea Cream. The successful stretching of the brand was based on the careful selection of new products that matched the brand's original personality both in Germany and the rest of Europe. This was used to evaluate potential product developments. The essential attributes and values used as the benchmark were as follows:

- other care and protection;
- be simple and uncomplicated;
- be mild;
- have natural active ingredients;
- have a subtle perfume;
- be of high quality;
- give value for money;
- be blue and white (the colours of the parent brand).

Maintaining this personality enabled Nivea successfully to launch a range of sun-care products that were number two in the UK market in the late 1990s. Meanwhile, in Germany, Nivea successfully launched a range of Nivea products for men. All these developments were a significant step away from the original product. With the exception of the UK, the sales of the original soap have benefited from these extensions to the range. In the UK, however, Nivea soap was a late entrant into an already crowded market and the benefits of these extensions were less significant.

Questions

1   Discuss how a brand extension can provide substantial support for an established brand name, as well as some examples of the negative impact of brand stretching.
2   Explain what is behind the meaning structure related to the levels of brand extension, namely, the characteristics and consequences levels, as well as lifestyle and values.
3   What are the basic conditions that a good brand extension must adhere to?

(A) *Problem 5.5* Brand equity

Introductory comments

Nevertheless, the concept of establishing a financial value for a brand, in other words its equity value, remains an attractive one. Notwithstanding the accounting debate, it is useful for those responsible for brands to be able to place a value on their brands for several reasons.

*   It focuses management's orientation away from short-term financial goals towards the development of a true sustainable competitive advantage.
*   It enables an objective choice to be made between alternative options for the investment of limited resources.
*   It helps management to place a value on potential licensing and merchandising deals.
*   It facilitates the evaluation of the potential return on the investment of strategic options such as brand extensions.

The value of a brand has been defined as the balance of both the assets and the liabilities that can be directly associated with it. On the assets side we might include such factors as follows. On the liabilities side we might include all the costs of maintaining the brand's competitive position.

Assests	Liabilities
The extent of brand loyalty	Average annual advertising and promotional costs
The perceived quality of the brand	Legal costs associated with the protection of
The brand's market share	patents, trade names, etc.
The extent of the brand's leadership compared with the number in the market	The costs of legislative changes – e.g. on packaging
Long-term trends in the market	Directly attributable staff costs
The existence and extent of patents and other legal protection	
The susceptibility of the brand to competition, technological change, etc.	
Average profitability	

The major problem with all these eminently sensible assets and liabilities is, of course, the problem of measurement. All the variables listed above contain, to varying degrees, an element of subjectivity in their assessment. The fact remains, however, that, without some form of systematic approach, decisions on the allocation of funds will be subject to hunch and personal bias. It is not surprising, therefore, that the topic of brand equity and how to measure it has become a focus for research, particularly in the USA. 'It is widely accepted that higher-share brands are less "deal elastic".'

BRAND VALUE

Recent work on brand names in marketing has dealt with the issue of brand equity (Farquhar, 1989; Schoker and Weitz, 1988; Tauber, 1988).

The concept of brand equity has gained much prominence both in academic and industry, especially because of the growing recognition of brands as valuable assets for the company. However, little consensus has emerged about how brand equity should be measured (Barwise, 1993). The literature proposes to measure brand equity (e.g. see Barwise et al., 1989), reflecting a wide diversity of conceptualisations about this concept. More than 25 measures have been proposed in the literature all named brand equity. The outcomes differ substantially depending on which measure is applied.

Many researchers view brand equity from a financial perspective, based on costs (Stobart, 1989), present and future earnings (Brasco, 1988), incremental cash flows relative to unbranded goods (Simon and Sullivan, 1990) or a comparison of the brand characteristics with those of representative (usually unbranded) competitors (Wertz, 1989).

Simon and Sullivan (1990) estimated the value of a brand's equity by distinguishing between the value of a company's tangible and intangible assets, brand equity being defined as an intangible asset.

From a firm's financial perspective, brand equity has been defined as 'the incremental cash flow resulting from a product with the brand name vs. the cash flow which would result without the brand name' (Shocker and Weitz, 1988). Alternatively, one can define it as the capitalised expected future profits because of the association of a brand name with existing and potential products and services (Simon and Sullivan, 1990).

One of the most elaborate procedures is that of the Interbrand Group, a London-based consulting firm. Interbrand multiplies average profitability over the past three years by a P/E (price/earnings) multiplier. This P/E multiplier is estimated as a function of a 'brand strength index' composed of subjective ratings of the brand on market leadership, brand stability, international presence, long-term trend and stability of the product category, trademark protection, and advertising and promotion support (Penrose, 1989). Another way of assessing the value for the company is through the brand's ability to maintain a long-run competitive advantage (Blackett, 1989; Murphy, 1989).

From a product policy perspective, brand value (or equity) is the outcome of long-term investments designed to build a sustainable, differential advantage relative to competitors (Doyle, 1990). Tauber (1988: 26) notes that, 'capitalizing on the equity in established brand names has become the guiding strategy of product planners.'

Barwise (1993) has provided an evaluative review of research to-date on brand equity. He stressed that the original emphasis of brand equity was on brands as financial assets and the aim was to counter financial 'short-termism'. However, he also argued that most academic research on brand equity has focused on consumer behaviour. Much has been achieved in the complex and important area of brand extensions research. Much less has been achieved on the financial, managerial and strategic aspects of brand equity.

The value associated with brand names (Farquhar, 1989; Shocker and Weitz, 1988) is directly related to the informational aspects of a market and the marketing actions of companies. Kirmani and Wright (1989) and Kirmani (1990) found empirical evidence that perceived advertising costs may lead to more favourable brand evaluations over some range of costs, which provides some empirical support for the signalling view of advertising.

Brand names function as signals in the marketplace, reducing consumer's perceived risk and information costs which, in turn, underlie 'the additional utility not explained by measured attributes', a definition of brand equity adopted by Louviere and Johnson (1988) and Kamakura and Russell (1993). In short, according to this view, additional utility is brand equity to consumers and enables firms to command premiums (e.g. additional revenues, increased distribution channel power, etc.) in the marketplace (Leuthesser, 1988).

Kamakura and Russell (1993) defined brand equity to be the utility intrinsic to a brand that cannot be captured through its tangible characteristics and its short-term price (i.e. akin to 'the additional utility not explained by measure attributes', as suggested by Louviere and Johnson, 1988). Specifically, they define the equity of a brand to be the brand-specific constant (hypothesised to capture the valuation of intangible characteristics of the brand).

The conceptual framework of brand equity postulated by Erdem and Louviere (1992) emphasises that brand equity is consumer-, not firm-, or trade-driven. The approach to modelling and measuring brand equity based on consumer utility functions developed by Swait et al. (1993) fits within a general information signalling framework, fully presented in Erdem and Louviere (1992).

Perceived fit has been considered to underlie transferability of brand equity in marketing literature (Aaker and Keller, 1990; Tauber, 1988). Sunde and Brodie (1993) concluded that consumer acceptance of a proposed brand extension depends on (i) quality, (ii) perceived fit (especially the transferability of skills and the complementarity of product categories), and to a lesser extent, (iii) the difficulty of making the extension.

Kamakura and Russell (1993) developed a method for evaluating a brand's consumer-based brand equity from real-world scanner data as opposed to questionnaire surveys or laboratory experiments. The method adjusts for the short-term effects of price variations (e.g. special offers) and recent advertising to give an estimate of the underlying brand value, a measure of the total equity of the brand and product in combination. This is then decomposed into a 'brand tangible value' (derived from consumers' perceptions and valuation of physical product attributes and 'brand intangible value' (obtained by subtraction). The 'brand intangible value' is a measure of 'separated' brand equity in the sense of the incremental value of the brand after allowing for the value of the physical product.

Swait, Erden, Louviere, and Dubelaar (1993) explored a complementary measure to Kamakura and Russell's using designed choice experiments. Swait et al. (1993) proposed a new measure of consumer-based brand equity, the equalisation price (EP). The EP is a monetary expression of the utility a consumer attributes to a bundle consisting of a brand name, product attributes and price. It is estimated for each consumer-based on her or his (a) brand perceptions and (b) responses to a designed choice experiment in which the researcher offers existing and/or extended brands at different prices representative of the price variation in the real market. The EP is the hypothetical price, derived from these data (assuming an appropriate choice model, e.g. Multinomial Logit), at which each brand would have the same market share in that consumer's purchases. It can then be averaged across consumers within segments or for the whole market. A brand with high consumer-based brand equity will thus have a high EP. The EP captures aspects of consumer brand equity in a single robust measure and, similar to Kamakura and Russell's Brand Value measure, could also be decomposed to separate the effects of price and physical product attributes.

Rangaswamy, Burke and Oliva (1993) explored the extendability of brand equity across product categories as it could influence financial valuation, especially in an acquisition context. Rangaswamy et al. (1993) decomposed a parent brand's utility into the utility of (i) its physical attributes, (ii) its name and (iii) the interaction of (i) and (ii), the implication is that, to increase a brand's extendability and strategic flexibility, marketers should emphasise intangible associations such as quality, durability and prestige.

Problem – example

Brands seek to capture both the hearts and minds of consumers and are central to the concept of the global company.

Brands are universal icons. Recognised the world over, they sell everything from cola to cars (see Table 5.3). They have a powerful pull on consumers in cosmopolitan cities

Table 5.3 The world's most valuable brands

Brand	Brand value ($ bn)
Coca-Cola	47.99
Marlboro	47.64
IBM	23.70
McDonald's	19.94
Disney	17.07
Sony	14.46
Kodak	14.44
Intel	13.27
Gillette	11.99
Budweiser	11.99
Nike	11.13
Kellogg's	10.67
AT&T	10.39
Nescafé	10.34
GE	10.29
Hewlett-Packard	9.42
Pepsi	9.32
Microsoft	8.99
Frito-Lay	8.99
Levis	8.17

such as New York and Sao Paulo. And they touch the lives of people living in remote rural communities across the globe. But global brands are about much more than logos and advertising campaigns.

Companies such as Coca-Cola, McDonald's, Walt Disney, Sony, Body Shop and Mercedes-Benz have become world leaders through the strength of their brands. By becoming synonymous with their products, they almost own their categories.

A well-established brand name can broaden a company's ambitions, allowing it to introduce new products or move into new markets. Walt Disney has stretched its brand well beyond films to cover books, clothing, toys, games and holidays.

People do not have to pay 30 per cent more for a Disney T-shirt, but they do so because the brand means more to them than just a T-shirt – it embodies the Disney magic. With more choice between suppliers, business customers are looking for consistency and trust. IBM fell into the trap of just selling computers. Now it realises it needs an ongoing relationship trust with its customers which a single global brand can help build.

Most large companies with diverse consumer products follow similarly diverse branding strategies. Nestlé, for example, has multiple layers of branding. Its dried milk is always sold under the company name and Nescafé is clearly of Nestlé provision (sub-brand).

Even in less diverse businesses where global branding makes sense, attention must be paid to local preferences. McDonald's, selling a US fast-food concept with a consistency that is almost chilling, serves wine and salads with its burgers in France. For the Indian market where beef products are taboo, it created a mutton burger: the Maharaja Mac.

Young urban professionals in London have more in common with their contemporaries in Singapore than with middle-class families in Berkshire. The latter have more in common with people living in the affluent suburbs of Sydney.

The challenge for marketing professionals is to link their product to individual needs. One way is product proliferation – so that Coca-Cola becomes Classic Coke, Diet Coke and Cherry Cola. Coca-cola remains the brand, but it is delivered by a variety of means.

General Motors has chosen four global brands for its cars, in Saab, Cadillac, Opel and Chevrolet. A single brand could not stretch from the Opel Astra to a performance car such as the Saab 9000 or a luxury saloon such as the Cadillac.

Another is to create an idea for a single brand that transcends such differences by identifying it with an attitude rather than a particular lifestyle. 'Good branding is about stirring emotions,' says Peter Farnell-Watson, European managing director at Landor Associates, the US branding consultancy. 'It sits in peoples minds and has an attachment in their hearts.'

Thus Nike is much more than a pair of trainers: it is about personal empowerment. Body Shop, the cosmetics retailer, offers ethical consumption in a world where the environment is under threat. And IBM offers solutions for the planet – it is a company that can enhance your business performance.

But establishing just what the big idea is needs to be taken seriously at the highest level in the company. The companies which have managed their brands best are those led by chief executives who take the keenest interest in branding: Roberto Goizueta at Coca-Cola, Michael Eisner at Disney and Lou Gerstner at IBM.

Questions

1   What is the meaning behind the value of a brand in terms of assets and liabilities?
2   Provide the definition of hard equity following a company's financial perspective.
3   What is the P/E multiplier developed by the Interbrand Group?
4   Discuss and elaborate on (i) the notion that brand names can function as signals in the marketplace as well as (ii) the argument that hard equity can be defined as the utility intrinsic to a brand.

(A) *Problem 5.6* Financial methods used in the new product development process

Introductory comments

A number of different financial methods are used to rank new-product projects and to decide whether they should be accepted to carry through in the development process and for inclusion in the capital budget of the organisation. Three of the most commonly used are as follows:

1   *Payback (or payback period)* This is the number of years required to return the original investment.
2   *Net present value (NPV)* This is the present value of future cash flows, discounted at the appropriate cost of capital, minus the cost of the investment. The NPV (and also the IRR) method is called a *discounted cash flow* (DCF) method.
3   *Internal rate of return (IRR)* This is the discount rate that equates the present value of the expected future cash flows to the initial cost of the new-product project. The IRR corresponds to the yield-to-maturity on a bond.

Future cash flows are, in all cases, defined as the expected annual net cash inflows from the investments.

Payback method

The payback period is defined as the number of years it takes a company to recover its original investment from net cash flows.

Prior to the 1960s, the payback was the most commonly used method for screening capital expenditure proposals. It is still widely used, but generally only for smaller replacement projects or as a risk indicator for larger projects. Some features of the payback, which indicate both its strengths and its weaknesses, are listed below:

1   *Ease of calculation* The payback is easy to calculate and apply. This was an important consideration in the pre-computer, pre-calculator days.
2   *Ignores returns beyond payback period* One glaring weakness of the payback method is that it ignores cash flows beyond the payback period. Ignoring returns in the distant future means that the payback method is biased against long-term projects.
3   *Ignores time value of money* The timing of cash flows is obviously important, yet the payback method ignores the time value of money. A pound in year 3 is given the same weight as a pound in year 1.

NPV Method

As the flaws in the payback method were recognised, managers began to search for methods of evaluating new-product projects that would recognise that a pound received immediately is preferable to a pound received at some future date. This led to the development of DCF techniques to take account of the time value of money. One such DCF technique is called the NPV method. To implement this approach, find the present value of the expected net cash flows of an investment, discounted at an appropriate percentage rate and subtract from it the initial cost outlay of the new-product project. If its NPV is positive, the project should be accepted; if negative, it should be rejected. If two projects are mutually exclusive, the one with the higher NPV should be chosen.

The equation for the NPV is

$$
\begin{aligned}
\text{NPV} &= \left[\frac{CF_1}{(1+K)^1} + \frac{CF_2}{(1+K)^2} + \cdots + \frac{CF_n}{(1+K)^n} \right] - C \\
&= \sum_{T=1}^{n} \frac{CF_T}{(1+K)^T} - C \\
&= CF_1(PVIF_{K,1}) + CF_2(PVIF_{K,2}) + \cdots + CF_n(PVIF_{K,n}) - C
\end{aligned}
$$

Here, CF_1, CF_2 and so forth, represent the annual receipts, or net cash flows; K is the appropriate discount rate or the project's cost of capital; C is the initial cost of the new-product project; and n is the project's expected life. The cost of capital, K, depends on the riskiness of the project, the level of interest rates in the economy and several other factors.

Present value of £1: $PVIF_{K,n} = 1/(1+K)^n$

The IRR

The IRR is the discount rate that equates the present value of the expected future cash flows, or receipts, to the initial cost of the project. The equation for calculating this rate is:

$$
\frac{CF_1}{(1-R)^1} + \frac{CF_2}{(1-R)^2} + \cdots + \frac{CF_n}{(1-R)^n} - C = 0
$$

$$
\sum_{T=1}^{n} \frac{CF_T}{(1+R)^T} - C = 0
$$

$$
CF_1(PVIF_{R,1}) + CF_2(PVIF_{R,2}) + \cdots + CF_n(PVIF_{R,n}) - C = 0
$$

Here we know the value of C and also the, CF_1, CF_2, ..., CF_n, but we do not know the value of R. Thus, we have an equation with one unknown and we can solve for the value of R. Some value of R will cause the sum of the discounted receipts to equal the initial cost of the project, making the equation equal to zero: this value of R is defined as the internal rate of return. In other words, the solution value of R is the IRR.

Notice that the IRR formula is simply the NPV formula, solved for the particular discount rate that causes the NPV to equal zero. Thus, the same basic equation is used for both methods, but in the NPV method the discount rate, K, is specified and the NPV is found, while in the IRR method the NPV is specified to equal zero and the value of R that forces the NPV to equal zero is found. Because IRRs can be calculated very easily by computers, many companies have computerised their capital budgeting processes and automatically generate IRRs, NPVs and paybacks for all projects. Even some hand-held calculators are programmed to compute IRRs. Thus, business firms have no difficulty whatever with the mechanical side of capital budgeting.

Problem

The example used is taken from the files of a major industrial firm, Miller Chemical Co. Miller's cash flow analysis for the compound X project is typical of that used in all types of business with sales in excess of about £10 million.

It is assumed that the annual sales volume will be 100,000 tons by the third year. This is 10 per cent of projected industry sales. These estimates are based on the results of a test marketing programme for the newly patented compound X and the market potential as projected for the next 15 years by the market research department. The net sales price will be £40 per ton. This estimate is based on present competitive price levels as determined by the marketing department. Selling and advertising expenses, which were estimated by the marketing department, are based on other products sold to the textile industry. An inflation rate of 8 per cent in labour and materials cost is expected. Sales prices will increase at this same rate. The capital needed to undertake the project can be raised at an average cost (average of debt and equity) of 10 per cent. Cash flow data are shown in Table 5.4 for projects S and L. The S stands for short and the L for long: project S is a short-term project and L a long-term one in the sense that S's cash inflows tend to come sooner than L's. For now, the company assumes that the projects are equally risky. Note that cash flows consist of both after-tax profits and depreciation, not profits alone. Also, most projects require both fixed assets and an addition to net working capital as in the compound X case; the investment outlays in Table 5.4 include any necessary working capital and the cash flow in the past year includes the return of these funds.

Table 5.4 Net cash flows (profit after taxes plus depreciation) for Miller Chemical Co.'s projects S and L (£000s)

Year	Project S	Project L
1	500	100
2	400	300
3	300	400
4	100	600
Total inflows	£1,300	£1,400
Investment outlay or initial cost at time	£1,000	£1,000

Questions

1   Calculate the payback periods for projects S and L.
2   Calculate the NPVs of projects S and L.
3   Calculate the IRRs of projects S and L by using the 'trial-and-error' method (i.e. with selected discount rates of 10 and 15 per cent).

(A) *Problem 5.7* Net present value/profitability index

Introductory comments

The net present value (NPV) of an investment project is defined as the present value of the stream of net cash flows from the project minus the project's net investment. The cash flows are discounted at the firm's required rate of return that is, its cost of capital. A firm's cost of capital is defined as its minimum acceptable rate of return for investment projects of average risk.

The NPV of a new-product development project may be expressed as follows,

$$NPV = PVNCF - NINV$$

where NPV is the net present value, PVNCF the present value of net cash flows and NINV the net investment.

Assuming a cost of capital, K, the NPV for a project with a five-year expected life would be the following:

$$NPV = \frac{NCF_1}{(1+K)^1} + \frac{NCF_2}{(1+K)^2} + \frac{NCF_3}{(1+K)^3} + \frac{NCF_4}{(1+K)^4} + \frac{NCF_5}{(1+K)^5} - NINV$$

Where $NCF_1 \ldots NCF_5$ are the net cash flows occurring in years 1 to 5. NCF_5 may be assumed to include any salvage value remaining at the end of the project's life. In general, the NPV of a project may be defined as follows,

$$NPV = \sum_{T=1}^{n} \frac{NCF_T}{(1+K)^T} - NINV$$

$$= \left\{ \sum_{T=1}^{n} NCF_T \times PVIP_{K,T} \right\} - NINV$$

Where n is the expected project life, and

$$\sum_{T=1}^{n} \left[\frac{NCF_T}{(1+K)^T} \right]$$

is the arithmetic sum of the discounted net cash flows for each year, T, over the life of the project (n years); that is the present value of the net cash flows. PVIF is the present value interest factor.

The NPV approach is superior to the payback method, because it considers both the magnitude and the timing of cash flows over a project's entire expected life. The NPV approach to treating the capital constraint problem is to invest the funds that are available in that set of new-product projects with the highest total NPV. That is, the goal is to maximise the NPV of the entire current investment.

If the company's investments do not provide a rate of return at least equal to the cost of capital (i.e. imply a positive NPV), they should be rejected as the company can earn the cost of capital by simply investing (lending) its funds in the market. No investment that is inferior to such market opportunities should be accepted.

The profitability index is a procedure that ranks the company's investments by the ratio of the NPV per pound of initial investment that they provide (NPV/I), and then selects those investments with the highest NPV/I until the budget is exhausted. NPV/I is referred to as the profitability index. This procedure selects for adoption the combination of investments within the budget constraint that has the highest total NPV.

The profitability index is also often defined as (NPV + I)/I = (present value of future net cash flows)/(initial outlay); this ratio is sometimes referred to as the bene-fit–cost ratio and using this ratio to rank investments leads to the same decisions as using the profitability index as defined here.

The profitability index (PI), or benefit–cost ratio, is the ratio of the present value of future net cash flows over the life of a project to the net investment. It is expressed as follows:

$$PI = \frac{\sum_{T=1}^{n} NCF_T/(1 + K)^T}{NINV}$$

The profitability index is interpreted as the present value return for each pound of initial investment. In comparison, the NPV approach measures the total present value pound return.

A project whose profitability index is greater than or equal to 1 is considered acceptable, while a project having a profitability index less than 1 is considered unac-ceptable. When a project has a profitability index equal to 1, the NPV of the net cash flows is exactly equal to the net investment.

The profitability index is useful when choosing among projects in a capital-rationing situation.

Problem

Imhoff Instruments (Zurich) Ltd has new-product projects it can adopt as shown in Table 5.5.

Questions

Assuming (a) the initial outlay is the only cash outflow for each new-product project, (b) the projects are not mutually exclusive and (c) the cash flows of the

Table 5.5 Imhoff Instruments (Zurich) Ltd: possible new-product projects

Project	Initial outlay (£)	NPV (£)
A	50,000	70,000
B	90,000	120,000
C	60,000	120,000
D	100,000	10,000
E	250,000	150,000
F	80,000	20,000
G	40,000	40,000

projects are not interdependent:

1 Rank the projects in order of desirability on the basis of the profitability index.
2 If the company has a limited capital budget of £550,000, which new-product projects should it choose?
3 The data for project D are revised as follows:

Project	Initial outlay	NPV
D	£100,000	£55,000

Now answer (1) and (2) again.

(A) *Problem 5.8* Application of decision trees in new-product development

Introductory comments

Many managerial problems have a rather long-drawn-out structure in that they consist of a whole sequence of actions and outcomes. For example, in a new-product development programme, a critical action is often test marketing and the action choice might be between intensive and gradual testing. Having taken this decision there is an outcome – perhaps the product reception is favourable, fair or poor. Given one of these outcomes (fair, say) one then has to decide between redesigning the product, an advertising campaign or withdrawing altogether. Given that decision, there will be an outcome that leads to another decision and so on. There are two important features to this kind of decision problem – time and uncertainty. In the real world each of these actions and outcomes takes some time to initiate or unfold. In total, the elapsed time may be very large. The effects of time on financial values can be incorporated very well by discounting, but the probabilities in the problem may also be influenced by the passage of time and the emergence of more information. In this case, the application of Bayes' theorem will allow us to modify probabilities in the light of further information.

The other factor is that uncertainty is made more severe by being compounded into a chain of events. It is hard enough to make an assessment of probabilities in the case of a single action with several outcomes but it is much more difficult to make a set of mutually consistent probability assessments for a whole chain of outcomes. Note that, despite the difficulties involved, the manager has to solve these problems in any case.

Regardless of whether he or she uses formulae or has ever heard of Bayes' strategies, he or she is balancing uncertainty in some way. The contention of decision theory is that it is better to have some formal procedure for dealing with uncertainty because that at least makes managerial judgement explicit and open to discussion by those involved.

Having said that complex decision problems have a sequential structure, it seems fairly obvious to represent them by diagrams that show the branching ramifications of the decision and outcomes involved. These diagrams are called *decision trees*.

CONSTRUCTING DECISION TREES

The squares in a decision-tree diagram are points at which decisions have to be made, the circles are points at which one of number of outcomes may occur and the dots are the ends of chains of events. These points are collectively called *nodes*.

The 'branches' between the nodes are either decisions or outcomes and each is labelled with an identification, a probability or a value, where appropriate. For convenience of explanation each node should be labelled. The numbers to be written above the nodes are expected values and the lines to be drawn across some of the branches ( ) should indicate optimal paths. There are no universal formulae for constructing decision trees because each one is tailored to an individual problem and its branches are as long and complex or short and simple as needed (note that the branches may be of different lengths if need be). We can, however, offer a few rules of thumb:

1   Use a fairly large piece of paper as the tree will almost certainly wander off a small one.
2   Divide it up from left to right into a series of vertical strips for actions and outcomes. Make the strips a couple of inches wide and allow for more than you think you will need. It is often useful to label these strips 'action', 'outcome', 'action', 'outcome' and so on, across the bottom of the sheet.
3   Start at the left-hand edge with a decision box, recalling that there are nearly always at least two possible decisions – 'do something' and 'do nothing', for example 'test' and 'abandon' as in the Robinson Home Appliances Co. case (later).
4   Try to follow each branch in turn across the page, writing down only the labels of actions and outcomes for a start. This process will, in itself, often stimulate new ideas for actions, a phenomenon that is at least half and probably much more of the value of the decision-tree technique.
5   When the tree is complete try to get someone to check it for omissions.
6   Now write down the probabilities. In reality you may have no idea of what the salutary experience will be like and also no idea of what the likelihoods of the various outcomes are. This is again a very useful practical feature of the tree because it may save you from blundering ahead with an action. There is a very real temptation to say 'the tree technique is useless because we don't know what the probabilities are'. This is putting the cart before the horse with a vengeance. Decision trees and the other techniques of decision theory are not intended to be number-crunching masters that have to be obeyed and fed with raw material. If the probabilities cannot be assigned to some particular set of outcomes then this means that you are in a situation where you are about to confront the future with no idea of what is likely to happen. This is bad managerial practice, not impractical managerial theory.
7   Working from right to left calculate the expected values – EVs – (payoff × probability) and determine the optimal acts at each decision stage. Remember to verify that the probabilities on the branches from each outcome node do add up to 1.00. Also, add these products, taking account of the sign. Care is needed with signs, and negative payoffs and their signs are best put in brackets to identify them.

8 Ensure that the whole thing makes some kind of sense, with due caution about relying too heavily on intuition in the very complex cases.

9 Even if the recommended strategies do make sense in the real world, but especially if they do not, recheck the probabilities. If in doubt, recalculate the tree with different probabilities and see how and where the optimal acts change. If you have to change the probabilities by fairly large amounts before the optimal path becomes different, then you have a fairly robust tree and the problem is fairly clear-cut. In many cases, however, there will be a point in the tree where quite small alterations in the probabilities will make fairly large changes in the optimal path, even reaching right back to the starting point because of the changed expected values. If this happens it focuses attention on the critical area and usually indicates the need for more study by, for example, marketing research methods.

10 Finally, do not get too involved with the decision-tree technique itself. It depends on probabilities and these are nearly always a matter of someone's opinion about what is likely to happen in the future. This does not invalidate the method because managerial decisions generally depend on someone's opinion. The great value of decision trees is that they bring these opinions into the open where they can be scrutinised for what they are as long as you are not too busy drawing squares and circles.

These introductory comments probably make decision trees seem an incredible amount of work. They are not but, like everything else, the first few take much longer than the later ones. With a little practice a decision tree can be written down directly from knowledge of the problem and can be amended as the sequence of events unfolds.

Problem

Robinson Home Appliances Co. have a new wonder product of which they expect great things. At the moment they have two courses of action open to them: to test market it or abandon it. If they test it, it will cost £100,000 and the response could be positive or negative with probabilities of .60 and .40. If it is positive they could either abandon the product or market it full scale. If they market full scale the result might be low, medium or high demand, and the respective net payoffs would be −200, 200 or 1,000 in units of £1,000 (i.e. the result could range from a net loss of £200,000 to a gain of £1,000,000). These outcomes have probabilities of .20, .50 and .30 respectively.

If the result of the test marketing is negative they have decided to abandon the product. If, at any point, they abandon it there is a net gain of £50,000 from the sale of scrap. All the financial values have been discounted to the present.

It is by no means easy to see from the description what Robinson Home Appliances Co. should do.

Questions

1 Construct the decision-tree diagram for the problem facing the company.
2 As a result of the construction and analysis of the decision tree, work out a contingency plan for Robinson Home Appliances Co.

(A) Problem 5.9 Application of the PERT/cost technique in new-product development

Introductory comments

A network is basically a graphical representation or description of a problem situation. By employing special network analysis algorithms, solutions can be obtained for the particular problems. Programme evaluation and review technique (PERT) and critical path method (CPM) and two well-known network analysis techniques used to assist managers in planning, scheduling and controlling large-scale research and development projects.

In many situations managers assume the responsibility for planning, scheduling and controlling projects that consist of numerous separate jobs or tasks performed by a variety of departments, individuals, etc. Often these projects are so large and/or complex that the manager cannot possibly keep all the information pertaining to the plan, schedule and progress of the project in his or her head. In these situations the techniques of PERT and CPM have proved to be extremely valuable in assisting managers in carrying out their project management responsibilities.

PERT and CPM have been used to plan, schedule and control a wide variety of projects, including research and development of new products and processes.

In projects such as these, marketing managers must schedule and coordinate the various jobs or activities so that the entire project is completed on time. A complicating factor in carrying out this task is the interdependence of the activities; for example, some activities depend upon the completion of other activities before they can be started. As new-product development projects have many specific activities, marketing managers and new-product managers look for procedures that will help them answer questions such as the following:

1   What is the expected project completion date?
2   What is the scheduled start and completion date for each specific activity?
3   Which activities are 'critical' and must be completed exactly as scheduled in order to keep the project on schedule?
4   How long can 'non-critical' activities be delayed before they cause a delay in the total new-product development project?

PERT and CPM can be used to help answer the above questions.

PERT was developed with an objective of being able to handle uncertainties in activity completion times. A distinguishing feature of CPM is that it enables time and cost trade-offs for the various activities in the project.

In today's usage the distinction between PERT and CPM as two separate techniques has largely disappeared. Computerised versions of the PERT/CPM approach often contain options for considering uncertainty in activity times as well as activity time/cost trade-offs.

The development of an accurate list of activities is a key step in any new-product development project. The immediate predecessors for a particular activity are the activities that must be completed immediately prior to the start of the given activity. The network consists of numbered circles interconnected by several arrows. In general network terminology, the circles are called *nodes* and arrows connecting the nodes are called *branches* or *arcs*. In a PERT/CPM network, the arrows correspond to the activities in the project, and the completion of several activities that lead into a node is referred to as an *event*. For example, in Figure 5.4 node 2 refers to the event that activity B has been completed, and node 3 refers to the event that both activities A and C have been completed.

The first step in the new-product development project scheduling process is to determine all the activities that make up the project as well as the immediate

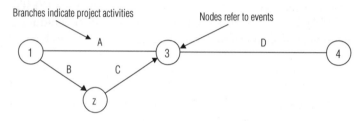

Figure 5.4 Example of a PERT/CPM network.

predecessors for each activity. Once we have established a network for the project, we will need ed in information on the time required to complete each activity. This information will be used for the calculation of the duration of the entire project and the scheduling of the specific activities. Accurate activity-time estimates are essential for successful project management.

The PERT procedure estimates the average time for each activity or expected time (T) from the following formula:

$$T = \frac{a + 4m + b}{6}$$

where T = the average time for each activity or expected time, a = optimistic activity-time estimate, b = pessimistic activity-time estimate and m = most probable activity-time estimate.

For uncertain activity times we can use the common statistical measure of the variance to describe the dispersion or variation in the activity-time values. In PERT we compute the variance of the activity times from the following formula:

$$\text{Variance of activity time } (\sigma_2) = \left(\frac{b - a}{6} \right)^2$$

The variance equation is based on the notion that a standard deviation is approximately 1/6 of the difference between the extreme values of the distribution $(b - a)/6$. The variance is simply the square of the standard deviation.

The difference between the pessimistic (b) and optimistic (a) time estimates greatly affects the value of the variance. Once we have the network and the expected activity times, we are ready to proceed with the calculations necessary to determine the expected project completion date and a detailed activity schedule. In order to arrive at a project duration estimate we will have to analyse the network and determine what is called its *critical path*. A path is a sequence of connected activities that lead from the starting node to the completion node. The longest path determines the expected total time or expected duration of the project. The longest-path activities are the critical activities of the project and the longest path is called the critical path of the network.

Summary of PERT Procedure

Let us now briefly review the process of analysing a new-product development project using the PERT procedure. In analysing any project using PERT, we perform the following steps:

Step 1 Develop a list of activities that make up the project, including immediate predecessors.

Step 2 Draw a network corresponding to the activity list developed in step 1.

Step 3 Estimate the expected activity time and the variance for each activity.

Step 4 Using the expected activity-time estimates, determine the earliest start time and earliest finish time for each activity. The earliest finish time for the complete project corresponds to the earliest finish time for the last activity. This is the expected project completion time.

Step 5 Using the project completion time as the latest finishing time for the last activity, work backwards through the network to compute the latest start and latest finish time for each activity.

Step 6 Compute the slack associated with each activity. The critical path activities are the activities with zero slack. *Slack* is defined as the length of time an activity can be delayed without affecting the completion date for the project. The amount of slack for each activity is computed as follows

$$Slack = LS - ES = LF - EF$$

where LS = latest starting time for a particular activity, ES = earliest start time for a particular activity, LF = latest finishing time for a particular activity and EF = earliest finish time for a particular activity (EF = ES + T; T = expected activity time for the activity).

Step 7 Use the variability in the activity times to estimate the variability of the project completion data; then, using this estimate, compute the probability of meeting a specified completion date.

Computer packages currently exist that carry out the steps of the PERT procedure, thus relieving the marketing manager from having to carry out the details of the technique using hand-calculation procedures.

PERT/cost

As you have seen, PERT and CPM concentrate on the time aspect of a project and provide information that can be used to schedule and control individual activities so that the entire project is completed on time. While project time and the meeting of a scheduled completion date are primary considerations for almost every project, there are many new-project development situations in which the cost associated with the project is just as important as time. In this section, we show how the technique referred to as PERT/cost can be used to help plan, schedule and control new-product development project costs. The ultimate objective of a PERT/cost system is to provide information that can be used to maintain project costs within a specified budget.

Planning and scheduling new-product development project costs

The budgeting process for a project usually involves identifying all costs associated with the project and then developing a schedule or forecast of when the costs are expected to occur. Then at various stages of project completion, the actual project costs incurred can be compared with the scheduled or budget costs. If actual costs are exceeding budgeted costs, corrective action may be taken to keep costs within the budget.

The first step in a PERT/cost control system is to break the entire project into components that are convenient in terms of measuring and controlling costs. While a PERT/CPM network may already show detailed activities for the project, we may find that these activities are too detailed for conveniently controlling project costs. In such cases, related activities that are under the control of one department (outside marketing research agency, etc.) are often grouped together to form what are referred to as *work packages*. By identifying costs of each work package, a marketing manager can use a PERT/cost system to help plan, schedule and control project costs.

In our discussion of the PERT/cost technique we will be treating each activity as a separate work package. Realise, however, that in large and complex projects we would almost always group related activities so that a cost-control system could be developed for a more reasonable number of work packages.

Problem

In order to illustrate the PERT/cost technique, let us consider the new-product development project network used by Scott Morton Ltd, as shown in Figure 5.5.

The company is assuming that each activity is an acceptable work package and that a detailed cost analysis has been made on an activity basis. The activity cost estimates, along with the expected activity times, are shown in Table 5.6. In using the PERT/cost technique the company is also assuming that activities (work packages) are defined such that costs occur at constant rate over the duration of the activity. For example, activity B (screening of new-product ideas), which shows an estimated cost of £30,000 and expected three-month duration, is assumed to have a cost rate of £300,000/3 = £10,000 per month. The cost rates for all activities are provided in Table 5.6. Note that the total estimated or budgeted cost for the new-product development project is £87,000.

Now let us assume that all activities begin at their earliest possible starting date. Using the monthly activity cost rates shown in Table 5.6 and the earliest start times, we can prepare the month-by-month cost forecast.

Provided the project progresses on its PERT or CPM time schedule, each activity will be started somewhere between its earliest and latest starting times. This implies that the total project costs should occur at levels between the earliest start and latest start costs schedules.

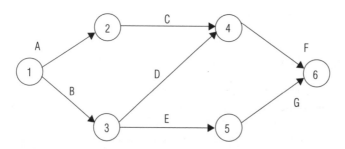

Figure 5.5 Scott Morton Ltd's new-product development project network.

Table 5.6 Activity time and cost estimates

Activity	Expected time (months)	Budgeted or estimated cost (£)	Budgeted cost per month (£)
A	2	10,000	5,000
B	3	30,000	10,000
C	1	3,000	3,000
D	3	6,000	2,000
E	2	20,000	10,000
F	2	10,000	5,000
G	1	8,000	8,000
Total project budget		87,000	

Questions

1 Using the expected activity times, compute the critical path and the resulting activity schedule for the project.
2 Develop a budget for the project that will show when costs should occur during the project duration (based on the calculated critical path) and prepare the month-by-month cost forecast. Assume that all activities are started at the earliest starting times.
3 Now calculate the budgeted total cost schedule (preparing again the month-by-month cost forecast) assuming that all activities are started at the latest starting times.

References and further reading

Jaffe, L. Berger, P. (1988), Impact on Purchase Intent of Sex-Role Identity and Product Positioning, *Psychology and Marketing*, fall, pp. 259–271.
Keller, Kevin Lane (2000), The Brand Report Card, *Harvard Business Review*, January–February.
Malcolm Gladwell (2000), *The Tipping Point*, New York: Little, Brown.
Nowlis, S. and Simmonson, I. (1996) The Effect of New Product Features on Brand Choice, *Journal of Marketing Research*, February, pp. 36–46.
Trout, Jack (1997), *The New Positioning: The Latest in the World's No 1 Business Strategy*, New York: McGraw-Hill.

6

Pricing

All profit organisations and many non-profit organisations set prices on their products or services. Price goes by many names:

Price is all around us. You pay *rent* for your apartment, *tuition* for your education and a *fee* to your physician or dentist. The airline, railway, taxi and bus companies charge you a *fare*; the local utilities call their price a *rate*; and the local bank charges you *interest* for the money you borrow. The price for driving your car on Florida's Sunshine Parkway is a *toll*, and the company that insures your car charges you a *premium*. The guest lecturer charges an *honorarium* to tell you about a government official who took a *bribe* to help a shady character steal *dues* collected by a trade associate. Clubs or societies to which you belong may make a special *assessment* to pay unusual expenses. Your regular lawyer may ask for a *retainer* to cover her services. The price of an executive is a *salary*, the price of a salesperson may be a *commission*, and the price of a worker is a *wage*. Finally, although economists would disagree, many of us feel that *income taxes* are the price we pay for the privilege of making money!

Throughout most of history, prices were set by buyers and sellers negotiating with each other. Sellers would ask for a higher price than they expected to receive, and buyers would offer less than they expected to pay. Through bargaining, they would arrive at a mutually acceptable price.

Traditionally, price has operated as the major determinant of buyer choice. And, although non-price factors have become more important in buyer behaviour in recent decades, price still remains one of the most important elements determining company market share and profitability. In fact, price has been experiencing considerable downward pressure in recent years. As consumers' real incomes stagnate or decline and they experience diminishing expectations, they shop more carefully, forcing retailers to lower their prices. Retailers in turn put pressure on manufacturers to lower their prices. The result is a marketplace characterised by heavy discounting and sales promotion.

Price is the only element in the marketing mix that produces revenue; the other elements produce costs. Price is also one of the most flexible elements of the marketing mix, in that it can be changed quickly, unlike product features and channel commitments. At the same time, pricing and price competition are the number-one problems facing many marketing executives. Yet many companies do not handle pricing well. The most common mistakes are these: pricing is too cost-orientated; price is not revised often enough to capitalise on market changes; price is set independent of the rest of the marketing mix rather than as an intrinsic element of market-positioning strategy; and the price is not varied enough for different product items, market segments and purchase occasions.

Companies handle pricing in a variety of ways. In small companies, prices are often set by top management rather than by marketing or salespeople. In large companies, pricing is typically handled by division and product-line managers. Even here, top management sets the general pricing objectives and policies and often approves the piece proposed by lower levels of management.

A firm must set a price for the first time when the firm develops or acquires a new product, when it introduces its regular product into a new distribution channel or geographical area, and when it enters bids on new contract work. The firm must decide where to position its product on quality and price.

Companies usually do not set a single price but rather a pricing structure that reflects variations in geographical demand and cost, market-segment requirements, purchase timing, order levels, delivery frequency, guarantees, service contracts and other factors. As a result of discounts, allowances and promotional support, a company rarely realises the same profit from each unit of a product that it sells. Here we will examine several price-adaptation strategies: geographical pricing price discounts and allowances, promotional pricing, discriminatory pricing and product-mix pricing.

After developing their pricing strategies, firms often face situations where they need to change prices. A price decrease might be brought about by excess plant capacity, declining market share, a desire to dominate the market through lower costs, or economic recession. A price increase might be brought about by cost inflation or over-demand. These situations may call for anticipatory pricing, delayed quotation pricing, escalator clauses, unbundling of goods and services, and reduction or elimination of discounts. There are also several alternatives to increasing price, including shrinking the amount of product instead of raising the price, substituting less expensive materials or ingredients, and reducing or removing product features. It is often difficult to predict how customers and competitors will react to a price change.

(M) *Problem 6.1* Determining price levels

Introductory comments

Whatever the pricing strategy and structure a company adopts, it ultimately has to arrive at price levels for specific items, target markets and periods. Such prices may be unilaterally specified by the company (fixed price levels), or may result from interactions between buyers and sellers. In this chapter we discuss methods for assessing fixed price levels, the basic principles of price negotiations, competitive bidding and then leasing.

FIXED LEVELS

To determine price levels, companies often make use of simple decision procedures that focus on one dimension of the pricing problem. We first discuss these simplified methods, and then touch on complex optimisation, simulation methods and price adjustments.

Simplified decision methods

Among the simplified decision procedures, cost-based methods are the most widely used approaches to pricing.

Cost-based methods have a common denominator: they start out from information on unit costs for the product, and take this as a 'floor' above which a pre-specified remuneration is charged by the company. In *mark-up* (MU) *pricing*, the company sets a price per unit equal to the cost per unit plus a pre-specified 'MU'. MUs are often specified as a percentage of unit cost, and vary widely between sectors and product categories. An alternative cost-based method is *target return pricing*. Here, the company starts out from a desired return on investment (ROI), and then calculates the premium to be charged over unit cost to realise this ROI. In *break-even pricing*, finally, the company computes the minimum price needed to cover fixed and variable costs (and, eventually, a pre-specified ROI) in view of the forecast demand level. Cost-plus pricing is used in a wide range of consumer and industrial settings, and is adopted by almost all retailers.

Competition-oriented rules of thumb concentrate on competitive price levels to determine the company's own price. The most simple procedure is that of *going rate pricing*, where the company simply aligns its own prices with those prevailing in the marketplace. A similar procedure is followed by some international companies, which try to maintain a 'global' competitive position by setting prices relative to competitors' price levels in each export market.

Demand-oriented methods take the customers' willingness to pay as the basis for pricing. A popular approach, especially in industrial settings, is *perceived-value pricing*. The basic idea is to set price in such a way that the ratio of perceived value to price for the company's product equals that of competitors. Perceived value can be calculated as a weighted average of the products' perceived attribute scores.

While the simplified pricing methods are extremely popular, they suffer from basic defects. Cost-plus pricing rules forgo the link between price and demand: they start out from estimated volume (and associated unit cost) to set price, but ignore the crucial impact that this price will have on ultimately realised volume. Competition-oriented approaches ignore differences in cost and demand between the company and its competitors. These methods rely upon the 'collective wisdom of the market', and their outcomes depend on the selection of competitors whose prices will be mirrored. Perceived-value pricing resolves some of these problems by allowing differences in perceived value to affect prices, yet it does so in a simplified manner. Multi-product and channel considerations, as well as market heterogeneity and dynamics, are ignored in each of the 'simplified' approaches discussed in this section.

Each of these procedures concentrates on one major environmental factor (cost, demand, competition), and basically ignores the others. As a result, each method separately yields only partial insights at best. At the same time, though, the approaches are complementary. Applied in combination they may provide an indication of the range of acceptable prices within which a specific price has to be selected.

Optimisation methods

Optimisation methods take on a different approach: they try to derive an optimal price level analytically or numerically. Optimisation methods start out with the specification and estimation of demand and cost functions. Occasionally, competitive and channel intermediary response functions are also formulated. Next, the pricing objective is identified. In a last step, optimal prices are derived using mathematical techniques. Optimisation methods can deal with a variety of complex situations. They can set prices for single products as well as product lines, and for single periods as well as multiple period sequences (trajectory models and optimal control theory). Competitive reactions and channel inter-dependencies (game theory) may be explicitly incorporated. Other complicating factors such as demand heterogeneity and uncertainty, asymmetric or limited information, and psychological effects can also be accounted for.

Yet in order to allow for analytical solutions, many optimisation methods rely on simplified models and assumptions. Others pursue numerical optima for less restrictive settings, but necessitate the use of extremely complex optimisation routines. In any of these approaches, one is confronted with the problem of a priori model specification. As pointed out by Kalyanam (1996): 'Demand functions are latent constructs whose exact parametric form is unknown. Estimates of price elasticities, profit maximising prices, etc. are conditional upon the parametric form employed in estimation. In practice, many forms maybe found that are not only theoretically plausible, but also consistent with the data, yet lead to different (optimal) pricing implications.' Solutions are currently suggested to reduce the impact of specification error, but none of these is widely applicable yet.

Simulation methods

Simulation methods are similar to optimisation methods, except that the price recommendations are obtained in a different fashion. No 'optimal' prices, but near-optimal or satisfying prices are derived from a comparison of alternative scenarios. Simulation methods are often used in combination with conjoint analysis, a technique for estimating 'utility' functions for existing or new products. Conjoint analysis is the basis for simulating demand in various price settings. Combined with cost functions, it can yield overall insights into profit implications of alternative price levels. Simulation may be applied to complex problems and settings. Yet, as for optimisation, simulation applied to comprehensive settings may become complex, and necessitate the collection of a large amount of information.

Price adjustments

While the previous methods, alone or in combination, help determine the appropriate amount to be charged to consumers, small adaptations may be needed to translate them into price levels. These adaptations are in line with practical requirements and originate from psychological pricing issues. In particular, principles of odd pricing and of price lining (the practice of using a limited number of price points to price products in a line) may be highly relevant here. As indicated earlier, both have psychological as well as practical implications, and therefore deserve managerial attention.

Problem

Illustration of cost-based pricing rules

A manufacturer of toothbrushes considers the following costs and demand level:

Production costs	£1,000,000	Fixed costs per month
	£20	Variable costs per unit
Expected demand	20,000 units	per month

1   To earn an MU of 20 per cent on price, the following unit price should be charged:

MU price = AC/(1 − MU)

MU is specified as a percentage of the selling price. Alternatively, MU can be defined as the margin by which price exceeds average costs (MU price = average cost × (1+MU)).

2   A target return of 8 per cent on investments (INV = £2,000,000) per month results in the following price level:

$$\text{Taret return price} = \text{AC} + \frac{\text{INV} \times \text{ROI}}{\text{Sales}}$$

3   The break-even price level at which total returns cover total costs, finally, equals:

Break-even price = total cost/sales

Questions

1   In the case example, if the manufacturer wishes to earn a MU of 20 per cent on price, what would be the unit price that should be charged?
2   What would be the resulting price level if the company wanted to achieve a target return of 8 per cent on investment?
3   Calculate the break-even price level at which total returns cover total costs.
4   Comment on the role of optimisation methods in the determination of price levels.

(M) *Problem 6.2* Perceived value pricing

Introductory comments

Price is the *value* that is placed on something. What is someone prepared to give in order to gain something else? Usually, price is measured in money, as a convenient medium of exchange that allows prices to be set quite precisely. This is not necessarily always the case, however. Goods and services may be bartered ('I will help you with the marketing plan for your car repair business if you service my car for me'), or there may be circumstances where monetary exchange is not appropriate, for example at election time when politicians make promises in return for your vote. Any such transactions, even if they do not directly involve money, are exchange processes and thus can use marketing principles. Price is any common currency of value to both buyer and seller.

Even money-based pricing comes under many names, depending on the circumstances of its use: solicitors charge fees; landlords charge rent; bankers charge interest; railways charge fares; hotels charge a room rate; consultants charge retainers; agents charge commission; insurance companies charge premiums; and over bridges or through tunnels tolls may be charged. Whatever the label, it is still a price for a good or a service, and the same principles apply.

Price does not necessarily mean the same things to different people, just because it is usually expressed as a number. You have to look beyond the price, at what it represents to both the buyer and the seller if you want to grasp its significance in any transaction. Buyer and seller may well have different perspectives on what price means. We now turn to that of the buyer.

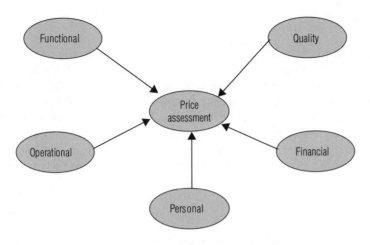

Figure 6.1 Factors influencing price assessment.

THE CUSTOMER'S PERSPECTIVE

From the buyer's perspective, price represents the value they attach to whatever is being exchanged. Up to the point of purchase, the marketer has been making promises to the potential buyer about what this product is and what it can do for that customer. The customer is going to weigh up those promises against the price and decide whether it is worth paying (Zeithaml, 1988).

In assessing price, the customer is looking specifically at the expected benefits of the product, as shown in Figure 6.1.

Functional

Functional benefits relate to the design of the product and its ability to fulfil its desired function. For example, a washing machine's price might be judged on whether it can handle different washing temperatures, operate economically and dry as well as wash.

Quality

The customer may expect price to reflect the quality level of the product (Erickson and Johannsson, 1985). Thus a customer may be prepared to pay more for leather upholstery in a car, or for solid wood furniture rather than veneer, or for hand-made Belgian chocolates rather than mass produced. Quality perceptions may be to do with the materials or components used in the product, as in these examples, or with the labour involved in making it. Quality may also, however, be a less tangible judgement made on the basis of corporate image. BMW, Heinz and Cadbury's are perceived as quality companies, and therefore they are perceived as producing quality products. The consumer can thus accept that those organisations might charge higher prices.

Operational

In organisational markets, price may be judged in relation to the product's ability to influence the production process. For example, a new piece of machinery might be assessed on its ability to increase productivity, make the production line more efficient or reduce the labour content of the finished goods. Even in a consumer market, operational issues might be considered. For instance, the purchase of a microwave oven increases the operational efficiency of the kitchen, both making it easier to cater for the staggered mealtimes resulting from the modern family's fragmented lifestyle, and giving the chief cook more time to pursue other interests.

Financial

Particularly in organisational markets, many purchases are seen as investments, and therefore the expected return on that investment is important in judging whether the price is worthwhile. New machinery, for example, is expected to pay for itself over time in terms of increased efficiency, output, labour saving, etc. Note that this judgement is made not only in terms of production outputs, but also in terms of long-term cost savings, efficiency gains and productivity improvements.

Personal

Personal benefit is a difficult category for the marketer to gauge, as it attempts to measure price against intangible, individual, psychological benefits such as status, comfort, self-image, etc. Some high-involvement products, such as perfumes, use high pricing deliberately as a means of amplifying the upmarket, sophisticated, exclusive images portrayed in their packaging, distribution and advertising strategies, thus increasing the status enhancement and 'feel good' factor of the purchase.

Remember too that organisational markets are not immune to the effects of personal factors. Purchasing can be influenced by the individual motivations of people involved and even by a desire to enhance a corporate self-image.

The problem is, of course, that different buyers put different values on different benefits. This endorses the need for market segmentation, which can begin to sort out groupings of like-minded customers so that appropriately tailored marketing mixes (including price) can be developed.

So far, it has been assumed that *price perceptions* and judgements of value are constant in the mind of the potential buyer. They are, however, variable according to circumstances. For example, a householder thinking of replacing water pipes would probably be very price sensitive and get quotes from a number of plumbers before making a decision. A burst pipe in the winter, however, would have that same householder paying almost any price to get a plumber round immediately. In any such distress purchase, the value placed on immediate problem solution justifies paying a *premium price*.

Another factor influencing price perception is scarcity. Where supply is severely limited and demand is high, prices can take on a life of their own and begin to spiral.

THE SELLER'S PERSPECTIVE

Price is a distinctive element of the marketing mix for the seller, because it is the only one that generates revenue. All the other elements represent outgoing costs. Price is also important, therefore, because it provides the basis of both recovering those costs and creating profit.

Profit = Total revenue – total cost,

when total revenue is the quantity sold multiplied by the unit price, and total cost represents the costs of producing, marketing and selling the product. Quantity sold is itself dependent on prices as well as on the other marketing mix elements. The motor industry has suggested that although a car dealership selling a large number of cars every year could well generate 80 per cent of its turnover from car sales, it is generating only just over one-third of its total profits from those sales. In comparison, the workshop might only generate 5 per cent of turnover, but 25 per cent of profit. This reflects the face that for some products, competitive pressures may keep margins tight. To increase profit in such areas, therefore, the organisation may have to find a way of either reducing the costs involved, or justifying higher prices.

The seller, however, must always take care to think about price from the perspective of the customer. In pure economic terms, it would be assumed that reducing a price would lead to higher sales because more people could afford that and want the product. A low price may be interpreted as making a negative statement about the product's quality, and a sudden reduction in price of an established product may be taken to mean that product's quality has been compromised in some way. Even petrol, the stereotypical homogeneous product, has been a victim of this.

Similarly, a high price may not always be a bad thing for a seller. If buyers equate price with quality (and in the absence of information or knowledge of the market, it may be the only indicator they pick up), then a higher price might actually attract customers. Part of the psychological benefit of the purchase for the customer might well be derived from its expense, for example in purchasing gifts where one feels obliged to spend a certain amount on the recipient either to fulfil social expectations or to signal affection. The higher the price, the more exclusive the market segment that is able to afford the product or service. Many more rail travellers, for example, choose to travel second class than in the higher-priced first-class accommodation.

The seller also needs to remember that sometimes the cost to the customer of purchasing a product can be much greater than its price. These broader considerations might have an inhibiting effect on purchase. A consumer buying a DVD player for the first time, for example, will not only look at the ticket price of the machine, but also weigh up the costs of replacing favourite video cassettes with discs. A business buying a new computer system has to consider the costs of transferring records, staff training and the initial decrease in productivity as they learn to find their way around the new system and the costs of installation (and of removing the old equipment). The whole marketing strategy for a product has to recognise the real old cost to the customer of accepting the offering and work to overcome such objections, whether through pricing, a better-tailored product offering or effective communication and persuasion.

Whatever type of market an organisation is in, whatever market segments it seeks to serve, it must always be aware that price can never stand apart from the other elements of the marketing mix. It interacts with those elements and must, therefore, give out signals consistent with those given by the product itself, place and promotion. Price is often quoted as a reason for not purchasing a product, but this reflects a tendency to use price as a scapegoat for other failings in the marketing mix. Price is a highly visible factor and at the point of purchase it hits the buyer where it hurts – in the pocket. As has been said before in this chapter, if the rest of the marketing mix has worked well up to the point of sale, then the price should not be too great an issue, because the buyer will have been convinced that the benefits supplied are commensurate with the price asked. Price is seen here as a natural, integrated element in harmony with the rest of the offering. It could be argued that a buyer who is wavering and uses price as the ultimate determinant of whether to purchase is either shopping in the wrong market segment or being ill served by sloppy marketing.

Example

The roller towel had been replaced by hot-air dryers and paper towels in many organisations' washrooms on the basis that these were cheaper, easier to service and more hygienic. The cotton towel industry has fought back, however, demonstrating that when consumables, transport, labour, dispenser costs and disposal are taken into account, the roller towel system can be up to 58 per cent cheaper to operate per month (Smith, 1994). Added to that, the industry has improved the design of roller dispenser cabinets and the laundering standards to overcome the poor hygiene image, and has proved that cotton is much more efficient and consistent at drying. In industries such as food processing, catering and pharmaceuticals where hygiene standards are becoming increasingly stringent, and in a world where environmental friendliness is a serious concern, it is not surprising that the combination of cost advantage and performance benefits found in cotton roller towels is irresistible!

Problem

Four companies W, X, Y and Z, produce electric can openers. Consumers were asked to allocate 100 points among the companies' products for each of four attributes. The results are shown below: (an average electric can opener sells for £20).

Importance Weight	Attribute	Company products			
		W	X	Y	Z
0.35	Durability	30	15	40	15
0.15	Attractiveness	20	20	30	30
0.25	Noiselessness	30	15	35	20
0.25	Safety	25	25	25	25

Questions

1   Comment on both the customer's and the seller's perspectives when dealing with the issue of perceived value pricing.

2 Discuss the elements of variability and continuity related to price perceptions in the mind of a potential buyer.
3 What should company W do about the pricing of its product if company Y charges £22?

(M) *Problem 6.3* Cash discounts

Introductory comments

A cash discount is a discount offered on the condition that the customer will repay the credit extended within a specified period of time. A cash discount is normally expressed as a percentage discount on the net amount of the cost of goods purchased (usually excluding freight and taxes). The length of the discount period is also specified when discount terms are offered. For example, credit terms of '2/10, net 30' mean that the customer can deduct 2 per cent of the invoice amount if payment is made within 10 days from the invoice date. If payment is not made by this time, the full invoice amount is due within 30 days from the invoice date (in some cases the discount period may begin with the date of shipment or the date of receipt by the customer). Like the length of the credit period, the cash discount varies among different lines of business.

Cash discounts are offered (or increased) in order to speed up the collection of accounts receivable and, by extension, reduce the company's level of receivables' investment and associated costs. Offsetting these savings or benefits is the cost of the discounts that are taken, which is equal to the lost pound revenues from the existing unit sales volume. The offering of a cash discount also may increase demand and sales, as some potential customers may view it as a form of price cut and be willing to purchase the product at this new, 'lower' price.

Problem

The Knoxville Record Co. is considering instituting a cash discount. The company currently sells to record distributors on credit terms of 'net 30' and wants to determine the effect on pretax profits of offering a 1 per cent cash discount on terms of '1/10, net 30'. The company's average collection period is now 50 days and is estimated to decrease to 28 days with the adoption of the 1 per cent cash-discount policy. It also is estimated that ~40 per cent of the company's customers will take advantage of the new cash discount. Knoxville's annual credit sales are £2,500,000, and the company's required pretax rate of return on receivables' investment is 20 per cent.

Questions

1 Develop an analysis of Knoxville's proposed cash-discount policy.
2 Calculate the earnings Knoxville expects to realise on the funds released by the decrease in receivables.

(A) *Problem 6.4* Predicting future pricing strategies using game theory

Introductory comments

As we all know, the competition in most industries does not come right out and indicate what strategies they will pursue. In most of these cases, managers have to use

171

subjective estimates based on the information previously collected and analysed. For example, Korean Steel has invested billions of dollars in the past few years to upgrade its flat-rolled steel facilities. Competitors were then able to forecast that this investment in highly efficient capacity would improve Korea's ability simultaneously to cut prices and protect margins.

One of the most useful approaches to forecasting competitors' possible actions is to simulate them. One can take existing data already collected, play the role of the competitor and develop competitor-action scenarios. When there are a small number of competitors, it is possible to use a combination of game theory and decision trees to predict competitive behaviour. To use these we assume that the objective of both firms is known and the same, such as annual profits.

GAME THEORY

Game theory is an approach to evaluating decision alternatives. Similar to statistical decision theory, it calls for identifying the decision alternatives, uncertain variables and the value of different outcomes. It differs from statistical decision theory in that the major uncertain variable is assumed to be a competitor, nature or some other force that is malevolent. The probability is 1.00 that each actor will do what is in its best interests. Consider the example in Figure 6.2. Given this game matrix, find the decision associated with the least bad outcome.

A toiletries manufacturer is trying to decide whether it should substantially improve the packaging of its line of deodorants. The managers of the company know that the competitor is also trying to make the same decision. The company estimates that if neither improves the packaging, neither will gain anything over the normal rate of profit. If the company changes the packaging of the product line and the competitor does not, the company will gain £20m over the competitor. We will assume the competitor loses £20m – that is, the gain to one company is a loss to the other. If the company does not improve the packaging of the line of deodorants and the competitor does, the company loses £10m. Finally, if they both change the packaging, the company gains £5m, and the competitor loses £5m, because the company is assumed to be better at package design.

| | | Competitor | |
		Keep old product package	Improve product packaging
Company	Keep old product package	£0	−£10m
	Improve product packaging	£20m	£5m

Figure 6.2 Game theory.

A solution is possible if we assume that both opponents will want to take the course of action that will leave them least badly off. Called the minimax regret criterion ('minimising the maximum loss'), it assumes that both opponents are conservative. This criterion would lead the company to prefer the package-improvement alternative. If it does not alter the packaging of the product, it might lose as much as £10m; if it does change the package, it will make at least £5m. The competitor would also prefer to change its packaging policy. If it does not change the product package, it might lose as much as £20m; if it does change the package, it cannot lose more than £5m. Hence both opponents will decide to change their product packages, which leads to a £5m gain for the company and a £5m loss for the competitor. Neither opponent can gain by switching unilaterally to a different strategy.

Problem

Air Nova, a small regional airline company, is planning a new pricing strategy for a route with a high passenger-load factor. For this particular decision-making situation, the company is examining two pricing alternatives: cut versus maintain current air fares.

Air Nova has calculated the profitability outcome to both market players – the company and its main competitor – as shown in Figure 6.3, which represents a 'game' between the two airline competitors.

Questions

1   Given the game matrix shown in Figure 6.3, find the decision associated with the least bad outcome.
2   Develop a decision tree depicting the situation where Air Nova moves first and the competitor responds, given the following estimated response probabilities (which were based on the competitor's analysis):

We cut prices	<	They cut prices = .9
		They maintain prices = .1
We maintain prices	<	They cut prices = .3
		They maintain prices = .7

Then compute the results of the two decisions.

	We cut prices	We maintain prices
They cut prices	Their profits/Our profits £30m £20m	Their profits/Our profits £240m £10m
They maintain prices	Their profits/Our profits £50m £180m	Their profits/Our profits £160m £100m

Figure 6.3 Air Nova's game theory illustration (pay-off matrix).

(A) *Problem 6.5* Price dispersion in online markets

Introductory comments

Pricing on the Internet has attracted much research attention (e.g. Bakos, 1997; Baye and Morgan, 2001; Brynjolfsson and Smith, 2000; Clemons et al., 2002; Degeratu, et al., 2000; Erevelles et al., 2001; Pan et al., 2001; Shankar et al., 2001; Smith and Brynjolfsson, 2001; Smith et al., 2000). The themes of much of the research have centred on whether price dispersion or price sensitivity is higher online than it is offline or on the drivers of price dispersion. *Price dispersion* refers to the distribution of prices of an item with the same measured characteristics across sellers, as an indication by measures such as range and standard deviation of prices.

It has been hypothesised that the online medium and the Internet lower search costs, make more price information available to buyers and electronic markets more competitive than conventional markets (Bakos, 1997). If electronic markets are highly competitive, we might expect price dispersion to be absent from these markets. This is because price dispersion is thought to be associated with incomplete information (e.g. Carlson and McAfee, 1983; Stigler, 1961), and buyers with low search costs should not face this in electronic markets.

Contrary to this expectation, however, Bailey (1998), Clemons et al. (2002) and Brynjolfsson and Smith (2000) have all found that price dispersion in electronic markets is substantial and no narrower than in conventional markets. That is, electronic markets offer the right information about prices of competing offerings at low search costs, and this should lead to greater price competition in these markets than offline markets. However, these studies did not control the possibility that the observed price dispersion is because of differences in the services offered by different e-tailers.

In the next section, we formulate economic models of price dispersion based on product differentiation, search costs and incomplete information.

MODELS OF PRICE DISPERSION

Much prior research on online price dispersion has been empirical. In contrast, we first propose an analytical model of online price dispersion based primarily on two theories – (1) product differentiation and (2) search costs and incomplete information – and follow this model with an empirical analysis.

Price dispersion due to product/service differentiation

As noted by Betancourt and Gautschi (1993), the value of an item bought from a retailer depends on a variety of distribution services, such as assortment, accessibility, ambience, availability of information and assurance of product delivery. These services provide value either by lowering the cost of acquiring items at retail (Ratchford and Stoops, 1998) or by lowering the cost of household production (Betancourt and Gautshci, 1993). These services have electronic counterparts, such as convenience of findings and navigating the web site, reliability of order fulfilment and convenience of returns, availability of information and quality of shipping.

Because these services add value or provide utility to the consumer, we can write the utility of any item bought from a given retailer or e-tailer as $U(x, s_1, \ldots, s_k)$, where x refers to a vector of attributes of the good and s_i refers to utility-providing service feature i. Rosen (1974) showed that if consumers are perfectly informed, the textbook model of perfect competition can be extended to the case in which consumers have different valuations of the various attributes $x, s_1, \ldots, s_k$ and producers have different costs of supplying $x, s_1, \ldots, s_k$. If we assume that producers and consumers act independently about how much to buy and how much to sell, then the key outcome of all of the independent decisions of producers and consumers is a functional relationship between prices and attributes of the following form:

$$p_j = p(x, s_{1j}, \ldots, s_{kj}),$$

where p_j refers to the price of the e-tailer or retailer j. The relationship in the above equation is often called the *hedonic price function*. If all attributes are measured correctly, the correct functional form is chosen, and if information is perfect, Rosen's (1974) model predicts and exact functional relationship between the prices of different retailers or e-tailers for a given item and the services that they provide with the item. Thus, price dispersion in this model is completely explained by differences in service offerings. Moreover, the model predicts that services that are positively valued will have positive signs in the hedonic relationship.

In practice, however, measurement errors and omitted attributes are likely to keep the estimated relationship between prices and service levels for a given item across e-tailers from being perfect. However, given a reasonably complete list of attributes, we should expect a high R^2 value and a small standard error from estimates of the equation if the status of information availability in a market is perfect or close to it.

Price dispersion due to search costs and incomplete information

The explanation of price dispersion as a result of incomplete information has a long tradition and dates back to the classic study by Stigler (1961). Subsequent studies have modelled price dispersion as an equilibrium outcome when some consumers find it too costly to locate the lowest price offered in a market (Burdett and Coles, 1997; Burdett and Judd, 1983; Carlson and McAfee, 1983; Salop and Stiglitz, 1982). Among these studies, the Carlson and McAfee (1983) model is perhaps the most insightful and easy to calibrate empirically (see Dahlby and West, 1986 for an empirical application). Carlson and McAfee defined a search as an inspection of one alternative and assumed that consumers search sequentially until the marginal cost of an additional search is more than the marginal gain. Carlson and McAfee also showed that if there is a distribution of search costs across consumers and if sellers also have different costs, price dispersion will be an equilibrium outcome. Price dispersion will increase if the highest search cost increases and if the distribution of search costs across consumers becomes more dispersed. The other studies of equilibrium price dispersion listed above obtain qualitatively similar results in which price dispersion results from differences in buyer search costs and the consequent differences in incentives to locate the lowest price.

Testing the explanations

Combining the two theories of price dispersion, we can write the price of an item sold by e-tailer j as

$$P_j = p(x, s_{1j}, \ldots, s_{kj}) + e_j + v_j,$$

where e_j is unmeasured service attributes that are specific to e-tailer j, v_j is idiosyncratic differences in price charged by j because of differences in cost or pricing policy, and the mean values of e and v are assumed to be 0. In a world with perfect information, v_j must be 0 because consumers would buy only at the lowest price for their preferred level of service, forcing all e-tailers to charge the same price.

If one can measure all the relevant service attributes and capture the functional form of the relationship between prices and attributes, we can make $e_j \to 0$.

Thus, if we denote the estimated price in a regression of price on service attributes as $\hat{p}_j = \hat{p}(x, s_{1j}, \ldots, s_{kj})$, we can define the *quality-adjusted* price as

$$p_j - \hat{p}_j \approx \hat{v}_j$$

Computing the variance of $\hat{v}_j$, $V(\hat{v}_j)$ across the sample of j e-tailers would provide a measure of pure price dispersion net of the effects of service quality. If v_j and $p(x, s_{1j}, \ldots, s_{kj})$ are independent, $\hat{v}_j$ will be an unbiased estimate of v_j, and $V(\hat{v}_j)$ will be an unbiased estimate of price dispersion. If they are not independent, the regression of prices on service attributes will explain some of the variance of v_j, leading $V(\hat{v}_j)$ to underestimate the true price dispersion. Thus, $V(\hat{v}_j)$ will be a conservative estimate of price dispersion after controlling for the effects of service quality. If this is found to be large after controlling for the effects of retail services on prices, one can conclude that imperfect information must be present in the corresponding market.

Market knowledge of the product or popularity of the item does not seem to have significant effects on e-tailer prices, but prices at pure-play e-tailers appear to be equal to or lower than those at bricks-and-clicks e-tailers, after controlling for e-tailer service quality for a majority of the categories. Pure-play e-tailers may charge less than bricks-and-clicks e-tailers because their awareness may be lower and because they may not offer consumers the opportunity to physically inspect, pick up or return an item.

Since e-tailer service attributes do not explain much of price dispersion, other factors such as online trust and brand may explain price dispersion and allow e-tailers to command price premiums. For example, an e-tailer with a stronger brand name and a more trusted web site (site that is perceived as more competent, easier to do business with, better protects privacy and offers better security of transactions) may be able to charge higher prices than one with a weaker brand and less-trusted site. Thus, online trust could be related to prices as well. Managers may want to focus attention on the role of online trust in pricing.

Citibank offers cheap loans

Citibank is offering the cheapest personal loans available in the UK in 20 years in a move that will increase pressure on banks and building societies to reduce their unsecured lending rates. The rates offered by Citibank, which has only three branches in the UK and operates mainly as a telephone bank, start at 13.9 per cent for loans of £3,000 but its cheapest rate is for large loans of £15,000 or more where the rate is 7.9 per cent. According to data provider MoneyFacts, the next cheapest lenders are Tesco, Royal Bank of Scotland Direct and First Direct – all non-traditional players in the banking industry. Citibank, which is based in the US, has 100,000 current account customers in the UK but aims, with the introduction of cheap loans, to widen its appeal beyond wealthy international professionals. About 20 per cent of new Citibank customers are opening accounts via the Internet. *Source*: *Financial Times* (17 July 1999)

Have a Cigar (Or A Beanie Baby, Or Some Erotica?)

Cigars are less easy to find on the Internet than Beanie Babies. At least, that's the opinion of Jango, the Internet shopping agent from Excite Shopping. On 5 August 1999 we searched for the best-value Arturo Fuente Brevas Royale cigars on the Web. Jango could only find two online retailers that sold them: Cigar Express and The Cigar Box. Beanie Babies were a different matter altogether. Although we specifically told Jango that he had to find the cheapest *Scoop the Pelican* beanie baby, it was no problem to our digital shopping assistant. Within seconds Jango returned with 353 results from a variety of Internet classified advertising sites and online auctions. For $7.00 we could purchase Scoop from one of Yahoo's classified advertisements. Alternatively we could choose from a variety of auctions, including 19 different Yahoo! auctions, all of which were due to start within eight hours. Guide prices range from $3.00 up to $9.00, the highest prices being reserved for Scoops with free heart-shaped tag protectors or similar value-added paraphernalia. If we were in a hurry, the online auction house eBay had an auction starting within six minutes and, yes, there was a *Scoop the Pelican* going for $9.99.

To go with the cigar and the beanie baby, some soothing music, perhaps? This time, we asked MySimon if he could find Madonna's Erotica CD (there's no accounting for taste). MySimon was almost as efficient as Jango, returning quickly with 73 results from 42 different merchants, including Amazon.com, Compact Disc Connection, Border.com, BestPrices.com, and even Wal-Mart. BestPrices.com even offered a choice between the clean version and the stickered version of the CD. Unfortunately, it was out of our price range at over $14.99. Eventually we settled for Amazon's offer of shipping within 24 hours for a mere $12.99.

All in all, a good evening's shopping. Now, where's that cigar? *Source*: O'Connor and Galvin (5 August 1999).

Questions

1　Define the concept of price dispersion.
2　What happens to price dispersion if the highest searcsh cost increases and if the distribution of search costs across consumers becomes dispersed?
3　What is the equation which defines the quality-adjusted price?
4　Why is it that pure-play e-tailers may change less than bricks-and-clicks e-tailers?

References and further reading

Ackerman, D. and Tellis, G. (2001), Can Culture Affect Prices? A Cross-Cultural Study of Shopping and Retail Price, *Journal of Retailing*, Vol. 77 pp. 57–82.

Cooper, R. and Kaplan, R. (1991), Profit Priorities from Activity-Based Costing, *Harvard Business Review*, May–June, pp. 130–135.

Erickson, G.M. and Johanson, J. (1985), The Role of Price in Multi-Attribute Product-Evaluations, *Journal of Consumer Research*, September, pp. 195–199.

Monroe, Kent B., (1973), Buyers' Subjective Perceptions of Price, *Journal of Marketing Research*, February, pp. 70–80.

Rajendran, K. and Tellis, G. (1994), Contextual and Temporal Components of Reference Price, *Journal of Marketing*, January, pp. 22–34.

7

Integrated Marketing Communication

Corporate communication is aimed at the public via a variety of interactive tools. These include corporate advertising, corporate publicity, public affairs, government relations and lobbying activities, issues management, city and analyst relations, and corporate sponsorship. The aim of such activities is to support and underpin image and identity.

Integrated communication at the corporate level implies that relationships with each of these public or groups need to be managed in a pluralistic, interactive manner and with a long-term relationship marketing perspective in mind:

1   Integrated communication, similar to marketing, needs to be *managed*. It is preceded by a sound understanding of the dynamic(s) of each public. Relationships have to be *planned*, then *implemented, monitored* and *adjusted* when necessary. This implies that different marketplaces may require different approaches and different strategic alliances and relationships while not losing sight of the strategic imperative for a globalised approach. Integrated communication is driven by the long term and the strategic vision. The process in not short term, or ad hoc. Reactive firefighting may occasionally be necessary but must always return to the strategic imperative.
2   Integrated communication is not about one activity. It is diverse in nature and may involve singular or multiple deployment of elements of the corporate communication arsenal.
3   It is not one-way communication but is two-way, interactive and aimed at mutual benefit. Thus it is concerned with identifying, establishing and maintaining relationships with various publics *nationally, regionally, internationally* and *globally*. These relationships pre-suppose regular monitoring of awareness, attitudes and behaviour inside and outside an organisation.
4   Publics able to impact organisational performance are not singular (i.e. consumers) but plural. This means analysing and adjusting corporate and marketing policies in line with public interests and with the concomitant focus on organisational survival and growth in a globalised market.

Integrated marketing communication (IMC) was the major communication development in the last decade of the twentieth century. Just as businesses do not spring full-blown into the arena as global combatants, businesses do not suddenly decide to become integrated. More and more firms are considering communication the key competitive advantage of marketing per se, and we agree with them.

IMC is a concept of marketing communication planning that recognises the added value of a comprehensive plan that evaluates the strategic role of a number of communication disciplines (e.g. general advertising, direct response, sales promotion and public relations) and combines these disciplines to provide clarity, consistency and maximum communication impact.

IMC itself has been evolving with input from academics and practitioners around the world. A more succinct definition for the twenty-first century is suggested by Schultz and Kitchen (2000):

IMC is a strategic business process used to plan, develop, execute and evaluate coordinated measurable, persuasive brand communication programs over time with consumers, customers, prospects, and other targeted, relevant external and internal audiences.

This definition first focuses on strategy – a strategy of communication that is clearly related to corporate mission, values and needs, but relates equally to brand mission, values and needs. At both levels executives will need to develop resonance and consonance in terms of brand identity.

Executives need to know the return on investment from any communication activity. For each delineated audience measurable outcomes need to be specified in advance. Also crucial will be an understanding of what is persuasive.

Integrated marketing communication offers you a way to meld image and brand meaning into a unified message – but it takes strategic and financial commitment to realise the potential of IMC.

(A) *Problem 7.1* Media selection

Introductory comments

Selecting media in which to place advertising is one of the most important decisions of a media plan. A number of preliminary decisions have to be made before media can be selected. The following is the approximate order of decisions that usually are made, and which lead to the selection process:

1   Devise media objectives:

- Select demographic targets.
- Check creative strategy for guidance in selecting media classes.
- Determine media budget.
- Set reach, frequency, and GRP goals for the total media plan.
- Set other media objectives.

2   Devise media strategy.
3   Media selection process begins here.

Contained in the decisions listed above, were certain terms that must be explained as follows:

1   Media: means broad classes of vehicles such as TV, newspapers, magazines, radio, etc.
2   Vehicles: (also called media vehicles). These are specific carriers of ads. For example, *Time* magazine is a vehicle and so is a Football League game, or the 11 pm news, or any TV programme.
3   Reach: means the number of target audiences exposed at least once to vehicles in a media plan. A 'reached' audience is also called 'unduplicated' because it is only counted as exposed, only once. We can say that the 11 pm news had a reach of 17.4 per cent of men aged 18–49. This means that 17.4 per cent of all men aged 18–49 were exposed once to a telecast of that news. At times the planner might want to know the number of times that an audience saw the same TV programme more than once in a month, and therefore would use a different measurement called 'frequency'.

- When reach is expressed as a percentage, the base on which it is calculated is the target market size. Example: If there are 5 million targets of a certain age in the country and the vehicles selected reach 2.5 million in a month, we would say that those vehicles had a 50 per cent reach.
- Finally, it is important to remember that reach is based on exposure to media vehicles, not ads in those vehicles. Of course there is an assumption that those who see the vehicles also will have an opportunity to see the ads.

4   Gross rating points (GRPs): any time we add TV ratings or reaches we have GRPs. Gross rating points means 'duplicated exposures' as contrasted with reach, which represents unduplicated exposures to vehicles. Here is an example: If a TV programme had an average weekly rating of 20, and it was broadcast four times a month, then we would simply multiply 20 times four for a GRP total of 80. GRPs are duplicated exposures.

5   Frequency: the average number of times an audience of vehicles in a media plan were exposed. Therefore, this is a measure of exposure repetition to vehicles. The formula for frequency is: GRPs divided by reach. Example: If the GRPs of the programme (mentioned above) were 80 per month, and the four-week reach were 40, then the average four-week frequency would be 2. The '2' means that the audience see that programme an average of 2 times a month.

6   Cost per thousand: this is a formula for comparing the cost efficiency of one or more vehicles with other vehicles. If there are two or more groups of vehicles that are being compared, and one of them has a lower cost per thousand than the other, then the lower CPM group is usually considered to be the most cost-efficient. The formula for CPM was given previously.

THE SELECTION PROCESS

The process begins with a search for all media vehicles that contain large numbers of target audiences in them, and at the same time meet the requirements of other media objectives. While each vehicle has its own reach, it is necessary to find the net, or combined, reach of various vehicle combinations in order to learn which combination meets the reach goal set in the objectives. Remember that the net reach represents unduplicated exposures.

To find the net reach, one has to use a formula, of which there are many to choose from. Also, computer companies such as Interactive Market Systems (IMS) have their own formulae for calculating the net reach of a combination of vehicles (which they sell to the public).

After the net reach is calculated, the planner usually checks to see whether that group of vehicles met the reach goal. Then the planner also checks to see whether that group of vehicles is the most cost-efficient. Are there some other combinations of vehicles that are more cost-efficient?

Ultimately a planner would like to find the group of vehicles that provide the most reach at the lowest cost per thousand. When that group is found, it must then be checked to see that other media objectives also have been met. When they have, a major part of the media selection process is finished.

There are other ways to select media vehicles, but the one described above is often used. The selection process consists of evaluating vehicles on the basis of meeting objectives and strategies which serve as constraints in decision making.

Problem – example

Assume that the target market is women aged 18–49. Also assume that the creative strategy requires both the use of television and magazines for the copy that will be written. The marketing strategy calls for national coverage because the product is distributed nationally. A planner may then set a reach goal of 65° a frequency goal of 1.2, and a GRP level of 78 per month (65 × 1.2 = 78). A budget of £195,000 may also have been set for one month.

Assume that the following list of network TV programmes and magazines was tentatively selected on the basis of their power to reach targets of women aged 18–49.

Vehicles	Reach of women 18–49	Per cent of targets reached	Cost per page or 30-second commercial
Network programme A	12,000,000[a]	23.6	£65,000
Network programme B	14,500,000[a]	2B.5	£70,000
Magazine C	16,000,000	31.5	£60,000
Magazine D	14,000,000	27.5	£55,000

Note
[a] 1 telecast a month (base of women aged 18–49: 50,850,000).

Step 1 Assume that the planner believes that it will only take three vehicles to attain the reach goal. Therefore, he chooses to examine only three of the four vehicles: A, B and C. The planner now calculates the net reach of the three formula. The following formula provides a very quick, but rough estimate of the net reach of the vehicles A, B and C. Here is the formula:

$$\text{Reach of } n \text{ vehicles} = 100.0 - (100.0 - R_1)(100.0 - R_2)(100.0 - R_n)$$

where R_1 = percentage reach of vehicle 1.
    To calculate the net reach:

1   First, subtract each reach from 1.000. (*Note*: We converted percentages to decimal form).

   A = .764 (1.000 − .236 = .764)

   B = .715 (1.000 − .285 = .715)

   C = .685 (1.000 − .315 = .685)

2   Multiply subtracted numbers: .764 × .715 × .685 = .374
3   Finally, subtract the product from 1.000, which results in a net reach of 62.6° (1.000 − .374 = .626).

Step 2 Evaluate the net reach. Is it adequate? The planner would now compare the 62.6° reach with the 65 per cent goal and find it inadequate. Perhaps if vehicle D were substituted for A, the net reach might be large enough to meet the 65 per cent goal requirement. All four vehicles could have been used, but this would substantially raise the cost.
    Recalculating the net reach of vehicles B, C and D, we find the new net reach to be 64.5 per cent (or 65 per cent) – enough to meet our goal (.715 × .685 × .725 = .355, and 1.000 − .355 = .645). We now have met our first goal.
    Step 3 Find the frequency by first finding the GRPs of this group of vehicles as follows: add the reaches of B, C and D:

   Add reaches: (B) 28.5 + (C) 31.5 + (D) 27.5 = 87.5 GRPs

Now calculate frequency as follows:

$$\frac{87.5 \text{ GRPs}}{64.5 \text{ reach}} = 1.4$$

Since the goal was a 1.2 frequency, the three-vehicle frequency meets a second goal. A third goal also was met when the GRP level of 87.5 was attained. The goal was 78 GRPs.

Step 4 Convert reach percentages to raw numbers (called gross impressions) in order to calculate CPMs, as follows:

Vehicle B = .285 × 50,850,000 = 14,492,000

Vehicle C = .315 × 50,850,000 = 17,798,000

Vehicle D = .275 × 50,850,000 = 3,984,000

Step 5 Calculate cost per thousand (CPMs) of the three-vehicle group.

Vehicles	Cost	Audience delivered
B	£70,000	14,492,000
C	£60,000	17,798,000
D	£55,000	13,984,000
Total	£185,000	46,274,000

CPM = £185,000 × 1000 .44,500,000 = £4.00

Step 6 Compare the B, C, D group with another group of vehicles (not shown) which have a £6.00 CPM and the same reach as B, C, D. Such a comparison would lead the planner to reject the latter group in favour of the former. The selection process is now finished and open for inspection by management (assuming all other criteria have been met).

Assume that you are the media planner and are faced with the same problem and constraints as described in the example shown on the previous pages. The only differences are that you have different reach and frequency goals as follows: reach needed is 75 per cent and frequency needed is 1.6 (GRPs obviously will be 120). Also you will have more money to spend than the planner had in the example. You will have a £375,000 budget for a month.

The vehicles that you may use are shown below (E, F, G, H). You may use any or all of those vehicles. They have the following reaches and costs:

Vehicles	Reach of women 18–49	Per cent reached	Cost per page or 30-second commercial
Network programme E	10,000,000	19.7	£60,000
Network programme F	18,000,000	35.4	£90,000
Magazine G	20,000,000	40.0	£120,000
Magazine H	10,000,000	26.0	£80,000

Note: Base of women aged 18–49 = 50,850,000.

Questions

1   The problem is this: For a maximum of £375,000 for one month only, which vehicles should you choose from among the four choices that will attain the objective listed above?

2   Show your answers in the following spaces:

   a   Names of vehicles chosen _____

   b   Cost per thousand of the chosen group _____

   c   Reach of the chosen group _____

   d   Frequency....... GRPs _____

   e   Show your calculations here for each of the answers listed above:

3   Suppose that you had to compare your media package in Question 1, with the medial package of vehicles shown in the earlier example (vehicles B, C and D). Which package would you select and why?

(I) *Problem 7.2* Effective reach

Introductory comments

GROSS RATINGS POINTS

The media buyer typically uses a numerical indicator to know how many potential audience members may be exposed to a series of commercials. A summary measure that combines the programme rating and the average number of times the home is reached during this period (frequency of exposure) is a commonly used reference point known as *gross ratings points* (GRP):

$$\text{GRP} = \text{reach} \times \text{frequency}$$

GRPs are based on the total audience the media schedule may reach; they use a duplicated reach estimate.

As marketers have budget constraints, they must decide whether to increase reach at the expense of frequency or increase the frequency of exposure but to a smaller audience. A number of factors influence this decision. For example, a new product or brand introduction will attempt to maximise reach, particularly unduplicated reach, to create awareness in as many people as possible as quickly as possible. At the same time, for a high-involvement product or one whose benefits are not obvious, a certain level of frequency is needed to achieve effective reach.

Effective reach represents the percentage of a vehicle's audience reached at each effective frequency increment. This concept is based on the assumption that one exposure to an ad may not be enough to convey the desired message. No one knows the exact number of exposures necessary for an ad to make an impact, although advertisers have settled on three as the minimum. Effective reach (exposure) is shown in the shaded area in Figure 7.1 in the range of 3–10 exposures. Fewer than 3 exposures is considered insufficient reach, while more than 10 is considered overexposure and thus ineffective reach. This exposure level is no guarantee of effective communication; different messages may require more or fewer exposures. For example, Jack Myers, president of Myers Reports, argues that the three-exposure theory was valid in the 1970s when consumers were exposed to approximately 1,000 ads per day. Now that they are exposed to 3,000 to 5,000 per day, three exposures may not be enough. Adding in the fragmentation of television, the proliferation

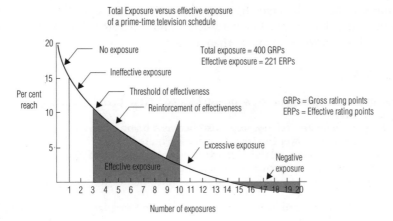

Figure 7.1 Graph of effective reach.

of magazines, and the advent of a variety of alternative media leads Myers to believe that 12 exposures may be the *minimum* level of frequency required. Also, Jim Surmanek, vice-president of International Communications Group, contends that the complexity of the message, message length and recency of exposure also impact this figure.

As they do not know how many times the viewer will actually be exposed, advertisers typically purchase GRPs that lead to more than three exposures to increase the likelihood of effective reach and frequency.

Problem

Determining effective reach is further complicated by the fact that when calculating GRPs, advertisers use a figure that they call *average frequency*, or the average number of times the target audience reached by a media schedule is exposed to the vehicle over a specified period. The problem with this figure is revealed in the following scenario:

Consider a media buy in which: 50 per cent of audience is reached 1 time; 30 per cent of audience is reached 5 times; 20 per cent of audience is reached 10 times; average frequency = 4.

In this media buy, the average frequency is 4, which is slightly more than the number established as effective. Yet a full 50 per cent of the audience receives only one exposure. Thus, the average frequency number can be misleading, and using it to calculate GRPs might result in underexposing the audience.

Although GRPs have their problems, they can provide useful information to the marketer. A certain level of GRPs is necessary to achieve awareness, and increases in GRPs are likely to lead to more exposures and/or more repetitions – both of which are necessary to have an effect on higher-order objectives. Perhaps the best advice for purchasing GRPs is offered by Ostrow, who recommends the following strategies:

1   Instead of using average frequency, the marketer should decide what minimum frequency goal is needed to reach the advertising objectives effectively and then maximise reach at that frequency level.
2   To determine effective frequency, one must consider marketing factors, message factors and media factors.

In summary, the reach-versus-frequency decision, while critical, is very difficult to make. A number of factors must be considered, and concrete rules do not always apply. The decision is often more of an art than a science.

Marketing factors

- *Brand history* Is the brand new or established? New brands generally require higher frequency levels.
- *Brand share* An inverse relationship exists between brand share and frequency. The higher the brand share, the lower the frequency level required.
- *Brand loyalty* An inverse relationship exists between loyalty and frequency. The higher the loyalty, the lower the frequency level required.
- *Purchase-cycles* Shorter purchasing cycles require higher frequency levels to maintain top-of-mind awareness.
- *Usage cycle* Products used daily or more often need to be replaced quickly, so a higher level of frequency is desired.
- *Competitive share of voice* Higher frequency levels are required when a lot of competitive noise exists and when the goal is to meet or beat competitors.
- *Target group* The ability of the target group to learn and to retain messages has a direct effect on frequency.

Message or creative factors

- *Message complexity* The simpler the message, the less frequency required.
- *Message uniqueness* The more unique the message, the lower the frequency level required.
- *New versus continuing campaigns* New campaigns require higher levels of frequency to register the message.
- *Image versus product sell* Creating an image requires higher levels of frequency than does a specific product sell.
- *Message variation* A single message requires less frequency; a variety of messages requires more.
- *Wearout* Higher frequency may lead to wearout. This effect must be tracked and used to evaluate frequency levels.
- *Advertising units* Larger units of advertising require less frequency than smaller ones to get the message across.

Media factors

- *Clutter* The more advertising that appears in the media used, the more frequency is needed to break through the clutter.
- *Editorial environment* The more consistent the ad is with the editorial environment, the less frequency is needed.
- *Attentiveness* The higher the level of attention achieved by the media vehicle, the less frequency is required. Low-attention-getting media require more repetitions.
- *Scheduling* Continuous scheduling requires less frequency than does flighting or pulsing.
- *Number of media used* The fewer media used, the lower the level of frequency required.
- *Repeat exposures* Media that allow for more repeat exposures (e.g. monthly magazines) require less frequency.

Questions

1 Comment on the given media buy scenario.
2 Discuss the specific GRPs measure in this case.
3 Critically introduce two marketing factors, two message or creative factors and two media factors which might be used to determine effective frequency.

(M) *Problem 7.3* Audience measures in broadcast media

Introductory comments

There are numerous terms rating services and media planners used to define a television or radio station's audience, penetration and efficiency. We will discuss some of these before examining some procedures used to buy television or radio time. TV households (TVHH) refers to the number of households that own television sets. For example, in the USA ~70 million households (over 98 per cent if all households) own television sets. By looking at the number of households that own TVs in a particular market we can gain a sense of the size of that market. Similarly, by looking at the number of TVHH tuned into a particular programme, we can obtain a sense of how popular the programme is and how many people our commercial is likely to reach.

The percentage of homes in a given area that have one or more TV sets turned on at any particular time is expressed as households using TV (HUT). If there are 1,000 TV sets in the survey area and 500 are turned on, the HUT figure is 50 per cent.

We are all familiar with TV shows that have been cancelled because their ratings slipped. What does that really mean? The percentage of TVHH in an area that are tuned in to a specific programme is called the programme rating:

$$\text{Rating} = \frac{\text{Number tuned into specific station}}{\text{TVHH}}$$

The networks are interested in high ratings because that is a measure of a show's popularity. If a show is not popular, advertisers will not want to advertise on it and a network's revenue will decrease. Similarly, local stations often make changes in their local news shows in order to increase their popularity and thereby, their ratings.

The percentage of homes that have sets in use (HUT) tuned in to a specific programme is called the programme's share of audience. A programme with only 50 viewers could have a 50 per cent share if only 100 sets are turned on. For that reason the programme ratings' figures are important because they measure the audience as a percentage of all TV households in the area, regardless of whether the TV set is on or off.

The total number of homes reached by some portion of a programme is referred to as total audience. This figure is normally broken down to determine audience composition (the distribution of audience into demographic categories).

Gross rating points

In television, gross rating points (GRPS) are the total weight of a media schedule against TVHH. For example, a weekly schedule of five commercials with an average household rating of 20 would yield 100 GRPS, or a total audience equivalent to the total number of TVHH in the area.

To give another example, a company determined that a schedule of 50 GRPS per week would be sufficient at the beginning of its television campaign. This might have been accomplished by buying 10 spots with an average rating of 5 or only 2 spots with an average rating of 25. The latter might have been feasible by using a highly rated prime-time programme, but then the frequency would have been very low. So the company opted to use the late evening newscasts, which had lower ratings against total TVHH but higher shares of those adults watching; it also afforded the company the ability to gain frequency.

The results of the company's decision demonstrated the wisdom of its choice. In key markets where the commercials ran, surveys were taken and the number of respondents who looked on the company as an attractive investment alternative increased by 20 per cent – to more than 60 per cent total. In control markets where the company's commercials did not air, the company's image remained virtually unchanged.

Selecting programmes for buys

To determine which shows to buy, the media buyer must select the most efficient ones in relation to the target audience. To do this, a simple computation is made of the cost per rating point (CPP) and the cost per thousand (CPM) for each programme, as follows:

$$CPP = \frac{Cost}{Rating} \qquad CPM = \frac{Cost}{Thousands\ of\ people}$$

Obviously, the lower the cost per thousand, the more efficient the show is against the target audience. The media buyer's task, therefore, is to compare the packages of each station, substituting stronger programmes for less efficient ones. The media buyer has to use the best areas each station has to offer to construct suitable packages.

Buying radio time requires a basic understanding of radio terminology. Naturally, much of the language used for radio advertising is the same as that used for other media. But radio also has numerous terms that are either peculiar to it or have a special meaning when applied to radio advertising.

The most common of these are the concepts of dayparts, average quarter-hour audiences and cumes (cumulative audiences).

Dayparts

The radio day is divided into five basic dayparts:

> 6 am to 10 am – morning drive
> 10 am to 3 pm – daytime
> 3 pm to 7 pm – afternoon (or evening) drive
> 7 pm to 12 am – night-time
> 12 am to 6 am – all night

The rating services measure the audiences for only the first four of these dayparts, because all-night listening is very limited and not highly competitive.

The heaviest radio use occurs during drive times (6–10 am and 3–7 pm) during the week (Monday–Friday). One exception to this is that easy listening (or 'good' music) stations traditionally have their heaviest use during daytime (10 am–3 pm). Otherwise, drive time is radio's prime time. This is important to advertising because usage and consumption vary for different products. Television advertising in prime time, for example, is seen when viewers are least likely to consume coffee. On the other hand, radio's morning drive time coincides perfectly with most people's desire for a steaming, fresh cup of coffee.

Radio stations base their rates on the time of the day the advertiser wants commercials aired. To achieve the lowest rate, an advertiser can order spots on run of station (ROS) basis, similar to ROP in newspaper advertising. ROP advertising rates entitle a newspaper to place a given advertisement on any newspaper page or in any position it desires – in other words, where space permits. However, this leaves total control of spot placement up to the station. Most stations, therefore, offer a total audience plan (TAP) package rate, which guarantees a certain percentage of spots in the better dayparts if the advertiser buys the total package of time.

Naturally, the subject of daypart advantages can be exhausting for the sophisticated advertiser who has the time, resources and facilities to study it in depth.

Average quarter-hour

This term is used to identify the average number of people who are listening to a specific station during any 15-minute period of any given daypart. The following is an example of an average quarter-hour listening estimate:

Station Radio Red Dragon, Cardiff, Wales.
Average quarter-hour, Monday–Sunday, 6 am–midnight; persons over 12 years old 4,200.

This means that any day Monday–Sunday, during any 15-minute period between 6 am and midnight, it is probable (more than likely) that 4,200 people over 12 years old are tuned into the Radio Red Dragon station.

This same idea can be expressed in terms of 'share' if station's audience is shown as a percentage of the total listening audience in the area.

Rating points

By extending our computations a little further, this same audience could be expressed in terms of rating points if we showed it as a percentage of the population. Determining the gross rating points of a radio schedule, therefore, simply requires multiplying the average quarter-hour rating by the number of spots.

Similarly, the GRPS could also be determined by multiplying the average quarter-hour audience rating by the number of spots and dividing by the population.

Cume audience

This capsule term for 'cumulative audience' describes the total number of different people listening to a radio station for at least one 15-minute segment over the course of a given week, day or daypart.

For example, we can generate 50,400 gross impressions with our schedule on a particular radio station, but that does not mean that 50,400 different people heard our commercials. Many people might have heard our commercial three, four or five times, depending on how long they stayed tuned to that particular radio station.

By measuring the cumulative number of different people listening to a radio station, the rating services can give is an idea of the reach potential of our radio schedule.

Thus, cume and average quarter-hour are important concepts. A high cume figure means that a lot of different people are tuning into the station for at least 15 minutes. A high average quarter-hour figure usually means that people are listening and staying tuned in.

It is important to remember one basic concept about these radio audience measurements. They are derived from the manipulation of statistical data, which involves a complex weighting of various members of the station's surveyed audience. These manipulations produce an important result: generating the average quarter-hour audience figure is dependent on the length of listening. The longer the survey respondent listens, the larger the average quarter-hour audience will be. The cumulative audience is dependent on numerous different people tuning in to the radio station. The more respondents that tune in, the higher the cume will be.

Thus, the most stable (accurate) number for estimating the size, scope and depth of a radio station is the cume. This is because, in the rating service's survey, the cume number is based on larger sample size.

Problem

Sunset Leisure, a company providing leisure-related activities in the north of England, is planning to air a concentrated advertising campaign using broadcast media. The advertising agency handling their account wants to place the company's advertising spots next to highly popular programmes destined to reach the same target audience. The company is particularly interested in targeting the city of Sheffield area with an advertising media plan based on local radio and local television.

Questions

1   For example, assume that the local programme, family Quiz, has a rating of 25, reaches 200,000 people in the primary target audience and costs £2,000 for a 30-second spot on Yorkshire Television Calculate the CPP and the CPM.

2   Sunset Leisure wants to use radio advertising in the Sheffield area through the placement of spots in Radio Hallam, which has an average quarter-hour listening estimate (Monday–Sunday, 6 am–midnight; persons over 12 years old) of 4,200 people. The advertising agency handling the company's account found that the total average quarter-hour listening audience for all stations in the Sheffield catchment area is 48,900. Calculate the average quarter-hour audience of Radio Hallam as expressed as an average quarter-hour 'share'.

3   As Radio Hallam is located in Sheffield (population, 600,000), we can now express and calculate its average quarter-hour audience as an average quarter-hour rating.

4   Sunset Leisure wants to run 25 spots in Radio Hallam during a two-week period. Determine the gross rating points (GRPS) that would result as a consequence of this radio schedule.

(A) Problem 7.4 Advertising effects and effectiveness measurement

Introductory comments

Advertising function is to change consumers' attitudes towards the advertised products or brands so as to increase the sales or market shares. Based on these primary functions, advertising should have some significant impacts on both consumer attitudes and sales. In this problem we would like to discuss the advertising effects on consumers' mind sets, sales and market shares.

In general, advertising effects can be separated into current effects and carryover effects. In the aggregate level, it can be classified into sales effects; market growth, market share and market size effects; as well as price premium effects. For the consumer level, advertising can create brand choice and brand loyalty effects. They are explained below.

Current effects

Generally speaking, current effects and carryover effects are broadly defined as advertising effects. According to the Bendixen (1993) research's findings, there are four kinds of advertising effects, namely current effects, carryover effects, brand loyalty effects and media effects. The first three effects are summarised in the following FCB Grid.

From Figure 7.2, the current advertising effects occur when products or services have a high consumer involvement in the purchase decision process, such as motor vehicles and jewellery. In this category, in accordance with the hierarchy-of-effects model, the consumer goes through the 'learn-feel-do' or 'feel-learn-do' process to evaluate a product. Thus, the evaluation process is long and the purchase behaviour is infrequent. It is obvious that advertising current effects are observed when advertising moves up consumer readiness to the behavioural stage by shortening the decision-making process and raising immediate action. Thus, current effects can reflect the existing of sales effects also.

Carryover effects

Next, carryover advertising effects are observed when advertising achieves product differentiation and bears it in consumers' minds. In this category, products or services have an intermediate consumer involvement in the purchase decision, such as gasoline and toilet soaps. Those products are psychologically differentiated through branding. Compared with the learn-feel-do or feel-learn-do process, consumer goes through

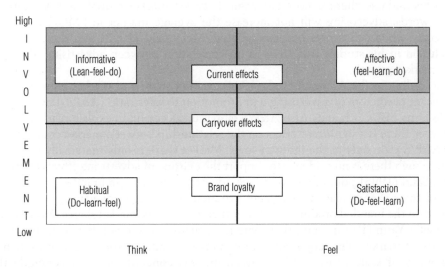

Figure 7.2 Advertising effects on the FCB Grid (Bendixen, 1993).

a relative short evaluation process. Besides, the carryover effects also can demonstrate the existing of the V-shaped sales response function.

Sales effects

As mentioned earlier, the sales effects can be found in the current period and substantially carry over. These results are supported by Assmus et al. (1984) and; Sethuraman and Tellis (1991). They also found that there is a significant effect of advertising on sales.

Owing to the carryover effects of advertising, the relationship between advertising expenditures and sales is V-shaped (Ackoff and Ermshoff, 1975). By using the adaptive information processing hypothesis, Hahan et al. (1992) demonstrated that the advertising carryover effects occur in the left side of the V-shaped curve.

The right upwards sloping side of the V-effect shows that consumers pay attention to ad content out of interest (Petty and Cacioppo, 1986). By increasing the exposures, consumers process ad contents and learn more about the advertised brand and its competitive offerings. As a result, sales can be enhanced by repetition for allowing consumers to extract novel content from the ad, as well as enticing the consumer towards the advertised brand (Berger and Mitchell, 1989).

For the left side of the V-effect, by using the adaptive information processing hypothesis, sales increase continuously even though advertising is reduced from current level. It is because carryover effects and brand loyalty effects exist (Hahn et al., 1992). Those will be illustrated in the later part.

MARKET GROWTH, MARKET SHARE AND MARKET SIZE EFFECTS

In addition to the V-shaped effects between sales and advertising expenditures, Yasin (1995) also studied the advertising to sales ratio (A/S) among market growth and size of market from branded products in fast-moving consumer goods (FMCG) markets. From his findings, there is no relationship between market growth and A/S ratio. In other words, advertising will not increase the average market in FMCG categories, especially when consumers become satiated. McDonald (1992) also drew the same conclusion in his studies that there is no correlation between advertising levels and total market growth.

According to the Ailawadi et al. (1994), market share and market growth are not significant predictors of advertising and promotion to sales ratio (A&P/S) over time or across firms, SBUs or brands. Also, A&P/S ratio is unsuccessful to explain market growth. However, there is a significant effect on the relationship between market concentration and A&P/S ratio only at the industry level. Market share is only marginally better.

Although there is no evidence to support the existing of advertising effects on market share, Yasin (1995) pointed out that high advertising weights in branded products can defend their shares against own label products. Also, high advertising weights can strengthen the branded products and lower their own labels' market shares (Yasin, 1995).

Finally, Yasin (1995) found that there is a negative correlation between advertising and size of market. The larger advertising budgets resulting from larger markets have economies of scale (Yasin, 1995). Based on this concept, one can conclude that advertising spending of market leader and well-developed brands is more efficient than new brands or market followers. Ailawadi et al. (1994) also pointed out that the overall relationship between market size and A&P/S ratio is not straightforward.

Price premium effects

Also, the price premium effects are observed and strongly supported by Yasin (1995).

Advertising enables a greater price premium to be sustained by advertised brands over unadvertised brands in the same market.

Generally speaking, advertising can increase the volume sold at a given price by shifting the demand curve for the advertised brand upwards. In addition to increasing the volume sold, Yasin (1995) also found that the price premium effects exist. By shifting the demand curve of the advertised brand to the right, the advertised brand can charge a higher price while selling at the same quantity.

Brand choice and brand loyalty effects

According to the Bendixen (1993) FCB Grid, products or services which have a low consumer involvement in the purchase decision, will be characterised by brand loyalty effects, such as foodstuffs and household products. Brand loyalty effects are observed when advertising moves the consumer through the cognitive, affective and behavioural stages to create brand loyalty in consumer mindset. It is because consumers go through do-feel-learn or do = learn-feel process. Then, brand loyalty is crucial for repeat purchasing.

Besides, the left side of V-shaped advertising response function also can explain the existence of brand loyalty effects (Hahn et al., 1992). First, having seen an ad in the recent past, a high impact ad should retain its novelty. When an ad is shown subsequently, consumers pay more attention on an ad and engage in in-depth processing of ad information. It leads to strengthen consumers' memory of the advertised brand and its positive attributes and benefits (Hahn et al., 1992).

Second, an impressive ad can work in favour of brand associations and consumers' memory by stimulating positive word of mouth (Hahn et al., 1992).

Third, when consumers are exposed to commercials of competing brands and other related stimuli, such as point of purchase display, they will retrieve the previous memory of ad and brand (Hahn et al., 1992).

Fourth, as interest value and distinctiveness are created by strong memory, these lead to self-cueing potential in consumers' mindsets (Eysenck, 1984). This self-cueing potential will increase for fewer exposures and strengthen the interest value and distinctiveness of the ad. Besides, these cueing mechanisms can reactivate perceptual or experience-based representations of the ad and brand in the memory of both brand switchers and brand loyals (Johnson and Raye, 1981).

Finally, as strengthening and reactivation of memory-based representations enhance the brand's salience, and stimulate consumers to think more about the brand, the self-persuasion occurs. This self-persuasion is more impressive than stimulation of an ad (Kardes, 1988; Petty and Cacioppo, 1983). Thus, consumers may retrieve and process the ad and brand more often to lead to creating more favourable brand attitudes, even though the advertising is reduced (Hahn et al., 1992).

Argument on advertising effects

According to Tellis and Weiss (1995), a new study based on disaggregate scanner data have estimated only weak or non-significant effects of advertising on sales and brand choice. If their results are reliable, heavy spending on advertising is questioned. By further analysing, some reasonable answers are mentioned in their research.

First, Tellis and Weiss (1995) agreed with the point of view that advertising serves as a source of information for consumers. Besides, advertising efforts can be treated as a supporting tool to charge in price premium (Yasin, 1995), to support the personal selling effort by creating awareness (Aaker et al., 1992: 91–3), as well as to motivate retailers to stock and promote the brand. Also, owing to budget setting, advertising expenditures are based on percentage of sales or competitive advertising so as to counterbalance the competitive interference (D'Souza and Rao, 1995; Kent and Allen, 1994).

Moreover, owing to the timing difference, distribution channels usually are less flexible and unable to match the advertising campaigns. So, the non-significant results are uncovered, specifically for current effects (Tellis and Weiss, 1995).

Furthermore, there is a weak or non-significant effect of advertising on brand choices (Tellis and Weiss, 1995). First, the concept of high loyalty resulting from high advertising is not enough to support the existence of brand choice effects because loyalty can be created by superior quality. Second, advertising does not influence consumers to choose the advertised brand when the message is fresh. Then, it is impossible to create any preference for a brand at a later time. Third, one of the roles of advertising is to attract new consumers to the market or the brand. However, the overall efficiency of spending heavily on mature categories for a slight increase in the numbers of new consumers looks very doubtful.

Advertising expenditures have some psychological effects on consumers' mindsets. Based on implied warranty concept (Crosier, 1983), for cutting the advertising expenditures of a brand, it is possible to harm its product image. Consumers will suspect that a brand is losing profit or shares in the market, or is no longer to be a market leader. In 1993, Honda withdrew from the formula one Grand Prix. Consumers suspected that its engine was falling behind its competitors Lotus, Renault and Ferrari or that their financial position was not strong enough to support a team anymore. Thus, it may be one of the reasons why firms keep on spending heavily on advertising, even though the brand choice effects are weak.

Advertising effectiveness

Advertising effectiveness can be broadly classified into an aggregate level and an individual level. From a management point of view, advertising effectiveness is an aggregate level target that links with the sales and relative expenditure. Although those figures can show how well the advertising campaign is, it cannot tell how an effective advertisement develops.

Should advertising effectiveness be seen as a means to an end, affective advertising needs to be effective in terms of resulting in a favourable evaluation of the advertised product or brand. Thus, the attitude towards the advertisement itself can directly condition the attitude towards the advertised brand. Many researchers therefore focus on the individual level to find out a benchmark for an effective ad. Thus, different models are developed so as to increase advertising effectiveness.

One of the main views studies have emphasised is the role of a person's message-relevant thinking as the central mediator of attitude change (Petty and Cacioppo, 1986). Advertising readers are assumed to be active information processors. Cognitive processing occurs, when individual's motivation and involvement are aroused resulting in the attitude formation or change process. Based on this concept, the Elaboration Likelihood Model (Petty and Cacioppo, 1983, 1986), the Triad Model (Poiesz, 1989) and the Advertising Response Model (Mehta, 1994) were developed. These models mainly pay attention on the ad content itself as to how best to affect consumers' attitudes towards the advertised product or brand.

In addition to these models, other factors are concerned as significant factors in persuasion. They are likeability of the ad, repetition of exposure, competitive interference in the exposure environment, media effectiveness and negative effects caused by readers' perceptions and biases.

Elaboration Likelihood Model (ELM)

The Elaboration Likelihood Model (Petty and Cacioppo, 1983, 1986) has two general conditions for persuasion to take place: motivation and ability. Motivation refers to the attractiveness of the message. Attraction is determined by the personal relevance of the product or by executional aspects. Ability refers to the sensory and mental ability to adequately perceive and understand the message, to both store and retrieve it from memory. The ELM specifies two routes to persuasion: the central and peripheral routes. The central route is followed if both motivation and ability are present. The peripheral route is followed if either or both motivation and ability are absent. In the central route, persuasion takes place after message arguments have been processed. In the peripheral route a small and brief affective reaction is produced by a persuasion cue that refers to a marginal message element not directly related to the message content (Mehta, 1994; Petty and Cacioppo, 1983, 1986; Poiesz et al., 1994). If no persuasion cue is present, no affect change is taking place.

Triad Model

The Triad Model (MacInnis and Jaworski, 1989; Poiesz, 1989) is strongly associated with ELM. It goes one step further to develop three conditions for effective communication to take place: motivation, capacity and the opportunity to process information of the ad. The later two factors can be more detailed to explain how internal and external factors can affect audience's process information. It separates the ELM's ability variable into capacity and opportunity, because it is believed that an ineffective ad is caused by either or both viewers (internal factors) and environmental characteristics (external factors). Capacity refers to the ability that is determined and constrained by internal factors. Opportunity refers to process information as determined by external factors.

These three variables are treated as necessary conditions, dependent on, and can be influenced by, one another at one point of time. If any one of three variables is unfavourable, it cannot be compensated by a very favourable one or a combination of other variables (Poiesz et al., 1994). Also, the Triad Model allows for the existence of an escape route. This route reflects the tendency of consumers to avoid or ignore advertising rather than to process it, if a combination of motivation, capacity and opportunity is unfavourable (Poiesz et al., 1994).

Advertising Response Model (ARM)

ARM suggests that information processing occurs along one or both of the two routes: central and peripheral (Mehta, 1994; Petty and Cacioppo, 1983, 1986). During central processing, the focus is on product or brand-related information. During peripheral processing, the consumer is more concerned with the executional factors of the ad. Central processing leads mainly to brand attitude to arouse buying interest or buying intention (Mehta, 1994). Peripheral processing mostly leads to ad attitude or ad liking to influence brand attitude and buying interest (Mehta, 1994).

Also, the involvement level can influence the processing route. For high-involvement product, audiences pay more attention on the brand-related information during information processing. Under the conditions of advertising message involvement, attitudes formed or changed tend to be more permanent (Mehta, 1994). For a low involvement product, respondents reply on peripheral cues, such as music and spokesperson (MacKenzie and Lutz, 1989; Muehling et al., 1991). Attitudes formed or changed tend to be more temporary in nature and may be lost when ad is not being seen anymore (Mehta, 1994). Therefore, repetition of exposure can reinforce the linkage between peripheral cues and attitudes towards the advertising brand (Mehta, 1994).

Likeability

Likeability can enhance the persuasion and recall in advertising (Aaker and Stayman, 1990; Biel and Bridgewater, 1990). Also, Biel and Bridgewater (1990) studied the relationship between likeability and sales effectiveness.

In the case of fast moving consumer goods (FMCG), people who like a commercial a lot were twice as likely to be persuaded by it than people who simply felt neutral towards the advertising.

Besides, Biel (1990) found that the overall persuasion of a commercial is enhanced if commercials which viewers like are made.

Consumers liking the ad itself can affect their attitudes towards the advertised brands and products because these attitudes are caused by affective and cognitive components which are emotional and utilitarian in nature (Batra et al., 1986). Both emotional and utilitarian factors can influence purchase intentions. Specifically, the affective reaction plays a significant role in buying decisions of low involvement product categories, such as FMCG (Batra et al., 1986). In addition, within an over-communicated environment, consumers are surrounded by information clutter. Thus viewers become to be in a low involvement advertisement reception situation (Batra et al., 1986) so that consumers tend to have less time for information processing. A likeable advertisement can give consumers a deeper impression during information processing.

Owing to the above-mentioned reasons, likeability plays an important role in the prediction and development of effective commercials (Aaker and Stayman, 1990). First, it can serve as a predictor of effective commercials (Biel and Bridgewater, 1990). Second, it also serves as a diagnostic tool to evaluate the comparative effectiveness of different commercials (Aaker and Stayman, 1990). Third, it can be a gatekeeper for further information processing through greater audience involvement with the commercial (Biel and Bridgewater, 1990).

In accordance with Leather et al. (1994), likeability can be created by five principal components to underpin viewers' reactions to the commercials. They are (1) stimulating, which includes interesting, clever, watchable, bright, attention grabbing, amusing and exciting; (2) relevance; (3) incorporated situational vignette, aid and abetment; (4) its music quality; and (5) its positive character distinctiveness.

First of all, a commercial should be able to stimulate and to communicate a product message to the audience. Thus, the most important factor is to reflect the principal function of advertising, as well as to predict overall evaluation of ads (Leather et al., 1994). Next, the relevance predicts intention to purchase. Both stimulation and relevance are interrelated within an advertisement. Stimulation can obtain and hold audience's attention amidst a clutter of competing stimuli. By further and deeper processing, purchasing intentions can be raised for achieving a satisfactory degree of relevance (Leather et al., 1994). Finally, the remaining components of music quality, positive character distinctiveness and originality can make audiences have a feeling of warmth, familiarity and liveliness. Then, these lead to enhance the likeability of ads (Aaker and Stayman, 1990; Biel and Bridgewater, 1990).

Repetition

According to D'Souza and Rao (1995), repletion of advertisements has significant effects on increasing top of mind awareness (TOMA), brand shares, brand preference and brand choice in mature product categories. Especially, TOMA is the most affected by repetition. Besides, Nedungadi (1990) found that consideration set formation is influenced by priming through repeating advertising. Also, Hawkins and Hoch (1992) revealed that when consumers believe that brand trivia statements are truth, brand preference can be created by repetition. It is because, in accordance with the accumulation of learning, new information accumulates beside the old so that the new can refresh the old and old can strengthen the new.

D'Souza and Rao (1995) also mentioned that the effectiveness of repetition is under constraints of the competition and the quality of an ad itself. In the competitive situation, the effectiveness of repetition is diluted by the existence of competitive interference that comes from both prior exposures and recent exposures (Burke and Srull, 1988). They are called *proactive interference* and *retroactive interference* respectively. Also, an effective ad wears in consumers' memory, then it wears out after the peak. However, an ineffective advertisement never wears in, so the effectiveness of repetition never occurs in this case.

Media effects

Media is a vehicle to determine the best environment for a presented message. Media effects are defined as the magnitude of the advertising effect for a particular medium. It is determined by the extent of usage of that medium and not by the medium itself (Bendixen, 1993). Besides, there is no right medium that is right for every advertisement. Based on this concept, the media tactics play a significant role in determining the advertising effectiveness. Understanding readers of different media and media limitations can increase the overall effectiveness. It is believed that TV has the highest coverage, so it may be the most efficient medium. However, Bendixen (1993) pointed out that the greater the extent of usage of a medium, the less the effectiveness of that medium is. In fact, the creative devices and content of an advertisement determines whether the advertisement will be effective.

Competitive interference

Competitive interference is caused by competitive clutter effects. According to associative network models of memory, when one is exposed to ads of competing brands, these contents are retained and overlapped in one's memory traces. This overlap can hinder consumers retrieving distinctive advertising information when sought elements become inaccessible or are confused with other information in contiguous storage (Burke and Srull, 1988). Also, when consumers are exposed to more competing brands advertising, they are less likely to recall a target advertisement. It is therefore believed that advertising effects will be diluted by competing brands, especially, for unfamiliar brands (D'Souza and Rao, 1995; Kent and Allen, 1994).

Based on Kent and Allen (1994), well-known brands take advantage of reputation and familiarity in marketplace advertising. Also, they found that consumers appear to have better memories for new product information of familiar brands, for familiar brands are less affected by exposure of competitive advertising. Therefore, it can explain why leading brands spend a lot on advertising to maintain a market share that exceeds their advertising share-of-voice. Also, it is one of the reasons why low share brands spend more on advertising to have a greater share of voice than their market share.

Undesirable advertising effects

According to the Triad Model (Poiesz, 1989) the escape behaviour from advertising exists. Also, it leads to undesirable effects. They include zapping behaviour, the attention shift after source identification, the dissociation of brand name and message, the misunderstanding of the message, the irritation caused by certain messages and the confusion of brand names.

Besides, some indirect effects of communication objectives are detected by consumers when they are exposed to the advertisements. It is possible for consumers to infer the quality of a brand from exposure frequency of advertising for this brand, or from the perceived advertisement execution costs. These undesirable effects are unexpected to influence consumers' attitudes towards a brand.

Problem – example

A common phenomenon in advertising is known as 'wear-out', where the advertisement loses the impact it had when it first appeared. This illustration shows the gains that can be made by understanding this phenomenon.

Suppose sales response to advertising is, initially:

Sales $= 10 + 10X - X^2$

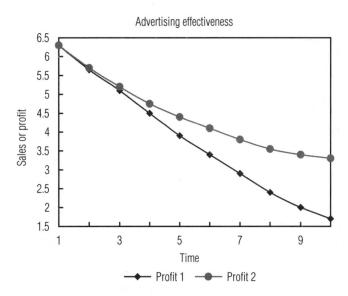

Figure 7.3 Optimal advertising policy (decreasing spending over time, Case 2) versus a constant spending policy when advertising effectiveness decreases over time.

If we assume margin = 0.3 (i.e. price − unit cost = 0.3), then the optimal advertising level is £3 ⅓ million per period.

Suppose, however, that the main advertising effectiveness coefficient, the coefficient of X (10 in the above equation) decays to value of about half its original level over ten time periods. If this decay takes place exponentially, that is, with the same proportional decay each period, then the effect can be modelled as:

$$X \text{ Coefficient} = 10 \, e^{-.07(t-1)}, \quad t = 1, \dots, 10$$

We then input a value for the X-coefficient in the Z-function of 10 * @EXP(−.07 * (T−1)). We run two cases, assuming no sales carryover effects (Alpha = 1; Lambda = 0):

Case 1: Advertise at the same level for ten periods, ignoring the decline. Thus, advertising = £3.33 each period.
Case 2: Advertise at the optimal level for each period, as follows:

					t					
	1	2	3	4	5	6	7	8	9	10
Optimal advertising level	3.33	3.00	2.68	2.39	2.11	1.86	1.62	1.40	1.19	1.00

Figure 7.3 plots the profit levels associated with Cases 1 and 2 above.

Questions

1   Explain the rationale behind the elaboration likelihood model (ELM) and the advertising response model (ARM).

2   Discuss the concept of 'competitive interference'.
3   Comment on the key managerial implications related to the study of advertising effects and its effectiveness measurement.
4   Based on Figure 7.3 which plots the profit levels associated with Cases 1 and 2, make a critical analysis on these results.

(A) *Problem 7.5* Estimating market response to sales promotion

Introductory comments

Marketing managers must have some estimate of sales response in order to set the tentative advertising budget. These estimates are even more critical in sales-promotion budgeting, for two reasons. First, some costs cannot be estimated without estimates of sales response. Second, unlike advertising objectives, sales objectives generally have a very direct link to sales volume. Product-trial, repurchase, inventory-building and traffic-building objectives are specifically sales-oriented. Promotional support and enquiries can be expected to result in increased sales with a small time lag. Consequently, the ability to predict response will enable the marketing manager to assess not only the profitability consequences but also the degree to which the programme objective will be achieved.

However, different kinds of sales responses can result, and these must be distinguished before managers can evaluate results or establish budgets. That is a single measure of total sales during the promotion period will be inadequate for three reasons:

1   *Displaced sales* Some of the sales made during a promotion will simply displace sales that would otherwise have been made to regular buyers at the normal price. Thus, sales must increase by a certain amount just to cover the reduced contribution margin on these sales.
2   *Borrowed sales (stocking up)* Some sales during the promotion will represent 'borrowed' sales from future periods, as consumers stock up on the product while sale prices are in effect. Accordingly, some post-promotion decline in sales can be expected as a result of inventory building, and this effect should be considered, then, the greater the long-run profitability of the programme.
3   *Conversion rates* Very frequently the sales promotion is designed to acquire new customers who will remain loyal after trial. The greater the number of conversions, then, the greater the long-run profitability of the programme. Accordingly, marketing managers should attempt to determine the potential increase in sales to these buyers in the post-promotion period.

Although some fairly sophisticated mathematical approaches have been developed for analysing and estimating these response factors, frequently it is impossible to estimate precisely the displacement, borrowed sales and conversion rates in advance. Accordingly, marketing managers may use payout analysis. In this method, the required level of sales to achieve a target profit is calculated under different assumptions. In general, then, two budgeting approaches are available. First, marketing managers can use payout analysis. Second, managers can attempt to estimate directly each type of response. Both methods are examined in the following example. Companies that use a given sales-promotion device frequently, and that carefully monitor the results in terms of these types of market response, will be able to develop a fairly high degree of accuracy in projecting the effects of the sales promotion. Companies with limited experience can use management's knowledge of market share, and of the buying process factors, in order to project displacement, conversion and stocking-up effects.

200

All companies can also use the experience of sales-promotion specialists in estimating, for example, coupon-redemption rates.

But no matter how extensive a company's experience, marketing managers should determine how sensitive the profitability results will be if slight errors in estimation are made.

One additional point should be emphasised. The use of consumer sales promotions for product-trial and conversion purposes will generally be less attractive to market-share leaders. One reason for this is the fact that leading brands stand to depreciate their brand's quality image by sensitising customers to price. Further, the larger the market share, the greater the chance that, for example, coupons or sale prices will be taken advantage of by regular buyers. By virtue of having a larger share, the market leader will almost inevitably have a higher displacement rate than will other brands because there are fewer competitors' customers. Further, regular buyers may be more likely to stock up, as they already know and (presumably) prefer the brand.

Problem

Allied Foods Inc. is a manufacturer of specialty prepared foods. The company is contemplating a one-month coupon sales promotion that is designed to attract new users to try its line of frozen dinners. Although sales of the product are somewhat seasonal, Allied Foods has developed an effective sales-forecasting system, and the unconditional sales volume for the coupon period has been estimated to be 1 million cases, at an average manufacturer selling price of £15 per case (there are 12 units per case). Variable production costs are £9.75 per case, so the normal projected pound variable contribution per month is:

$$(\pounds15 - \pounds9.75) \times 1 \text{ million} = \pounds5.25 \text{ million}$$

The coupon promotion involves the distribution of 10 million coupons at a cost of £50,000. Consumer savings attributable to the coupon will be £1.80 per case (or 15 pence per item) and redemption costs will be 45 pence per case (3.75 pence per item).

In order to determine the budgetary feasibility of the sales promotion, Allied Foods has examined the profitability consequences in two ways: by looking at a payout analysis of the 'worst-case' downside risk, and by a profitability analysis based on the company's estimates of market response to the coupon programme.

Evaluating the worst case

The worst case will occur where all current buyers gain access to and use the coupons and no new buyers are reached. If this were to occur, management would want to know the required increase in sales to offset the lower contribution margin and the increase in direct costs. In other words we would employ the same analysis used to evaluate the simultaneous impact of a price cut plus an increase in direct costs. That is,

$$\begin{array}{l} \text{Required sales to} \\ \text{maintain current} \\ \text{target total contribution} \end{array} = \frac{\left[\begin{array}{l} \text{Current total} \\ \text{contribution} \end{array} + \begin{array}{l} \text{Current} \\ \text{direct costs} \end{array} + \begin{array}{l} \text{Increase in} \\ \text{direct costs} \end{array} \right]}{\text{New percentage variable contribution margin}}$$

$$\text{Current variable} = \frac{\text{Contribution margin} + \text{Increase in direct cost}}{\text{VCM per case} \div \text{Selling price}}$$

Estimating market response

Allied Foods' estimate based on previous company and industry experience is that about 12 per cent of the coupons will be redeemed. Additionally, Allied Foods believes that about 20 per cent of those redeeming the coupons will be regular users. Although this estimate will be very difficult to determine with any precision, Allied Foods' managers know that the company currently has a 15 per cent market share and that regular buyers are slightly more likely to use the coupons than non-users of the Allied Foods brand. Given these percentages, then, the estimated total sales resulting from coupon redemption will be: number of coupons distributed × redemption rate = number redeemed or 10 million × 12 per cent = 1.2 million. Further, 20 per cent of these sales will be 'displaced' sales purchased by regular users. Therefore, 20 per cent of the total number of cases would have been purchased at regular prices had the coupon promotion not been in effect. This means that the remaining 80 per cent of coupon sales come from new buyers.

In evaluating allied Foods' proposed promotion using these estimates, management would, of course, raise the question, 'Was the objective achieved?' That is, does an increase of 80 per cent of coupon sales to new users constitute an acceptable level of performance, given that attracting new triers was the objective? After all, 80 per cent of coupon sales out of a normal volume of 1 million represents only a small increase in total sales.

As Allied Foods' current market share is 15 per cent is this sufficient percentage of new customers to be attracted to meet the sales-promotion programme objective? Additionally, managers should examine the profitability consequences of these results. This can be done by determining *the net impact of the promotion on the total contribution to indirect cost and profit* as follows:

1 *Determine the normal monthly pound contribution.*
2 *Determine the pound contribution during promotion*: (a) contribution on new sales equals coupon sale to new buyers' time contribution on coupon sales per case plus (b) contribution on displaced sales equals coupon sales to regular buyers' time contribution on coupon sales per sales plus (c) contribution on regular sales equals regular (non-coupon) sales (normal-displaced) pound contribution.
3 *Calculate the direct cost of promotion.*
4 *Calculate the net profit impact*: promotion-month variable contribution minus normal-month variable contribution equals increased contribution minus total direct cost of promotion equals net increase in pound contribution to indirect cost and profit.

Questions

1 Calculate the variable contribution margin (VCM) per case on coupon sales.
2 Calculate the required sales volume to maintain Allied Foods' current target total contribution.
3 Taking into account the coupon prices and redemption costs, calculate the pound contribution on the estimated total sales resulting from coupon redemption.

4   Determine the pound contribution during the sales promotion period and the net impact of the promotion on the total contribution to indirect cost and profit.

5   Make your own recommendations to the company based on the projected profitability analysis of the sales-promotion campaign.

(M) *Problem 7.6* Sponsorships – event marketing and publicity

Introductory comments

The company's general advertising for its products or services may be complemented or replaced by advertising-like activities in the form of sponsorships, event marketing or company-initiated positive publicity.

Sponsorship refers to the company's financial support of a media, social, sporting cultural activity in return for exposure of its brand or brands. Media activities included TV programmes, radio programmes, or special editions or supplements in print media. Social activities include support for hobbyist or outdoor interest clubs, or charitable support for organisations for the disabled, children or the elderly. Sporting activities include the support of sports organisations, sports teams and sports venues. Cultural activities include support of the visual or performing arts.

Event marketing is distinguished from sponsorship only in that it refers to financial support of a particular *short-duration* activity, such as the Super Bowl, the Olympic Games, or a specific art exhibition or concert performance.

Publicity refers to news media reportage about the company and its products or services, and is here used to refer to *company-initiated*, *positive* medial reportage. Coverage of the activity or event in the news media is usually part and parcel of sponsorship or event marketing.

Sponsorships, event marketing and publicity are related here as a single advertising-like communications activity. They are related because event marketing is simply a short-term form of sponsorship; and sponsorship, in turn, can be defined as payment in cash or kind, such as free products or services, to an organisational activity in return for publicity. This publicity takes the form of *intermediaries'* advertising, such as by retailers, or 'free' publicity in news media (in actuality, publicity rarely is free because a good deal of management time is devoted to it, making it a cost for the company). (*Note*: in the following analysis, we will use the term *sponsorship* generically to cover all three activities, although event marketing and publicity will be identified specifically when appropriate).

Sponsorship is an alternative to general advertising – making it larger than the smallest general advertising medium, outdoor (and poster) advertising. In most countries, there has been a growth in sponsorship as a complement to, or a substitute for, general advertising. The highest proportional expenditure is in Italy, where marketers spend the equivalent of about 8 per cent of their advertising expenditure on sponsorship, most of it on football.

For some companies, sponsorship is used as almost a complete substitute for general advertising. An example of almost complete reliance on sponsorship is Cornhill Insurance Company in the UK. Cornhill, a virtually unknown competitor in the insurance category, spent £2 million (perhaps £4 million if entertainment costs are included) over 5 years to sponsor test-match cricket, which is enormously popular in England. By careful tracking, the company estimated that brand recall of Cornhill as an insurance company rose from 2 per cent to 21 per cent over the 5-year period, and that the return in terms of insurance sales by the company was on the order of £15 to £20 million. To have achieved these results with advertising may have cost ~£50 million over the 5 years. Most tellingly, Cornhill 'merchandised' the sponsorship very thoroughly by obtaining exclusive rights to the televised coverage of the cricket matches; by placing its logo on the sports grounds where the matches were played (indeed, on the actual grass of the grounds, which no other companies were allowed to do); and by printing its name very prominently (and tastefully) on the tickets for the games.

For most companies, however, sponsorship is a *complementary* activity alongside general advertising and other forms of promotion.

If the marketer undertaking the sponsorship is also distributing the product through retailers, it has been estimated that ~70 per cent of sponsorships are followed by *retail* promotions, such as retail advertising, special displays or promotional pricing by the retailer. These tie-in activities illustrate the necessity for customer timeline integration when using the IMC approach.

Sponsorships are undertaken not just to increase awareness or create goodwill but to product a measurable result in terms of sales, and local trade follow-through is instrumental in achieving this goal. Similar to advertising campaigns, sponsorships have to be carefully selected and planned rather than opportunistically rushed into, because they have approximately a 50 per cent failure rate. Among the successes have been Volvo's sponsorship of tennis and later golf, and also the Jaguar and Cornhill examples mentioned earlier. But there have been some notable apparent failures of sponsorship. For instance, Ford spent £2.5 million a year to sponsor English national football and £300,000 a year to sponsor European football, with no apparent effect. At the end of the 5-year sponsorship, only 1 per cent of the public could link the Ford name with football.

From a brand attitude perspective, the correct measurement procedure is to use the *company* as the cue and ask which events *it* is associated with – a connection which would thereby enhance the company's 'image' if the event were appropriately selected. The first measure means little, so we should not strictly use this as proof of sponsorship failure.

Sponsorship is more likely to succeed if it is planned and evaluated as an advertising campaign. For details, see chapter appendix 11D, Planning and Evaluating Sponsorships.

Sponsorships also provide excellent opportunities for public relations contacts through corporate entertainment at sponsored events.

BUDGETING FOR A SPECIFIC IMC ACTIVITY

In the IMC 'activities mix' budgeting decision described above, the manager will have used the task matrix method to estimate the main and interactive effects of each of the activities. Having decided on each particular activity, there are now *implementation costs* to be considered. With non-traditional advertising and promotions activities especially, as well as with advertising campaigns, there is a likelihood that the manager will have misestimated the numbers in the stages of effects, or that the communication activity or promotion, once implemented, does not work as well as planned and may have to be terminated – usually to be replaced by another activity for achieving the same stage of effects.

The budgeting formula developed by Thomas L. Powers is very useful for identifying implementation costs. The formula is an elaboration of the 'leverage' principle of target audience selection. Power's formula is as follows:

$$P = S (L) (M) - (UF + OF + V [S] [L] + T [E])$$

where P = expected profit, S = sales increase (expressed as a fraction of the base level of sales), L = base level of sales in pounds, M = product margin (unit profit expressed as a fraction of unit selling price), UF = up-front costs, OF = ongoing fixed costs, V = variable costs, T = termination probability and E = termination expense.

Most of the terms in this formula should be self-explanatory; however, examples of the less familiar terms will help. Suppose the manager is considering a telemarketing campaign as an IMC activity. Up-front costs (UF) for telemarketing would include fees paid to an agency or specialised telemarketing contractor for developing the tele-marketing 'script' to be used in the campaign. Ongoing fixed costs (OF) would include rental of the telephone lines for the campaign as well as salary and expenses for a super-visor. Variable costs (V) for the telemarketing would be the hourly rates paid to the telemarketing operators, perhaps with bonuses or commissions paid as well. Termination expense (E) for the telemarketing campaign would include the cost of cancelling the supervisor before the contract has expired and cancelling the rental agreement for the telephone lines. Whereas these costs are by no means complete and are only indicative, they cover the main factors that should be taken into account in estimating the contribution of a particular IMC activity.

One point to clarify about Power's formula is that the sales increase – S in the formula – has to be interpreted as the sales increase that would result from the inclusion of that activity in the *overall* IMC programme, not as a solo activity – unless, of course, it *is* the only activity for the brand. For instance, if publicity is to be added to the overall IMC programme, the manager has to estimate what the sales increase would be, above and beyond that generated by the other components of the programme, that is added by the publicity component alone. Clearly this is not an easy estimate to make, because publicity will probably not simply add to but rather will *interact* with other activities in the programme such as general advertising. Therefore, the best way to make this sales increase estimate is simply to forecast the sales expected *with* the activity in place, *taking into account the interaction*, and then subtract the sales forecast *in the absence of* that activity. Then express this sales difference as a decimal fraction of the latter sales forecast. For example, if the sales estimate *with* the activity in place is £110 million, and the sales estimate *without* the activity is £100 million, then the sales difference would become S = 0.10 in the formula.

In particular, we have referred to advertising in general and to various other IMC activities without carefully considering their suitability and *capability* of delivering the required communication effects. To make an informed decision here, the manager has to understand the capabilities – not just the costs – of alternative advertising communi-cations and promotions media.

Perhaps another realisation has occurred, too. With IMC programmes, the media planning decision is moved considerably *earlier* in the manager's planning stages than when using general advertising alone. With IMC, the manager is essentially considering media options before thinking about creative strategy, in many cases. Although this book places creative strategy *before* media strategy, in reality there is a good deal of simultaneous planning; and we therefore recommend an iterative 'propose and revise' procedure in practice.

Problem

You are a cereal manufacturer and you decide to sponsor the nation champion junior woman swimmer, hoping she will make it to the next Olympic Games. You expect that your sponsorship association with her progress will increase sales of the designated cereal brand by 5 per cent in the first year on a base level of sales of £10 million. The product's unit profit margin is 30 per cent. UF costs for the sponsorship are £500,000; ongoing fixed costs are £20,000 per month; and variable costs are zero. You estimate the termination probability at the end of the first year to be .2 and the termination expense, in the form of a straight-out donation to her programme in the event of your termination as £50,000.

Question

Using Power's formula, calculate the expected profit on this sponsorship for the first year.

References and further readings

Aaker, D., Barta, R. and Myers, J. (1992) *Advertising Management*, Englewood Cliffs, NJ: Prentice-Hall.

Aaker, D.A. and Stayman, D.M. (1990) Measuring audience perceptions of commercials and relating them to ad impact, *Journal of Advertising Research*, 30 (4): 7–17.

Ackoff, Russell L. and Emshoff, J.R. (1975) Advertising research at Anheuser-Busch Inc. (1963–68), *Sloan Management Review*, Winter 1–15.

Ailawadi, K.L., Farris, P.W. and Parry M.E. (1994) Share and growth are not good predictors of the advertising and promotion/sales ration, *Journal of Marketing*, 58 (1) (January): 86–97.

Assmus, G., Farley, J.U. and Lehmann, D.R. (1984) How advertising affects sales: meta-analysis of econometric results, *Journal of Marketing Research*, 21 (February): 65–74.

Batra, R. and Ray, M.L. (1986) Situational effects of advertising repetition: the moderatin influence of motivation, ability, and opportunity to respond, *Journal of Consumer Research*, 12 (March): 432–45.

Berger, I.E. and Mitchell, A.A. (1989) The effect of advertising on attitude accessibility, attitude confidence, and the attitude–behaviour relationship, *Journal of Consumer Research*, 16 (December): 269–79.

Biel, A.L. and Bridgewater, C.A. (1990) Attributes of likeable television commercials, *Journal of Advertising Research*, 30 (3): 38–44.

Burke, R.R. and Srull, T.K. (1988) Competitive interference and consumer memory for advertising, *Journal of Consumer Research*, 15 (June): 55–68.

Crosier, K. (1983) Towards a praxiology of advertising, *International Journal of Advertising*, 2: 215–32.

D'Souza, G. and Rao, R.C. (1995) Can repeating an advertisement more frequently than the competition affect brand preference in a mature market?, *Journal of Marketing*, 59 (2) (April): 32–42.

Eysenck, M.W. (1984) *A Handbook of Cognitive Psychology*, Hillsdale, NJ: Lawrence Erlbaum.

Gardner, M.P. and Shuman, P.J. (1987) Sponsorship: an important component of the promotions mix, *Journal of Advertising*, 16(1): 11–17.

Hahan, M., Park, C.W. and MacInnis, D.J. (1992) The adaptive information processing hypothesis: accounting for the V-shaped advertising response function, *Journal of Advertising*, 21(2) (June): 37–46.

Hawkins, S.A. and Hoch, S.J. (1992) Low-involvement learning: memory without evaluation, *Journal of Consumer Research*, 19 (September): 212–25.

Jack, M. (1993) More is indeed better, *Media Week*, September 6: 14–18.

Jim, S. (1995) One-hit or miss: is a frequency of one frequently wrong?, *Advertising Age*, November 27: 46.

Johnson, M.K. and Raye, C.L. (1981) Reality monitoring, *Psychological Review*, 88 (January): 67–85.

Joseph, W.O. (1984) Setting frequency levels: an art or a science?, *Journal of Advertising Research*, 24 (August/September): i9–11.

Kardes, F.R. (1988) Spontaneous inference processes in advertising, *Journal of Consumer Research*, 15 (September): 225–33.

Kent, R.J. and Allen, C.T. (1994) Competitive interference effects in consumer memory for advertising: the role of brand familiarity, *Journal of Marketing*, 58(3) (July): 97–105.

Leather, P., McKechnie, S. and Amirhanian, M. (1994) The importance of likeability as a measure of television advertising effectiveness, *International Journal of Advertising*, 13(3): 265–80.

Louisa Ha (1995) Media models and advertising effects: conceptualisation and theoretical implications, *Journal of Current Issues and Research in Advertising*, Fall: 1–15.

MacInnis, D.J. and Jaworski, B.J. (1989) Information processing from advertisements: toward an integrative framework, *Journal of Marketing*, 53: 1–23.

MacKenzie, S.B. and Lutz, R.J. (1989) An empirical examination of structural antecedents of attitude toward the ad in an advertising prestest context, *Journal of Marketing*, 53(2): 48–65.

McDonald, C. (1992) *How Advertising Works*, The Advertising Association, NTC Publishing (Chicago, Illinois).

Mehta, A. (1994) How advertising response modelling (ARM) can increase ad effectiveness, *Journal of Advertising Research*, 34(3) (May/June): 62–74.

Nedungadi, P. (1990) Recall and consumer consideration sets: influencing choice without altering brand evaluations, *Journal of Consumer Research*, 17(3): 263–76.

Petty, R.E. and Cacioppo, J.T. (1983) Central and peripheral routes to persuasion: application to advertising, in Percy, P.L and Woodside, A.G. (eds) *Advertising and Consumer Psychology*, Lexington, MA: Lexington Books: pp. 3–23.

Petty, R.E. and Cacioppo, J.T. (1986) *Communication and Persuasion: Central and Peripheral Routes to Attitude Change*, New York: Springer-Verlag.

Poiesz, Th.B.C. (1989) *De Transformatie van een Karikatuur*, Inaugural Lecture, Tilburg University.

Poiesz, Th.B.C. and Robben, H.S.J. (1994) Individual reactions to advertising: theoretical and methodological developments, *International Journal of Advertising*, 13(1): 25–53.

Schultz, D.E. and Kitchen, P.J. (2000) *Communication Globally – An Integrated Marketing Approach*, Chicago, IL: NTC Business Books.

Sethuraman, R. and Tellis, G.J. (1991) An analysis of tradeoff between advertising and price discounting, *Journal of Marketing Research*, 28 (May): 160–74.

Sponsorship fails for Ford (1994) *Marketing* (Australia), March: 9.

Stewart, D.W. and Koslow, J. (1989) Executional factors and advertising effectiveness: a replication, *Journal of Advertising*, 18(3): 21–32.

Tellis, G.J. and Weiss, D.L. (1995) Does TV advertising really affect sales? The role of measures, models, and data aggregation, *Journal of Advertising*, 24(3) (Fall): 1–12.

This case was originally written up by F. Dinsmore, Cricket sponsorship (1980) *The Business Graduate* (UK), Autumn: 68–72; and further reported in T. Meenaghan (1991), The role of sponsorship in the marketing communications mix, *International Journal of Advertising*, 10(1): 35–47; and Witcher, B., Craigne, J.G. Culligan, D. and Harvey, A. (1991) The links between objectives and function in organisational sponsorship, *International Journal of Advertising*, 10(1): 13–33.

Williams J.D. (1983) Industrial publicity: one of the best promotional tools, *Industrial Marketing Management*, 12(3): 207–11.

Yasin, J. (1995) The effects of advertising on fast-moving consumer goods markets, *International Journal of Advertising*, 14(2): 133–147.

8

Internet Marketing

The scale of the Internet's potential influence is dramatically illustrated by a research project commissioned by the US corporation Cisco Systems and undertaken by the University of Texas (Internet Indicators, 1999). The researchers concluded that during 1999, within just the US economy, the Internet generated an annual revenue of £332 billion and supported almost 1,400,000 jobs. These figures are rendered even more dramatic when it is realised that revenues on this scale put this sector among the top 20 economies in the world, almost equal to the entire GDP of Switzerland. Another observation that can be drawn from these data is that although the World Wide Web was only launched around five years ago, its total market size already rivals well established sectors such as energy, car manufacturing and telecommunications.

It is critical for organisations to recognise that exploiting this new technology goes way beyond just putting a brochure online. Essentially what is happening on a global basis is that technologies such as telecommunications, satellite broadcast, digital TV and computing are converging. As a result of this convergence, the world is being offered a more flexible, more rapid and extremely low cost way of exchanging information. Thus when discussing this new technology, it is safer not to restrict any assessment of opportunity to the role of the Internet.

E-commerce marketing is usually based around applying established marketing management principles as the basis for defining how new technologies are to be exploited. Additionally, in many organisations e-commerce proposals involve building upon existing offline activities as the basis for providing new sources of information, customer–supplier interaction and/or alternative purchase transaction channels.

The degree to which e-commerce marketing objectives are defined can vary tremendously. Some organisations merely restrict aims to increasing the effectiveness of their promotional activities. Others may specify overall forecasted e-sales and desired e-market share. Some organisations may extend this statement by breaking the market into specific e-market target segments and detailed aims for e-sales, e-expenditure and e-profits for each product and/or e-market sector.

The e-marketing strategy defines how, by positioning the company in a specific way, stated marketing objectives will be achieved. The marketing-mix section will cover how each element within the e-commerce mix (product, price, promotion and distribution) will be used to support the specified strategy. In relation to the product, it is necessary to determine whether the e-commerce offering provides an opportunity for product enhancement. Such opportunities include improvements in customer service, expansion of product line, and reductions in delivery times. In pricing, thought must be given to whether offline and online prices will be different, and to the potential implications of any price variation on existing offline customers. The promotional mix is reviewed in relation to how the website provides information and the investment which may be needed for offline promotion to build market awareness for the e-commerce operation.

If online transactions are to be on offer to customers, the implications of new distribution methods need to be examined. Finally, after the marketing-mix issue has been resolved, these variables provide the basis for specifying the technological infrastructure needed to support the e-commerce operation.

Control systems should permit management, upon e-market plan implementation, to identify rapidly variations of actual performance from forecast, and be provided with diagnostic guidance on the cause of those variations. To achieve this aim, the control system should focus on measurement of key variables within the plan, such as targeted e-market share, e-customer attitudes, awareness objectives for e-promotion, e-market distribution targets by product, and the expected and actual behaviour of competition.

E-commerce innovation, especially if concerned with revising internal organisational processes, is not a simple task. First, the developers are dependent upon compatibility in the software system operated by the company, suppliers and customers. Most e-commerce software developers can tell stories of the months spent achieving software compatibility between standard platforms and specialist architectures (e.g. linking brand name word processing and graphic software to an automated document imaging system), only to find that a supplier or the customer's IT department innocently installs an upgraded version of a standard software platform with the immediate effect of crashing the entire system.

The second complexity in the innovation management process is the need for e-commerce system to (1) be linked into every database within the organisation and (2) run data interchange on a real time basis. This goal demands that all departments are oriented towards giving priority not to their own information needs but the effective operation of the organisation's e-commerce system. Even in offline companies, efficient interdepartmental communication during the execution of an innovation project is rarely an easily achieved goal. Once the communication requirements are for real time data interchange, seeking to establish effective communication flows usually becomes many times more difficult.

The third complexity within e-commerce innovation is that in many cases the developers will need to draw upon new technologies from a very diverse range of sources, such as computing, telecommunications and optoelectronics.

(I) *Problem 8.1* e-Business gets personal

Introductory comments

Personalisation Once a relationship is the marketing goal, an important step is to identify individual customers (Peppers and Rogers, 1993) and to gather information about them, which is the foundational concept of personalisation (Peppers and Rogers, 1997). Personalisation, then, is defined to be any form of customisation that occurs because of specific recognition of a given customer. For example, a cookie placed on the visitor's computer can allow a site to deliver a homepage low in graphical content if the user appears to be on a slow dial-up modem. Such personalisation is a matter of degree. A conceptual personalisation quotient based on the degree that the website exercises has been developed:

(a) customisation – the system's ability to customise items by allowing individual users to set their own preferences,

(b) individualisation – the system's ability to customise itself to the user based on the user's exhibited behaviour, and

(c) group characterisation – the system's ability to customise itself to the user based on the preferences of other users with similar interests.

PERSONALISATION DOES NOT GUARANTEE LOYALTY

Many conventional and online retailers have invested in customer relationship management, personalisation, and one-to-one marketing programmes in the hopes of building customer loyalty and increasing customer retention. Retailers believe that by tailoring their marketing activities to the unique needs and wants of individual shoppers, they can do a better job of serving their customers.

While personalisation can create customer value and reinforce loyalty, most applications have been simplistic and retailer-centric. The 16 personalisation features tested in this research represent some of the common techniques used in retailing. From this set, there were only 2 that most consumers thought retailers must or should provide and another 4 that more than 40 per cent of shoppers desired. Seven features were disliked by more than 10 per cent of consumers. There are several reasons why personalisation programmes have failed to achieve their goals.

Convenience One of the most popular methods of personalisation is the frequent-shopper programme that rewards repeat customers with price discounts. Some programmes require shoppers to carry a special loyalty card and present it at the point of purchase so that their purchases can be tracked across all forms of payment. Others require consumers to save their receipts and turn them in at a special service desk. For people who do participate, this reduces the convenience of shopping by adding extra steps to the process. For those people who do not, it raises issues of fairness by charging higher prices. It is not surprising that some of the most popular personalisation options increased the convenience of shopping, such as saving a transaction log to simplify returns and warranty repairs.

Privacy Most people do not have to pay their friends to reveal their names, addresses and hobbies. Yet, this is what most retailers do when they sign shoppers up for their frequent-shopper programmes. They give people a discount in exchange for information. Why? Because shoppers often do not see any other tangible benefit for participating in these programmes. Quite the contrary, consumers worry that the information will be distributed to other companies without their knowledge and permission, which may lead to unwanted junk mail, spam and telephone solicitation.

For personalisation to be effective, retailers must build trust with the consumer. Shoppers want to know what information is being collected and how it will be used. They would like the option to view and edit personal information and to control its dissemination. Shoppers expect to see tangible benefits for providing personal data that are commensurate with the amount and type of data provided.

Prediction At the core of most personalisation programmes is an algorithm that attempts to predict which products, services and messages a consumer will respond most favourably towards. Often, this prediction is based on a statistical model of the shopper's past purchases and demographic profile. While this approach can improve the chances that shoppers will respond to an offer, most consumers still receive a mountain of irrelevant and potentially irritation product recommendations and promotional messages. Prediction is poor because (1) the forecasts are based on an incomplete record of shoppers' category purchases, (2) the purchase history may include items purchased for someone other than the shopper, (3) consumers' needs change over time and across situations and (4) purchase histories and demographic profiles may not reflect consumers' attitudes and lifestyles.

Retailers need to move away from the practice of just offering consumers more of what they bought the previous time (or giving them an incentive to switch to a competing product). Retailers need to understand the full constellation of consumer needs and the role of variety seeking so they can filter out what consumers truly have no interest in yet retain a selection of items that will satisfy and potentially delight shoppers. They also need to expand the concept of personalisation to include situational influences and the life stage of shoppers, both of which are important purchase drivers.

In addition, personalisation can be done based on rules provided by experts. For example, if the customer buys shirt A, then recommend pant B, or if the customer is from corporation X, then provide a discount of Y per cent, and so on. From this discussion, it is apparent that personalisation can be applied across any aspect of the e-marketing mix and is, therefore, overlapping and moderating with regard to the effect those other functions have on the customer experience.

Privacy The collection of information forces the marketer to decide how this is to be used, particularly regarding access to it – decision about privacy. Note that privacy-revisions are inescapable (or, in the terms of this, 'basic') once the marketer collects information about individuals and stores it.

Security Another 'essential' function of e-marketing, once we move beyond the concept of simply a transaction, is the issue of security. There are at least two aspects to security, the first being security during the transaction. An example of the first type of security is to ensure that a third party is not hijacking aspects of the transaction. The need for credit card numbers and other critical information on the Internet exposes the customer to risks beyond just the current transaction and therefore involves a trust in the marketer that goes well beyond just the probity and punctuality of the current transaction, heightening the relationship nature of these digital interactions. This trust now encompasses beliefs about the security-related diligence of the marketer. The second aspect of security is regarding the data that are being recorded about the individual (e.g. providing adequate security to the consumer that a third party cannot break into the database). There is a constant battle between methods of security (e.g. encryption) and the sophistication of hackers. It is the marketers' responsibility and competitive necessity to keep ahead in this technological race. A lapse in the security domain could easily be the end of a company.

Customer service Many early marketing mix taxonomy specifications (e.g. Borden 1964) included customer service as a support function often needed to make a transaction happen (and therefore a situational function). The introduction of 'time' into the exchange paradigm (the driving factor in moving to a relationship perspective) means that the marketer is forced to consider providing support to the customer *over time*. This necessitates consideration of customer service (in its broadest sense) as an ongoing and essential function. Interestingly, customer service is typically shown as a necessary function (a key element) in the retail mix (Levy and Weitz, 2001). This suggests that an ongoing direct interaction with customers requires support as an essential function. Furthermore, the support can be about any aspect of the e-marketing mix. It can be an issue about product availability, service plans, pricing or promotions. Hence, customer support is an overlapping function.

The preceding discussion regarding e-marketing functions can be summarised into the following:

- The basic relational e-marketing functions are anytime, anywhere access; personalisation; security; privacy; and customer service.
  - These functions map into the following e-marketing elements, respectively: site, personalisation, security, privacy and customer service.

Following van Waterschoot and Van den Bulte (1992), it is important to realise that while all of the marketing-mix elements are to be coordinated in terms of their interacting and potentially synergistic influence on the customer experience, some functions take place *mostly* through their interaction with other more basic functions and very much moderate the effect of those basic functions. These functions are termed *overlapping functions* and lead to the summary:

Site, customer service, personalisation, privacy, security, sales promotion and community moderate e-marketing mix functions and are designated overlapping.

THE RESULTING E-MARKETING

Mix taxonomy

The preceding propositions lead to the e-marketing taxonomy portrayed on a cube in Figure 8.1. Functions that do not moderate other functions as much (non-overlapping) are shown on the surface of the cube. The overlapping functions are placed in the lower part of the cube to convey that they operate mainly by moderating any of the functions on the surface in addition to moderating each other. The resulting e-marketing mix is expressed in the following acronym: $4Ps + P^2 C^2 S^3$, where P stands for product, price, place, promotion, personalisation and privacy; C stands for customer service and community; and S stands for site, security and sales promotion functions (following the distinctions drawn in van Waterschoot and Van den Bulte, 1992) are as described in the traditional marketing mix. We note that most of the new elements are considered essential from an e-marketing perspective and overlap across the other elements.

We are able to classify all e-marketing tools based on their function to one of the e-marketing mix elements. Figure 8.2 presents this classification. The e-marketing functions allow the categorisation of tools that are otherwise hard to categorise or have a tendency to be arbitrarily categorised. For example, consider registries and wish lists. Many retailers consider these 'services' that are offered to the customer. However, as per our analysis, registries and wish lists allow customers to communicate their preferences to other customers; in other words, they are a community function.

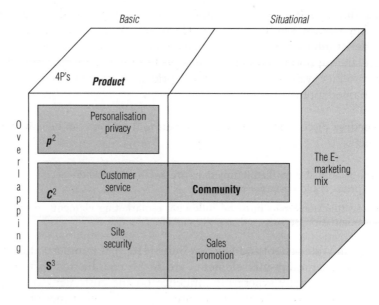

Figure 8.1 The e-marketing mix = 4Ps + $P^2 C^2 S^3$.

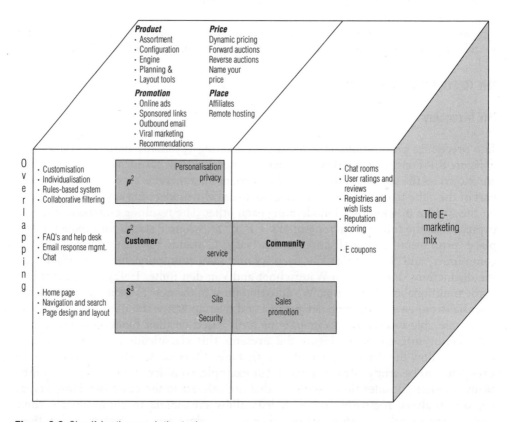

Figure 8.2 Classifying the e-marketing tools.

Merchants and buyers often provide recommendations based on their expert judgement and knowledge, and retailers tend to classify them under assortment. However, our analysis suggests that these are simply communications and hence should be classified under the promotion element. Furthermore, even if a recommendation were personalised, it would still be a communication, except with personalisation moderating it. Again, thinking in terms of e-marketing functions provides a basis for the categorisation.

Techniques for tracking website visitor activity and for monitoring and logging their interests are becoming increasingly powerful.

It's long been understood that it's significantly cheaper to sell to an existing customer than to find a new one. The growth of electronic business has not changed this and recently the US-based Boston Consulting Group calculated from a survey that the cost of selling to a new electronic customer was £34 while to sell to an existing customer was a fifth of that figure at £6.80. Hence to ensure that marketing spend is efficient and that existing customers can be retained, it is important to know what customers want and what your marketing efforts mean to them personally.

It is also very important that web activities should not be divorced from the company's other activities. For most organisations, Internet-only companies excepted, the Web should be seen as only one facet of an overall marketing strategy. Web customers and visitors are simply using a particular medium at a certain point in time and information about them needs to be brought into the relevant databases or customer relationship management (CRM) systems just as much as existing information is used to tailor websites appropriately. In many cases the information will be anonymous but is no less valuable in determining company strengths and weaknesses as well as opportunities for increasing sales to particular segments.

Perhaps the most significant lesson which organisations need to learn is that while the Internet opens up opportunities for increasing sales to new geographical markets, it simultaneously opens up domestic markets to external competitors. One major consequence of this is that the balance between customers and companies supplying them has shifted greatly in the direction of the buyer. It is no longer good enough to rely on customer inertia and companies which do so will fail.

Conversely, organisations which take the trouble to understand their customers' needs and tailor their communications – whether through web pages, e-mail or more conventional mechanisms – to what their customers want will be far better placed to retain them.

Profiling is a means of tracking, identifying and recording visitor activities and preferences so that something approaching a one-to-one dialogue can subsequently take place. This may mean that websites become more dynamic, offering different customers different views according to the customer's specific interests. These dynamic views may be completely personal to individuals or they may be constructed to meet the wishes of those in particular sectors to which anonymous visitors belong. There are now extremely sophisticated mechanisms available, both to gather information and to tailor sites carefully in ways which window displays, print advertising or even personalised direct mail simply cannot match.

Mechanisms for gathering information tend to overlap and most developers offer products which combine two or more techniques. However, the four categories into which Web profiling mechanisms broadly fall are filtering, tracking, response analysis and demographic correlation. These are all variously used in traditional marketing but filtering and tracking in particular are now used to great effect in electronic commerce.

Filtering

The form of filtering enabled by computer power and now widely used on websites is what is known as automated collaborative filtering (ACF). This works by combining the opinions of a large number of people and matching these, duly weighted, with a user's own opinions to attempt predictions. It is particularly useful where little is known about individual visitors and where the area being considered is fairly limited – books, music, clothing, food and the like. However, it is less suitable where correlations are difficult to establish or where scalability is essential.

Another product using ACF is Firefly, now owned by Microsoft. Users who register are given an electronic passport which allow them access to particular sites which are dynamically tailored according to their individual profiles. They can reveal more or less personal data according to their own wishes thereby maintaining a balance between privacy and benefiting from directly tailored offerings. Firefly supplies aggregate anonymous data to retailers and others who use this to construct sites reflecting the interest of particular groups.

Tracking

Tracking mechanisms have been used virtually since the start of the Web and are now becoming extremely sophisticated. They can be used anonymously or can be tied to visitor identities if these are given at some point. Typically they provide information on pages visited; the order in which this happened; how long users spent browsing a particular section of a website; where and how often they clicked; where they came from and where they went to.

Such information can be of considerable value not only for building personalised sites but also for identifying problems in site design or clarifying which mechanisms may work better in getting orders or enquiries.

Tracking and related methods of measurement are used also as crude measurements of site or page popularity by identifying the numbers of accesses, perhaps with the aim of charging advertisers or others on a sliding scale. Much tracking is carried out using what are known as 'cookies' which are small text files placed on the user's computer and subsequently interrogated and updated by the website system.

Beware of the measurement unit 'hit', particularly by those less scrupulous about how they justify high rates. A hit is nothing more than a particular page element, perhaps a graphic, and is meaningless except in context, whereas data on pages viewed or numbers visiting a site usually have more relevance in measuring interest and value.

One particular mechanism which is really in a class of its own but which shares some similarities with other tracking mechanisms is that developed by the Cambridge company Autonomy. The eponymous product is unique in that it offers very sophisticated mechanisms for identifying text according to context and irrespective of language, dialect and jargon. As part of its process, it can track a user's activities whether through reports or other documents or browsing and searching for particular material. This is used to build a sophisticated profile which can change dynamically with changes in user interest and which is then used to offer appropriate items such as reports or research documents.

Demographic analysis and questionnaires

Each of these mechanisms has been in use for some considerable time but has been given new impetus with the development of the Internet. Two of the major companies involved in profiling and personalisation, BroadVision and ATG, each offer products which combine a number of different techniques including response analysis.

It is extremely important, when seeking information from users, that sites do not put barriers in the way of access or of accuracy. A remarkable number of sites not only require registration but also insist on having lengthy questionnaires filled out before a visitor can get anywhere or do anything. This approach is both naive and foolish and has the effect, as research repeatedly shows, of turning away potential customers and of getting information which is flawed and, hence, costly to use as the basis for marketing initiatives.

Registration and questionnaires have their place but it is essential that information be accurate and gathered with the willing cooperation of the visitor. With the new shift in power to the consumer it is essential for companies to understand clearly what their customers want and to get as close to a one-to-one dialogue as is practicable. This has to be done within the context of respecting privacy, both in the formal sense of taking account of the requirements of the new Data Protection Act and in the wider sense of acting in ways with which visitors feel comfortable.

Mechanisms for profiling visitors and customers, whether as identifiable individuals or as anonymous members of particular interest groups, are becoming extremely powerful and can transform a company's marketing effort. However, both the profiling data gathered and the subsequent personalisation of the site for individual visitors should be recognised as being an integral part of the company's overall marketing strategy and not some technical matter handled in isolation.

Problem – example

Levi Strauss

The clothing manufacturer and retailer, Levi Strauss, uses on its website what it calls 'Style Finder', a mechanism to suggest to visitors products which might fit their personal style and tastes determined by answers to questions on preferences in other areas such as music, sports and appearance. Style Finder uses collaborative filtering, powered by Macromedia's LikeMinds personalisation engine, to compare expressed preferences with other customers and then to make recommendations.

A survey of customers found high levels of satisfaction with Style Finder, 93 per cent saying that it was 'fun' and 'easy to use' and 84 per cent commenting that the recommendations were 'right on'. Possibly of even more interest were Levi's figures showing that the average spend rate increased by 33 per cent; that the repeat visit rate increased by 27 per cent and the average length of the shopping session nearly doubled from four to seven minutes with the average number of products viewed rising from six to ten.

Freeserve

The business model for Internet service providers (ISPs) is shifting as new ISPs emerge and as the income streams from call charges and from subscriptions come under threat on account of competition forcing pricing downwards. This means that new revenue must be found and this, in turn, means that accurate information about visitor interest and patterns of browsing needs to be determined in order to justify costs charged to advertisers and to web retailers accessed through portal sites.

Freeserve, part of the Dixon's group, was one of the first UK ISPs to offer a subscription-free service and now has nearly two million registered accounts, an extremely valuable resource of interest to a variety of electronic businesses. It uses WhiteCross Systems tools to monitor user behaviour and to identify customer needs and preferences. These reports are then used by Freeserve to provide demographic data, usage patterns, information on website stickiness and matters such as potential interest in new product lines, to negotiate terms with its corporate customers and so maintain revenue through advertising and related marketing initiatives.

Questions

1 Discuss the notion of a conceptual personalisation quotient (CPQ).
2 At the core of most personalisation programmes is an algorithm that attempts to predict which products, services and messages a consumer will respond most favourably towards, still, why is prediction a poor instrument of analysis?
3 On the basis of the Kalyanam and McIntyre's Framework depicting the e-marketing mix, classify and discuss the marketing tools related to personalisation.
4 Comment on the concept of 'filtering'.
5 Refer to the Levi Strauss case study and critically assess the advantages and disadvantages of the recommendations tool used to encourage customers to repeat purchases.

(I) *Problem 8.2* Digital marketing research

Introductory comments

The Internet represents both continuity and innovation in marketing research. Although it brings considerable new opportunities to market researchers, it is not without its problems and challenges. Some of these are technical, others are ethical, and yet others are political. With less than a decade of solid experience behind it, Internet marketing research is still in its infancy. Although it is now relatively clear how to use the medium to investigate Internet users, it is still not quite so clear how it can be used to research offline activities.

Perhaps the single greatest challenge of the Internet lies in the way that it promises to break down the artificial barriers that currently exist between marketing research and most of the other activities involved in marketing. The Internet provides an opportunity to close the loop, not only between data gathering and data reporting but also between marketing research and selling, and even between marketing research and the product or service design process. Unlike traditional media, the Internet encompasses the entire 'sales' process. Therefore online advertising can be (and is being) integrated with all the other processes of selling, and is becoming an essential element of the broader technology of customer relationship management (CRM).

For online marketing, research need no longer be an episodic and expensive activity, involving teams of interviewers descending on people with clipboards or tape recorders in hand. Rather, it can take place frequently, wherever crucial consumer views are required. The Internet can also close the loop between survey research and reporting. Where Web questionnaires are used, for example, it is possible to post interim results back on the Web or deliver them to sponsors in real time, though the co-existence of interim results and a live questionnaire (as in the currently popular website polls) raises all kinds of methodological issues.

New technology now impacts on every aspect of our lives and the way that we do business, and so it was only ever a matter of time before it was incorporated into market research. A look at the current players who are using new technology shows a polarity emerging in terms of its use. At one end, there are those who focus on the development of computer-based technology for use under strict supervision. At the other end are those who have adopted websites, e-mail, and now mobile phones as means of communication with research participants who can be anywhere, and respond at any time they choose. Others are mixing their methodologies to get the results they want.

Research International, BMRB and MORPACE International are using e-mail, online questionnaires and online focus groups, with Research International currently piloting the use of mobile phone data collection in Japan.

One of the attractions of Internet-based research is that participants can be anywhere, and answer questions at any time, as long as they have access to a PC, but whilst this can solve logistical headaches it can throw up concern about the nature of responses. People taking part in research using the Internet tend to treat it as a family affair, and can consult with others when answering questions. When it comes to buying toilet tissue, for example, we want to know what mum actually does when she's on her own in the supermarket. Results from Internet-based research simply do not replicate consumer behaviour.

Still, the issues of accuracy and the importance of constructing a proper sample are exactly the same when you use the Internet as when you use any other research methodology.

Up to 40 NPD ideas, or ads, promotions, packaging, or names, can be tested in just one three-hour session amongst a sample of up to 200. As total turnaround time is just three weeks, clients do not need to put their programmes on hold. Clients enjoy the increased speed of turnaround; ease of set up; the benefits of real-time dynamic reporting and how they can more effectively reach geographically dispersed audiences.

There may also be other interesting effects of using new technology in research that could not have been foreseen. Because the respondents are, in effect, giving their answers to a computer rather than to another individual, there is no incentive to exaggerate or attempt to impress as is often the case. This is well illustrated by our standard question regarding personal income, (which is) notoriously difficult to glean, and often grossly inaccurate. Our comparisons with national income statistics indicate a high degree of correlation.

Great care must still be taken when using the Internet for survey research when researching consumer markets that are non-Internet related, such as in most FMCG research. The profile of Internet users does not currently match the population profile of the UK, and is unlikely to do so for some time to come. Groups such as women, those over 45, and C2DE respondents are still significantly less likely to have Internet access. To an extent (the use of new technology) has always been restricted by the profile and number of people with access to the technology, although this is getting better. It is generally good for any group with a high Internet penetration, or where you have a defined list of contacts, such as the youth or technical market, or when you are looking at business-to-business or males between the ages of 18 and 35, but it can be less effective for national samples.

Problem

Many of the problems of carrying out marketing research on the Internet are common to conventional marketing research. Those problems that are more likely to be associated with Internet surveys are summarised below.

Lack of universal access to the Internet Less than 20 per cent of the world's population currently has access to the Internet, and most of these are concentrated in the countries of the developed world. Within particular countries, there is also an in-built bias towards early Internet adopters.

Poor online sampling frames There is no global list of e-mail addresses, so online surveys have to make do with alternatives, such as conventional sampling frames (e.g. printed directories or member lists), Internet-based lists (e.g. website visitors and e-mail address lists) and newsgroups. Automatically harvested lists of e-mail addresses (e.g. from newsgroups) often contain a high proportion of out-of-date or spurious addresses. Even where correct email addresses are available, other problems still reduce their effectiveness as a sampling frame: the growing number of people who have multiple email addresses; people who change their email addresses (e.g. switching from one ISP to another to benefit from low-cost start-up offers); users who fail to check their email regularly; and many consumers belong to a number of different online environments.

Sampling problems Even within countries that have a relatively large online population, sampling is made difficult because of biases in the characteristics of people who currently have Internet access – until recently, early Internet adopters in the USA and the UK were white, male, aged 18–59, of above average social–economic and educational status, and either white-collar or professional workers. This makes it difficult to extrapolate Internet survey findings to the entire population.

It is possible to adjust sampling methods to account for this kind of bias. For example, the demographic profile of early Internet adopters tends to be different from the population at large. Knowing the demographic profile of this group, various steps can be taken to counter this bias: adjust samples to include more laggards; sift responses to weed out those from ineligible groups; weight results to boost the results for under-represented sub-populations; or combine online surveys with conventional surveys that have biases in the opposite direction.

The 'open-to-all' Web survey suffers from the same lack of sample knowledge that affects the use of self-completion mail cards inserted in magazines or left on aeroplanes. However, it is not just differential access to the Internet that poses sampling problems and problems of sample representativeness. Bradley (1999) makes the important point that the capabilities of the hardware and software that people use to access the Internet (e.g. PC, TV, Internet-enabled phone) also need to be taken into account, as do the different levels of user capability in relation to the Internet (e.g. do they know how to extract an email attachment?), and user behaviour in the online environment (e.g. frequency, time and place of access). All of these affect whether a survey instrument will get through to an individual, and thus the structure of the online sample. Because these additional factors are still not well understood, this makes it difficult to draw properly constituted samples from online populations. Because of this problem, some restrict online research to online populations, such as visitors to a website, members of an online forum, or members of a business extranet.

Response rate problems If a sampling frame is unavailable, then it is difficult to estimate the online survey response rate, and to ascertain whether a sample quota has been achieved. Although Internet surveys can obtain equally good response rates as conventional surveys, very low response rates (in the 1–5 per cent range) are not uncommon, even in well-designed and highly targeted surveys. Poor response rates in online surveys can be attributed to several reasons: bad vibes, caused by spamming; fears over security and lack of anonymity; and survey fatigue.

Data quality issues The value of data gathered online can be compromised by unreliable responses (e.g. users entering spurious details on website registration forms), and the lack of geographical specificity (i.e. not knowing where email or Web respondents live).

Ethical issues Internet marketing research shares many of the ethical problems that surround various forms of conventional survey and observational research. However, the Internet has thrown up additional problems, the chief of which is the lack of anonymity of email, the selling of people's email addresses and personal information, and the dangers of data integration (i.e. the collation, integration or fusion of disparate sources of individual data gathered over the Internet).

When to use – and not to use – online marketing research

There are several situations where the Internet is a good choice:

- To survey people in distant areas/countries, or dispersed common interest populations.
- To investigate sensitive subjects. There is some evidence, for example, that consumers enjoy the perceived anonymity that Web shopping brings, not only to the obvious acquisition of porn but also to car buying and medical diagnosis. In face-to-face encounters, there is always the possibility that some consumers will feel ashamed or embarrassed, and the same feelings may apply when they are polled for their views. The mediating influence of an Internet encounter can reduce or eliminate these potentially negative feelings.
- For studying people who are early technology adopters or regular Internet users (e.g. academics or young people) – that is those who are *au fait* with the technology, and who are more likely to respond to online questions.
- To study people's online activities – for example their use of websites.

There are also circumstances where it is probably inadvisable to use the Internet. The Internet is probably not the best choice when it is necessary to draw a representative sample of people whose characteristics, behaviour and attitudes need to be extrapolated to the population at large. Another situation is where it is important to involve naturalistic (i.e. non-mediated) interaction – for example where the observation of an individual's body language or of interpersonal reactions is significant. Finally, the Internet may not be effective where respondents need to have physical contact with a product that is being evaluated.

Questions

1   Comment on the following key problem areas related to online surveys (a) lack of universal access to the Internet, (b) sampling problems, (c) response rate problems and (d) ethical issues.
2   Discuss several situations where the Internet is a good choice for marketing research.

(I) *Problem 8.3* B2C e-marketing mix

Introductory comments

High levels of interactivity enable retailers to provide exactly the type of information about products, services and pricing that the individual customer wishes to receive. High levels of interactivity also encourage customers to provide exactly the type of information about themselves that retailers want – including credit card numbers, email addresses, shipping address, personal preferences and purchase histories.

Product strategies

As offline consumers, we purchase impulse items, shopping goods and occasionally speciality items. Some of these purchases require little concentration (low involvement) while others demand much more mental and/or emotional investment (high involvement). Up until now, e-tailers have been reasonably successful selling middle-of-the-road shopping goods (e.g. CDs, books, travel bookings) and also relatively low-involvement speciality goods (e.g. computer games, software and auctions). As technology develops further and e-consumer confidence inevitably builds, we may well witness a significant rise in the availability and purchase of impulse items as well as high-involvement shopping and speciality products. Buying lottery or cinema tickets online or even a new automobile or home may be quite commonplace a few short years from now.

Not very long ago, brands were categorised as pure offline or online brands. Brands such as Coca-Cola, UPS and Sony enjoyed a very distinct position in relation to Yahoo!, AOL and Amazon. But

as the Internet expanded, we began to observe the crossover of offline brands into the online world, and the transition of online brands into the offline world. The end result is a blurring of the distinction between pure offline and pure online brands. (Rayport and Jaworski, 2001: 188)

Brands such as Netscapé, Microsoft and Nintendo are promoted across all available media, the world over.

Place strategies

Although many products may not always be deliverable online, e-consumers are now requiring the use of more non-traditional logistical solutions for non-hope commerce. Increasingly, these customers will want to collect their purchases at tube/rail stations, the workplace, the post office and the petrol station.

e-Marketers, sometimes called 'electronic stallholders', have already seen that automatic cash machines (ATMs), automated kiosks (used for selling CDs, videos or performance tickets, for example) and other online technologies can provide excellent alternative to traditional distribution methods. Banks, auction houses and hospitality businesses are introducing online tools at a fast-growing rate. As they do this, strategists are finding that they need to ask themselves a fundamental question: what blend of offline and online distribution activities is right for our particular industry in order to maintain a high degree of customer satisfaction while keeping our distribution costs low?

Pricing strategies

In this new model, information or content is not merely transmitted from a sender to a receiver, but instead, mediated environments are created by participants and then experienced. (Hoffman and Novak, 1996)

In terms of pricing, this means that e-consumers are empowered by the very nature of online technologies. e-Tailing, by definition, necessitates unprecedented levels of transparency on the part of the vendor. Company information, product features, after-sales support and, of course, pricing/payment terms and conditions must all be presented clearly for easy access by a prospective buyer or his or her 'intelligent agent' (discussed earlier). Websites such as *www.PriceScan.com, www.BotSpot.com* and *www.consumerreports.org* provide excellent product/price comparison opportunities for e-consumers of all ages (Kardes, 2002). The key question one might ask at this point is this: if online customers really do 'want it all', will the average etailer be able to afford to offer such great price deals on an ongoing basis? As is the case for offline marketing, e-tailers must learn to develop very different strategies when attempting to commercialise highly price-sensitive products.

Communications mix

We have seen that ICTs facilitate 'many-to-many' communication exchanges (Hoffman and Novak, 1995). Interactive TV shopping channels, Internet banner ads and pop-up windows, short message service (SMS) marketing and webcasting (or multicasting) are but some of the e-marketing tools recently developed to help e-taliers communicate with netizens. But how can e-tailers maximise the effectiveness of their Internet-based communications? Nicovich and Cornwell (in Richardson, 2001: 155) support the view that traditional mass marketing processes do not appear to fit neatly with Internet culture. The authors recommend that marketers should:

contact users and elicit information without violating the norms exhibited about commercial speech. The way to accomplish this is for marketers to become members of the communities in which they wish to communicate. In this manner, marketers will learn the social values and attitudes exhibited by the community as well as garner a greater appreciation of the communications they present.

e-Tailing is changing rapidly and, in the process, changing the way consumers and marketers look at commerce itself. We are witnessing the rise of 'the experience economy'. In a book of the same name, Pine and Gilmore suggest that more and more companies are staging, marketing and delivering 'memorable experiences' rather than ordinary goods and services. From Niketown to Sony's Metreon (an interactive entertainment experience) the consumer is being exposed to brand/product-related feelings and sensations as never before. We are witnessing the rise of a new breed of retailer, and strategists who ignore this trend may experience tough challenges ahead.

Problem – example

Together we stand

In the comment piece of October's issue of *Marketing Business*, I read that CIM studies show that marketers are losing control of websites to 'an unlikely rival. The customer services department'.

Now call me an old fuddy-duddy if you wish, but I was brought up to see all aspects of a company's interaction with its customers as 'marketing'. And CIM, the lead body of marketing, is frequently harping on about effective customer relations management as part of marketing. So, I ask, how is customer services – which can only be part of the overall task of looking after relationships with customers – seen as a rival? Shouldn't all the customer-related people be operating as one under the heading of marketing people? Isn't this idea of all working together to 'delight the customer' what marketing is supposed to be about?

What's needed is to have practical realism to wipe away the clouds of hype and for good teamwork to make it happen. We need IT to properly explain what can be done, customer services to explain what they think is needed on their part, sales to explain what they think needs doing and for marketing management to ground the whole thing with good solid marketing principles of anticipating and identifying customer needs and wants, and satisfying (nay exceeding) them profitably.

A complete waste of time

In my experience, it is a total waste of time making enquiries on the Internet (unless they are directly related software technical enquiries) as no one bothers to reply.

The commercial websites want your money, but they do not want to hire the staff needed to physically attend to all the incoming and outgoing email messaging.

I have requested technical specifications, availability and VAT refund details several times without ever receiving any reply.

So, what is my reaction? Quite simply, I shall continue to bring my good old fashioned Index and Argos catalogues with me to Saudi Arabia and then when I return (e.g. at Christmas) pre-plan all my shopping from these. So much for all the hype and drivel about how shopping online will threaten the old traditional methods. It is mostly pure hype and propaganda to persuade the punters!

Questions

1   Critically discuss the concept of 'electronic stallholders'.
2   Comment on the views expressed by Nicovich and Cornwell (2001) in which they stated that traditional mass marketing processes do not appear to fit neatly with internet culture.
3   Should all the customer-related people be operating as one under the heading of marketing people?
4   Critically analyse the common complaint that 'it is a total waste of time making enquiries on the Internet as no one bothers to reply'.

(I) *Problem 8.4* e-Distribution management

Introductory comments

Distribution of products usually involves some form of vertical system in which transaction and logistic responsibilities are transferred through a number of levels. In terms of distribution management, Stern and El Ansary (1988) propose that the following factors will need to be considered in the selection of an appropriate system:

1   The capability of intermediaries in the logistics role of sorting goods, aggregating products from a variety of sources and breaking down bulk shipments into saleable lot sizes.

2   The capability of intermediaries in routinising transactions to minimise costs.
3   The capability of intermediaries in minimising customer search costs (e.g. a computer store having available information and demonstration models from a range of different suppliers).

A common convention in Western economies during the twentieth century was that retailers perceived scale benefits in purchasing directly from suppliers, 'cutting out the middleman' and establishing vertically integrated procurement, warehousing, distribution and retailing operations.

Exploitation of this ahead of competition provided the basis for the establishment of what are now considered highly conventional trading dynasties such as Sears Roebuck in the US and Marks & Spencer in the UK.

After decades of being virtually ignored as an important aspect of the marketing management process, in the mid-1980s organisations began to realise that effective management of distribution channels can actually provide additional opportunities to gain advantage over competition. A number of factors contributed to this situation.

Possibly two of the more important have been (1) the impact of new or improved technology in the reduction of transportation costs and/or delivery times (e.g. the construction of motorway networks in Europe that have made it feasible for a manufacturer based in one country to service effectively from one single plant the needs of customers in all other European countries) and (2) exponentially declining prices for IT systems across all facets of the distribution process (e.g. the linking of supermarket computers with the production scheduling systems of key suppliers, to manage more effectively the process of matching production to demand).

Rangan et al. (1993), in reviewing the future strategic implications of new approaches to channel management, suggest that managers must now view the flow of goods and services in relation to the questions of whether exploitation of alternative channels can serve to create competitive entry barriers, enhance product differentiation and enable greater customer intimacy. These authors' proposal is that it is now necessary to 'unbundle' the channel functions of information provision, order generation, physical distribution and after-sales service. The next step is to then determine how customer needs can best be met by channel members working together as a team of channel partners each performing those tasks in which they excel.

E-commerce distribution

The advent of e-commerce is causing many companies to reassess their approach to using distribution systems to acquire and sustain competitive advantage. Even prior to the arrival of the Internet, Moriaty and Moran (1990) refer to the exploitation of new electronic technologies as an opportunity for building 'hybrid marketing systems'. They perceive these technology-based systems as offering new, more customer-oriented, entrepreneurial approaches to channel management. They present the example of IBM, which over the years has moved from a single channel based around its own sales force, to being a hybrid operation involving dealers, value-added resellers, a catalogue selling operation, direct mail and tele-marketing. In the past ten years this has resulted in a doubling of the size of its own sales force and the opening of 18 new channels to serve the highly diverse nature of customer need.

One approach to determining an optimal strategy for selecting an optimal e-commerce distribution channel is to assume that there are two critical dimensions influencing the decision; namely, whether to retain control or delegate responsibility for transaction management, and to retain control or delegate, responsibility for logistics management. This concept can be visualised in the form of an e-commerce channel option matrix of the type shown in Figure 8.3.

An example of an e-commerce market sector in which the supplier tends to retain control over both distribution dimensions is online banking services, because supplier banks usually retain absolute control over both the transaction and delivery processes.

Possibly the most frequently encountered e-commerce distribution model is one in which control over transactions is retained and distribution delegated. It is the standard model used by most online tangible goods retailers. These organisations, having successfully sold a product to a website visitor, will use the global distribution capabilities of organisations such as Federal Express or UPS to manage all aspects of distribution logistics.

In the majority of offline consumer goods markets the commonest distribution model is one in which both transaction and logistics processes are delegated (e.g. major brands such as Coca-Cola being marketed via supermarket chains). This can be contrasted with the online world, in which absolute delegation of all processes is still a somewhat rarer event. The reason for this is that many companies, having decided that e-commerce offers an opportunity for revising distribution management practices, perceive cyberspace as a way to regain control over transactions by cutting out intermediaries and selling direct to the end-user customers. As already mentioned, the process by which traditional intermediaries are squeezed out of channels is usually referred to as 'disintermediation'.

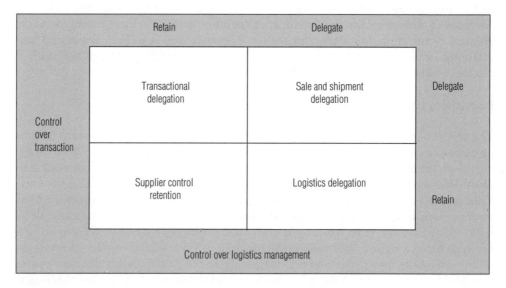

Figure 8.3 An e-commerce distribution option matrix.

It must be recognised, however, that delegation of transactions and logistics may offer ways to improve market service provision, through the exploitation of opportunities made available through 're-intermediation' (Pitt et al., 1999).

Pitt et al. (1999) propose that in assessing e-commerce distribution strategies there is the need to recognise that the technology has the following implications:

1 Distance ceases to be a cost influencer because online delivery of information is substantially the same no matter the destination of the delivery.
2 Business location becomes an irrelevance because the e-commerce enterprise can be based anywhere in the world.
3 The technology permits continuous trading, 24 hours-a-day, 365 days-a-year.

By combining these implications with the basic roles of intermediaries (assortment management, transaction routinisation and the reduction of customer search activities), Pitt et al. have evolved an e-commerce strategic distribution option matrix of the type shown in Figure 8.4. The authors recommend that marketers use this type of matrix to identify potential competitive threats caused by other actors within a market system exploiting e-commerce technology to enhance the distribution process. They also propose that in the future, because of the interactivity of e-commerce, marketers will begin to replace the phrase 'distribution channel' with a new term, 'distribution medium'.

	Technology implications		
	Minimal delivery cost	Location irrelevance	Continuous operation
Minimizing customer search	On-line airline reservation systems	On-line insurance companies	On-line employment recruitment agencies
Transaction routinazation	On-line cross-border banking	On-line OEM procurement networks	On-line catalogue companies
Assortment management	On-line music stores offering customised Cd-ROMS On-line ROMS	On-line manufacturers of customised PCs	On-line educational institutions

Figure 8.4 An e-commerce strategic distribution option matrix (modified from Pitt et al., 1999).

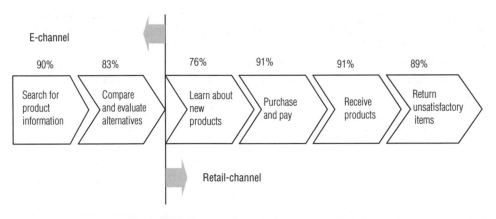

Figure 8.5 Consumer preference for multichannel shopping.

Eventually e-commerce may lead to a major increase in the total number of companies offering products and services across world markets. As this occurs, markets will become more efficient, and many products will be perceived as commodities, with a consequent decline in average prices.

Consumers were most enthusiastic about shipping in conventional retail stores and on the Internet. However, the survey revealed that the various media can play different roles in moving shoppers through the purchase process (see Figure 8.5). On one hand, consumers preferred to visit a retail store to learn about new products (76 per cent), purchase and pay for merchandise (91 per cent), receive products (91 per cent), and return unsatisfactory items (89 per cent). On the other hand, they were most enthusiastic about using the Internet to search for product information (90 per cent) and compare and evaluate alternatives (83 per cent).

Consumers preferred using media that could accurately portray the characteristics of the specific products they were buying. For example, consumers liked using the Internet to find out about and search for information on products such as music, movies, books and consumer electronics, presumably because of the detailed information that is available online. Catalogues were more popular for weekend apparel and furniture and lighting, for which visual quality is important. Television was a preferred medium for learning about products that have a sensory or entertainment element such as toys, games, music and videos. In-store visits were more appealing for expensive and infrequently purchased items such as appliances, furniture, hardware, paint and wallpaper, as well as weekday apparel and groceries.

Problem – example

The e-milkman cometh

E-shopping should be easy, but how do you get the goods delivered?

Shopping on the Internet just has not lived up to its promises. The convenience. The time-saving. All at the click of a mouse.

If you do manage to master all those high-tech ways of persuading you to part with your money – computer and modem, WAP phone and interactive digital television – the last step in the e-commerce chain remains annoyingly low-tech.

You wait for hours for the goods to arrive, pop out to buy a paper and then find a note saying: 'We tried to deliver but you were not in. Please pick up delivery up from the depot.' It is enough to send us all back to the supermarket check-out queues.

These setbacks could soon be a thing of the past. Internet companies have finally realised that online shoppers do not have time to wait for the goodies to turn up.

The finest minds in Internet retail are now dreaming up a range of solutions. In the not too distant future, the lawn-mower you bought from a dot.com could be brought to you by the milkman.

Or you could pick up your new evening dress from the late-opening Costcutter while your supermarket shopping will be safely deposited in the chilled Deliver-e box outside your home.

e-milkmen

Milk floats are being beefed up to allow milkmen to deliver everything from televisions and DIY equipment to fine wines and beauty products right to your doorstep.

Every day, about 4,000 floats deliver milk to 2.2 million households. These milkmen also drive past another 5.5 million homes. In all, about 40 per cent of British homes could be reached by milk floats delivering all your Internet shopping.

'Bundling deliveries together is very environmentally friendly. It also means your milkman becomes your local community delivery agent,' says Andrew Day, chief operating officer at M-box, the company which has linked up with Express Dairies to provide the service.

The company has yet to announce which online traders and mail-order companies will be using the service.

The corner shop

If the e-milkmen do not reach your home or you are never there when the floats drive past, you may be able to pick up your delivery from a late-opening corner shop. Spar, Londis and Costcutter are some of the convenience stores which have agreed to receive deliveries on behalf of Internet shoppers. The idea will work rather like the National Lottery franchise. It will be up to local shopkeepers to decide whether to provide the service; then M-box will vet each outlet to see whether the premises are suitable to take part in the scheme.

If they meet the standards, each corner shop will have a special computer terminal connected to the central M-box hub to keep track of deliveries. When the shopkeeper receives your parcel, the barcode will be scanned into the computer and you will be sent an e-mail to say your shipping is ready for collection.

The Roving Porter

Many shoppers many still prefer to cut out the middlemen and receive goods directly at home. Urbanites living in a block of flats could hire the modern equivalent of Jeeves – a Roving Porter.

This service already exists but the downside is that the cost may wipe out any savings made by shopping online.

For £25 an hour, Luxury Home Management will send a real person to wait for deliveries at your home. Given that few companies promise an exact delivery time, hiring a Roving Porter to hang around our home for the afternoon is likely to burn holes in your pockets.

However, the service could be value for money if flat owners club together and split the costs. Roving Porters can organise your domestic life from collecting dry cleaning to booking theatre tickets for visiting relatives while waiting for your case of wine to arrive.

The Delivery Dock

Property developer Laing has developed its own solution to the problems of Internet delivery in the form of a Delivery Dock.

The dock is 1 metre high and 1.7 metres wide: deliveries are made through an external door opened by a security code while the homeowner has access through an internal door.

The dock is big enough to hold a supermarket trolley and has three compartments at different temperatures to ensure that your ice-cream stays frozen, your milk is kept chilled and biscuits are stored at room temperature.

At the moment, the only Delivery Dock in the country is a £7,000 prototype attached to a five-bedroom Laing home at a development at Richmond Heights in London. But the company says the price will drop once the system is in full production, and smaller docks will be also available.

Deliver-e box

Not everyone will want to knock an extra door through one of their external walls. Nor could you install a dock if you live in a flat. But you may be able to use a Deliver-e Box. It works on the same principle as the dock but can be installed anywhere you like, provided it is connected to the electricity mains.

Internet Delivery Solutions (iDS), the company behind Deliver-e box, says the stand alone 'smart boxes', like fridges, will be available in a variety of sizes including a special model designed as a bank of lockers for blocks of flats. As with docks, these boxes can be customised to fit in with the surroundings. Expect to pay around £400 for each unit. But they are not in the shops just yet. iDS is not planning to sell the units until it has completed a full-scale pilot next spring.

Questions

1. Comment and give examples of the advent of 'hybrid marketing systems'.
2. Discuss one approach to determining an optimal strategy for selecting an optimal e-commerce distribution channel.
3. Comment on the effectiveness of the 'corner shop', 'the Delivery Dock' and 'Deliver-e box' approaches.

References and further reading

Quelch, J. A. and Klein, L. (1996), The Internet and International Marketing, *Sloan Management Review*, Spring, pp. 60–75.

Rayport, J. F. and Sviokla, J. (1994), Managing in the Marketspace, *Harvard Business Review*, November–December, pp. 75–85.

Rayport, J. F. and Sviokla, J. (1995), Exploiting the Virtural Value Chain, *Harvard Business Review*, November–December, pp. 141–150.

9

Sales and Distribution Management

Sales management programmes and activities do not exist in a vacuum. Effective sales management programmes must be designed to respond to a firm's environmental circumstances, and they must be consistent with the objectives and content of the business's competitive and marketing strategies. Sales management also plays a crucial role in implementing those higher level strategies. Good sales management policies and practices are essential ingredients for ensuring the success of a firm's competitive and marketing strategies.

Effective management requires a solid understanding of the activities one is trying to manage. Unfortunately, many people have misconceptions about the selling process, the activities carried out by salespeople, and the personal characteristics necessary for a successful career in professional sales. In part, these misconceptions arise because different types of selling jobs involve different kinds of tasks and require different skills and abilities from the people who do them.

Sales management involves three interrelated processes: (1) the formulation of strategic sales programme, (2) the implementation of the sales programme and (3) the evaluation and control of sales force performance.

A sales programme constitutes only one part of a marketing plan, and the marketing plan is only one element of the total strategic planning process in most firms. This is particularly true for companies with multiple divisions and those that have divided their operations into strategic business units to improve planning and the allocation of company resources across related groups of products or markets. Because such firms involve multiple 'businesses', their overall strategic planning process typically occurs in several stages and involves a series of different plans to guide activities at different levels of the organisation. This hierarchy of strategic plans commonly includes the corporate strategic plan, the strategic business unit plan, marketing plans, and programmes for individual marketing functions.

The values of society also affect marketing and sales programmes in a variety of ways. Social values set standards for ethical behaviour. Ethics is more than simply a matter of complying with the laws and regulations.

Marketing channel decisions are among the most important decisions that management faces. A company's channel decisions directly affect every other marketing decision. The company's pricing depends on whether it uses mass merchandisers or high-quality speciality stores. The firm's sales force and advertising decisions depend on how much persuasion, training and motivation the dealers need. Whether a company develops or acquires certain new products may depend on how well those products fit the abilities of its channel members. Companies often pay too little attention to their distribution channels, however, sometimes with damaging results.

Distribution channels are more than simple collections of firms tied together by various flows. They are a complex behavioural system in which people and companies interact to accomplish individual, company and channel goals. Some channel system consist only of informal interactions among loosely organised firms; others consist of formal interactions guided by strong organisational structures. Moreover, channel systems do not stand still: new types of intermediaries surface, and whole new channel systems evolve.

In designing marketing channels, manufacturers struggle between what is ideal and what is practical. A new firm usually starts by selling in a finite market area. Because it has limited capital, it typically uses only a few existing intermediaries in each market – a few manufacturers' sales agents, a few wholesalers, some existing retailers, a few trucking companies and a few warehouses. Deciding on the best channels might not be a problem: the problem might simply be how to convince one extra few good intermediaries to handle the line.

If the new firm is successful, it might branch out to new markets. Again the manufacturer will tend to work through the existing intermediaries, although this strategy might mean using hybrid marketing channels. In smaller markets, the firm might sell directly to retailers; in larger markets, it might sell through distribution. In one part of the country, it might grant exclusive franchises because that is the way merchants normally work; in another, it might sell through all outlets willing to handle the merchandise. In one country, it might use international sales agents; in another, it might partner with a local firm.

Thus, channel systems often evolve to meet market opportunities and conditions. However, for maximum effectiveness, channel analysis and decision making should be more purposeful. Designing a channel system calls for analysing consumer service needs, setting the channel objectives and constraints, identifying the major channel alternatives, and evaluating them.

Once the company has reviewed its channel alternatives and decided on the best channel design, it must implement and manage the chosen channel. Channel management calls for selecting and motivating individual channel members and evaluating their performance over time.

In today's global marketplace, selling a product is sometimes easier than getting it to customers. Companies must decide on the best way to store, handle and move their products and services so that they are available to customers in the right assortments, at the right time and in the right place. Logistics effectiveness will have a major impact on both customer satisfaction and company costs; poor distribution system can destroy an otherwise good marketing effort. Here consider, *the nature and importance of marketing logistics, goals of the logistic system, major logistics functions and the necessity of integrated logistics management.*

The integrated logistics concept recognises that improved logistics requires teamwork in the form of close working relationships across functional areas inside the company and across various organisations in the supply chain. Companies can achieve logistic harmony among functions using cross-functional logistics teams, integrative supply managers, and senior-level logistics executives with cross-functional authority. Channel partnerships can be cross-company teams, shared projects, and information sharing systems.

(I) *Problem 9.1* Marketing objective and structure for the sales force

Introductory comments

Even when the strategic conditions and communications tasks faced by a firm favour the allocation of substantial promotional resources to the salesforce, the specific marketing objectives that salespeople are asked to pursue vary widely across firms facing different market and competitive situations. A company's sales personnel might be asked to focus on one or more of the following objectives: (1) winning acceptance of new products by existing customers, (2) developing new customers for existing products, (3) maintaining the loyalty of current customers by providing good service, (4) facilitating future sales by providing technical services to potential customers, (5) facilitating future sales by communicating product information to potential customers or influencers and (6) gathering market information. Table 9.1 summarises these selling objectives, the specific activities involved in achieving them, and the conditions under which they are likely to be appropriate.

It is interesting to note that several of these personal selling objectives – such as maintaining customer loyalty, providing technical service, and communicating product information – are all related to the broader marketing objectives of retaining and increasing sales to current customers; objectives that Nabisco's salespeople have tackled quite successfully in recent years. Clearly, the ability to effectively service existing customers is crucial to a firm's continued success. In one recent study of nearly 200 firms across a variety of industries, for instance, firms that reported they were successful in retaining existing customers and in increasing their share of the purchases made by such customers were nearly twice as profitable as the average company in the survey. Unfortunately, fewer than two-thirds of the responding firms considered themselves effective at retaining existing customers, and only about a third felt they were doing a good job of gaining share or selling new products to established accounts. These results suggest that not all salesforces are as effective at servicing customers and building enduring relationships with them as Nabisco's. This, in turn, suggests that some firms may need to adjust salesforce objectives and/or provide the sales management policies and support needed to help achieve those objectives.

TYPES OF SALES JOBS

Each of the above objective demands a somewhat different set of activities from the salesforce. Because different firms pursue different objectives, the nature and content of the industrial sales job varies widely across companies. Researchers have classified sales jobs in more than 100 different ways. The most useful classification scheme identifies four types of sales jobs found across a wide variety of industries.

Trade selling

The salesforce's primary responsibility is to gain and maintain support for the firm's products within the distribution channel by providing merchandising and promotional services to the channel members. Such salespeople also play a critical role in gaining distribution support for new products by making effective sales presentations to

Table 9.1 Personal selling objectives

Objective	Activities involved	Conditions where appropriate
Winning acceptance for new products	Sales reps build awareness and stimulate demand for new products or services among existing or potential customers	Business pursuing prospector strategy: potential customers arge in size lor few in number; company's promotional resources limited; firm pursuing *push* distribution strategy
Developing new customers	Sales reps find and cultivate new customers and/or expanded distribution for business's products or services	Target market in growth stage or firm wishes to increase share of mature market; potential customers large in size or few in number; company's promotional resources limited; firm pursuing *push* distribution strategy
Maintaining customer loyalty	Sales reps work to increase value delivered to customers by providing advice or training on product use, expediting orders, and facilitating product service	Business pursuing differentiated defender strategy; firm has large share of mature market and wants to maintain loyalty of existing customers; product technically complex and/or competition for distribution support is strong
Technical service to facilitate sales	Sales reps work to increase value to customers by helping integrate product or service with customer's other equipment or operations and by providing design, installation and/or training	Product technically complex; customers (or dealers) relatively few in number and large in size; product or service can be customised to fit needs of individual customers; products sold as parts of larger systems
Communicating product information	Sales reps work to increase understanding of product's features and application as basis for possible future sales and to educate people who may influence final purchase	Product technically complex and/or in introductory or at growth stage of life cycle; lengthy purchase decision process; multiple influences on purchase decision
Gathering information	Sales reps provide reports on competitors' actions, customers' requests or problems, and other market conditions and conduct marketing research or intelligence activities	Appropriate under all circumstances, but especially useful in industry introductory or growth stage, or when product technology or other factors are unstable; business pursuing a prospector strategy

wholesale or retail buyers. As we saw in the Nabisco Biscuit example, some firms divide their trade-selling activities between two positions: sales representatives concentrate on gaining acceptance for new products and expanded support for established products; *retail merchandisers* support the selling effort by providing merchandising and promotional services, such as building displays, in individual stores.

Missionary selling

The salesforce's primary purpose is to build and maintain volume from current customers – and perhaps to facilitate new product introductions – by giving purchase decision-makers product information and service assistance. Missionary salespeople often do not make sales to customers directly but persuade them to buy the firm's products from wholesalers or retail suppliers. Examples include brewers' reps who call on bar owners and encourage them to order a particular brand of beer from the local distributor, and medical detailers who call on doctors as representatives of pharmaceutical manufacturers.

Technical selling

The salesforce's primary objective is to increase business from both past and potential customers by providing technical product information and technical design and engineering services needed to facilitate sales. Sales engineers for machine-tool and telecommunications equipment manufacturers are examples of people engaged in technical selling.

New business selling

The salesforce's primary responsibility is to identify, establish relationships with, and obtain business from new customers that the firm has not dealt with before. This is a particularly important kind of selling in firms pursuing prospector strategies and in industries with rapidly changing technology and newly emerging product applications.

Each type of sales job involves different objectives and tasks, and each requires different skills and capabilities on the part of the salesperson. Thus, a firm's sales management policies – including its selection criteria, training programmes and compensation plans – must be consistent with its objectives and the kinds of selling activities necessary to achieve them. One set of activities, however, is common to nearly all kinds of sales jobs (with the exception of missionary selling), namely, the activities involved in actually making a sale to a customer.

SALESFORCE ORGANISATION

There are several common bases for organising a firm's sales efforts. Each has unique advantages that make it appropriate under specific strategic circumstances.

The first organisational issue to be resolved is whether the firm should hire its own salespeople or rely on outside agents, such as manufacturers' representatives. When a firm decides to hire its own salespeople, it can organise its salesforce in a number of different ways. The major alternatives include: by geographic area, by product type, by customer and by selling function.

Geographic organisation

The simplest and most common way to organise a salesforce is to assign salespeople to separate geographic territories. Each salesperson is then responsible for performing all the activities necessary to sell all the products in a company's line to all types of customers in that territory.

One of the major strengths of this approach is its relatively low cost, an advantage that is particularly attractive to smaller firms. Besides, as only one sales rep calls on each customer, there is seldom any confusion about who the customer should talk to if problems arise.

The major disadvantage of geographic organisation is that it does not provide any of the benefits of specialisation and division of labour. Each salesperson is a jack-of-all-trades who must be knowledgeable about all the firm's products and all types of customers, and who must be competent in performing a full range of selling and customer service activities. For these reasons it is unusual for larger firms to rely exclusively on geographic organisation, although they often use it in conjunction with other organisational forms. Thus, a firm may have separate salesforces for different product lines, but the members of each salesforce are likely to be assigned geographic territories.

Product organisation

Many larger firms – particularly those in high-tech industries – have separate salesforces for their different products or product lines, as outlined in Figure 9.1. Nearly every division at the 3M Company, for instance, has its own salesforce.

The primary advantage of a product organisation is that salespeople become familiar with the technical attributes, applications and effective selling methods associated with a specific type of product or service. It also enables sales management

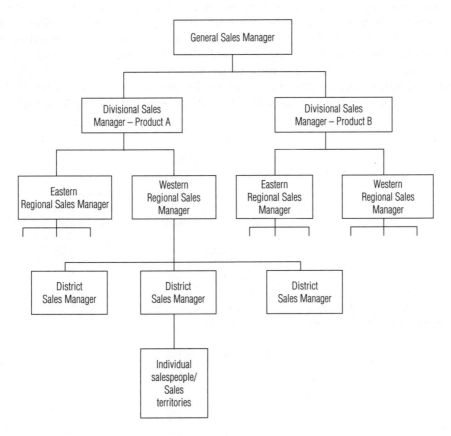

Figure 9.1 Salesforce organised by product type.

to control the allocation of selling effort across products. If management decides to devote more effort to a particular product line, it can simply assign more people to the appropriate salesforce.

The major disadvantage of organising by product is duplication of effort. Salespeople from different product divisions assigned to the same geographic territories may call on the same customers.

Customer organisation

In recent years, increasing numbers of firms have organised their salesforces by customer type, as shown in Figure 9.2. For example, General Electric at one time organised its salesforce by products (fan motors, switches). Later GE changed its structure to allow salespeople to specialise in a particular industry, such as air-conditioner manufacturers or auto makers. This approach is a natural extension of the concept of market segmentation. By specialising in serving a particular type of customer, a salesperson can better understand their unique needs and requirements. Managers can also control the allocation of selling effort to different markets by varying the size of the specialised salesforces.

The disadvantages of customer organisation are the same as those of a product-oriented structure. When customer firms have different departments or divisions operating in different industries, two or more salespeople may end up calling on the same customer. This duplication of effort can lead not only to higher selling and administrative costs but also to customer confusion. Nevertheless, these structures are increasingly popular among large firms whose products have different applications in different industries, or who must use different selling approaches to reach different types of customers (as when products are sold to both the government and to private industry).

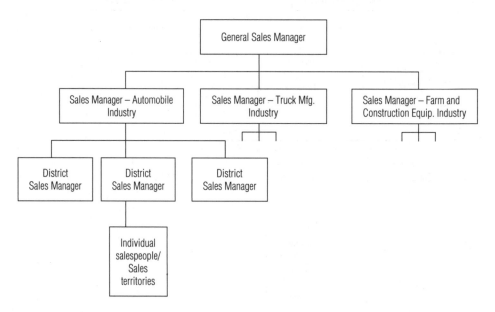

Figure 9.2 A salesforce organised by customer type.

It is also a useful organisational form when a firm's objectives include penetrating previously untapped markets.

One specific form of customer-oriented organisation that has enjoyed a rapid recent increase in popularity is *national account management*. In this form a firm designates its largest customers or potential customers as national accounts (sometimes also called *key accounts* or *house accounts*) and assigns them to special high-level sales managers or sales teams. Xerox, for example, handles about 250 of its largest customers through a separate force of national account managers. Black & Decker has even established separate power tool divisions to cater to its fastest growing national accounts – Wal-Mart and Home Depot. In each, a vice president oversees an account service team composed of salespeople, a marketer, an information systems expert, a sales forecaster and a financial analyst.

National account management is growing in popularity for several reasons: Mergers and acquisitions have produced greater concentrations of large firms in many industries. Some companies find that a mere 10 per cent of their customers account for well over half their sales volume. Also, many large corporations are centralising more of their purchases to increase their bargaining power over suppliers. Those suppliers, in turn, are forced to devote more attention to such customers. Finally, the typical sales representative may not always have sufficient authority or expertise to deal effectively with the high-level managers from various functional departments who constitute the buying centres in many large corporations.

Given this rationale, a firm's national account managers should have several characteristics. They should hold relatively high-level positions within the company hierarchy. They should have the knowledge and experience – or the technical support – to deal effectively with buying influences from different functional areas. And they should have the authority to coordinate the efforts of departments within their own company – such as R&D and production – playing crucial roles in meeting the requirements of the firm's national accounts.

Organisation by selling function

Because different selling tasks require different skills and abilities, it may make sense in some cases for different salespeople to specialise in different functions. One such functional organisation has one salesforce prospecting for and developing new accounts, while a second maintains and services old customers. Nabisco Biscuit's approach of hiring retail merchandisers to take over some stocking and display duties and free salespeople to spend more time selling is another example of a functional organisation. In view of their high costs, though, such structures are justified only when the complexity of the selling task or the effort required to service accounts increases the value of specialisation.

Problems and Questions

A sales manager for a large consumer package goods firm argues that £350,000 should be cut from the media advertising budget of the firm's various products and used to hire five more company salespeople. Her rationale is that at today's media prices five more salespeople can generate more sales volume than spending £350,000 in advertising.

1   How would you evaluate this argument? Under which conditions might the sales manager be right? Under what conditions might she be wrong?

The 100-member salesforce of the firm mentioned in Question 1 calls on national, regional and local supermarket chains. They are responsible for gaining authorisation for purchases from the chain headquarters and winning shelf space in, and providing merchandising service to, individual stores in each chain. The company's product line consists of 10 varieties of cookies, 7 kinds of crackers and 5 snack products. Suggest two ways in which such a salesforce might be organised. What are the benefits and limitations of each?

2   Which would you recommend and why?
3   Which type of sales job are the salespeople working for the company described in Questions 1 and 2 involved in? What objectives and activities are likely to be most important in such a job? What kind of skills and personal characteristics should the company look for when hiring new salespeople?

Problem 9.2 Sales force management

Introductory comments

Recruiting and selecting sales personnel

Recruiting is the activity of locating skilled salespeople and 'selling' them on applying for employment. Companies use many means to recruit a salesforce – newspaper advertisements, announcements in trade publications, conventions, referrals by salespeople and other employees, and college placement offices.

The selection of a salesforce is basically a matching process. Many methods are used to evaluate potential salespeople including application forms, references, credit reports, psychological tests, physical examinations and aptitude tests. These and other devices help screen out unsuitable candidates, but the most common selection method is still the personal interview. This allows an organisation to evaluate a candidate's personality, drive, ability to meet and deal with people and ability to think and react quickly. Few, if any, salespeople have been hired without first undergoing a personal interview.

Training the salesforce

Sales training is required to turn candidates into effective salespeople. The methods used vary widely. Some companies – especially those that market products from door to door – provide little formal training; they expect new salespeople to learn from experience. But other companies invest thousands of dollars in sales training. And they provide frequent refresher courses to keep the sales force motivated and up-to-date.

A training programme should focus on providing (1) *product information*, which allows salespeople to fit the product to the customer's needs; (2) *sales techniques*, which enhance salespeople's persuasiveness; (3) *general information* about the company – its history, policies and procedures – to help salespeople understand the organisation they represent; and (4) *competitive information*, which enables salespeople to better understand the strengths and weaknesses of competitors.

Motivating salespeople

The job of selling can be very frustrating. Customers can be unpleasant; the word *no* is frequently heard; travelling takes time and saps energy. Research has shown that about 80 per cent of 'new business' is obtained only after five sales calls. In short, selling can be a big headache, and sales managers must constantly motivate the salesforce. This can take the form of both financial and psychological encouragement.

Many companies set sales quotas for their salespeople, and financial compensation is tied to fulfilment of the quota. Generally such quotas are set higher than expected sales levels in order to give the salesperson extra incentive. In addition, many companies establish a programme for acknowledging the accomplishments of their salespeople. They also encourage salespeople through such means as formal sales meetings, conventions, bulletins in company publications and trips and other prizes for top performers.

Compensating the salesforce

Certainly a major way to motivate the sales staff is to offer financial rewards. An organisation's compensation progrmme can both motivate salespeople and keep them from leaving for greener pastures elsewhere.

There are many ways to compensate a sales staff, but they all tend to reward employees for time, productivity or both. If time is the main factor, salespeople receive a *salary*. This makes sense when salespeople are new to the job or when many non-selling tasks must be performed. A salary is appropriate for the less creative sales jobs described earlier in the chapter. Productivity, on the other hand, is most often rewarded by means of *commissions* or *bonuses*. A *straight commission plan* is the opposite of a salary; it is directly related to performance. The commission rate is either fixed or based on a sliding scale that is applied to sales or profits generated. *Bonuses* are generally given for special efforts or achievements. Most companies offer a combination of these approaches. (See Table 9.2)

Designing a compensation programme is not a simple matter. Management desires a plan that is flexible and financially reasonable and allows sufficient control over the salesperson's activities – yet at the same time provides incentives for greater effort. The salesforce wants an equitable plan that provides a steady income and at the same time offers rewards for outstanding performance. Some middle ground between the desires of both parties needs to be found.

Supervising the salesforce

The 'outside' salesforce often is quite distant from company headquarters. Some means of supervision is necessary to ensure that the work is carried out and to let salespeople know that the organisation cares about their work and their productivity. Supervision involves seeing that the sales objectives are being met in the field. The sales manager can provide technical assistance and help salespeople voice their problems and

Table 9.2 Percentage of companies using plan

Method	All industries		Consumer products	Industrial products	Other commerce/ industry
	1984	1983	1984	1984	1984
Straight salary	17.1%	20.4%	12.4%	14.2%	27.4%
Draw against commission	6.8%	5.4%	5.1%	6.5%	8.4%
Salary plus commission	29.0%	30.9%	21.2%	32.5%	25.9%
Salary plus individual bonus	33.6%	30.1%	46.0%	33.4%	25.9%
Salary plus group bonus	2.3%	1.9%	4.4%	2.0%	1.5%
Salary plus commission plus bonus	11.2%	11.3%	10.9%	11.4%	10.9%
Total	100.0%	100.0%	100.0%	100.0%	100.0%

complaints to the company. Because of their 'middleman' position, sales managers can have a tremendous impact on salespeople's attitudes and morale.

The lines of communication between the salesforce and the company should be kept open. Memos, letters, reports and various publications all help accomplish this. Most important, however, is the personal supervision that brings a human element to the relationship between the organisation and the sales force.

Evaluating salespeople

Evaluation of each salesperson's performance is a key step in sales force management. It entails measuring results against a specific set of standards. This process is complicated by the amazing number of uncontrollable factors that influence salespeople's performance. For this reason, qualitative judgements must enter into the evaluation process.

Sales managers obtain information about the salesforce from many sources. The most important is the sales report. Additional information comes from letters of complaint and praise, customer questionnaires, conversations with other salespeople and personal observation. Sales or call reports often show plans for the future as well as past activities; they are generally submitted weekly. (Some examples are shown in Figure 9.3.) Such reports give the status of customer accounts and provide information for follow-up. Salespeople also submit expense reports and special reports on new business or new products. These reports allow the sales manager to evaluate the salesperson on the basis of average number of sales calls made, average length of sales call, sales volume per sales call, average order size, sales by product line, number of new customers per time period and number of customers lost per time period. Salespeople must know what performance standards they are expected to meet; otherwise, their efforts may be misdirected and they may become dissatisfied with the management.

Call Report

_____   _____
Company   Date

Person and title _____

Address _____

Objective of Call
_____

Result of Call
_____

☐ Follow-up
_____

Target Account Call Report

_____   _____
Company   Date

Person and title _____

Address _____

Potential Order _____

Current status	Objective this call	Next action to be taken	Problems to be over

Key Account Call Report

_____   _____
Company   Date

Person(s) contacted _____

Address _____

Stage of sales process	Action taken this call	Result	Next action and call back date

Call Report

Reason for call:	☐ Appointment secured
☐ First call (Prospecting qualifying)	☐ Complete information secured
☐ Needs analysis	
☐ Presentation	☐ Proposal accepted
☐ Proposal/cost analysis	☐ Follow-up
☐ Close	

Figure 9.3 Tailoring commission plan measurement to fit component objectives.

Problem

Cove Inc.

Cove Inc.'s chairman, John Mackay, and its president, Peter McKinlay, depend on a dedicated and professional direct salesforce to market their company's products. However, recent social and economic changes have made recruiting and retaining salespeople far more difficult today than they were a few years ago. Cove Inc.'s profits are suffering as a result.

Cove Inc., which manufactures and sells its own line of cosmetics, food supplements and household products, experienced downturns in the past but was able to recover. In 1996, the company raised its prices by 10 per cent, thereby pushing dealers' prices to a level 50 per cent higher than that of competing vitamins and food supplements. Sales collapsed, and Mckinlay, the then company president, ordered a price freeze. Profits continued to fall, however, so McKinlay moved all vitamin production to a new plant, doubled the research budget to £5 million, and dropped many low-profit cosmetic and household cleanser items from the product line. More important, he shifted the company's emphasis to nutritional products. This strategy earned Cove Inc. modest sales gains for the next two years.

In 2001, Cove Inc. entered the diet market with Focus, a high-protein meal substitute drink. Cove Inc. salespeople sold £67 million worth of Focus, breaking previous company records for a new product and boosting overall sales by 14 per cent, to £539 million. The company's stock price leaped to a record high of £42 per share.

The recovery proved short-lived, however. In 2002, Focus sales dropped by 38 per cent, to £40 million, reducing the company's total sales by 15 per cent and its profits by 59 per cent. Third-quarter earnings were 70 per cent below the previous year's figure, and Cove Inc.'s stock price sank to a low of £13.38.

Mackay and McKinlay realised that the temporary profit surge had masked Cove Inc.'s real problem: recruiting and retaining salespeople. Cove Inc. had tried to increase its profits by maximising productivity instead of by improving its salesforce. As a result, in 2002 the number of company salespeople was 7 per cent less than the 2001 peak of 13,400, and sales suffered accordingly. Other direct-sales companies – including Avon Products, Mary Kay cosmetics and Tupperware suffered similar salesforce reductions and, consequently, a dramatic drop in 2002 earnings.

Analysts blame the death of direct salespeople on a number of factors. It was difficult to earn a living in direct sales during the recession years of the early 1990s to mid-1990s. As the economy improved, many direct salespeople discovered that they could make money more easily at other kinds of work. Also, the pool of 'housewife' sellers shrank as more women entered the labour force.

Mackay and McKinlay hope to solve the problem by changing their recruiting tactics and providing more enticing incentives to remain with the company. They plan to attract new dealers from the ranks of career women and middle-class couples seeking additional income. The proposed incentive programme offers salespeople 50 per cent of their sales revenues and adds more steps to the top of the company's direct-selling structure so that salespeople can earn the rewards of advancement more quickly.

Despite the havoc that economic and social factors have played with direct selling, Mackay and McKinlay have no intention of abandoning it for another marketing strategy. The new incentive programme may solve Cove Inc.'s salesforce problems. However, Mackay and McKinlay plan to hedge their bets by investing some of the company's £70 million of available cash in pharmaceutical, fitness and personal-products companies.

Questions

1 Outline the marketing and personal-selling problems facing Cove Inc.
2 What strategic and tactical recommendations would you make to Cove Inc.'s managers?
3 With respect to sales management, how might the recruitment problem be approached?

(I) *Problem 9.3* Development of a sales commission plan

Introductory comments

A commission is payment for achieving a given level of performance. Sales people are paid for results. Usually, commission payments are based on the salesperson's dollar or unit sales volume. However, it is becoming more popular for firms to base commissions on the profitability of sales to motivate the sales force to extend effort on the most profitable products or customers. The most common way is to offer salespeople variable commissions, where relatively high commissions are paid for sales of the most profitable products or sales to the most profitable accounts. Variable commission rates can also be used to direct the sales force's efforts towards other straight sales objectives such as introduction of a new product line.

Advantages

Direct motivation is the key advantage of a commission compensation plan. There is a direct link between sales performance and the financial compensation the salesperson earns. Consequently, salespeople are strongly motivated to improve their sales productivity to increase their compensation, at least until they reach such high pay that further increases become less attractive. Commission plans also have a built-in element of fairness (if sales territories are properly defined with about equal potential), because good performers are automatically rewarded, whereas poor performers are discouraged from continuing their low productivity.

Commission plans have some advantages from an administrative view. Commissions are usually easy to compute and administer. Also, compensation costs vary directly with sales volume. This is an advantage for firms that are short of working capital because they do not need to worry about paying high wages to the sales force unless it generates high sales revenues.

Limitations

Straight commission compensation plans have some important limitations that have caused many firms to abandon them. Perhaps the most critical weakness is that management has little control over the sales force. When all their financial rewards are tied directly to sales volume, it is difficult to motivate salespeople to engage in account management activities that do not lead directly to short-term sales. Consequently, salespeople on commission are likely to 'milk' existing customers rather than work to develop new accounts. They may overstock their customers and neglect service after the sale. Finally, they have little motivation to engage in market analysis and other administrative duties that take time away from actual selling activities.

Straight commission compensation plans also have a disadvantage for many salespeople. Such plans make a salesperson's earnings unstable and hard to predict. When business conditions are poor, turnover rates in the sales force are likely to be high because salespeople find it hard to live on the low earnings produced by poor sales. And agency theory, a conceptual framework developed in economics, suggests such problems are likely to be even more severe when a firm's salespeople are relatively risk averse; that is, when they prefer a predictable future income stream to one that offers uncertain chances to earn either unusually high or unusually low levels of income.

To combat the inherent instability of commission plans, some firms provide their salespeople with a *drawing account*. Money is advanced to salespeople in months when commissions are low to ensure they will always take home a specified minimum amount of pay. The amount of the salesperson's 'draw' in poor months is deducted from earned commissions when sales improve. This gives salespeople some secure salary, and it allows management more control over their activities. A problem arises, however, when a salesperson fails to earn enough commissions to repay the draw. Then the person may quit or be fired, and the company must absorb the loss.

A series of steps are required to establish the foundation on which a sales commission plan can be built. These steps are as follows:

(A) Determine specific sales objectives of positions to be included in plan

For a sales commission plan to succeed, it must be designed to encourage the attainment of the business objectives of the component division. Before deciding on the specific measures of performance to be used in the plan, the component should review and define its major objectives. Typical objectives might be:

* Increase sales volume.
* Do an effective balanced selling job in a variety of product lines.
* Improve market share.
* Reduce selling expense to sales ratios.
* Develop new accounts or territories.
* Introduce new products.

Although it is probably neither desirable nor necessary to include all such objectives as specific measures of performance in the plan, they should be kept in mind, at least to the extent that the performance measure chosen for the plan are compatible with and do not work against the overall accomplishment of the component's business objectives.

Also, the relative current importance or ranking of these objectives will provide guidance in selecting the number and type of performance measure to be included in the plan.

(B) Determine quantitative performance measure to be used

Although it may be possible to include a number of measures in a particular plan, there is a drawback to using so many as to overly complicate it and fragment the impact of any one measure on the participants. A plan that is difficult to understand will lose a great deal of its motivation force, as well as be costly to administer properly.

For those who currently have a variable sales compensation plan(s) for their salespeople, a good starting point would be to consider the measures used in those plans. Although the measurements used for sales managers need not be identical, they should at least be compatible with those used to determine their salespeople's commissions.

However, keep in mind that a performance measure that may not be appropriate for individual salespeople may be a good one to apply to their manager. Measurements involving attainment of a share of a defined market, balanced selling of a variety of products and control of district or region expenses might fall into this category.

Listed in Table 9.3 are a variety of measurements that might be used to emphasise specific sales objectives.

For most components, all or most of these objectives will be desirable to some extent. The point is to select those of greatest importance where it will be possible to establish measures of standard or normal performance for individuals, or at least small groups of individuals working as a team.

If more than one performance measurement is to be used, the relative weighting of each measurement must be determined. If a measure is to be effective, it must carry enough weight to have at least some noticeable effect on the commission earnings of an individual.

As a general guide, it would be unusual for a plan to include more than two or three quantitative measures with a minimum weighting of 15–20 per cent of planned commissions for any one measurement.

(C) Establish commission payment schedule for each performance measure

1 *Determine appropriate range of performance for each measurement* The performance range for a measurement defines the percentage of standard performance (%R) at which commission earnings start to the point where they reach maximum.

The minimum point of the performance range for a given measurement should be set so that a majority of the participants can earn at least some incentive pay and the maximum set at a point that is possible of attainment by some participants. These points

Table 9.3 Tailoring commission plan measurements to fit component objectives

Objectives	Possible plan measurements
Increase sales/ orders volume	Net sales billed or orders received against quota
Increase sales of particular lines	Sales against product line quotas with weighted sales credits on individual lines
Increase market share	Per cent realisation (%R) of shares bogey
Do balanced selling job	%R of product line quotas with commissions increasing in proportion to number of lines up to quota
Increase profitability	Margin realised from sales
	Vary sales credits to emphasis profitable product lines
	Vary sales credit in relation to amount of price discount
Increase dealer sales	Pay distributor *salespeople* or sales manager in relation to realisation of sales quotas of assigned dealers
Increase sales calls	%R of targeted calls per district or region
Introduce new product	Additional sales credits on new line for limited period
Control expense	%R of expense to sales or margin ration. Adjust sales credit in proportion to variance from expense budget
Sales teamwork	Share of incentive based upon group results

will vary with the type of measure used and the degree of predictability of individual budgets or other forms of measurement. In a period where overall performance is close to standard, 90–95 per cent of the participants should fall within the performance range.

For the commission plan to be effective, most of the participants should be operating within the performance range most of the time. If a participant is either far below the minimum of this range or has reached the maximum, further improvement will not affect his or her commission earnings, and the plan will be largely inoperative as far as he or she is concerned.

Actual past experience of %R attained by participants is obviously the best indicator of what this range should be for each measure used. Lacking this, it is better to err on the side of having a wider range than one that proves to be too narrow. If some form of group measure is used, the variation from standard performance is likely to be less for the group in total than for individuals within it. For example, the performance range for total district performance would probably be narrower than the range established for individual salespeople within a district.

2 *Determine appropriate reward to risk ration for commission earnings* This refers to the relationship of commission earned at standard performance to maximum commission earnings available under the plan. A plan that pays 10 per cent of base salary for normal or standard performance and pays 30 per cent as a maximum commission would have a 2 to 1 ration. In other words, the participant can earn twice as much (20 per cent) for above-standard performance as he or she stands to lose for below-standard performance (10 per cent).

Reward under a sales commission plan should be related to the effort involved to produce a given result. To adequately encourage above-standard results, the reward to risk ratio should generally be at least 2 to 1. The proper control of incentive plan payments lies in the proper setting of performance standards, not in the setting of a low maximum payment for outstanding results that provides a minimum variation in individual earnings. Generally, a higher percentage of base salary should be paid for each 1%R above 100 per cent than has been paid for each 1%R up to 100%R to reflect the relative difficulty involved in producing above standard results.

Once the performance range and reward to risk ratios have been determined, the schedule of payments for each performance measure can then be calculated. This will show the percentage of the participant's base salary earned for various performance results (%R) from the point at which commissions start to maximum performance. For example, for measurement paying 20 per cent of salary for standard performance:

Per cent base salary earned		Per cent of sales quota
1% of base salary for each + 1&R	0%	80% or below
	20%	100% (standard performance)
1.33% of base salary for each + 1%R	60%	130% or above

(D) Prepare draft of sales commission plan

After completing the above steps, a draft of a sales commission plan should be prepared using the outline below as a guide.

Keys to effective commission plans

1   Get the understanding and acceptance of the commission plan by the managers who will be involved in carrying it out. They must be convinced of its effectiveness to properly explain and 'sell' the plan to the salespeople.

2   In turn, be sure the plan is presented clearly to the salespeople so that they have a good understanding of how the plan will work. We find that good acceptance of a sales commission plan on the part of salespeople correlates closely with how well they understood the plan and its effect on their commission. Salespeople must be convinced that the measurements used are factors they can control by their selling efforts.

3   Be sure the measurements used in the commission plan encourage the salespeople to achieve the marketing goals of your operation. For example, if sales volume is the only performance measure, salespeople will concentrate on producing as much revenue as possible by spending most of their time on products with high volume potential. It will be difficult to get them to spend much time on introducing new products with relatively low volume, handling customer complaints, and so on. Even though a good portion of their compensation may still be in salary, you can be sure they will windup doing the things they feel will maximise their commission earnings.

4   One good solution to maintaining good sales direction is to put at least a portion of the commission earnings in an 'incentive pool' to be distributed by the sales manager according to his or her judgement. This 'pool' can vary in size according to some qualitative measure of the sales group's performance, but the manager can set individual measurements for each salesperson and reward each person according to how well he or she fulfils the goals.

5   If at all possible, you should test the plan for a period of time, perhaps in one or two sales areas or districts. To make it a real test, you should actually pay commission earnings to the participants, but the potential risk and rewards can be limited. No matter how well a plan has been conceived, not all the potential pitfalls will be apparent until you have actually operated the plan for a period of time. The test period is a relatively painless way to get some experience.

6   Finally, after the plan is in operation, take time to analyse the results. Is the plan accomplishing what you want it to do, both in terms of business results produced and in realistically compensating salespeople for their efforts?

A point system for basing bonus payments on two performance dimensions

An industrial chemical manufacturer pays its salespeople a base salary of £15,000 per year. An annual sales quota is established for each salesperson, and the sum of the quotas equals the firm's annual sales forecast.

The incentive plan is divided into two parts. Part I provides that each sales rep who meets or exceeds quota receives 10 bonus points. In addition, for each 2 per cent of sales in excess of quota, each salesperson receives an additional bonus point up to a maximum of 20 points per year on Part 1 of the plan.

Part II of the plan provides bonus points for bringing in new accounts. A new account is defined as one that has not placed an order during the preceding 36 months. Bonus points are granted to salespeople for new accounts as follows:

Annual purchase volume by new account	Sales rep bonus points
£5,000–25,000	1
25,001–50,000	2
50,001–100,000	3
100,001 and up	4

Each salesperson is limited to a maximum of 20 bonus points per year on Part II of the plan. Bonus earnings are calculated and paid annually. For each bonus point earned, the salesperson receives 1 per cent of the salary. Thus, each salesperson can earn bonus payments up to a maximum of 40 per cent of the salary.

Questions

1   Discuss the advantages and limitations of the straight commission compensation method.
2   Analyse possible plan measurements associated with the following specific sales objectives: (1) increase sales/orders value, (2) increase market share, (3) increase profitability and (4) the introduction of a new product.
3   How can a sales manager determine the appropriate reward to risk ration for commission earnings?

(M) *Problem 9.4* Choosing among alternative distribution-channel structures

Introductory comments

Given the number of alternatives for a distribution-channel structure, management needs a rational, formalised approach to determine the best arrangement for specific needs. Various techniques are possible, but here we discuss only two of the more popular methods.

Weighted factor score method

Management begins the weighted factor score method by identifying factors important in the choice of a distribution channel alternative. Such factors might include selling ability, market coverage, customer knowledge and others, as presented in Table 9.4. Weights are assigned to each factor according to its importance to management in the channel selection decision. The weights add to 1.0. Channel alternatives are then rated in terms of their strength on each factor. The importance weights assigned by management are multiplied by their perceptions of the strength of each channel alternative on the factors of importance. Management usually chooses the distribution channel alternative with the highest score.

Hierarchical preference ordering method

The hierarchical preference ordering method requires management to rank each selection factor by its importance in the choice of a distribution channel alternative and to set a minimum 'pass' level for each factor, as shown in Table 9.5. Management initially evaluates each distribution channel alternative on the most important factor. Next, management evaluates each channel alternative according to the second factor, then the third and so forth through all factors. Channel alternatives rated below the minimum level of acceptance for a factor are eliminated.

Problem

Lee Matthews Technology Ltd is an industrial manufacturer of precision equipment products. The management of the company has decided to revise its distribution policy in order to increase the overall level of effectiveness of the corporate strategy. As shown

Table 9.4 Weighted factor score method of channel selection – the Lee Matthews Technology Ltd case

Factor	Factor importance to management	Channel member strength as perceived by management*										
		.0	.1	.2	.3	.4	.5	.6	.7	.8	.9	1.0
Selling ability	0.10				x						y	
Inventory	0.15		y								x	
Market coverage	0.20							y			x	
Control	0.05			x				y				
Selling	0.05							x				y
Customer knowledge	0.25							x		y		
Investment	0.20		y							x		
Total score	1.00											

Note
* x = rating of the distributor; y = rating of the representative.

Table 9.5 Hierarchical preference ordering method (applied to five distribution alternatives) – the Lee Matthews Technology Ltd case

Factors in order of importance	Level					
	Minimum pass	Alternative 1	Alternative 2	Alternative 3	Alternative 4	Alternative 5
Amount of investment involved	.3	.8	.6	.2	.9	.9
Amount of profit if this alternative works well	.5	.5	.8	.6	.5	.4
Ability of the company to cut short its losses	.5	.7	.6	.1	.8	.8
Effectiveness in reaching key end-use customers	.3	.3	.7	.8	.6	.3
Experience the company will gain in industrial marketing	.4	.2	.5	.6	.2	.4

in Table 9.4, two channel alternatives – an industrial distributor and a manufacturer's representative – are being evaluated.

The managers involved in this decision-making process have also used the hierarchical preference ordering method to evaluate five possible channel alternatives (three new types of industrial distributors in addition to the same two channels being considered). They have rated the amount of investment involved as the most important factor in the assessment of both alternative channels.

Table 9.5 introduces the evaluation of the different channel alternatives according to the utilisation of the hierarchical preference ordering method made by the managers of Lee Matthews Technology Ltd.

Questions

1 Calculate the ratings allocated to the two channel alternatives (industrial distributor and manufacturer representative) based on the importance weights and perceptions of strength assigned by the management of the company. Which channel alternative should be favoured in this case?

2   What are the limitations associated with the use of the weighted factor score method?
3   Determine the 'pass' and 'fail' levels on each factor of importance achieved by the five alternative channels on the basis of the judgement made by the management of the company when applying the hierarchical preference ordering method and allocate the appropriate final ranking of the possible distribution channels.
4   What are the limitations associated with the use of the hierarchical preference ordering method?

(I) *Problem 9.5* Retailing strategies

Introductory comments

Retailing strategies

Two broad theoretical concepts drive retailing strategies: theories of institutional (structural) change and store location. *Theories of structural change* include the retail life cycle concept, wheel of retailing, retail accordion, dialectic process, adaptive behaviour and scrambled merchandising. Retailers who understand these theories can develop proactive and adaptive strategies that enable them to remain profitable in a rapidly changing environment.

The *retail life cycle* is similar to the product life cycle but refers specifically to changes in the structure of retail institutions over time. Like products, retail institutions progress through four identifiable stages of indeterminate length from inception to demise: innovation, accelerated development, maturity and decline, as illustrated in Figure 9.4.

The *wheel of retailing theory* describes the evolution of retail institutions as a wheel-like or cyclic progression. It explains the upward spiral of retail innovators who enter the market as low-priced, low-margin, no-frills, low-status operators. Over time, competitive pressures cause the retailer to add more upscale products, more services, and more attractive store surroundings. This results in loss of the original price-conscious consumers, making way for new low-price innovators to enter the market (see Figure 9.5).

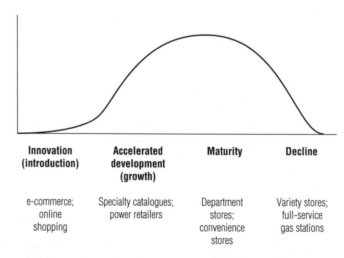

Innovation (introduction)	Accelerated development (growth)	Maturity	Decline
e-commerce; online shopping	Specialty catalogues; power retailers	Department stores; convenience stores	Variety stores; full-service gas stations

Figure 9.4 Retail life cycle.

Note: Actual length of each stage may vary.

252

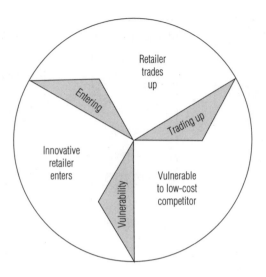

Figure 9.5 Wheel of retailing.

General ⟶	Specific	⟶ General	
General store	Department store	Single-line; speciality store	Superstore
Wide assortment	More specialised than general store	One or a few merchandise lines	Wide assortment
One-stop shopping;	Urban-dense populations	Drug stores, bookstores	One-stop shopping:
Rural/sparse populations			Serve large populations

Figure 9.6 Retail accordion.

The *retail accordion* concept refers to a general-specific-general pattern of expansion and contraction of merchandise lines, although each type of store exists today. The general store that offered broad assortments of unrelated merchandise to early US colonists lost popularity as department stores emerged to fill more specialised needs. Eventually, a broad spectrum of speciality stores evolved to fill these same needs, focusing on a single product line or a few related lines of merchandise. The accordion idea continues as superstores and mass merchants offer one-stop shopping to a diverse customer base (see Figure 9.6).

Distinctly different forms of retail institutions emerge as old and new, or substantially different, types of retail institutions adapt to one another. This can be explained as a *dialectic process* with three stages: thesis (original form of retail operation), antithesis (completely different form) and synthesis (innovative combination of old and new), as shown in Figure 9.7.

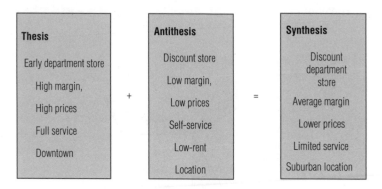

Figure 9.7 Dialectic process.

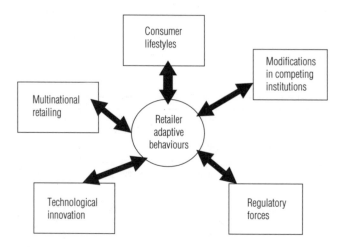

Figure 9.8 Adaptive behaviour.

The *adaptive behaviour theory* of changing retail institutions has its roots in Darwin's theory of natural selection (survival of the fittest). Retailers who anticipate changes in their environments and develop winning competitive strategies will survive and prosper. In an overcrowded retail marketplace, often the only place to gain new business is to take it away from competitors (see Figure 9.8).

THEORIES OF STRUCTURAL CHANGE IN RETAILING

Scrambled merchandising

Scrambed merchandising refers to the practice of adding unrelated goods and services to a retailer's traditional product assortment to increase sales and profits through quick selling of higher-margin items that often are purchased on impulse. Examples include the addition of sunglasses and snack foods at a gasoline service station and milk and eggs at a drugstore.

Store location strategies

Store location strategies are related closely to manufacturer and wholesaler distribution strategies and to the evolution of retail structures. The complex theories of retail location and site selection are beyond the scope of this problem. However, location can be viewed from the perspectives of competition and development. Strategic positioning involves not only perceptual comparisons with competitors but also physical placement of retail facilities relative to those of other retailers that compete for the same consumer dollars. For example, fast-food restaurants find it advantageous to locate relatively close to one another. Most discount stores and mass merchandisers operate in free-standing locations with large parking areas, preferably near a large shopping mall in a high-traffic location. Stores that sell shopping goods such as jewellery, furniture and cars tend to locate near one another to facilitate customers' need to compare merchandise and deals. Malls and strip shopping centres are home to many specialty retailers and large department stores.

Trends and issues in retailing

The retailing industry is experiencing change in major areas: store formats and operations, channel relations and customer characteristics. The trend in *store formats and operations* is towards more nonstore retailing, greater specialisation, and more superstores. Many retailers and their customers bypass physical storefronts altogether with direct-response techniques, such as direct marketing (e.g. telemarketing, catalogues, vending machines, and a computerised and electronic commerce). Perhaps the most compelling trend is the rapid acceleration of electronic commerce, made possible by advances in technology, communications, and customer databases.

Speciality stores that serve nearly every product category and consumer lifestyle are proliferating. Many are small boutiques that carry everything from sunglasses to souvenirs of your favourite sports team. Others are megaretailers that focus on one product category. Category killers like Toys 'R Us and Home Depot carry luggage assortments of a particular product line and sell at low prices, making it difficult for department stores and smaller specialty stores to compete with them in that category. Following the 'bigger is better' trend, acquisitions and mergers in all retail categories have accelerated retail consolidation for greater domestic and global coverage. At the other end of the spectrum, entrepreneurs continue to develop innovative concepts that change the usual way of doing business such as grocery shopping over the Internet, fast-food delivery services and one-product kiosks in malls.

Retailers are under pressure from all sides to cut operating costs by adopting operating methods that are most efficient or lose their competitive advantage. Point-of-sale scanning, computerised order processing, improvements in logistics and other state-of-the-art applications have become more sophisticated. More demands are placed on suppliers to provide services such as prewrapping delicatessen products or preticketing apparel. At the same time, consumers demand greater value and lower prices, making it necessary to increase profit margins by lowering costs, partially through performing more of the distribution functions in-house.

Trends in *channel relations* focus on heightened competition, building stronger relationships with suppliers and customers, and developing synergies in the supply chain.

Many channel relationships have been formalised through acquisitions and mergers that increase consolidation within the industry. Many of these changes are evolving in response to the demands of a changing marketplace.

Shifts are occurring in *customer characteristics*. Customers are better informed and more value conscious. They come from increasingly diverse ethnic and socio-economic backgrounds and have different shopping preferences. They expect more service, more convenience or hassle-free shopping and lower prices. Increasingly retail customers expect to be entertained while shopping and are attracted to the ambience of the store.

Problem – example

High street heroes lose to superstore

The traditional high street is under threat and there will be smaller and fewer retailers in the feature, according to a recent Mintel report.

Mintel says the high street is suffering at the hands of out-of-town retail parks and superstores and although it will survive into the next century, its role is changing.

The report follows the Government's *volte face* on town development. In the past developers have been encouraged by government and relaxation of planning regulations, to build large out-of-town complexes, but the government is now encouraging town centre, high-street investment. A government paper published this summer identified a 'sequential approach' to planning ensuring developers gave preference to town centres.

However, much of the development and the future of the high street depends upon consumer behaviour. Increased car ownership has made consumers more mobile and given them more choice about where to shop (and park). However, it is the less mobile and affluent pensioners and benefit groups that are most loyal to the high street.

Added to this is the demand by retailers for better quality sites which are often not found in town centres but in new complexes. To survive, smaller high-street retailers, particularly food stores, will have to develop upmarket niches to compete with the more convenient grocery superstores on the outskirts of town, says the Mintel report. Non-food retailers are advised to focus on those, generally more affluent, consumers who use the high street for 'top-up shopping'. But with out-of-town sites with planning permission still to be built the general outlook for smaller retailers is bleak. The number and choice of the traditional high street-based retail businesses will inevitably decline as a consequence of changing shopping habits determined by preferences to shop elsewhere (*Marketing Business*, 1995; Dec/Jan).

Questions

1   Which of the theories of structural change in retailing describes best the case discussed in the problem example above?
2   Taking into account the specific conditions of the competitive environment (e.g. saturation of markets, low growth rates, high competitive intensity, high business failure rates, the increased number of 'multidimensional' competitors) which of the models of structural change in retailing explains this scenario more accurately?
3   Comment on the retailing trend conceived with store formats and operations.
4   Discuss the impact of the new characteristics of the new consumer on the future of retailing.

(I) *Problem 9.6* Merchandising strategies

Introductory comments

Store image and atmosphere are also affected by the retailer's approach to *layout* and *display*, which can influence both the customer's behaviour within the store and their perception of the retailer's positioning. They affect how people move around the store, which items attract their attention and their propensity to interact with the merchandise. Retailers might, however, be restrained in what they can do with layout and display by the kind of factors shown in Figure 9.9.

STORE LAYOUT

McGoldrick (1990) suggests that most store layouts conform to one of three broad types, or combine elements of them. The alternative layouts are shown in Figure 9.10.

Grid pattern

The grid pattern is the kind of layout adopted by most supermarkets, with systematically arranged aisles. These tend to lead the shopper around the retail space along a largely predictable route that covers most of the store. Supermarkets try to prevent the shopper from taking short cuts by making sure that staple items such as sugar, bread and milk are placed well apart from each other and scattered around the store. Thus the shopper who only wants a few basic things still has to pass lots of tempting items that might just lead to a few extra, impulse purchases. Routine-response staple items are also piled high to reduce the frequency of shelf refilling, and are placed in narrow

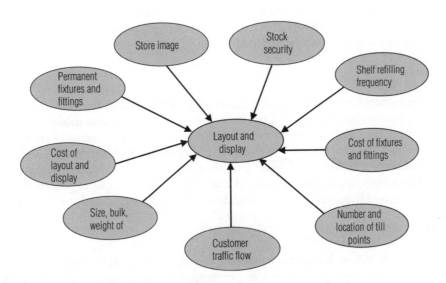

Figure 9.9 Consideration sets of layout and display.

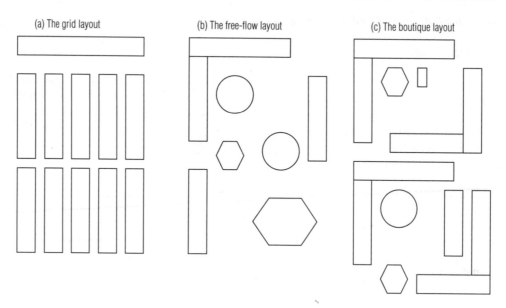

Figure 9.10 Three types of store layout.

aisles to keep shoppers moving, as they do not need to browse around these goods. In contrast, wider aisles are used for the more exotic, less frequently purchased premium goods, such as ready meals, so that shoppers can move more slowly, have their attention captured and browse comfortably.

Grid layouts do make sure that the shopper covers as much of the store as possible, and they are easy and cheap to install and maintain. They can, however, be rather boring and regimental, giving the impression of 'functional' shopping. The shopper might also be inclined to associate them with 'pile it high and sell it cheap' discount approaches to retailing, although the fixtures and fittings and the lighting used by some supermarket chains do give a better-quality feel.

Free flow

The free flow pattern is more irregular, involving a variety of different sizes, shapes and heights of fixtures and fittings. Shoppers are free to take any route around the store, and can thus either browse around everything in any order they choose, or cut through directly to one display at the back of the store if they prefer. Fashion retailers and others trying to achieve a strong visual 'look' that stimulates customers but encourages them to take their time browsing use this kind of layout. It can, however be expensive to set up and maintain, and it does not use the available floor space as efficiently as a grid layout.

Boutique

Whereas in a free flow layout the customer perceives the selling area as essentially a single space, in a boutique layout the perception is a number of discrete, separate spaces. This might be particularly useful in a large selling space, such as a department store, where very different departments and concessionaires want to create their own unique and more intimate character.

Many stores combine elements of the three types of layout. A superstore might well use a grid layout for its groceries and other fast-moving lines, but use a free flow approach for clothing, books or videos, for example. Similarly, a variety store such as Boots will vary its approach. Boots uses a supermarket-style grid layout for fast-moving, staple items such as tights, shampoos, soaps and sticking plasters, but a free flow approach for gift-orientated toiletries, toys and household goods. In some larger stores, the gift department, for example, might even be a boutique layout.

DISPLAY

Whatever the type of layout adopted, the retailer also has to think about the way in which merchandise is displayed within it. Rosenbloom (1981) suggests five alternatives.

Open display

Open displays make the merchandise easily accessible to shoppers and encourages them to pick up and examine goods closely. Fashion stores in particular prefer to encourage such involvement, so that customers can feel the texture and quality of the fabric, can hold a garment up in front of themselves to check its length or whether it suits them, or can be encouraged to try it on.

Theme display

Themes are commonly used in all kinds of retailers to create a focal point to attract a customer's attention. Events such as Christmas, Easter and Mother's Day all provide natural themes for the display of gifts and other merchandise. A supermarket might perhaps build an end-of-aisle display around a theme such as Chinese cookery. These displays are usually temporary and thus provide something new and different for the regular customer to look at, as well as bringing in related merchandise together.

Lifestyle display

Lifestyle displays try to create a more natural setting for the product, giving an idea of how it might be used or by whom, through the subtle use of pictures and other props. IKEA and other furniture retailers, for example, show their goods in room settings, with books in the bookcases, lamps on the tables and pictures on the walls. Fashion retailers also use lifestyle displays, perhaps using large photographs at the point of sale showing a particular type of person in a particular type of setting wearing a particular outfit. The mail-order catalogues have, of course, been doing this sort of thing for years.

Co-ordinated display

A coordinated display is similar to lifestyle and themed displays in that it brings together related goods. In a coordinated display, goods that are usually sold or used together are displayed together. Thus a women's clothing store might display coordinating jackets, skirts and trousers together, or include accessories in a clothing display. Even supermarkets might use coordination, for example by displaying marzipan, icing sugar, ready-made icing, food colourings and edible cake decorations together near the flour, dried fruit and other home baking goods.

Classification dominance display

The aim of a classification dominance display is to suggest specialisation and expertise within a particular product group through the sheer choice of goods displayed. Thus a branch of W.H. Smith, for instance, might have a display of biros and fountain pens covering a wide range of prices, colours, designs and brands. Displays such as this are meant to give the customer the impression that *this* is the only place to shop for these kinds of goods.

Problem – example

House of brands

Selfridges won the 2002 Phoenix Award for transforming itself from an uninspiring department store to a stylish destination.

In 1909 Selfridges founding father, Gordon Selfridge, opened his store in Oxford Street, London, declaring that Selfridges was 'for everyone'. The retailer remained successful for the best part of a century, but by the mid-1990s had worn out its appeal. In 1997, a major programme to relaunch the brand began. Its key objective was to attract a new customer base and to provide a solid platform for the brand to move into other regions outside London. The main challenge was to move Selfridges from 'famous building' status to 'famous brand' status.

'A key driver in the repositioning was the concept of shopping as entertainment', says marketing director James Bidwell. Radical changes to the brand included investment of more than £100 million in store layout and design; more directional supplier brand mix; new corporate identity; and deployment of windows as brand advertising vehicles (versus traditional product sales tools). 'Selfridges' strategic positioning in the market-place is 'the House of Brands'. 'We firmly believe in the power of the brand, as opposed to the traditional department stores, where layout was historically dictated by product groupings,' says Bidwell.

Advertising agency BBH worked with Selfridges to create the ad campaign 'It's Worth Living in London' – designed to act as a wake-up call and shock consumers out of their traditional perceptions of the brand. The campaign featured no product (highly unusual for department store retailers) and was designed to position Selfridges as being at the heart of metropolitan life.

This concept was also delivered through events in store (Spice Girls book signings, club nights in the Selfridges car park in conjunction with Kiss FM etc.), collaborations with artists and designers through window displays, and a series of sponsorship initiatives with galleries such as the Serpentine, Barbican and Hayward.

In 1999, Selfridges' advertising share of voice was 8 per cent, against Harrods' 18 per cent, Harvey Nichols' 2 per cent and Liberty's 4 per cent.

Measuring effectiveness

The effectiveness of Selfridges' relaunch is evident across all key indicators: latest sales growth increased by 6 per cent in Oxford Street (52 weeks by February 2001) and 23 per cent Manchester in a depressed sector. The market overall saw 2 per cent, according to British Retail Consortium.

- share price growth – up 35 per cent (320.0£ 3 February 2001 versus 236.5£ July 1998).
- Increase in conversion to purchase – 48 per cent in 2001 versus 46 per cent in 2000 and rising to 63 per cent in added value promotional periods.
- Increase in footfall of up to 28 per cent in London, 58 per cent in Manchester as a result of major events.

Selfridges continues to capitalise on market trends and will be investing £25 million over the next two years to fund eight new departments in its two stores.

In September 1998, Selfridges opened a store in Manchester. Expansion plans continue – another store will open in Manchester Central in 2002 and, following a £40 million investment, 2003 will see a store in Birmingham. Further sites are being sought. Plans have also been announced to develop the back of the Oxford Street site. It will be designed by Sir Norman Foster and will include 100,000 square feet of additional retail space, a new hotel, leisure facilities, store offices and a car park.

Factfile

Name of parent company:
Selfridges Retail Ltd
Brand name:
Selfridges & Co
Original launch:
Oxford Street Store, 1909;
  Manchester Store, September 1998
Date of national relaunch:
1997
Market category:
Retail

Brand share	1998	1999
Selfridges	2.8	3.4
Harrods	3.9	4.0
Liberty	0.6	0.6
Harvey Nichols	1.1	1.1

Questions

1 Comment on the concept of 'grid pattern'.
2 What is the rationale behind the multisection of lifestyle displays?

3   What was the main driver associated with Selfridges' repositioning strategy? Discuss some of the radical changes implemented by the company.

4   Analyse the key indicators used to measure effectiveness in the case of the Selfridges relaunch strategy.

(M) *Problem 9.7* The total cost approach to distribution

Introductory comments

The more management focuses on the company's efforts on cutting distribution costs, the less successful it is likely to be in reducing the real costs of distribution. This apparent paradox is no abstract or armchair play on phrases. It explains why so many companies have diligently pruned distribution costs – in the warehouse and in inventory, in order processing and in transportation – only to find that these hard-earned savings are somehow not translated into improved profit margins. They have been watered down or actually washed out by increases in other costs scattered throughout the company.

It is these 'other costs,' motley and miscellaneous as they first seem, that turn out on closer analysis to be the *real* cost of distribution. They never appear as distribution costs on any financial or operating report, but show up unidentified and unexplained at different times and in assorted places – in purchasing, in production, in paper-work processing – anywhere and everywhere in the business. When the gremlin-like costs are traced to their roots, however, one finds that they are, in fact, all intimately interrelated, linked together by one common bond. They all result from the way the company distributes its products.

It is this aggregation of distribution-related costs – rather than what management usually mean when they complain about the cost of distribution – that represents the important and increasing drain of distribution on earnings. These are the costs – rather than those usually defined and dealt with as distribution costs – that have eluded even the most earnest cost-cutting drives. Because of its size and its elusiveness, this cost complex remains for many companies a promising profit-improvement potential.

THE TOTAL COST APPROACH

When to use it

For earnings-minded management, the dimensions of this profit potential, and a practical technique for tapping it, have now been tested and proved. A handful of companies have faced up to the across-the-board impact of distribution on costs and profits. They have accomplished this by applying an approach – we call it the 'total cost approach' that is designed to convert these intangible and intricate cost interrelationships into tangible dollar-and-cents improvements in profit margins. A major food manufacturer, after applying effectively an assortment of rigid cost-cutting techniques, has found that this new approach is enabling the company to add 1.7 per cent to its margin on sales.

A major merchandiser, already enjoying the benefits of advanced distribution techniques, found that this same new approach could cut from its corporate costs an additional £7.5 million – 3 per cent of the sales value of its products – while at the same time significantly improving service to customers.

At Du Pont, a company well known for its general management excellence, this same new approach underlies the announcement that programmes recently instituted are expected to cut £30 million from its total cost, a 10 per cent reduction of the costs attributed to distribution.

These success stories shed some light on how distribution drains profits – and on what can be done about it:

The real impact of distribution on profits is much greater than most management think. In companies in which distribution-connected costs have been studied, they turned out to be significantly greater than management estimated – as much as from a third to a half of the selling price of the product.

This untapped profit-improvement potential exists because these costs lie in a managerial no man's land, where they can increase because they are outside the scope of responsibility or control of any operating executive. These distribution-related costs are not strictly the responsibility of the man in charge of distribution, because they are costs of purchasing, manufacturing or some other function of the business. But they cannot be dealt with effectively by the executive in charge of these other functions because they are actually caused by distribution decisions, for which only the man in charge of distribution has any responsibility. They are the result of complex interrelationships involving all of the functions of the business. Distribution lies at the crossroads of these complex interactions, and that is what is so different about distribution. In no other function of the business can decisions made at the operating level look so right and be so wrong.

The real cost of distribution

The real cost of distribution includes much more than what most companies consider when they attempt to deal with distribution costs. In a sense, any major distribution decision can affect every cost in the business and each cost is related to all the others. Our experience indicates that the following ten cost elements and interrelationships are the ones most likely to prove critical in evaluating the impact of alternative distribution approaches on total costs and total profits.

Warehousing

To provide service through the company's chosen channels of distribution, some warehousing is required, involving from one in-plant warehouse to a multiple-unit network dispersed across the country. Service usually becomes better as the number of warehouses is increased, at least up to a point. However, as the number of warehouses increases, their average size decreases; this will begin to reduce the efficiency of service to customers. Also, costs increase. Thus, any change in the three variables – number, type, or location of warehouses – will affect both service and costs.

Inventory carrying

The ownership of inventory gives rise to costs for money, insurance, occupancy, pilferage losses and custodial services, and sometimes inventory taxes. Depending on the business involved, this group of costs may range from 10 per cent to 30 per cent of average annual inventory value. Customer service will be improved by keeping inventory at many storage points in the field near to customers, but this will increase total inventory and the cost of carrying that inventory. Thus, inventory carrying cost is closely linked to warehousing cost and customer service.

Inventory obsolescence

If (at a given level of sales) total inventory is increased to provide better customer service, then inventory turnover is decreased. Also, the greater the 'pipeline fill' in the distribution system, the slower the inventory turnover. This automatically exposes the owner to greater risks of obsolescence and inventory write-down. This is a particularly important cost for companies having frequent model changeovers, style changes or product perishability.

Production or supply alternatives

Production costs vary among plants and vary with the volume produced at each individual plant. Plants have different fixed and different unit variable costs as volume is increased. The decision of which plant should serve which customers must give weight not only to transportation and warehousing costs, but also to production and supply costs; these will vary significantly with the volume allocated to each plant.

Cost concessions

A special aspect of production or supply alternatives arises from the fact that distribution decisions can affect costs otherwise incurred by suppliers or customers. For example, when a retailer creates his own warehouses, this may free suppliers from packing and shipping small quantities or from maintaining small local warehouses in the field. A retailer who establishes his own warehouse network may be able to recoup some of these costs by negotiation with the supplier.

Channels of distribution

The choice of distribution channels profoundly affects the nature and costs of a company's sales organisation, its selling price and gross margin structure, its commitment to physical distribution facilities. These in turn will affect production and supply costs.

Transportation

Changing the number or location of warehouses changes transportation cost, sometimes in unanticipated and complex ways. For example, an increase in the number of warehouses may initially reduce total transportation costs, but past some determinable point, the cost trend may reverse because of the decreasing ratio of carload to less-than-carload tonnage.

Communications and data processing

These costs vary with the complexity of the distribution system and with the level of service provided, including costs for order processing, inventory control, payables, receivables and shipping documents. These costs rise as more distribution points are added to the system. Additionally, as the cycle time or response time of the communications and data processing system is shortened, costs of this service are increased.

Alternative facilities use

Changes in inventory requirements or in other aspects of the distribution operation will change space requirements and utilisation in a plant-warehouse facility or a retail store. Space used for distribution may be convertible to selling space which yields incremental sales and profits. In the case of retail business, this is actually a variation of the customer service factor as it increases the availability of goods with which to fill customer requirements.

Customer service

Stock-outs, excess delivery time or excess variability of delivery time all result in lost sales. Any change in the distribution system will influence these elements of customer service and therefore must either gain or lose sales for the company. These effects, while difficult to measure, must be considered part of the real cost of distribution.

These costs *will* not respond to the usual cost-cutting approaches. Management has achieved near miracles in cutting costs in one function of the business after another, including costs within the distribution function, notably in warehousing, transportation and order-filling. But conventional cost-cutting approaches are limited to costs that fall within any one operation of the business; for cutting these costs, management can hold some executive responsible. Distribution-related costs are organisational orphans, beyond the reach of even the most diligent, skilful cost-minded executives.

These costs will respond only to a high level across-the-board re-examination of how distribution affects the total costs and total profits of the business, and of what management action is necessary to tap this profit opportunity.

Thus the problem and the opportunity are deposited squarely on the desk of the chief executive. The pursuit of these added profits has to get its start, its support and its sanctions at the top management level. With this high-level effort, even companies that have tightened and tidied their distribution operations can greatly increase earnings by a frontal attack on the basic framework of their distribution decisions and practices.

This broad, basic approach has a continuing pay-off, for once the most profitable pattern of distribution has been defined for the present operations of the business, management has in its hands a yardstick for measuring the impact on total profits of any proposed management move. This makes it possible to define the impact on total profits of a new plant or a new product, or a cluster of new customers, and so makes it possible to determine what changes in distribution – if any – will ensure peak profits from these new ventures.

What is this total cost approach? What is new about it? Why have we not heard more about it?

The approach simply stated

This approach sounds simple. First, analyse the distribution impact on each cost of the business, and select for more detailed study those activities the cost of which is significantly affected by distribution policies and practices. Second, develop the data necessary to measure the profit impact that alternative distribution decisions would have on each of these activities. Finally, determine which distribution decisions will maximise profits.

Obviously, if it were as simple as it sounds, more companies would long ago have beaten a path to this better mousetrap. Three sets of facts explain why this has not been so:

1   The impact of distribution on costs is more difficult to unravel than is the effect of other business decisions. All functions of a business are somewhat interrelated, but distribution is more complexly intertwined with each. And it is these interrelationships – rather than the costs of the distribution functions per se – that are the cause of high distribution costs and the key to understanding and reducing these costs.
2   Because corporate accounting has historically been orientated to finance and production, rather than to marketing or distribution, the operating reports that guide managerial action do not tot up in any place the full impact of distribution on costs. The real cost of distribution never stares management in the face.
3   Even where management have become aware of these costs and their impacts on profits, there was until recently very little that any one could do about the pervasive effects of distribution. Even a relatively simple problem in distribution system design can involve hundreds of bits of information that interact in thousands of ways. So there was no way of dealing with the distribution cost complex until techniques were developed to manipulate this mass of material as a single integrated entity.

This final point is, in fact, the major reason why these distribution-related costs have continued to rise and to depress profit margins throughout our economy. And for that same reason the total cost concept remained until recently a topic for textbook discussion, theoretically provocative but of little practical use. But techniques have been developed to deal with information in these quantities and interrelationships of such complexity. They have converted this sound but previously unworkable concept into a practical management approach.

The example traces the step-by-step process involved in the analysis of the factors that enter into the application of the total cost approach in a business engaged primarily in the retail distribution of a wide range of consumer products; the second shows how this complex array of information is analysed and manipulated to provide management with profitable answers to some familiar distribution problems.

At its very inception, the total cost approach is different in a number of ways from the traditional functional approach to distribution management. In the first place, it deals with the impact of distribution decisions on business costs wherever these costs appear. Second, many important cost factors and many critical relationships between distribution and other parts of the business are not usually translatable to quantitive terms. Customer service is a classic example.

The first step was to determine what distribution-related factors contribute significantly to total costs, trace the interrelationships of these factors, and then quantify both the factors and the interrelationships. This process has to be repeated anew for each company because of the important differences from industry to industry and even from one company to another in the same industry.

Then each of these have to be translated into a common denominator, so they can be measured and compared. If impact is measured in dollars, a unit that meets these requirements, it is possible to reduce all of the cost and profit considerations and all of these intricate interrelationships to one final total cost for each alternative course of action.

The significance of this for management is indicated for each major activity affected, the impact of different field warehouse systems on the total cost of this operation. It clearly indicates that for each factor of costs, a certain number of warehouses would yield the lowest costs and the maximum profit. Because each of these factors has its own built-in logic, each curve takes on its own configuration. The sum of all of these curves – each with its own optimum – is one final curve that defines the total cost. That in turn defines the optimum number of warehouses for this operation, when all considerations are taken into account. Except by chance coincidence, this point will differ from the optimum of each of the component curves. Obviously, a piece-metal approach to cost reduction will not yield the maximum profit impact achieved by this total cost approach.

It is difficult to conceive of a distribution problem in a company of any substantial size that could not show near-term benefits from this kind of analytical approach; the approach does much more than offer a one-time solution to what is actually a perennial problem.

Every time management makes a decision of any magnitude, it ought to be in a position to get an answer to the question, 'How will it affect distribution costs throughout the company?' The total cost approach puts the company in a position to make continuing gains by applying a rigid yardstick to any proposed corporate venture. Whenever manufacturing management designs a new plant, develops a new production process, or turns to a new source of raw material, the pattern of distribution-related costs will be changed throughout the business. Similar far-flung changes will take place whenever marketing management adds a new product or a promising new group of customers. The total cost approach enables management to define how these changes will interact with distribution to affect the company's total cost and its total profits. It tells management what distribution decisions need to be made to avoid the loss of potential profits, or to add to them. So both short-term and long-term benefits result from management's recognition of these complex cost and profit relationships.

Problem

What makes distribution different?

Consider the problem facing the management of a large company whose business consists of a widely dispersed chain of retail stores and a few factories that produce some of the merchandise sold in these stores. This company has shipped directly from its suppliers and its factories to its stores, but wants to determine whether there would be any profit advantage in shifting to a national system of field warehouses.

When this company looked at the combined cost of warehousing and of transportation that would result from introducing various combinations of field warehouses, it appeared, as that the lowest cost system was one with six warehouses.

Table 9.6 Profit impact of distribution-gains (losses) (in millions of dollars)

Warehousing	(14.4)
Transportation	0.5
Total distribution costs	(13.9)
Inventory	
Carrying costs	1.4
Obsolescence costs	4.3
Value of alternative use of facilities	7.8
Production and purchasing	
Production and raw materials costs	0.2
Reduced cost of purchased finished goods	6.7
	6.9
Data processing	(.02)
Marketing	
Channels of distribution	0.2
Customer service	1.4
	1.6
Total profit impact of distribution-related items	21.8
Pretax profit increase	7.9

But this would *increase* its distribution costs by £12.9 million. Thus, on the basis of apparent distribution costs alone, there was no profit advantage in any field warehouse system.

However, when this study investigated how alternative distribution networks would affect other costs in the company, the answer was quite different. As shown in Figure 9.14, the most efficient warehouse system turned out to be one with five, rather than six, field warehouses. And this five-warehouse system would cut the total costs of the company by £7.7 million: an increase of 1.4 per cent on sales.

Looking at distribution from a standpoint of total costs, this company discovered an opportunity to increase its profits that it could not have identified or taken advantage of in any other way.

The actual figures from this company's calculations for the five-warehouse system are shown in Table 9.6.

Because this company distributes mostly through its own retail outlets, the channels of distribution are not currently an important variable. They involve only the small amount of its product that it makes in its own factories but sells to other customers. The availability of field warehouses, however, would make it possible to sell and ship more of the output of these plants direct to customers rather than through local jobbers. As it turned out, the £200,000 it added to profitability was just about what it cost to design and engineer this whole new distribution system.

In this case, the company had good reason for considering the significance of distribution channels.

Questions

1   What explains the difference? What legerdemain turned up this handsome profit potential that represented a 22.4 per cent return on the investment required to design and install this field warehouse system?

2   What happens if one or several elements of the distribution cost are cut to these lowest practical level?
3   How do you assess the consequences of a reduction in warehousing and transportation?
4   Evaluate the possibility for the company of developing a strategy of backward integration?

(M) *Problem 9.8* Economic order quantity (EOQ) model

Introductory comments

Given the significance of the benefits and costs associated with holding inventories, it is important that the company efficiently control the level of inventory-investment. There are a number of inventory-control models available that can help in determining the optimal inventory level of each item. These models range from the relatively simple to the extremely complex. Their degree of complexity depends primarily on the assumptions made about the demand or usage for the particular item and the lead time required to secure additional stock. In the 'classical' inventory models, which include both the simpler deterministic models and the more complex probabilistic models, it is assumed that demand is either uniform or dispersed and independent over time. In other words, demand is assumed either to be constant or to fluctuate over time because of random elements. These types of demand situation are common in retailing and some service operations. Dependent demand models, in contrast, assume that demand tends to be 'lumpy', or to occur at specific points in time.

The simpler deterministic inventory-control models, such as the economic order quantity (EOQ) model, assume that both demand and lead times are constant and known with certainty. Thus, deterministic models eliminate the need to consider stockouts. The more complex probabilistic inventory-control models assume that demand, lead time or both are random variables with known probability distributions.

In its simplest form, the EOQ model assumes that annual demand or usage for a particular item is known with certainty. It also assumes that this demand is stationary or uniform throughout the year. In other words, seasonal fluctuations in the rate of demand are ruled out. Finally, the model assumes that orders to replenish the inventory of an item are filled instantaneously. Given a known demand and zero lead time for replenishing inventories, there is no need for a company to maintain additional inventories, or safety stocks, to protect itself against stockouts.

The assumptions of the EOQ model yield the saw-toothed inventory pattern shown in Figure 9.11.

The vertical lines at the 0, T_1, T_2 and T_3 points in time represent the instantaneous replenishment of the item by the amount of order quantity, Q, and the negatively sloped lines between the replenishment points represent the use of the item. Because the inventory level varies between 0 and the order quantity, average inventory is equal to one-half of the order quantity, or $Q/2$.

This model assumes that the cost of placing and receiving an order is the same for each order and independent of the number of units ordered. It also assumes that the annual cost of carrying one unit of the item in inventory is constant regardless of the inventory level. Total annual inventory costs, then, are the sum of ordering costs and carrying costs. The actual cost of the item (i.e. either the price paid for items purchased externally or the production cost for items manufactured internally) is excluded from

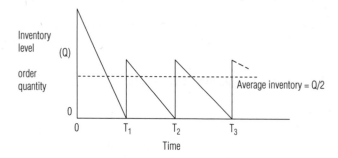

Figure 9.11 Certainty case of the inventory cycle.

this analysis, as it is assumed to be constant regardless of the order quantity. The primary objective of the EOQ model is to find the order quantity, Q, that minimises total annual inventory costs.

Algebraic solution

In developing the algebraic form of the EOQ model, the following variables are defined:

Q = The order quantity, in units.
D = The annual demand for the item, in units.
S = The cost of placing and receiving an order, or set-up cost.
C = The annual cost of carrying one unit of the item in inventory.

Ordering costs are equal to the number of orders per year multiplied by the cost per order, S. The number of orders per year is equal to annual demand, D, divided by the order quantity, Q. Carrying costs are equal to average inventory, Q/2, multiplied by the annual carrying cost per unit, C.
   The total annual-cost equation is as follows

   Total costs = ordering costs + carrying costs

By substituting the variables just defined into the above equation, the following expression is obtained:

   Total costs = (number of orders per year × cost per order) + (average inventory × annual carrying cost per unit)

or, in algebraic terms,

$$\text{Total costs} = \left(\frac{D}{Q} \times S\right) + \left(\frac{Q}{2} \times C\right)$$

The EOQ is the value of Q that minimises the total costs given in the above equation. The standard procedure for finding this value of Q involves calculus. The optimal solution, or EOQ, is equal to the following:

$$Q^* = \sqrt{\frac{2SD}{C}}$$

Another item of information that is sometimes useful for planning purposes is the optimal length of one inventory cycle, that is, the time between placements of orders for the item. The optimal length of one inventory cycle, T^*, measured in days, is equal to the economic order quantity, Q^*, divided by the average daily demand, $D/360$ (assuming 360 days per year), as follows:

$$T^* = \frac{Q^*}{D/360}$$

This equation can be rewritten as follows:

$$T^* = \frac{360 \times Q^*}{D}$$

Graphic solution

The order quantity that minimises total annual inventory costs can be determined graphically by plotting inventory costs (vertical axis) as a function of the order quantity (horizontal axis). As can be seen in Figure 9.12, annual ordering costs, DS/Q, vary inversely with the order quantity, Q, as the number of orders placed per year, D/Q, decreases as the size of the order quantity increases. Carrying costs, $CQ/2$, vary directly with the order quantity, Q, as the average inventory, $Q/2$, increases as the size of the order quantity increases.

The total inventory cost curve is found by vertically summing the heights of the ordering cost and carrying cost functions. The order quantity corresponding to the lowest point on the total cost curve is the optimal solution – that is, the economic order quantity, Q^*.

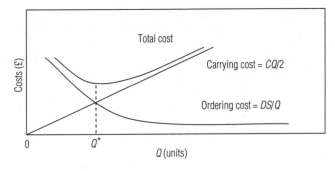

Figure 9.12 Graphic solution to the EOQ model.

271

Problem

Penny Mart Department Stores sells Sleepwell mattresses through its retail outlets located in the Manchester metropolitan area. All inventories are maintained at the company's centrally located warehouse. Annual demand for the Sleepwell standard-sized mattress is 3,600 units and is spread evenly throughout the year. The cost of placing and receiving an order is £31.25.

Penny Mart's annual carrying costs are 20 per cent of the inventory value. Based on a wholesale cost of £50 per mattress, the annual carrying cost per mattress is $.20 \times £50 = £10$. Because Sleepwell maintains a large regional distribution center in Manchester, Penny Mart can replenish its inventory virtually instantaneously. If the company wishes to determine the number of standard-sized mattresses it should periodically order from Sleepwell in order to minimise the total annual inventory costs.

Questions

1 Calculate the EOQ.
2 Calculate the total annual inventory costs of this policy.
3 Determine Penny Mart's optimal inventory cycle for the mattresses.

References and further reading

Barry Farber and Joyce Wycoff (1991) Customer service: evolution and revolution, *Sales and Marketing Management*, May: 44–51.

Barton A. Weitz, Stephen B. Castleberry and John F. Tanner (1992) *Selling: Building Partnerships*, Homewood, III: Richard D. Irwin.

Britt, S., Boyd, H., Davis, R. and Larreche, J. (1983) *Marketing Management and Administrative Action*, New York: McGraw-Hill.

Davidson W., Bates A., and Bass S. (1976) The retail life cycle, *Harvard Business Review* (November–December): 89–93.

Fredrick Trawick I., John E. Swan, Gail W. McGee and David R. Rink (1991) Influence of buyer ethics and salesperson behaviour on intention to choose a supplier, *Journal of the Academy of Marketing Science*, Winter: 17–23.

Herbert L. Seeger, Jr. (1970) *Sales Promotion Planning*, Chicago: Dartnell Corp.

Jan Heide and George John (1992) Do norms matter in marketing relationships, *Journal of Marketing*, April: 32–44.

Jerome A. Colletti and Gary S. Tubridy (1987) Effective major account sales management, *Journal of Personal Selling and Sales Management*, August: 1–10.

Karl A. Boedecker, Fred W. Morgan and Jeffery J. Stoltman (1991) Legal dimensions of salesperon's statements: a review and managerial suggestions, *Journal of Marketing*, January: 70–80.

McGoldrick, P. (1990) *Retail Marketing*, New York: McGraw-Hill Higher Education.

Rosenbloom, B. (1981) *Retail Marketing*, New York: Random House.

Sellers, 'How to Remake Your Salesforce': 102.

Tomkins (1997a) Wal-Mart goes shopping in Europe, *Financial Times*, 20 December: 15.

10

International Marketing

Markets have become truly global. If you stand still in your domestic market, you will probably be trampled by competitors from around the world. As one globe-trotting executive put it, 'if you don't act right now, somebody else will always do it for you at your expense ... and quickly'.

The term, 'global', epitomises the competitive pressure and market opportunities from around the world and the firm's need to optimise its market performance on a global basis. Whether a company operates domestically or across national boundaries, it can no longer avoid the competitive pressure and market opportunities. For optimal market performance, the firm should also be ready and willing to take advantage of resources on a global basis.

A number of broad forces have led to growing globalisation of markets. These include:

1   *Growing similarity of counties* Because of growing commonality of infrastructure, distribution channels, and marketing approaches, more and more products and brands are available everywhere. Similar buyer needs thus manifest themselves in different countries. Large retail chains, television advertising and credit cards are just a few example of once-isolated phenomena that are rapidly becoming universal.
2   *Falling tariff barriers* Successive rounds of bilateral and multilateral agreements have lowered tariffs markedly since World War II. At the same time, regional economic agreements, such as the European Union (EU), have facilitated trade relations.
3   *Strategic role of technology* Technology is not only reshaping industries but contributing towards market homogenisation. For example, electronic innovations have permitted the development of more compact, lighter products that are less costly to ship. Transportation costs themselves have fallen with the use of containerisation and larger-capacity ships. Increasing ease of communication and data transfer make it feasible to link operations in different countries. At the same time, technology leads to an easy flow of information among buyers, making them aware of new and quality products and thus creating demand for them.

Realistically speaking, there are more similarities than differences across many countries. In many cases, most of us tend to focus too much on cultural differences rather than similarities; or else, completely ignore differences or similarities. If you look only at cultural differences, you will be led to believe that country markets are uniquely different thus requiring marketing strategy adaptations. If, on the other hand, you do not care about, or care to know about, cultural differences, you may be extending a culture-blind, ethnocentric view of the world. Either way, you may not benefit from the economies of scale and scope accruing from exploiting cultural similarities – and differences.

Total world trade volume amounts to more than £4 trillion today. Today's environment is characterised by much more competition from around the world than in the past. As a result, many executives are feeling a much more competitive urgency in product development, materials procurement, manufacturing and marketing around the world. The same competitive pressure equally applies to executives of foreign companies.

The fluid nature of global markets and competition makes the study of global marketing not only interesting but also challenging and rewarding. The term *global* epitomises both the competitive pressure and the expanding market opportunities around the world. It does not mean, however, that all companies have to operate globally like IBM, Sony, Philips or Asea Brown Boveri (ABB). Whether a company operates domestically or across national boundaries, it can no longer avoid competitive pressure from around the world.

With a certain level of purchasing power, people, *irrespective of their nationality*, tend to enjoy similar educational levels, academic and cultural backgrounds, lifestyles and access to information. As these cultural and social dimensions begin to resemble each other in many countries, people's desire for material position, ways of spending leisure time and aspirations for the future become increasingly similar.

It is increasingly difficult for companies to avoid the impact of competition from around the world and the convergence of the world's markets. As a result, an increasing number of companies are drawn into marketing activities outside their home country.

Companies generally develop different marketing strategies depending on the degree of experience and the nature of operations in international markets. Companies tend to evolve over time, accumulating international business experience and learning the advantage and disadvantages associated with complexities of manufacturing and marketing around the world.

Therefore, knowing the dynamics of the evolutionary development of international marketing involvement is important for two reasons. First, it helps in the understanding of how companies learn and acquire international experience and how they use it for gaining competitive advantage over time. This may help an executive to be better prepared for the likely change needed in the company's marketing strategy. Second, with this knowledge, a company may be able to compete more effectively by predicting its competitors' likely marketing strategy in advance.

Global marketing refers to marketing activities by companies that emphasise (1) reduction of cost inefficiencies and duplication of efforts among their national and regional subsidiaries, (2) opportunities for the transfer of products brands and other ideas across subsidiaries, (3) emergence of global customers and (4) improved linkages among national marketing infrastructures leading to the development of a global marketing infrastructure.

Global marketing is a proactive response to the intertwined nature of business opportunities and competition that know no political boundaries. However, global marketing does not necessarily mean that companies should market the same product in the same way around the world as world markets are converging. To the extent feasible, they probably should. Nonetheless, global marketing is a company's willingness to adopt a global perspective instead of country-by-country or region-by-region perspective in developing a marketing strategy for growth and profit.

(M) *Problem 10.1* The comparative analytical approach in international marketing

Introductory comments

Although an understanding of the difficulties of collecting information for foreign markets will help to increase the quality of information obtained, an overall conceptual framework is necessary to provide the analyst with the relevant questions to ask. Consequently, a framework is needed that can guide international marketing managers in formulating market research studies.

Pioneered by T.A. Hagler in the late 1950s, comparative research actually led to the establishment of international marketing as a discipline. Comparative marketing focuses on the entire marketing system, but this macro-approach becomes less important as specific problems at the company level need to be analysed. However, the comparative approach can be adapted to specific micro-marketing problems.

MARKETING AS A FUNCTION OF THE ENVIRONMENT

The comparative marketing analysis emphasises the study of the marketing process in its relationship to the prevailing environment. Marketing is not viewed as an independent process separated from environmental influences. Instead, the marketing process (P) is viewed as a direct function of environment (E), or $(P) = f(E)$. Under changed environmental conditions, the existing marketing processes are also expected to change. As shown in Figure 10.1, in a dual-country analysis employing the comparative approach, the marketing environment (E_1) in country 1 is investigated with respect to its causal effect on the marketing process (P_1). The resulting functional relationship is transferred to a second country whose environment (E_2) may be known but whose marketing process (P_2) will be assessed based upon the earlier developed functional relationships:

$$P_1 = f(E_1)$$

The resulting analysis can be represented as

$$P_1 : E_1 = P_2 : E_2$$

where P_2 is the unknown. The marketing process (P) can also be referred to as the marketing mix. This macro-level approach can be extended to the managerial level, as illustrated in Figure 10.2. Let us assume the possible transfer of a marketing mix $(MMIX_1)$ from the home country to the host country. The unknown is the required nature of the marketing mix $(MMIX_2)$ as a function of the new environment (E_2). The comparative approach is based upon an assessment of the existing relationship between the present programme $(MMIX_1)$ and the environment (E_1).

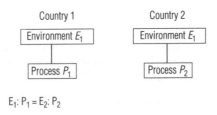

$E_1 : P_1 = E_2 : P_2$

Figure 10.1 Comparative approach.

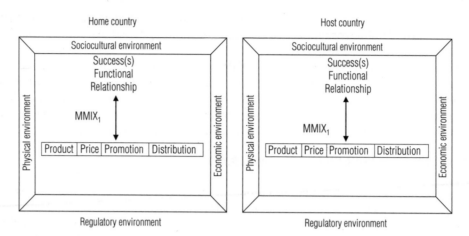

Figure 10.2 Managerial approach to comparative analysis.

The results of such an analytic assessment are transferred into the environment (E_2) of the host country whose environmental conditions are known, or have been researched, by the company. The unknown component, the desired marketing mix ($MMIX_2$), will therefore be estimated based upon the known functional relationship $MMIX_1 = f(E_1)$, with E_2 given, or $MMIX_2 = f(E_2)$.

What is different about the comparative analytic approach is its focus on the situational and its method of selecting the salient environmental variables that may affect the product's and/or service's success in any country. Because the selected environmental variables are the ones most clearly related to a product's and/or service's success in the home country, they can be referred to as success factors.

Traditionally, marketers have viewed success factors as variables under marketing management's control. With the comparative analytic approach, success factors are treated as a function of a given scenario of outside factors not always subject to management's control. Typically, marketing programmes succeed because managers take advantage of opportunities or positive constellations of success factors. This reversed view results in a greater appreciation of the role environmental variables play in marketing and also tends to avoid traditional tendencies to overestimate the impact of management's own actions in the marketplace.

The comparative analytical approach provides a methodology for marketers to analyse their success in current markets as a function of the marketing mix and the environment. It also provides an approach for isolating the critical environmental variables. These variables become the focus of the international market research process.

Problem

We can illustrate the concept by using an example familiar to most of us. McDonald's has achieved a tremendous success in the USA (its home country) by way of an aggressive and well-structured marketing mix ($MMIX_1$). The elements may be described as follows:

- *Product/service design* A standardised product of high and consistent quality emphasising speed of service and long opening hours.
- *Price* A low price policy.

- *Distribution* Placing restaurants in areas where customers primarily live – suburban and urban locations.
- *Promotion* A strong advertising campaign focused on the consumer, particularly young people, via heavy use of television.

With this $MMIX_1$, as described above, McDonald's has been extremely successful in the USA. In the early 1970s, several foreign countries were targeted for possible expansion and an assessment had to be made as to the best approach for McDonald's to pursue. The traditional approach would view success (S_1) as a function of McDonald's effective marketing strategy ($MMIX_1$) or as a direct result of the company's own efforts. The comparative analytic approach advanced here, however, views McDonald's success as a function of a given set of marketing-mix variables ($MMIX_1$) that were effective only due to the home-country environment (E_1). This view places a key emphasis on the environmental variables that allowed McDonald's marketing mix to become successful:

$$S_1 = f(MMIX_1)$$

$$MMIX_1 = f(E_1)$$

The difference between the two approaches is important. The comparative analytic view sees McDonald's primarily as having been able to take advantage of an existing opportunity (E_1), whereas the traditional approach sees McDonald's success primarily as a direct result of its own efforts.

Viewing the marketing mix as a function of the existing environment emphasises an environmental view of the marketing process. The emphasis is now on the existing environment that enables a given marketing mix to be successful. That view is of great importance, as success is no longer defined as unilateral or solely a function of the marketing mix. By looking at $MMIX_1$ in the home country, underlying environmental factors (E_1) are uncovered that enable success. Thus the company is viewed as taking advantage of a given opportunity rather than creating one by its own actions. The first step is to look at the environmental factors and to understand the components of the marketing environment. The critical environmental variables may be grouped into four major categories: physical, social, economic and regulatory. In the McDonald's case, the environmental variables analysed were population density, the family structure, and role of the mother, income levels and the availability of advertising media to reach children.

Question

Comment on the environmental variables' (physical, sociocultural, economic and regulatory) contribution towards McDonald's success in the home country that was later translated to worldwide success.

(I) *Problem 10.2* International target market selection

Introductory comments

A crucial step in developing a global expansion strategy is the selection of potential target markets. Companies adopt many different approaches to pick target markets. A flowchart for one of the more elaborate approaches is given in Figure 10.3.

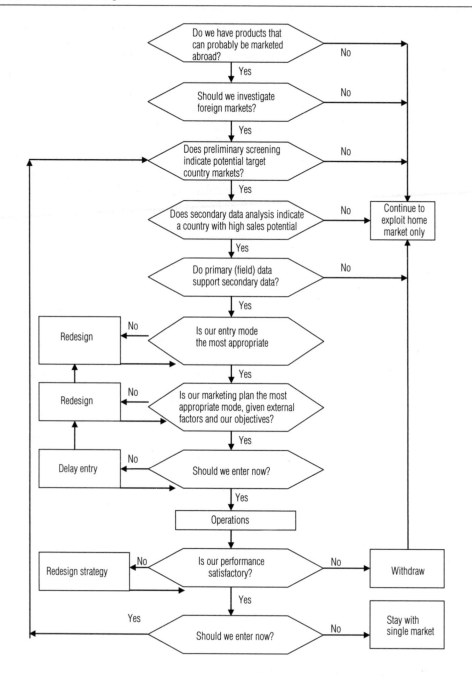

Figure 10.3 A logical flow model of the entry decision process.

To identify market opportunities for a given product (or service) the international marketer usually starts off with a large pool of candidate countries (say, all Central European countries). To narrow down this pool of countries, the company will typically do a preliminary screening. The goal of this exercise is twofold: you want to minimise the mistakes of (1) ignoring countries that offer viable opportunities for your product and (2) wasting time on countries that offer no or little potential. Those countries that make the grade are scrutinised further to determine the final set of target countries. Here is a four-step procedure that you can employ for the initial screening process:

Step 1: Indicator selection and data collection

First, you need to pick a set of socio-economic and political indicators you believe are critical. The indicators that a company selects are to a large degree driven by the strategic objectives spelled out in the company's global mission. Colgate–Palmolive, for instance, views per-capita purchasing power as a major driver behind market opportunities. Nestlé sees prospects in countries with population and buying power growth. McDonald's starts with countries that are similar to the USA in lifestyle, with a large proportion of women working, and shorter hours for lunch. Information on these country indicators can easily be gathered from publicly available data sources. Typically, countries that do well on one indicator (say, market size) rate poorly on other indicators (say, market growth). Somehow, you need to combine your information to come up with an overall measure of market attractiveness for these candidate markets.

Step 2: Determine importance of country indicators

The second step is to determine the importance weights of each of the different country indicators identified in the previous step. One common method is the 'constant-sum' allocation technique. Here, you simply allocate one hundred points across the set of indicators according to their importance in achieving the company's goals (e.g. market share). So, the more critical the indicator, the higher the number of points it gets assigned. The total number of points should add up to 100.

Step 3: Rate the countries in the pool on each indicator

Next, you give each country a score on each of the indicators. For instance, you could use a 100-point scale (0 meaning very unfavourable; 100 meaning very favourable). The better the country does on a particular indicator, the higher the score.

Step 4: Compute overall score for each country

The final step is to derive an overall score for each prospect country. To that end, simply sum up the weighted scores that the country obtained on each indicator. The weights are the importance weights that were assigned to the indicators in the second step. Countries with the highest overall scores are the ones that are most attractive. An example of this four-step procedure is given in Table 10.1.

Table 10.1 Method for pre-screening market opportunities: example

Country	Per-capita income	Population	Competition	Political risk	Score
M	50	25	30	40	3400[a]
N	20	50	40	10	3600
0	60	30	10	70	3650
P	20	20	70	80	3850
Weights	25	40	25	10	

Note
[a]$(25 \times 50) + (40 \times 25) + (30 \times 35) + (40 \times 10) = 3400$.

Problem – example

Wrigley, the US chewing gum maker, was not interested in Latin America until recently because many of the local governments imposed ownership restrictions. In that case, the four-step procedure would be done only for the countries that stay in the pool.

When the product has already been launched in some regions, the firm can substantially reduce the subjectivity by using a variant of the screening procedures just described. The alternative method leverages the experience the firm gathered in its existing markets. It works as follows: suppose the MNC currently does business in Europe and is now considering an expansion into Asia.

Step 1: Collect historical data on European market

Go back to your files and collect the historical data for the European markets on the indicators you plan to use to assess the market opportunities for the Asian region. Let us refer to these pieces of information as X_{iec}, that is, the score of European country ec on indicator i;

Step 2: Evaluate the MNC's post-entry performance in each of its existing European markets

Assess the MNC's post-entry performance in each European country by assigning a success score (e.g. on a 10-point scale). If performance is measured on just one indicator, say, market-share achieved five years after entry, you could also simply use that indicator as a performance measure. Let us refer to the performance score for country ec as S_{ec}.

Step 3: Derive weights for each of the country indicators

The next step is to come up with importance weights for each of the country indicators. For this, you could run a cross-sectional regression using the European data gathered in the previous two steps. Our dependent variable is the post-entry success score (S_{ec}) while the predictor variables are the country indicators (X_{iec}):

$$S_{ec} = a + w_1 X_{1ec} + w_2 X_{2ec} + \cdots + w_1 X_{1ec} \quad ec = 1,2,\ldots, \text{EC}$$

By running a regression of the success scores, S_{ec}, on the predictor variables, X_{iec} ($i = 1,\ldots,I$), you can derive estimates for the importance weights of the different indicators.

Step 4: Rate the Asian countries in the pool on each indicator

Each of the Asian candidate markets in the pool is given a score on each of the indicators that are considered: X_{iac}.

Step 5: Predict performance in prospective Asian countries

Finally, predict the post-entry performance in the prospective Asian markets by using the weights estimated in step 4 and data collected on each of the indicators (the X_{iac}'s) for the Asian countries. For instance, the regression estimates might look like:

$$\text{Performance} = -0.7 + 6.0(\text{market size}) + 2.9(\text{growth}) - 1(\text{competition})$$

By plugging in the ratings (or actual values) for the Asian markets in this equation, you can then predict the MNC's performance in each of these countries.

Other far more sophisticated methods exist to screen target markets. Kumar and colleagues, for example, developed a screening methodology that incorporates multiple objectives of the firm, resource constraints and its market expansion strategy. Figure 10.4

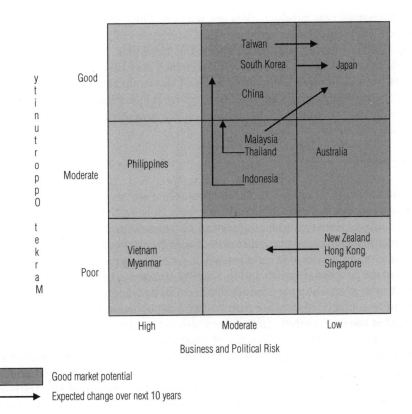

Figure 10.4 Opportunity matrix for Henkel in the Asia Pacific.

Source: Reprinted from Hellmut Schutte, 'Henkel's strategy for Asia Pacific', *Long Range Planning*, vol. 28, no. 1: 98. Copyright 2005, with kind permission from Elsevier Science Ltd, The Boulevard, Langford Lane, Kidlington, OX5 1GB, UK.

shows the opportunity matrix for the Asia-Pacific division of Henkel, a German conglomerate. The shaded area highlights the countries that look most promising from Henkel's perspective.

Questions

1 Select and discuss some of the critical stages included in a logical flow model of the entry decision process.
2 Compare the four initial pre-screening stages with the five stages associated with the case where a company possesses experience in existing markets and wishes to embark on an expansion strategy.
3 Explain the possible use of a cross-sectional regression model as in the case – when the analysis is deriving the weights for each of the country indicators.

(A) *Problem 10.3* Screening and concept testing for new global products

Introductory comments

Screening

Evidently not all new product ideas are winners. Once new product ideas have been identified, they need to be screened. The goal here is to weed out ideas with little potential. This filtering process can take the form of a formal scoring model. One example of a scoring model is New Prod, which was based on almost two hundred projects from a hundred companies. Each of the projects was rated by managers on about fifty screening criteria and judged in terms of its commercial success. A regression model was derived using these managerial judgements as data points. The results of the regression are shown in Table 10.2.

Concept testing

Once the merits of a new product idea have been established, it must be translated into a product concept. A product concept is a fairly detailed description, verbally or sometimes visually, of the new product or service. To assess the apparel of the product concept, companies rely on focus group discussions. Focus groups are a small group of prospective customers, typically with one moderator. The focus group members discuss the likes and dislikes of the proposed product and the current competing offerings. They also state their willingness to adopt the new product that were to be launched in the market.

A more sophisticated procedure to measure consumer preferences for product concepts is *conjoint analysis* (sometimes also referred to as *trade-off analysis*). Most products and services are a bundle of product attributes. The starting premise of conjoint analysis is that people make trade-offs between the different product attributes when they evaluate alternatives (e.g. brands) from which they have to pick a choice. The purpose, then, of conjoint is to gain an understanding of the trade-offs that consumers make. The outcome of the exercise will be a set of utilities (part-worth) for each attribute level, derived at the individual household or consumer segment level. This information allows the company to answer questions such as how much their customers are willing to pay extra for additional product features or superior performance.

Table 10.2 New product screening model (NPSM)

		Product
$CS_1 = \alpha + \beta_1$ (product superiority, quality and uniqueness) 1.744(F, 68.7)	*as defined*	• is superior to competing products • has unique features for user • is of higher quality than competitors' • does unique task for user • reduces customers' costs • is innovative – first of its kind
$CS_2 = \alpha + \beta_2$ (overall project/resource compatibility) 1.138(F, 30.0)	*as defined*	A good 'fit' between needs of project and company resource base in terms of • managerial skills • marketing research skills • sales force/distribution resources • financial resources • engineering skills • production resources
$CS_3 = \alpha + \beta_3$ (market need, growth and size) 0.801(F, 12.5)	*as defined*	• high need level customers for product class • large market (S volume) • fast-growing market
$CS_4 = \alpha + \beta_4$ (economic advantage of product to end user) 0.722(F, 10.2)	*as defined*	• product reduces customers' costs • product is priced lower than competing products
		Project takes the firm into new areas in the form such as:
$CS_5 = \alpha + \beta_5$ (newness to the firm (negative)) −0.354(F, 2.9)	*as defined*	• new product class to company • new sales force/distribution • new types of users' needs served • new customers to company • new competitors to company • new product technology to firm • new production process to firm
		A good 'fit' between needs of project and company resource base in terms of
$CS_6 = \alpha + \beta_6$ (technology resource compatibility) 0.342(F, 2.5)	*as defined*	• R&D resources and skills • engineering skills and resources • intense price competition in market
$CS_7 = \alpha + \beta_7$ (market competitiveness (negative)) −0.301(F, 2.0)	*as defined*	• highly competitive market • many competitors • many new product intros into market • changing user needs
$CS_8 = \alpha + \beta_8$ (product scope) 0.225(F, 0.9)	*as defined*	• market-driven new product idea • not a custom product, that is more mass appeal • a mass market for product (as opposed to one or a few customers)
$CS_9 = \alpha + \beta_9$ (constant) 0.328		

Source: Adapted from Robert G. Cooper, Selecting new product projects: using the new prod system, *Journal of Product Innovation Management*, 2(1) (March 1985): 39.

Note: CS: commercial success.

The tool can also be used to examine to what degree a firm should customise the products it plans to launch in the various target markets.

Problem – example

To illustrate the use of the conjoint for the design of products in an international setting, let us look at an example. In what follows, we focus on the use of conjoint analysis in the context of global NPD. Imagine that company SATEL considers selling satellite TV dishes in two Southeast Asian countries: Thailand and Malaysia.

The first step is to determine the salient attributes for the product (or service). Exploratory market research (e.g. a focus group discussion) or managerial judgement can be used to figure out the most critical attributes. At the same time, we also need to consider the possible levels ('values') that each of the attributes can take. In our example (see Table 10.3) four attributes are considered to be important: (1) the number of channels, (2) the purchase price (in the example we assume that no middlemen will be used, so the retail price is the same as the ex-factory price), (3) the installation cost and (4) the size of the dish (in terms of inches). Each of the attributes has three possible levels.

For instance, the diameter of the dish could be 18, 25 or 30 inches. The next step is to construct product profiles by combining the various attribute levels. Each profile would represent a hypothetical product configuration. In most applications it is unrealistic to consider every possible combination, as the number of possibilities rapidly explodes. Instead, one uses an experimental design to come up with a small but manageable number of product profiles. This number varies from study to study. Obviously, the number of profiles will depend not only on the number of attributes and attribute levels, but also on other factors like the amount of information you want to collect. In most studies, the number of profiles ranges between 18 and 32. An example of such a profile is given in Table 10.4.

Once the profiles have been finalised, you can go into the field and gather the desired information. In each country several prospective target customers will be contacted. Every subject in your sample is shown each of the product profiles and asked to state

Table 10.3 Salient attributes and attribute levels for satellite dishes

Product attributes	Attribute levels
Number of channels	(1) 30 (2) 50 (3) 100
Selling price	(1) £500 (2) £600 (3) £700
Installation fee	(1) Free (2) £100 (3) £200
Size of dish	(1) 18" (2) 25" (3) 30"

Table 10.4 Example of a product profile

Product Profile 18

(1) Number of channels: 30
(2) Price: £500
(3) Installation fee: £100
(4) Size of dish: 25″

Table 10.5 Results of conjoint analysis for satellite dishes

Attributes	Thailand	Thailand	Malaysia	Malaysia
	Segment I	Segment II	Segment I	Segment II
Number of channels				
30	0.0	0.0	0.0	0.0
50	1.5	3.4	1.4	1.8
100	3.2	5.6	3.0	2.5
Purchase price				
£500	0.0	0.0	0.0	0.0
£600	−3.2	−1.5	−2.8	−2.5
£700	−4.6	−2.0	−4.8	−3.0
Installation				
Free	0.0	0.0	0.0	0.0
£100	−1.5	−0.2	−1.4	−1.0
£200	−1.8	−0.4	−2.1	−1.7
Size of dish (diameter)				
18″	0.0	0.0	0.0	0.0
25″	−0.5	−1.0	−0.4	−2.0
30″	−0.8	−1.5	−1.0	−5.0
Size of segment	12,000	28,000	15,000	16,000

his or her preferences. For instance, you might ask the respondent to rank the product profiles from most to least preferred. In addition, other data (e.g. demographic, lifestyle) are collected that often prove useful for benefit segmentation purposes.

Once you have collected the preference data, you need to analyse them using a statistical software package. The outcome of the analysis will be a set of 'utilities' that each segment (or respondent) derives from each of the attribute levels. Results for our example are shown in Table 10.5. Each country has two segments: a price-sensitive and quality-sensitive segment. The entries in the columns represent the utilities (part-worth) for the respective attribute levels. For instance, the utility of 100 channels in Thailand would be 5.6 for segment II, compared with 2.5 for Malaysia's performance segment II. The results can be used to see which attributes matter most to each of the segments in the different target markets. The relative range of the utilities signals the attribute importance. In this example, price is most critical for the first Thai segment (utility range: 0 to −4.6), whereas the number of channels (utility range: 0 to 5.6) matters most for the second Thai segment. The technical nitty-gritty is less important here, but we would like you to get a flavour of how conjoint can be used to settle product design issues in a global setting. Let us consider the standardise versus customise issue.

To standardise or not to standardise For the sake of simplicity, suppose that currently there is one incumbent competitor, ABC, in the satellite dish industry in Thailand and Malaysia. The ABC brand has the following features:

Number of channels	30
Selling price	£500
Installation fee	Free
Size of dish	30″

SATEL is looking at two possibilities: (1) sell a uniform product (model SATELST) or (2) launch a customised product for each of the two markets (models SATEL/TH and SATEL/MA). The standardised product (SATEL/ST) has the following profile:

Number of channels	50
Selling price	£600
Installation fee	£100
Size of dish	25″

The customised products would have the following characteristics:

Attribute	Product SATEL/TH (Thailand)	Product SATEL/MA (Malaysia)
No. of channels	100	30
Price	£700	£700
Installation	£200	Free
Size of dish	25″	18″

In this example, the selling price for the standardised product is less than the price for the customised product because of scale economies. By computing the overall utility for each of the alternatives we are able to estimate the market share that each product would grab in the two countries. This overall score is simply the sum of the utilities for the attribute levels. The respective utilities for the various product configurations are shown in Table 10.6.

Table 10.6 Utilities for respective alternative derived via conjoint study

Alternative	Thailand Segment I	Thailand Segment II	Malaysia Segment I	Malaysia Segment II
ABC (competitor)	−0.8	−1.5	−1.0	−5.0
SATEL/ST (standardised)	−3.7[a]	0.7	−3.2	−3.7
SATEL/TH (customised for Thailand)	−4.0	2.2	Not offered	Not offered
SATEL/MA (customised for Malaysia)	Not offered	Not offered	−4.8	−3.0

Note
[a] 1.5 + (−3.2) + (−1.5) + (−0.5) = −3.7.

Assuming that each customer will pick the alternative that gives the highest overall utility, we can derive market share estimates in the two countries for the two product alternatives. For instance, looking at the uniform dish in Thailand, we find that customers in the quality segment II would prefer it over the competing model (because $0.7 > -1.5$). On the other hand, the first segment in Thailand would pick ABC (because $-3/7 < -0.8$). Hence, the market share for the standardised model (SATEL/ST) in the Thai market would equal 70 per cent: the number of households in the quality segment, 28,000 – see bottom row of Table 10.5 – divided by the entire market size for satellite dishes in Thailand, 40,000. In the same manner, we can compute SATEL's market share for the standardised model in Malaysia and for the customised models in the two countries:

Market share standardised product SATEL/ST in Malaysia = 51.6% (16,000/31,000)
Market share customised product SATEL/TH in Thailand = 70% (28,000/40,000)
Market share customised product SATEL.MA in Malaysia = 51.6% (16,000/31,000)

In our example, the market share estimates for the two alternatives (standardised versus customised) end up being equal. Once we have cost estimates for the manufacturing and marketing of the different alternatives, we can come up with an estimate of their expected profits. For instance, let us assume that the variable costs are equal (say, £400 per unit) but the fixed costs (combined across the two markets) differ: £5 million for the standardised product option as opposed to £10 million for the customised product option.

Questions

1 Explain the concept behind the conjoint analysis technique.
2 Plugging in the market share and the cost estimates, calculate the profit potential of the various options.
3 Assess the overall strategic alternatives with regard to the Thai and Malaysian markets faced by SATEL.

(I) *Problem 10.4* International price setting

Introductory comments

International pricing is affected by such factors as differences in costs, demand conditions, competition and government laws. The impact of these factors on pricing is figured in by following a particular pricing orientation.

Companies mainly follow two different types of pricing orientation: the cost approach and the market approach. The cost approach involves first computing all relevant cost and then adding a desired profit mark-up to arrive at the price. The cost approach is popular because it is simple to comprehend and use and leads to fairly stable prices. This approach, however, has two drawbacks. First, definition and computation of costs can become troublesome. Second, this approach brings an element of inflexibility into the pricing decision.

This approach arrives at a tentative price based strictly on costs. The final price emerges after making adjustments, dictated by considerations of government, demand, competition, company objectives and others. The principal emphasis, however, continues to be on costs, which forces inflexibility. More than that, a problem arises in defining the meaning of cost. Should all (both fixed and variable) costs be included or only variable costs? What proportion of fixed costs should be included, if any? Particularly, should costs related to R&D and parent corporation administrative overhead costs be included? The answers to these questions are far from easy.

Full Costing Versus Incremental Costing

A conservative attitude would favour using full costs as the basis of pricing. On the other hand, an incremental cost pricing could allow for seeking business otherwise lost. The difference between the two decision methods results from the treatment of fixed costs. The full costing method includes the fixed cost in the cost per-unit calculation. The incremental cost method recognises that no additional fixed costs will be incurred if additional units are produced. Therefore, fixed costs are not considered in the decision process.

The incremental costing method compares additional costs to be incurred with the additional revenues that will be received if the offer is accepted. The following problem is an illustration of the full costing and incremental costing methods.

Under the market approach pricing starts in a reverse fashion. First, an estimate is made of the acceptable price in the target market segment. An analysis is performed to determine if this price would meet the company's profit objective. If not, then the alternatives are either to give up the business or to increase the price. Additional adjustments in price may be required to cope with competitors, host-country government, expected cost increases and other eventualities.

Both the cost and market approaches essentially consider common factors in determining the final price. The difference between the two approaches involves the core concern in setting prices. The market approach focuses on pricing from the viewpoint of the customer. Unfortunately, in many countries it may not be easy to develop an adequate price-demand relationship, and therefore implementation of the market approach may occur in a vacuum. It is this kind of uncertainty that forces international marketers to opt for the cost approach.

In theory, export pricing is based on either of the two pricing approaches. In most cases, however, the cost approach turns out to be a more viable approach. The difficulty of gaining adequate knowledge of the foreign market and the desire to ensure satisfactory profit on export transactions lead companies to choose the cost approach.

Problem

The Concorde Co. has production capacity of 20,000 units per year. Presently the company is producing and selling 15,000 units per year. The regular market price is £15.00 per unit. The variable costs are as follows:

Material	£5/unit
Labour	£4/unit
Total variable cost	£9/unit

The fixed cost is £40,000 per year. The income statement reflecting the situation above would appear as follows:

Income statement		
Sales (15,000 @ £15.00)		£225,000
Cost: variable cost (15,000 @ £9.00)	£135,000	
Fixed cost	£40,000	£175,000
		£50,000

Questions

1 Now suppose the company has the opportunity to sell an additional 3,000 units at £10.00 per unit to a foreign firm. This is a special situation and would not have an adverse effect on the price of the product in the regular market. If the Concorde Co. uses the full costing method to make its decision, what would be your final recommendation?

2 If the incremental costing method is used by the company, what would be your final recommendation?

(I) *Problem 10.5* Organising for international advertising

Introductory comments

The firm has basically three organisational alternatives: (1) It can centralise all decision making for international advertising at headquarters, (2) it can decentralise the decision making to foreign markets or (3) it can use some blend of these two alternatives. Of course, the question of organising for international advertising cannot be separated from the company's overall organisation for international business. The firm is unlikely to be highly centralised for one function and decentralised for another. Here we consider the special factors affecting organisation for international advertising.

Centralisation

Complete centralisation of international advertising implies that campaign preparation, media and agency selection, and budgeting are all done at headquarters. This might be necessary if the firm's international business is small or if it is confined to dealing with distributors or licensees. Complete centralisation is less likely when the firm operates through foreign subsidiaries. In reality, control at headquarters of international advertising is seldom complete. We use the term *centralised* to refer to the situation where headquarters plays a major coordinating role, as in the Goodyear example cited earlier, or the ITT example below.

Centralised control of advertising is more feasible when the firm works with one international agency that has branches covering all of its markets, when the firm has standardised international advertising, and when market and media conditions are similar from market to market. As we saw, these conditions were met by American Express when it used Ogilvy & Mather to carry its message around the world.

On the personnel side, centralised control implies that staff at headquarters know foreign markets and media well enough to make appropriate decisions. Communications must be adequate for controlling the actual placement of the advertising in each market. It might be possible to rely on an international agency for help. Industrial marketers such as Timken, Rockwell and Du Pont rely on the US office of their international agency.

When subsidiaries are involved, there must be some authority over the subsidiary personnel, just as the agency works with its own people in the same market.

The centralised approach creates demands for advertising personnel at headquarters but minimal demands for them at the subsidiary level. Economies of scale in staffing and in administration are arguments for centralisation. The potential dangers are rigidity, failure to adapt to local needs, and stifling of local initiative, which can lead to morale problems in the subsidiary.

The trend is increasing for centralising international advertising as more companies push for regional or global marketing. The European Single Market has increased centralised control for European firms, as we have seen. Continuing integration of world markets is leading US and Japanese multinationals in the same direction. For US firms with well-established foreign subsidiaries, the main resistance comes from subsidiary managers who view global advertising as a threat to their autonomy.

Decentralisation

With complete decentralisation of international advertising, each market would make all its own advertising decisions. When this laissez-faire method is company policy, it may result from several considerations: (1) the volume of international business and advertising is too small to warrant attention at headquarters; (2) the communications problems between home and field render a centralised approach impossible; (3) the firm believes that local decision making gives a more national image; and (4) the firm believes that nationals know the local scene best and will be more highly motivated if given this responsibility.

Decentralised control is likely to be associated with national rather than international advertising campaigns and with the employment of independent local agencies in each market. It requires more expertise and personnel at the subsidiary. In markets where the firm does not have subsidiaries, performance depends on the advertising skills and interest of the firm's licensee or distributor. The advantages of decentralisation are the motivation given to the national operation and the possibility of getting more effective tailor-made advertising programmes. The dangers are duplication of effort and ineffective advertising, especially in smaller markets. Honeywell was a practitioner of the decentralised, or 'hands off' approach, and when Microsoft entered Europe in the mid-1990s, its advertising was also prepared by national marketing teams. This is quite a contrast to the coordination practised by ITT.

A compromise approach

Between the extremes of complete centralisation and complete decentralisation are programmes that use elements of both approaches. A compromise approach should entail finding the appropriate division of labour between headquarters and country operations, with each making its contribution according to its comparative advantage. One expert has called this *coordinated decentralisation*. However, this same expert emphasises the coordination more than decentralisation. IBM, Matsushita and Philips follow this approach, for example.

In a compromise approach, headquarters usually plays the more important role, being 'more equal' than the national operations. The central advertising manager is responsible for international advertising policy and guidelines. The basic creative work and selection of overall themes and appeals are generally centralised. Headquarters also works with the coordinator from the international agency, if such an agency is used.

When the Kodak Instamatic was introduced around the world, the Kodak vice-president for marketing and the Instamatic account executive of J. Walter Thompson not only planned strategy together, but they also travelled around the world together, visiting local subsidiaries and agencies. Rank-Xerox had a similar collaboration with Young & Rubicam in Europe.

The advertising manager at headquarters establishes standard operating procedures and prepares a manual for subsidiary advertising management, including budget and reporting forms, as at ITT. Common formats make budgets comparable from country to country for better evaluation. The manager also acts as a clearing house, transferring relevant experiences between countries and from domestic operations, and organising meetings of advertising personnel.

CPC International has held annual worldwide marketing conferences to help advertising coordination. These meetings sometimes took place in the USA, sometimes abroad. In addition, meetings were held on a regional basis where marketing personnel discussed advertising programmes and agency operations. The company used more than one agency in many markets because of the number of different brands it sold. In Europe, the company's largest region, the firm had a consumer goods policy council, whose duties included selection of agencies and coordination of advertising programmes.

In this compromise approach, the role of subsidiary personnel is strongest in media selection and in the adaptation of advertising appeals to local needs, while the role of headquarters is greatest in setting objectives and establishing the budget. Subsidiaries do not have major creative responsibilities, but they do have a voice in the decisions related to their own market. As compared with a decentralised approach, this compromise requires a smaller staff and less expertise within the subsidiary.

Using cooperative advertising

A firm that sells through licensees or distributors can choose one of three ways to advertise in its foreign markets: (1) It can handle such advertising itself; (2) it can cooperate with the local distributor; or (3) it can try to encourage the distributor or licensee to do such advertising by itself. The last alternative is not really feasible, so the choice is primarily between going it alone or cooperating.

When the firm chooses to handle its own advertising for distributor markets, it must arrange for the complete advertising programme at home with few inputs from the markets concerned. Going it alone poses some difficulty because the firm is not very familiar with those markets where its only contact is a licensee or distributor. This problem is alleviated somewhat when the firm's agency has offices in those markets. However, the agency's network is unlikely to mesh very closely with the company's foreign markets. The agency tends to have offices in the larger markets, whereas many of the firm's distributors are likely to be in smaller markets. The company may have its own subsidiaries in the larger markets.

In spite of the problems in centralised management of advertising for distributor markets, some firms choose this approach, implementing it through an international agency. Their understanding is that even with its limitations, this way offers more control and greater effectiveness than the alternatives. Working on a centralised basis with its agency gives the firm a voice in the management of the advertising and general control over its quality and placement even in distant markets.

Cooperative local advertising

Many other firms choose the alternative of developing their foreign advertising programmes in cooperation with their local distributors. They do so in an attempt to obtain the advantages claimed for coordinated decentralisation – the appropriate division of labour and a contribution from each party according to its comparative advantage.

Several advantages are claimed for the cooperative approach. For one, the exporter hopes to get more advertising for the money, either through a greater amount of advertising or through the same amount done on a shared basis rather than solely by the exporter. Furthermore, the cooperative programme itself may motivate the distributor to do more promotion. In markets where the distributor is well known, the exporter can trade on the distributor's reputation. The distributor, through knowledge of the local market and media, can help choose the advertising that best fits the local situation. The distributor may also get better media rates as a national.

One problem with cooperative advertising is that advertising quality is uneven from country to country. If the advertising is poor, it could be a waste. A related difficulty is that distributors sometimes emphasise their own business rather than the exporter's. Also, it is difficult to ascertain whether distributors actually spend their advertising allowance on advertising.

The problems of cooperative advertising need not prevent its being used. The manager can minimise the problems. Working with an agency with good foreign-market coverage can help to control distributor placement of ads. Development of prototype advertising helps standardise the quality. The exporter's partial payment of the cost provides for some control. Still another way to combat the problem of uncooperative distributors is to establish agreed-upon guidelines. If the firm can implement these steps, it has a good chance with a cooperative programme.

Problem – example

ITT provides an example of strong headquarters coordination of international advertising. ITT headquarters is in New York and so is its global advertising department. Under this office are advertising staff in the area organisations: Europe, Latin America, the Far East and the Pacific. The department also monitors the efforts of the various advertising agencies for ITT worldwide. The global budget is over £400 million. The department's responsibilities include selection of ad agencies around the world and hiring and indoctrination of ad managers for ITT divisions.

Coordination starts with an annual subsidiary advertising plan, which is explained in its *Standard Planning Guide*. The guide also spells out standard practices. Another control device is the monthly progress report from each unit's ad manager. A final form of communication is the annual face-to-face group meeting. It is a two-day session where staff from New York meet with ad managers from the four regions.

The three US auto companies practice central coordination, but in differing degrees and with different approaches. For example, General Motors markets in 176 countries on a regional basis, that is, for Latin America, Europe and Asia. McCann is GM's agency in 35 countries. Other agencies are used elsewhere, but they are in consultation with McCann and regional and corporate marketing staff in GM. Though control is regional, Detroit has final approval on campaign budgets. In Europe, McCann's office in Zurich coordinates European advertising in conjunction with GM's European headquarters there.

Ford, on the other hand, markets in 185 countries and uses more agencies, although J. Walther Thompson, Ogilvy & Mather and Young & Rubicam have 25 major country accounts among them. Rather than using a single agency for coordination as GM does, Ford has its own international coordinating group in Detroit that coordinates, counsels, advises and assists the other agencies. It does this through regular advertising exchange, including videos, advertising cost reviews and annual agency reviews.

In a completely different approach, Chrysler is basically only an export marketer abroad. Thus, it uses a US international agency, Bozell, Jacobs, Kenyon & Eckhardt, to handle its international promotion. BJKE has an office in Detroit to work with Chrysler's international arm there.

The Culligan Company prepared three different advertising approaches with its domestic agency. Then it met with its European licensees to review them. A majority vote by the licensees decided which approach should be used. The licensee's agency placed the ads.

Another success story involved the MEM Company (maker of English Leather products), which distributed US ad copy to licensees and allowed them discretion as to its use. Many did use these advertisements, finding them well done and convenient. If the licensee used its own ad material, it had to have it approved by MEM. Of course, to have this kind of control, the firm must pay for at least part of the local advertising. For example, both Culligan and MEM paid one-half of the expense.

Questions

1 Discuss some of the conditions that might favour a decision towards decentralisation.
2 Describe the role played by subsidiary personnel when a company is pursuing a 'compromise approach'.
3 Analyse some of the advantages and problems associated with cooperative local advertising.

(I) *Problem 10.6* International selling

Introductory comments

Personal selling takes place whenever a customer is met in person by a representative of the marketing company. When doing business internationally, companies will have to meet customers from different countries. These customers may be used to different business customs and may speak in a different language. Personal selling in an international context is therefore extremely complex and requires some very special skills on the part of the salesperson.

We will differentiate between international selling and local selling. When a company's sales force travels across countries and meets directly with clients abroad, it is practising international selling. This kind of selling requires the special skill of being able to manage within several cultures. Much more often, however, companies engage in local selling; they organise and staff a local sales force made up of local nationals to do the selling in only one country. Managing and operating a local sales force involves different problems from those encountered by international salespersons.

Purchasing behaviour

In industrial selling, one of the most important parts of the job consists of finding the right decision-maker in the client company. The seller must locate the key decision-makers which may differ from company to company or from country to country. In some countries, the purchasing manager may have different responsibilities or engineers may play a greater role. The international salesperson thus must be able to deal effectively with buying units that differ by country.

A Japanese study investigated the purchasing process of a large corporation for packaging machinery. The entire decision-making process took 121 days and involved 20 people from the purchasing company. In Japan, middle management is given considerable authority for purchasing. However, the staff departments responsible for the purchasing process will involve all interested and affected departments in the decision-making process. In the case of the company purchasing packaging machinery, the process involved the production manager and the entire production department staff, the new product committee, the laboratory of the company, the marketing department, and the department for market development. For a detailed chart see Figure 10.5.

Buying criteria

Aside from the different purchasing patterns found, the international salesperson may have to deal with different decision criteria or objectives on the part of the purchases. Buyers or users of industrial products in different countries may expect to maximise different goals. However, it should be pointed out that for standardised uses for specific industries, relatively little difference between countries applies. Particularly for high technology products, such as production equipment for semiconductor components used in the electronics industry, the applications are virtually identical regardless of whether the factory is located in Korea or in the USA.

Language

Overcoming the language barrier is an especially difficult task for the international salesperson. The personal selling effort is substantially enhanced if the salesperson speaks the language of the customer. For some of the products marketed by an international sales force today, two trends are evident. First, the dependency on the local language for many industries is not as strong today as it was just one or two decades ago. For many new and highly sophisticated products, such as in the electronics or aerospace industry, English is the language spoken by most customers. Consequently, with more and more executives speaking English in many countries, more firms have been in a position to actually market their products directly, without local intermediaries. English

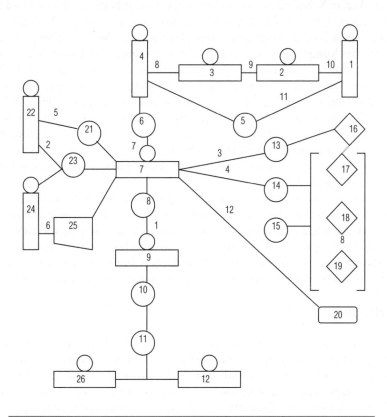

Figure 10.5 Decision-making flow.

Source: Adapted from 'Japanese firms use unique buying behaviour', *The Japan Economic Journal*, 23 December 1980: 29.

Management decision making (MDM)
  1. President
  4. Production chief
  24. Foreman

Functionality management input (FMI)
  2. Financial dept
  3. Sales headquarters
  7. Production dept
  12. Product development dept
  16. Makers design and technical staff
  22. Research staff
  26. Marketing dept

Group consensus (GC)
  6. Discussion production and sales plans
  9. New products development committee
  10. Request for consultation
  13. Discussion on design of prototype machines

Process management (PM)
  8. Production of packing process plan
  11. Production of new product marketing plan
  25. Production of draft plans

Operational element (OE)
  14. Prototype machine
  15. Placement of orders

Value chain input (VCI)
  17. Supplier A
  18. Supplier B
  19. Supplier C

Operational input (OI)
  20. Overseas machine exhibitions
  21. Request for testing of prototype machines
  23. Production of basic design

Outcome
  5. Decision

is widely spoken in Scandinavia and in Europe, just as it is the leading second language in Asia and Latin America. Consequently, we now see a trend in which the ability to speak a number of foreign languages is less of a necessity. More important is an ability to appreciate the foreign cultural context, which is helped by understanding a language but which can also be gained by better understanding the foreign culture itself.

In industries where knowledge of the local language is important, companies tend to assign sales territories to salespersons on the basis of language skills. A European multinational manufacturer of textile equipment assigns countries to its salespersons according to the languages they speak such as French, Spanish, German, Italian or English. This is more important in the traditional industries such as textile manufacturing, where businesses are more local in orientation and where English is not spoken that well by management.

Even executives who speak fairly good English may not understand all the details of product descriptions or specifications. As a result, a company can make an excellent impression by having its sales brochures translated into some of the key languages. European companies routinely produce company publications in several languages. Such translations may not be needed for Scandinavia, but might go a long way in other parts of the world where the level of English-language skills is not that high.

Business etiquette

International marketers selling to overseas markets are likely to encounter a diverse set of business practices as they move from one country to another. Because interpersonal behaviour is intensely culture bound, this part of the salesperson's job will vary by country. Many differences exist in how an appointment is made, how (and whether) an introduction is made, and how much lead time is needed for making appointments. The salesperson must also know whether gifts are expected or desired. When a salesperson is travelling to the same area repeatedly, familiarity with local customs can be expected. But for newcomers or experienced executives travelling to a new area, finding out the correct information is necessary.

For example, visiting businesspersons must attend long banquets when engaging in negotiations with the Chinese. These banquets may start in the late morning or early in the evening. Sitting mostly at a round table, the visitors will normally be seated next to the host who is expected to fill the visitor's plate at regular intervals. Foreign businesspersons are cautioned that frequent toasts are the norm and that many Chinese business hosts expect that the guest should become drunk; otherwise, the guest is believed not to have had a good time. Business etiquettes can change from one country to another. While it is acceptable for visitors to arrive late in China, India or Indonesia, arriving late in Hong Kong is not. Lateness causes the visitor to 'lose face', which is an extremely serious matter among Hong Kong businesspersons.

Important information can be obtained from special sources, as no manager can be expected to know the business customs of every country. For one, the company's own foreign-market representatives or sales subsidiary can provide important information or suggestions. Also, when such access is not available, governments tend to collect data on business practices through their commercial officers posted abroad. For example, the United States Department of Commerce (DOC) publishes a regular series, 'Doing Business in....' with a wealth of helpful suggestions. Some business service companies, such as accounting firms or international banks, also provide customers with profiles of business practices in foreign countries. Learning some foreign customs will help generate goodwill towards the company and can therefore enhance the chance of doing business.

Negotiations strategies

Negotiations in the international arena are complicated because the negotiating partners frequently come from different cultural backgrounds. As a result, misunderstandings or misjudgements can occur leading to failure. To maximise the outcome in often difficult, long and protracted negotiations, international sales personnel must be in tune with the cultural differences.

Although a myriad of negotiation strategies exist, concentrating on the mutual needs rather than the issues is a much practised approach. In international marketing, the salesperson, or negotiator, must first determine the true objectives and needs of the other party. When negotiating within an unknown cultural setting, this is often a challenging task. Careful assessment of the negotiating party's needs can, however, enhance the chance for success.

For successful negotiation, understanding the *mindscape* of the counterpart can be very important. Wenlee Ting, a noted anthropologist, defined mindscapes as 'a structure of reasoning, cognition, perception, design, planning, and decision making that may vary from individual to individual and from culture to culture'. Ting developed mindscape models based upon earlier work by another anthropologist, Maruyama. Building on Maruyama's work, Ting identified three common mindscapes for Hong Kong executives. Executives with an H-type mindscape tended to be interested in structured competition and the scientific organisation of business. The tendency of executives with the I-type mindscape was to see separation of individual efforts as a key to higher efficiency. The G-type mindscape considered heterogeneity as a basis for mutually beneficial competition and tended to encourage differences among units. I-type mindscapes were said to be predominant among players in international finance or real estate; H-type mindscapes were predominant in family businesses; and G-type mindscapes were typical in international trading and business.

The evidence further suggested that Hong Kong businesspersons negotiate well in Eastern and Western cultures. Skilled Hong Kong negotiators are able to engage in reasoning with Western counterparts while simultaneously employing other reasoning and negotiation techniques when dealing with local groups, family members and other business associates. This suggests that successful negotiation may depend on the foreign businessperson's ability to scout out the mindscape of his or her foreign counterpart's mindscape. Careful preparation of the cultural norms prevalent in the foreign country would be a starting point to successful negotiations and selling.

Timing is also an important aspect for negotiating abroad. In some countries, such as China, negotiations tend to take much more time than in the USA or some other Western countries. One European company that operated a joint venture in China observed that during one annual meeting, two weeks were spent in a discussion that elsewhere might have only taken a few hours. In this situation, however, much of the time was used for interdepartmental negotiations among various Chinese agencies rather than for face-to-face negotiations with the European company.

In another instance, a European firm negotiated with a Middle-Eastern country over several months for the delivery of several hundred machines. When the company representatives reached that country for the final round of negotiations, they found that the competing firm had already been there several weeks before their arrival. The European firm's representatives decided to prepare themselves for long negotiations and refused to make concessions, figuring that the competitor had most likely been worn out in the previous weeks. As it turned out, that assessment was correct and the European company won the order by outstaying its competitor in a rather difficult negotiating environment. Obviously, unprepared sales executives might lose out to competitors if they do not understand the negotiation customs of a foreign country as they relate to the amount of time necessary to conclude a deal.

Local selling (single country sales force)

When a company is able to maintain a local sales force in the countries where it does business, many of the difficulties of bridging the cultural gap with its clients will be minimised. The local sales force can be expected to understand the local customs, and the international company typically gains additional acceptance in the market. This is primarily because local sales forces are usually staffed with local nationals. However, many challenges remain, and the management of a local sales force often requires different strategies from those used in running a sales force in the company's domestic market.

Role of local sales force and control

When a company has decided to build up a local sales force, the decision has already been made for forward integration in its distribution effort. Establishing a sales force means that the company has moved to assume the full role of a local sales subsidiary, sidestepping the independent distributor. Depending on the distribution strategy adopted, the company might sell directly, as might be the case for many industrial products or business services, or indirectly through local wholesalers, as would be the case for many consumer products and services. Although international companies will not make such a move unless present business volume justifies it, there are substantial benefits for a company in having its own sales force.

Control over a firm's sales activities is a frequently cited advantage for operating a company-owned local sales force. With its own sales force, the company can emphasise the products it wants to market any time; and the company has better control over the way it is represented. In many cases, price negotiations, in the forms of discounts or rebates, are handled uniformly rather than leaving these decisions to an independent distributor with different interests. Having a company sales force also ensures that the personnel is of the necessary level and qualification. Control over all of these parameters usually means higher sales compared with using a distributor sales force.

Also, the local sales force can represent an important bridge with the local business community. For industries where the buying process is local rather than international, the sales force speaking the language of the local customer, can be expected to understand the local business customs, and can thus bring the international firm closer to its end users. In many instances, local customers, though not objecting to buying from a foreign firm, may prefer to deal with local representatives of that firm. As a result, the ability of the international company to make its case heard with prospective customers is substantially enhanced.

However, local sales forces are single-country, or single-culture, by nature. While they do speak the language of the local customers they often do not speak any other language. As many firms have experienced, the local sales force abroad may have a very limited understanding of English, and its understanding of the head-office language is, in general, not sufficient to conduct business in that language. Furthermore, a local sales force cannot be expected to speak the languages of neighbouring countries sufficiently in order to deal directly with such customers. In Europe, where this problem is particularly acute, language competency usually precludes a German firm from sending its sales force into France, or a French firm from sending its sales force into Italy or Spain. In some countries, there are several different languages spoken and this tends to further reduce the mobility of a sales force.

Local sales job

The type and extent of local sales effort a company will need is dependent on its own distribution effort and the relationship to the other communications mix elements. For firms who still use distributor sales forces to a large extent, a missionary sales force with limited responsibilities may suffice. This missionary sales force would concentrate on visiting clients together with the local distributor's sales force. If the international company's sales force needs to do the entire job, a much larger sales force will be necessary. As for the international firm's domestic market, the size of the local sales force depends to a large extent on the number of clients and the desired frequency of visits. This frequency may differ from country to country, which means that the size of the sales force would differ from country to country.

Problem – example

When Bausch & Lomb introduced its then new soft lenses line into Japan, the company had targeted influential eye doctors in each sales territory for its introductory launch. The assumption was that once these leading practitioners signed up for the new product, marketing to the majority of eye doctors would be easier. One salesperson was quickly dismissed by a key customer. The doctor said that he thought very highly of Bausch & Lomb equipment but preferred regular lenses for his patients. The salesperson did not even have a chance to respond; but he decided, as it was his first visit to this clinic, to stay around for awhile. He talked to several assistants at the clinic and talked to the doctor's wife who was, as was typical for Japan, handling the administration of the practice.

The next morning, the salesman returned to the clinic and observed that the doctor was very busy. He talked again with the assistants and joined the doctor's wife when she was cooking and talked with her about food. When the couple's young son returned from kindergarten, the salesman played with him and even went out to buy him a toy. The wife was very pleased with the well-intentioned babysitter. She later explained to the salesman that her husband had very little time to listen to any sales presentations during the day, so she invited him to come to their home in the evening. The doctor, obviously primed by his wife, received the salesman very warmly and they enjoyed *sake* together.

Table 10.7 Cross-cultural business behaviour

	Latin approach	Angol-saxon approach
Point of contact	Connections count heavily in this market. Trade shows and official trade promotion missions are good ways to make initial contact. The alternative is to arrange for a formal introduction to potential customers, distributors or partners. Ask your country's embassy to introduce you. France is definitely a country of personal networks. You get things done more quickly by working through inside contacts than by 'going through channels'. The French want to know a good deal about you before discussing business, but building rapport involves less small talk than in some other cultures. Showing a knowledge of French history, literature, art and philosophy is a good way to build rapport.	Famously a land of old school-ties and the old boys' network, Britain is a market where referrals, recommendations and testimonials are extremely useful. Write in English with basic information about your company and your product, adding that you will contact them soon to set up an appointment. Follow this with a phone call requesting a meeting two or three weeks hence. Your British counterpart will suggest the time and place.
Contextual communication	The French use many more hand and arm gestures than Asians and Anglo-Saxons. Always shake hands when meeting and when leaving someone.	The British use far less body language in comparison to the French. Eye contact tends to be less direct than in expressive cultures such as the Italians. Two Englishmen in conversation will often stand at a 90-degree angle to each other rather than facing each other directly. A very direct gaze may be interpreted as rude and intrusive.
Power distance	Level of education along with family background and wealth determine status in France. French bosses tend to run their companies in an authoritarian style. Managers are expected to be highly competent and to know the answer to virtually every question that arises. They are often reluctant to delegate authority.	Status in Britain is largely determined by one's regional origin, social class, family background and accent. Personal achievement is regarded as less important. The existence of relatively large status distinctions explains the formality in social interaction. The British usually prefer to stay with Mr or Mrs until at least the second or third meeting. Visitors, however, find that younger British business people are becoming less formal.
Face postulation	Handshake with moderate pressure and steady eye contact. Among males the older or higher status person should initiate the handshake. Women of any rank can decide whether to offer their hand.	While men exchange light to moderate handshakes, some women choose not to offer their hand. Men should always wait for the woman to extend her hand.
Degree of formality	Greet your local counterparts with monsieur, madame or mademoiselle without the person's name. Always use the *vous* (formal) pronoun rather than the informal *tu*.	Use Mr, Mrs, Miss or Ms until your counterpart suggests switching to given names.

(Table 10.7 continued)

Table 10.7 Continued

	Latin approach	Angol-saxon approach
Selling process	Avoid hard-sell tactics, hyperbole and flippant humour. Prepare a sober presentation with a logical sequence of arguments. If you encounter forceful disagreement on some points, be prepared to respond with factual counter-arguments. Vigorous disagreementwith specific issues does not necessarily signal lack of interest in your overall proposal.	Accustomed to understatement, British buyers are turned off by hype and exaggerated claims. Presentations should be straightforward and factual. Humour is acceptable, but visitors from abroad should remember that it rarely translates well.
Negotiation	Be prepared for long, relatively unstructured negotiating sessions punctuated frequently with verbal confrontation. Your counterpart may also attack the thought process behind your bargaining position. The French pride themselves on their logical thinking and often seem to relish faulting the logic of others. Expect decision making to take longer than in Anglo-Saxon countries.	English negotiators have been doing business all over the world for hundreds of years. They may put a safety margin in their opening position so as to leave room for substantial concessions during the bargaining process. Time-is-money Americans may find the British process too time-consuming, but for the rest of the world's business cultures it is quite normal. Expect emphasis on the legal aspects and the fine points of the written agreement.

Source: Adapted from Gesteland, R. (1999) *Cross-Cultural Business Behaviour: Marketing, Negotiating and Managing across Cultures*, Copenhagen, Copenhagen Business School Press.

The doctor listened patiently to the sales presentation and responded that he did not want to use the soft lenses on his patients right away. However, he suggested that the salesman try them on his assistants the next day. So on the third day, the salesman returned to the clinic and fitted soft lenses on several of the clinic's assistants. The reaction was very favourable, and the doctor placed an order on the third day of his sales call.

It is probably fair to say that salespersons in many countries would have taken the initial negative response as the final answer from the doctor and would have tried elsewhere for success. In the context of Japan, however, the customer expects a different reaction from the salesperson. Japanese customers often judge from the frequency of the sales calls they receive whether the company really wants to do business. When the salesperson of one company makes more frequent calls to a potential customer than the frequency of his/her competitors, he or she may be regarded as more sincere.

This also means that companies doing business in Japan have to make frequent sales calls to their top customers often only for courtesy reasons. Customers get visited twice a year, usually in June and December, without necessarily discussing any business. Although this may occasionally be only a telephone call, the high frequency of visits significantly affects the staffing levels of the company-owned sales force.

Selling in Brazil

Ericsson do Brazil was the Brazilian affiliate of L.M. Ericsson, a Swedish multinational firm with a strong position in the telecommunications industry. The company marketed both central switching equipment for telephone companies and private exchanges (PBXs) to individual firms. The sales force for the PBX business numbered about one hundred persons and was organised geographically. In the southern sector of Brazil where industry was concentrated, the sales force was divided into specialists for either large PBXs, with up to two hundred external lines and several thousand internal lines, or for smaller systems called *key systems*, which could accommodate up to 25 incoming lines or up to 50 internal lines. In the northern, more rural part of Brazil, this specialisation could not be achieved because of fewer accounts. As a result, the northern sales offices had sales representatives that sold both large and small systems.

Ericsson's sales force was compensated partially with a fixed salary and partially through commissions. Fixed monthly salaries amounted to about £400. A good salesperson could earn about £2,000 per month when the 4 per cent sales commission was added to the base salary. Special government regulations required that each salesperson be assigned an exclusive territory. If a salesperson were reassigned, the company was then liable to maintain his or her income for another twelve months. As a result, changes in sales territory had to be considered carefully. When Ericsson do Brazil was faced with the introduction of a new paging system that was to be sold to corporate clients, most of whom also bought telephone equipment, the company found it difficult to assign territories to each of its present salespersons. If it wanted to reassign territories later on once it became clear who was good at selling paging systems over and above the telephone systems, the company would not be able to easily reassign territories without incurring compensation costs. In the end, Ericsson decided to assign the new paging system to its salespersons on a temporary basis only, thus preserving the chance to make other assignments later on without extra costs.

Wiltech India

Selling in India is very different from selling in other countries. India, with the second-largest population in the world, is an example of a typical developing country. Wiltech, a venture between the British company Wilkinson and a large Indian conglomerate, was founded to market razor blades in India based upon Wilkinson technology. Founded in the early 1980s, the company needed to build up its sales force to compete against local competition. In India, there are more than 400,000 retailers or distributors of razor blades, and about 20 per cent of them carry Wiltech blades.

The sales force of sixty persons primarily concentrates on urban markets. The sales representative working in a big metropolitan city directly handles one distributor and about 600–700 retail outlets. He or she is expected to visit the distributor every day and to make another 40–60 sales calls per day. The sales representative accomplishes this largely on foot because the sales outlets are relatively small and are clustered close to each other. The goal is to see important retailers at least twice per month and smaller retailers once a month. The sales representative working in smaller cities might cover about a dozen distributors and some 800 to 1,000 outlets. He or she would see distributors once or twice per month and see from 35 to 40 outlets per day. Travel would be by railway or by bus, whichever is more convenient.

Wiltech sales representatives are paid a fixed salary of 800 rupees to 1,200 rupees per month (about US £70 to US £100). Sales representatives that achieve their quotas and productivity targets can earn another 400–500 rupees per month in bonus.

Expenses are paid on the basis of daily allowances for transport, lunch and hotel stays when necessary. For sales representatives selling from a fixed location, this daily allowance amounts to 30 rupees per day. When travelling away from home, the daily allowance amounts to 50 rupees plus the actual transportation costs for first-class train fare or bus fare. Although these costs might appear very low compared with typical salaries and travel expenses paid for in a developed country, they nevertheless represent a very good income in India where per capita GNP cost of living is very low by Western standards.

Questions

1 Discuss some of the main trends associated with the role of language within international selling.
2 Critically comment on the 'British Style' of business behaviour with regard to non-verbal communication, meeting and greeting, as well as forms of address.
3 Comment on the concept of (a) 'mindscape' and (b) on the 'British style' business behaviour applied to the bargaining style of negotiation.
4 Assess some of the key implications, related to the Bausch & Lomb example of selling in Japan.

(M) *Problem 10.7* Multinational product portfolio analysis

Introductory comments

One of the most important requirements in multinational strategic planning is the development of a product-by-country portfolio. The purpose is to position products in foreign markets by the opportunity for profits and the company's ability to exploit the opportunity. Positioning products/countries on a product portfolio then allows the company to determine whether products should be candidates for further growth, for selective investment or for harvesting and eventual divestment. The portfolio will also help management determine the potential sources for investment on the basis of projected cash flows. Thus, the strength of a well-known brand in a domestic market may be a source of cash for entry of the brand into additional international markets. In short, the objectives of product portfolio analysis in a multinational context are the same as those related to the General Electric (GE) market attractiveness/business position matrix, except that products in the international portfolio are positioned by country or region.

Because of the range of environmental and market factors required to evaluate products in foreign markets, the GE/McKinsey approach should be the basis for multinational portfolio analysis. This approach utilises a broad range of variables to analyse both market opportunities and the company's ability to exploit them (the company's business position).

Business position can be evaluated in the same manner as marketing opportunity. Management defines several variables that indicate the company's resources and the product's position relative to competition.

Problem

A hypothetical multinational portfolio for Lady Godiva International Co. is illustrated in Figure 10.6 using the GE/McKinsey approach. Four product lines are represented

Business position
(capability to exploit market opportunity)

		High	Medium	Low
Market attractiveness (market opportunity)	High	X Women's toiletries (UK) X Women's cosmetics (UK) **1**	**2**	X Women's cosmetics (Europe) X Health products (Latin America) **3**
	Medium	X Health products (UK/Europe) **4**	X Luggage products (Europe) **5**	**6**
	Low	X Luggage products (UK) **7**	**8**	X Women's toiletries (Europe) **9**

Figure 10.6 Multinational product-portfolio matrix for Lady Godiva International Co.

in various areas of the world by their market attractiveness (market opportunity) and business position (the company's ability to exploit the market opportunity).

The determination and evaluation of market opportunity was carried out on a formal basis by listing key evaluative variables and weighting them by importance. The international marketing opportunity analysis (MOI) undertaken by the company included market variables such as market size, market growth, level of competition, cyclicality as well as the norms and values of the target segment. The MOI approach used by Lady Godiva International Co. also included environmental variables such as barriers to entry, price controls, product standards, political stability, social attitude towards foreign business and rate of inflation. An importance weight was assigned to each variable on the basis of managerial judgement. The company placed greatest value on market growth, minimal competition, market size and the likelihood that the target market segment's values and norms conform to the prospective positioning of the product. Lady Godiva International Co. has considered market variables significantly more important than environmental variables.

Regarding environmental variables, the greatest emphasis was given to trade and political factors that facilitate market entry (lack of tariff barriers, quotas and so forth). Price controls and product standards were singled out but were given less weight. The company also gave political stability little weight.

Outcomes for each variable were found on the basis of a scaling procedure. The most desirable outcome was valued at 10 and the least desirable at 1. An overall opportunity score for a product in a country can be computed by multiplying the importance weight by the value of the outcome for each variable and summing the results across variables. Such a score would then be compared with scores for alternative foreign investment opportunities. For example, if the total market-opportunity rating for a particular brand in a particular country or world region was 466 and, assuming that the average for other international investment opportunities was 350, the brand's entry into that country or world region would then be evaluated positively.

This type of market opportunity analysis is very similar to the evaluation of investment attractiveness in the GE portfolio approach.

Each product-country is positioned on the vertical axis by an analysis of the market potential and environmental conditions based on a number of key variables. Products in each region should also be positioned by the company's business position in that particular market. The horizontal axis shows whether the company has the physical, human and financial resources and the know-how to exploit the market opportunity.

Assume Lady Godiva International Co. follows the successful introduction of its women's line of cosmetics in the UK with an attempt to market them in Europe. After two years it assesses its current business position, using the variables in Table 10.8.

The table lists two types of variables, those dealing with the product's market position and those dealing with the company's resources. Market position represented by market share, sales share of the leading competitor and ROI. Company resources are measured by the strength of the distribution system local market support

Table 10.8 International marketing business position analysis – the Lady Godiva International Co. case

Market position variables	Product – country value	Importance weight	Company resource variables	Product – country value	Importance weight
Market share		10	Channels of distribution		8
20% or more	10		• Strongest channels in the country	10	
15–19%	8				
10–15%	6		• Equal to leading competitor	8	
. . .	. . .		. . .	. . .	
*2–4%	2		*• Weak support	2	
1% or less	1		*• No support	1	
Sales		10	Local marketing support		8
£75 million or more	10		• Best in country	10	
£50–74 million	8		• Equal to leading competitor	8	
£30–49 million	6				
. . .	. . .		. . .	. . .	
£6–10 milion	3		• Weak support	2	
£5 million or less	1		• No support	1	
Return on investment (ROI)		10	Plant capacity		4
			• Excellent	10	
25% or more	10		*• Good	8	
20–24%	8		• Fair	5	
			• Poor	2	
. . .	. . .		• None	1	
*10% or less	1				
Market share of leading competitor		6	Capital requirements		6
			• None	10	
2% or less	10		*• Low	8	
3–5%	8		• Medium	5	
6–9%	5		• High	1	
. . .	. . .				
*20% or more	1				

Note
*Indicates the rating for Lady Godiva's cosmetics line in Europe.

(local personnel, use of local advertising agency), plant capacity and current capital requirements.

The company has not yet established a strong local representation in Europe. As a result, the cosmetics line receives a low overall rating in business position (right-hand side of the matrix in Figure 10.6). But an analysis of marketing opportunity based on the variables described earlier shows strong potential for women's cosmetics in Europe. AS a result, the product line is positioned in the upper right-hand part of the matrix in Figure 10.6.

Investment strategies

Once the products have been positioned by a country or world region, the company can determine whether various countries warrant investment for growth (boxes 1, 2 and 4 in Figure 10.6), investment to maintain current position (boxes 5 and 7) or a reduction in effort through harvesting and possible divestment (boxed 6, 8 and 9). Box 3 presents a problem because the company is not sure whether to move towards divestment because of the poor business position or to invest for growth because of the market opportunity.

Questions

1   What are the limitations associated with the international marketing opportunity analysis approach used by the company?
2   Calculate the total business position score for Lady Godiva's cosmetics line in Europe. Assume that the average business position score for other Lady Godiva product lines in foreign markets is 350 and rate the business position for the cosmetics line in Europe.
3   Based on the international marketing business position analysis and the multinational product portfolio matrix developed by the company, recommend specific investment strategies that could be implemented by Lady Godiva International Company.

References and further readings

Alf H. Walle (1986) Conceptualising personal selling for international business: a continuum of exchange perspective, *Journal of Personal Selling and Sales Management*, November: 9–17.

Franklin R. Root (1994) *Entry Strategies for International Markets*, New York: Lexington Books, p. 55.

Franklin R. Root, *Entry Strategies for International Markets*. Copyright © 1994 Jossey-Bass Inc., Publishers. First published by Lexington Books. All rights reserved.

Guanxi spoken here, *Forbes* (November 8, 1993): 208–210.

Hellmut Schutte, Henkel's Strategy for Asia Pacific, *Long Range Planning*, 28 (1): 98. Copyright 1995, with kind permission from Elsevier Science Ltd, The Boulevard, Langford Lane, Kidlington, OX5 1GB, UK.

Jean-Pierre Jeannet (1983) *Ericsson Do Brasil: Ericall System*, IMEDE, International Management Development Institute, Lausanne, Switzerland, M-296.

Jean-Pierre Jeannet (1987) *Wiltech India*, case in progress, Babson Collect.

Kumar, V., Stam, A. and Joachimsthaler, E. A. (1994) An interactive multicritera approach to identifying potential foreign markets, *Journal of International Marketing*, 2(1) (1994) : 29–52.

Lifestyle Flux Lures McD's to Mideast, *Advertising Age International* (November 21, 1994): 1–20.

Lloyd C. R. and Sam C. Okoroafo (1996) On the way towards developing a global screening model, *International Marketing Review*, 13(1): 46–64.

Paul E. G. and Yoram W. (1975) New ways to measure consumers' judgements, *Harvard Business Review*, 53: 107–17.

Robert G. C. (1985) Selecting new product projects: using the newProd system, *Journal of Product Innovation Management*, 2(1) (March): 34–44.

Wenlee, T. (1980) *Business and Technological Dynamics in Newly Industrialised Asia* (Greenwood, 1985); and Magorah Maruyama, Mindscapes and social theories, *Current Anthropology*: 589–608.

11

Issues and Trends

Brands on the balance sheet, intellectual property, databases, information warehouses, intellectual capital, the 'learning company' – buzz words such as these all reflect the IT revolution's far-reaching effects on business. Do not underestimate it. But do not be fooled by it either. Its profoundest effects are likely to be precisely opposite to those suggested by the new conventional wisdom.

The fundamental shift is not towards a so-called 'information age', but an imagination age. For all the breakneck advance of modern computing and communication technologies, what's really driving commercial success – including the performances of companies – is not hardware and software, but 'wetware': people and their ability to 'sense, judge, create and build relationships'.

Fundamentally, it opens up new dimensions for branding: what drives businesses internally increasingly sells them externally too. As customers seek out the people 'behind' the brand, the most powerful communication channel moves from media to flesh and blood contact with customers through day-to-day operations. Brands which lack this contact risk being seen as two-dimensional. For brands which have it, management becomes an altogether more all-embracing, challenging – and fascinating – task.

As we look at the world of business today, we see national borders blurring; suppliers and customers are everywhere. Lurking right beside them are our competitors. In business the race is not always to the swift, but that is the way to bet. The company that knows where customers are going and can supply them with the ever-changing needs of the trip in the twenty-first century will be the victor.

Product development for the twenty-first century will be most effective when the marketing, R&D, manufacturing, and engineering functions cooperate and when they understand one another.

In the twenty-first century, marketing will experience as much pressure as the factory to improve productivity. Zero-defect principles applied to marketing's processes offer the promise of re-engineering systems for the benefit of both the firm's customers and its own sales and marketing work force.

As we approach the twenty-first century, the economic borders of the world are shrinking, and the need for competitive awareness on a global perspective has increased.

Ironically, marketing as we know it today could disappear as a distinct function with its own box on the corporate organisation chart.

The best days for the business marketing function lie ahead, but getting there will not be half the fun. To prosper in the next millennium, companies serving business customers will face major changes in the way they go to market. Current trends have eroded the established role of marketing in the industrial firm, pushing it to the forefront of corporate business strategy. By the mid-1990s, down-sized corporate staff, leaner marketing budgets, global marketplaces and parsimonious buyers forced smarter firms to adopt new tools for battling price erosion, channel discord, foreign competition and finicky customers. The future suggests that companies hewing to traditional model in years to come will not be around to see how it all turns out in the twenty-first century

Robust fundamental issues help keep the field of marketing centred on its essentials and lessen susceptibility to distraction. The four fundamental issues have shown their versatility by guiding the field through past transformations. But what of the future? Will the non-linear, disruptive 'new economy', based on silicon, computers and networks, therefore change the ground rules because these questions are no longer useful? Five themes are emerging that are especially salient to markets and marketing:

- the connected knowledge economy;
- globalising, converging and consolidating industries;
- fragmenting and frictionless markets;
- demanding customers and consumers and their empowered behaviour;
- adaptive organisations.

Thus the field of marketing should be pursuing many new directions as it starts the millennium.

Index

Note: Page numbers in italics denote figures and tables.